Vade Mecum

Essays, Reviews & Interviews

Vade Mecum

Essays, Reviews & Interviews

Richard Skinner

zero books

Winchester, UK
Washington, USA

First published by Zero Books, 2015
Zero Books is an imprint of John Hunt Publishing Ltd., Laurel House, Station Approach,
Alresford, Hants, SO24 9JH, UK
office1@jhpbooks.net
www.johnhuntpublishing.com
www.zero-books.net

For distributor details and how to order please visit the 'Ordering' section on our website.

ISBN: 978 1 78535 024 5
Library of Congress Control Number: 2015930440

A CIP catalogue record for this book is available from the British Library.

Design: Stuart Davies

Printed and bound in the USA by Edwards Brothers Malloy

CONTENTS

Interviews

"A loose sally of the mind; an irregular undigested piece; not a regularly and orderly composition."
Dr Johnson's definition of an essay

Acknowledgements

For originally publishing some of these pieces, my thanks go to Matthew Apperley, Wayne Burrows, Clare Carlin, Daniela Cascella, Paolo Inverni, Richard Kelly, Annalena McAfee, Frances Spurrier, Dimitris Tsomokos & Owen Vince. For their love and friendship, special thanks to Jacqueline Crooks, Maria Fusco & Christian Patracchini.

Kazuo Ishiguro—"A master in the art of narration"

In December 2010, Kazuo Ishiguro accepted an invitation from myself and my co-tutor to speak to the students on the six-month 'Writing a Novel' course at the Faber Academy. It was a riveting two hours for the students and us tutors alike. During his talk, he offered access-all-areas to his thoughts on writing and his work practices, which was inspirational and which provoked a lot of discussion for weeks afterwards.

One of the key points dealt with was his use of the 'unreliable narrator'—the literary trope for which he is perhaps best known. The point he made was that unreliable narrators are often a result of people reassessing their lives and the disappointment of them and, if the feeling of disappointment was too great, narrators might choose to leaven it in order to make it manageable. He went on to say that he auditions all his characters before deciding which one to offer the role of narrator. Imagine the Sherlock Holmes stories with Holmes himself as the narrator, he said—they just wouldn't have worked. The point of the Holmes stories is that we are in the same boat as Watson with regard to the amount of information we have. Like Watson, we are in the dark most of the time. With regard to his own work, think of *The Remains of the Day* and how different it would have been had Miss Kenton narrated the story. Her self-awareness and emotional articulacy, which Stevens so obviously lacks, would have meant that the pleasure of the text would have to have come from some other place entirely. So, adopting different characters as narrators produces different kinds of books.

The other key point he made is that he feels each of his novels has grown out of its predecessor. He feels that writers have to learn 'on the job', but that they should treat every book as their masterpiece. There are a finite number of books in a writer, he said, so they need to pay attention to the shape and single impact of each narrative. Ishiguro clearly practices what he preaches: he has won the Booker Prize once—with *The Remains of the Day*—and no less than four of his six published novels have been shortlisted for Booker Prize. *Four*. No one (with the possible exception of Peter Carey) has had a greater hit rate at that particular prize and he is one of the most highly-regarded writers in the world. His advice and insight was so inspiring that my class and I decided to go away, revisit his work and have a mini-conference on it at the end of the course. To prepare for that, I thought it would be interesting to read his novels in the order he wrote them, which took me three months and which is one of the most rewarding reading experiences I've ever had.

The narrators of Ishiguro's first three novels—*A Pale View of Hills, An Artist of the Floating World* and *The Remains of the Day*—all share a very profound unreliability. Etsuko, Ono and Stevens are all ordinary figures living in extraordinary times and places and, although the stories they tell are complex, the stories themselves feel curiously incomplete and their conclusions are highly ambiguous. These three narratives, all set just before or after the Second World War, are deeply embedded in their historical moments but their narrators choose, for whatever reason, to tell the story at a tangent to those moments in history. The impression is that Etsuko, Ono and Stevens are traumatised, and their sense of self as narrators is paralysed. Indeed, the sense is even stronger than that—it is as though these characters are 'haunted'. It is almost as if, as individuals, they are not proper, rounded subjects but merely ghostly actors and performers inhabiting roles that are allocated to them by the context in which they find themselves. And yet, whatever was the cause of their original trauma remains absent from their account, either because it is beyond their ability to describe or because they cannot recall precisely. They are ghostly presences telling a story that is uncertain in its source, detail or outcome. The effects for the reader paying careful attention to how these stories are narrated are stunning.

Among those 'And Now For Something Completely Different' moments in an author's career, perhaps none has been more dramatic than *The Unconsoled*, about which Ishiguro said: '*The Unconsoled* received a hail of abuse, but it was what I needed. I was ready to embrace controversy. I'd just had a bestselling novel [*The Remains of the Day*], won the Booker Prize and the film of it had just been nominated for eight Oscars. I could easily have continued producing well-shaped novels that would get kind reviews, but I felt if I was going to do something different and difficult, now was the time.'

What can one say about this novel? It is delightful yet frustrating. It doesn't obey the laws of Euclidean geometry. Its forebear is clearly Kafka, and it shares certain similarities with Murakami's wild-goose-chase novels, yet it is a one-off. I think the key to reading this novel is not to ask too many questions of it because, if you do, you can only expect to get the wrong answers. It is a Derrida-esque story of endless delay and deferral and is highly 'overdetermined' in the sense that its plot possesses a multiplicity of causes and suggests a plurality of meanings. Rather than searching for answers to questions that an implied reader imagines are being asked, it is perhaps more useful here to accept that there might simply be nothing to say. Avoiding such over-interpretation may hopefully lead to an 'excess of wonder', a position *vis-á-vis* the text that leads to an exciting awareness of our role in finding and joining in the play of meaning. Not least of these is an amusing running joke whereby certain places and many of the minor characters are named after footballers who have appeared in World Cup finals or who have appeared in Josef von Sternberg's film, *Der Blaue Engel*.

When We Were Orphans is my particular favourite of the novels. As a result of his thoughts on the Sherlock Holmes stories, perhaps Ishiguro was keen to attempt a novel narrated from the detective's point of view, but we remain in the dark as ever regarding how Christopher Banks actually solves any crimes. Indeed, in place of being aligned with a narrator who can never quite grasp the reasoning process of the great detective (e.g. Watson), our perspective is shifted to a detective-narrator whose subjectivity and emotion often overwhelm the rational aspects of his role as detective. Banks's narrative has all the trappings of the detective story, but none of the internal logic. He is another ghostly, haunted narrator, an actor who wrongly interprets the reality around him. Like Stevens, Banks is unable to grasp the political complexity of Britain's position in the 1930s. Banks and Stevens are both confronted by the slow realisation that their social roles impose a restricted perspective on reality, one which limits their worldview and contributes to their lack of self-awareness and the sense of puzzlement they instil in others.

Along with *The Remains of the Day*, Ishiguro's sixth novel—*Never Let Me Go*—is his most commercially successful and it was also made into a well-liked film. Both novels also share a similar mode of narration in that both stories are narrated as though being spoken rather than written. There are no lines in either book that would not sound out of place if recited. There is no 'artfulness' in the narration (indeed, Ishiguro told us that he goes to great lengths to make sure that every word in his books can be easily translated). However, the narrator of *Never Let Me Go*—Kathy H—is not so much an unreliable narrator, as an *inadequate* narrator. Unlike Stevens, she does not keep her feelings hidden but she is instead openly puzzling about feelings that have not been made clear to her. The reader feels this narratorial flatness very keenly and it was interesting to hear Ishiguro himself tell us that he had, in fact, abandoned *Never Let Me Go* not once, but twice. In the novel's first manifestation, the young people in the novel were students and it wasn't until, many years later, he heard a radio piece on cloning that he hit upon the idea of turning the students into clones. The novel then miraculously came to life.

For me, however, it's the least interesting of his novels, precisely because the narrator is less unreliable than usual. My favourite novels of his are those that are set in the Far East. They are the ones that play with unreliable narration to the most startling, dazzling effect. After moving through the upper echelons of pre-war English society, the strange, dislocated vistas of an unnamed Eastern European state and a dystopian vision of the near future, and even after having spent most of his life in the UK, one senses that a greater part of his narrative heart still beats somewhere in the Orient.

Originally posted on Faber's Thought Fox blog, August 2012.

Alice Munro—"On the darker side of humanity"

Alice Munro's stories have always presented us with dazzling pictures of post-war North American life, but the dramatic tensions in them rest on the way her characters have always belied that North American dream. The lighter the surface texture, the darker the shadows. In her latest collection of stories, Munro's prose takes on even darker gleamings.

The title story of her new collection, *The Love of a Good Woman*, has a brutal homicide lying deep within a family life. It begins with three boys finding a car in a local lake with a drowned man inside. The man is the town's optometrist, a gentle, well-loved figure. Structured almost as a mystery, the story shifts its point of view until the enigma surrounding his bleak, humane death is unearthed. The manner in which this story ends is characteristic of the collection as a whole. There is a sense of inevitability to it, not as a consequence of a decision made but exactly the opposite. These characters are not in control of their lives, and they are subject to contingency and circumstance. They drift, dream and wonder what is happening to them.

"Before the Change" is an epistolary story written by a woman to 'R', a man who rejected her when she gave birth to his child. While she is staying with her father, she gradually finds out that her father is running an illegal abortion house. After she has helped him with a particularly grisly termination, she tells him about her child, which she gave away for adoption. 'So isn't that ironic', she says. This woman, like many of her father's patients, remains anonymous throughout the story. Her experience of childbirth has left her feeling that 'dying and living were both irrelevant notions, like favorite movies'. She recalls ballads learned at school with eponymous titles such as "Patrick Spens" and "Solomon Grundy". Upon hearing his daughter's news, the father has a massive coronary and dies—irony is collapsed and emptiness sweeps in.

The depth and scope of these stories is impressive. With modernist ease, Munro scrambles time according to the demands of characterisation. Almost every sentence in each story probes the recesses of character like a tendril, linking 'a well-peopled and untranslatable past' to the mute present and, perhaps, a lonely future.

"Jakarta", for example, begins with two young women, Kath and Sonje, having an argument on a beach. Kath is hesitant and unfulfilled with her husband Kent, while Sonje lives with a Marxist radical called Cottar. At first, it is Kath's story, centred on her fascination with and fear of Sonje and Cottar's open relationship. Kent, by contrast, is portrayed as a leaden conservative.

Decades later, Kent takes his young girlfriend to visit Sonje and we quickly learn that Kent is a widower and that Cottar has died of a tropical disease in Jakarta. The story now becomes Sonje's, as she details a theory to Kent that Cottar is not in fact dead. Lastly, the story becomes Kent's, with his admission to us that Kath is not dead either, and may have run off with Cottar. Told in a series of flashforwards and flashbacks, the net result is a four-way relationship founded on uncertainty and discontent.

An added dimension to all this is Munro's careful patterning of character to mood and setting. Environment and atmosphere are fleshed out by perception. A woman, who has not yet registered her departure from her family, sees a truck while waiting to cross a road. 'But not just a truck—there's large bleak fact coming at her. And it has not arrived out of nowhere.'

Munro has often been hailed as a great short story writer—and there is a strong sense that she is working hard with the form, pushing it to make it do more than usual. This superb collection gives credence to that claim—she is a writer at her peak.

Financial Times, January 1999.

Rupert Thomson—"Grim lives tangled in the city"

Rupert Thomson's *Soft* is a book about the brightness of colour, about heightened awareness—where the winter wind smells like 'knives', vodka wraps your brain in 'silver' and the pages of holiday brochures are as 'slippery as fish'.

Kwench! is a new orange-coloured soft drink that young Jimmy Lyle is employed to advertise. Through a series of events—a conversation overheard on the London underground, a present of some weird jelly babies—Jimmy hits on the idea of subliminal suggestion. His boss, the shady Connor, likes the idea, elbows Jimmy out of the picture and sets up a polysomnography programme to indoctrinate his volunteer victims.

One of those victims is Glade, a dreamy 23-year-old waitress who is more than happy to be paid to sleep. When she is released from the clinic, though, she starts seeing orange everywhere. She collects orange things in boxes and dyes her hair orange. She turns sicker and madder before our eyes, and when a journalist makes allegations of impropriety against Jimmy's company on her behalf, the Kwench! campaign goes into fallout.

Hired to 'take care' of Glade is Barker, a washed-up forty-something bouncer newly arrived in London. The city we see through his eyes is unbearably grim, but we experience it through images that are hypnotic and only just this side of reality. We sense his rootlessness and resignation as he moves around the city, trying to eke out a living. Neon signs, remote control buttons and slogans all leap off the page and act as interstices of hopelessness. His is an impressive, downbeat portrayal.

Perhaps most impressive of all is the novel's chronology. It is with Barker that we start, then we move on to Glade and her problematic relationship with a lawyer living in Miami, and finally on to Jimmy and his affair with a synchro swimmer. If it sounds tortuous, it isn't—the points of view move smoothly and boldly, with several brief flashbacks supplying background information. Thomson handles the novel's London specificity very well, transforming off-kilter landscapes into the exotic and hyper real and the prose style—hallucinatory, sensual and gripping—is a dream.

Originally published in the Financial Times, March 1998.

Keith Ridgway's *Hawthorn & Child* & Denis Johnson's *Train Dreams*

Two books published in 2012 stood out for me. The first is Keith Ridgway's *Hawthorn & Child,* which is challenging and exhilarating in equal measure. The novel starts out as a police procedural with a shooting in north London but, rather than develop that story, the subsequent sections follow the tangential paths of a cocky driver/pickpocket and his young love, an anonymous psychiatric patient, a gay orgy in a sauna, Estator, Prince of Wolves… Rarely does a novel make the reader work so hard to follow the action and fill in the gaps. The dog-leg narrative gathers together ideas that it cannot contain, leaking all the time, spilling story and seemingly making no sense. Rather than trying to present a conventional story, the novel works on the reader as a kind of 'consciousness', powered by dark matter and mental disorder. I saw Ridgway read from his novel recently and I hadn't realised how funny it is, too, in a jet-black kind of way. *Hawthorn & Child* won't be to everyone's taste but, as a contemporary novel, it pushes the form harder than anything else I've read and is pretty much where it's at.

The other book that leapt out at me this year was Denis Johnson's *Train Dreams*. This short novel couldn't be more different to *Hawthorn & Child* in terms of story and style. As straight and true as the spruce trees that feature so heavily in it, the book's short, linear narrative rockets through the long life of Robert Grainier, a logman working in the 1910–20s on the construction of America's great mid-west railroads. The book begins with a group of railwaymen trying to throw a Chinaman off a bridge spanning the Moyea River and thereafter follows Grainier's life of love, loss, natural disaster and solitude. One of the most striking scenes is with a child who may or may not have been brought up by wolves; another is the ending, set in a travelling show, which is one of the strangest and most transformative endings you're ever likely to read.

Originally posted on Faber's Thought Fox blog, December 2012.

Keith Douglas—"Into battle through the looking glass"

My grandfather, Captain Alexander Greig, served in North Africa during the Second World War. He fought in the battle of El Alamein with the 8th Army, one of the divisions affectionately known as the 'Desert Rats'. I have a picture of him in uniform sitting on a camel. My grandfather died when I was a small child and I don't remember him, but every time we visited my Nana, I would look at his small collection of books that she kept in a locked glass cabinet. These books were mostly about Rommel and my Nana told me that my grandfather always expressed enormous respect for the German field marshal. Ever since then, the word 'Alamein' has had a tremendous significance in my family.

So, when I came across a copy of *Alamein to Zem Zem* in a secondhand bookshop more than 20 years ago, I immediately bought it. I knew of and loved Keith Douglas the poet, but had no idea he had written a memoir of his wartime experiences, and what a stunning memoir it is—written immediately after the events it depicts, Douglas's prose is lucid and direct and sounds so fresh that it feels as though it could have been written yesterday. It is entirely free of that kind of dated English language we now associate with contemporary works such as Noël Coward's *Brief Encounter* or Evelyn Waugh's *Brideshead Revisited*.

As well as being the finest English poet to emerge from the Second World War, Douglas was also a talented graphic artist and he possessed an artist's mix of detachment and curiosity, which meant that he could get up-close and personal to the horrors of the war without flinching. His memoir is full of the most incredible drawings and linguistic images: 'Every man had a white mask of dust in which, if he wore no goggles, his eyes showed like a clown's eyes'. Laying down to sleep out in the cold desert night, he describes the lights in the sky as 'starshells, tracers of orange, green, blue, and a harsh white, and the deeper colour of explosions'.

His account is also very good at capturing the physical sensations of being in battle. A few hours before his first engagement, he describes his feelings as the 'unstable lightness which is felt physically immediately after putting down a heavy weight'. The view from his moving tank he says is like 'a camera obscura or a silent film ... which led me to feel that the country into which we were now moving was a strange land, quite unrelated to real life, like the scenes in *The Cabinet of Doctor Caligari*'.

Keith Douglas was born on 24th January 1920 and was fascinated by all things military as a child, perhaps because his absent father had been an army captain during the First World War. He went to Christ's Hospital school and later read English & History at Oxford. He was impulsive, precocious and developed a profound disregard for authority, resulting in a near expulsion from Christ's Hospital over a stolen training rifle. His antipathy towards the establishment continued at Oxford, where he wrote vaguely anti-war poems and yet, as soon as war broke out, he joined the Sherwood Rangers as a cavalry officer. This contradiction was typical of Douglas's complex nature.

After an administrative spell with the Sherwood Rangers in Palestine, Douglas was due to be sent back to England for more training. He was desperate for the experience of war and so, against direct orders, he famously made his own way to his unit, which was now in theatre in Egypt. He rejoined them in October 1942. No one immediately seemed to notice his absence and Douglas remained in the Middle East with the Sherwood Rangers until 1943, when he returned to England to retrain for the D-Day invasions. On 6th June 1944, Douglas took part in the main assault on the Normandy beaches. Three days later, he was killed by mortar fire near Tilly-sur-Seulles while returning from a patrol. He was just 24 years old.

The war for Douglas was a Nietzschean self-examination of willpower and endurance and he mentions several times that his reasons for joining up were not just ideological, but also highly personal. As a soldier, he was passionate, uncompromising—the kind of person you would want as a leader in wartime. As his batman said to him, 'I like you sir. You're shit or bust, you are.'

As in his poems, there is a meditation on the metaphysical that runs throughout the book, almost as though he were a criminal, feeling for his own pulse whilst in the middle of a crime. Death was, for Douglas, a moment of transformation. He describes his experiences in this beautiful memoir as like 'having walked through the looking-glass which touches a man entering a battle'. My grandfather would have concurred, I'm sure.

Originally published as the preface to 'Alamein to Zem Zem' (Faber Finds, 2014).

Werner Herzog's *Of Walking in Ice*

The day after I found stuffed between two seats a bag of heroin the size of a bag of sugar, I found this book. It was the summer after my A levels and I was cleaning planes at Gatwick airport. It was a great job: 747 tails protruding from hangars at sunset; hitching rides on planes as they were moved around the gates; learning how the bowser truck worked and avoiding catching a shift on it. I handed in the drugs, but smuggled the book off airside in a gash bag and took it home. I'd never heard of the book and had no idea who the author was, so when I found out that the author was also a film director, I was curious. I caught *Fitzcarraldo* at the Duke of York's in Brighton, and *Nosferatu* at the old Everyman Cinema in Hampstead. I didn't like Herzog's films—far too operatic and overwrought for me—but his book came to hold an enormous power over me, although I wasn't sure why.

The story behind *Of Walking in Ice* is simple. While in Munich during the winter of 1974, Werner Herzog learned that Lotte Eisner, the famous German film critic and writer, was dying in Paris. '*Es muss nicht sein*', he said. Taking out a map, he drew a line from Munich to Paris and made a pledge to walk the line in order to keep her alive. It took him 21 days to complete and the book is a record of his journey. Herzog never intended for his account to be read by others, but he finally relented and Tanam, a tiny press in New York, eventually published it in English in 1980.

I don't think I've ever actually read the book through from start to finish; it is full of longueurs, lists and dull accounts of drab fields and anonymous woods. Not writing for anyone other than himself, Herzog had written in a deliberately 'matte' style, reaching quickly for the first words that came to mind as he sat huddled in some cold barn or other, the wind whistling outside.

No, the book was galvanising for other reasons.

Firstly, the photograph on the cover—of a fully-clothed man in a wintry landscape caught in mid-air doing a somersault—seemed impossible and mysterious. Who was he? Why was he there? Where was he going? Secondly, Herzog's walk was an act of shamanism, a trial by ordeal that Herzog endured, survived and was now recounting (Eisner knew of his march and stayed alive until the day after his arrival in Paris, so the story goes). Thirdly, the book was short. I didn't know books could be that short and I have tried to keep mine as short as possible ever since.

It was everything about the book apart from the writing that cast a spell over me. Ever since finding it that day at the airport, my copy of *Of Walking in Ice* has become my talisman, a *vade mecum,* not because of what it is, but because of what it stands for: decision, resolve, tenacity in the face of adversity. It bothers me, niggles me, like a stone in the shoe; it remains in my body like a potential blood clot to the heart—'Onwards! Onwards!'—and has taught me that books can matter, so much so that they can keep a person alive.

Zoë Skoulding's *The Museum of Disappearing Sounds*

Writing on her staff profile page for Bangor University, where she is Senior Lecturer in the School of English, Zoë Skoulding says: 'I perform poetry with field recordings and electronic music as an exploration of relationships between language and the physical environment'. This cross-art nature of her work is the clear driving force in this intriguing and highly-disciplined collection, shortlisted for the 2013 Ted Hughes award for new work in poetry.

To expand further on Skoulding's remit: the poems here deal with sounds that are all around us, but that don't necessarily reach our ears. The poems attempt to capture the sounds of enclosed spaces, extended open spaces, environmental sounds, voice characteristics and the vibrations of responsive surfaces. They are not concerned with delivering point-blank, bull's eye statements, but each operates instead as a kind of investigatory net that is cast over a location. The mesh of sound connections that is drawn in as a result is what is on offer. The resultant work is a 'synchronicity' of times and places rather than a 'causality'; a promotion of a process over product.

The collection is divided into several smaller clusters of poems. The opening suite of five poems is a response to the question posed by Canadian writer and musician R Murray Schafer, 'Where are the museums for disappearing sounds?', and each one of these 'exhibits' reads as a sound installation, full of the 'crackle of static', 'the wind on the microphone' and rhythm that 'turns to pitch and sinks to drone'.

"Inventory" is a mini-collection of eight poems that examines with a forensic eye the forms and functions of everyday objects, including a colander, a Singer sewing machine and a casserole dish. My favourite of these is "television", which ends with the lines:

> ... the stars
> are humming quietly in
> skies that haven't reached us yet

Equally impressive is the suite of three poems set under the title "In Search of Lost Time", which, Skoulding tells us in her notes, makes use of search engine results for Proust's title. Here, Skoulding investigates how broken software, unreliable data, jet-lag and migraines cause us to maintain an uncertain, bewildering relationship to the actual passage of time. The sequence ends beautifully with the lines: 'Between accident and absence / the world had changed into something unrecognisable'.

There is a suite of three poems written from the point of view of a narrator and his/her interaction with the voices/ghosts of three French poets. On a trip down into the Parisian sewers, Baudelaire turns to the narrator and says: 'I'm so/tired of embracing clouds'. Paul Valéry, encountered in 'the cemetery by the sea', beseeches the narrator: 'Don't you/realise how beautiful silence can be'. Rimbaud is met out at sea as a 'drowned man insisting *je est je est je est*'.

The collection concludes with its main suite of poems, entitled "The Rooms" (the word 'stanza' derives from the Italian word for 'room'). This suite of 14 poems could be renamed "Fourteen Ways of Looking at a Room", for the similarity to Wallace Stevens' poem is striking. But instead of a blackbird, the focus of Skoulding's suite is once again sound itself. In the first, "Room 321", the narrator says: 'It's here that everything / is happening twice / once in the body / and once in the words for it'. In the second, "Room 201", this idea is developed: 'When entering the room he's listening for / the two silences / the one inside and / the one outside the window'.

In her notes, Skoulding acknowledges the influence of

American composer Alvin Lucier's work on "The Rooms". Lucier's most famous work is *I am sitting in a room*, a sound piece in which Lucier recorded himself in a room saying 'I am sitting in a room', then playing back the line into the now empty room and recording that, then playing back that line into the room and recording that, and so on. Gradually, the original speech fades and merges with the resonant frequencies of the room itself, which eventually take over. Lucier's piece demonstrates that the listener is no longer merely the passive recipient of meaning, but rather the place in which meaning is created, and this is Skoulding's modus operandi too.

In between these suites, there are single poems of great beauty, which also explore the soundscapes of single locations. These resemble the work of another sound artist, Luc Ferrari, who made field recordings of places and then edited them down into highly compressed, narrative-driven sound pieces. "Gwydyr Forest" and "Easy Listening (Penmon, Anglesey)" are poems that investigate the 'lattices of molecules' and 'skin and blood vessels' and posit such phenomena as 'the surface as / *écoute*'.

All these poems share a spectral, haunting beauty. They are fine-spun and well-balanced, but material and granular too. They seem fragile at first, but repeated readings reveal their tensile strength—pull a poem in one direction and the poem bends, but doesn't break. While reading them, the poems reminded me of many other things: the black glassiness of obsidian, the intricacy of filigree, the ghostliness of X-rays, the blasted music of Thomas Köner and Mika Vainio. Skoulding is one of the most adventurous, elegant and controlled poets working today and *The Museum of Disappearing Sounds* is a tremendous achievement.

Originally published on the WriteOutLoud website, April 2014.

Italo Calvino—"Utopias, the city and the Orient"

As a young man, Italo Calvino had read Marco Polo's account of his travels to the Orient and had always wanted to write about them but he never knew how. Many years later, he found himself writing numerous microtexts of imagined cities. He had the idea of framing these descriptions with Marco Polo's fabulous voyage to the Orient. At around this time, Calvino was invited to join OULIPO and his fiction began to incorporate that movement's obsession with building complex mathematical structures into literary texts.

Invisible Cities (1972) is at the crossroads of all these passions and obsessions. In it, Marco Polo is at the court of Kublai Khan and is describing to him all the cities he has seen in the world. Over the nine chapters, Marco Polo describes a total of 55 cities. The cities are divided into 11 thematic groups of five each: Cities & Memory; Cities & Desire; Cities & Signs; Thin Cities; Trading Cities; Cities & Eyes; Cities & Names; Cities & the Dead; Cities & the Sky; Continuous Cities & Hidden Cities. In the following diagram, number 1 represents Cities & Memory, number 2 Cities & Desire, number 3 Cities & Signs, and so on. As Polo describes the cities, he moves back and forth between the groups, while moving down the list, in a rigorously mathematical way:

```
I:     1
       21
       321
       4321
II:    54321
III:    54321
IV:      54321
V:        54321
VI:        54321
VII:        54321
VIII:        54321
IX:           5432
               543
                54
                 5
```

The above diagram—a symmetrical lozenge or a diamond—has also been described as a sine wave and a city skyline. In Chapter IV, Kublai Khan says, '... my empire is made of the stuff of crystals, its molecules arranged in a perfect pattern ... a splendid hard diamond ...', which is of course exactly what is produced by Calvino's ordering of the cities.

In the italicised dialogue at the beginning of Chapter VI (roughly half way through the book), Polo says 'Every time I describe a city I am saying something about Venice'. Although Polo never actually mentions Venice, the city is present in every description he recounts. When Khan requests a description of Venice, Polo replies, 'Memory's images, once they are fixed in words, are erased'. So Polo is simultaneously describing one city, all cities and no city.

Polo realises that the further he travels the more he understands his past, so the more he travels in space the further he proceeds in time, and therefore each person he sees in a city could have been himself had he taken a different path at various crossroads, an idea that recalls Borges' idea of forking paths, namely that every decision taken excludes a large number of other choices and destinies:

> Marco enters a city; he sees someone in a square living a life or an instant that could be his; he could now be in that man's place, if he had stopped in time, long ago; or if, long ago, at a crossroads, instead of taking one road he had taken the opposite one, and after long wandering he had come to be in the place of that man in that square. By now, from that real or hypothetical past of his, he is excluded; he cannot stop; he must go on to another city, where another of his pasts awaits him, or something perhaps that had been a possible future of his and is now someone else's present. Futures not achieved are only branches of the past: dead branches.

Calvino believed strongly in the idea of a work of art as a map of the universe and the sum of all knowledge, a vocation in Italian literature that he said had been handed down from Dante to Galileo. *Invisible Cities* is no exception. He pared down his style to the Borges-like clipped descriptions of cities and minimal dialogue. Calvino called his book a *poema d'amore* to the city and it was the work with which Calvino himself said he was most satisfied because he was able to concentrate all his meditations onto a single symbol. Its multifaceted structure allows for multiple, non-hierarchical readings. It is the single work that embraces all his previous works as well as alluding to the Bible, classical literature, medieval texts, oriental literature and utopian/dystopian literature from Thomas More and Aldous Huxley. Most of all, it displays what Calvino learned best from Borges, namely that brevity can encompass infinity.

William Burroughs—"Behemoth of Beat"

The Psychic Cosmonaut, the Junkie Who Lived, The Literary Outlaw, Godfather of Punk, King of the Beats. So many epithets have been attributed to William Burroughs, so much has been said about his life that it is hard to separate the man from the myth. Was he misrepresented by the media? Was he at odds with his public image? After reading Graham Caveney's biography, *The Priest They Called Him*, and the collection of interviews, essays and other curios entitled *My Kind of Angel*, the answer is clear—he didn't care. As Paul Bowles said, 'When I got to know him I realized the legend existed in spite of him and not because of him: he didn't give a damn about it'.

Most will know something about Burroughs' life—that he accidentally shot and killed his wife, Joan; that he wrote one of the most controversial books ever, *Naked Lunch*. But most will not know that, on a trip to Europe in 1937, he met and married Ilse Klapper, an Austrian Jew fleeing the Nazis. Or that, towards the end of his life, he wept at the thought of his beloved cats being wiped out by a nuclear explosion.

Burroughs was born in 1914, in St Louis. After Harvard, which he hated, he drifted, did odd jobs and some postgraduate work. After a brief stint in the Navy, he drifted again, eventually becoming a bug exterminator in the roach-infested apartments and run-down rooming houses of Chicago. Less than a year later, he relocated to Greenwich Village, New York, where he met two young Columbia students named Allen Ginsberg and Jack Kerouac and started his 40-year addiction to drugs.

In *My Kind of Angel*, Michael Horovitz argues that the Beat movement was 'a final fling of an old-style literary bohemia' of which Burroughs wasn't really a part. Whereas Ginsberg and Kerouac were into jazz, eastern religions and social protest, Burroughs appealed to a very different kind of audience, one which was hooked on hard drugs, new forms of communication and which had a profound mistrust of the whole state apparatus. Ginsberg's 'songs of himself' recalled the epic poetry of Walt Whitman and Kerouac's romantic vision of the road resurrected the spirit of Huckleberry Finn, but Burroughs' forebears came from the old world: De Sade and Dostoevsky, Eliot's *The Wasteland,* the vaudeville of Dada, George Bataille and Jean Genet. The Beats were all-American boys but Burroughs was always more Hipster than Beat. When asked if he shared Ginsberg's non-violent forms of social protest, Burroughs replied, 'Most emphatically no'.

Burroughs met Joan Vollmer during this time and, after several ill-conceived relocations, they moved to Mexico City to try to kick their habits. It didn't work. It was during one of their long, booze-fuelled afternoons that Joan was killed. The Mexican courts only charged Burroughs with *imprudencia criminal* and released him on bail 13 days later. To his dying day, Burroughs deeply regretted the whole affair and said that 'the death of Joan brought me into contact with the invader, the Ugly Spirit and manoeuvred me into a lifelong struggle, in which I have had no choice except to write my way out'.

Burroughs fled to Tangier. By now, he was shooting Eukadol into his arm every two hours, but he travelled to London and successfully underwent an apomorphine cure. As he remarked later, the cure was 'the turning point between life and death. I would never have been cured without it. *Naked Lunch* would never have been written.' He returned to Tangier clean and began assembling his musings and outpourings into what would become *Naked Lunch*. 'Nothing but work and weed all day', he wrote to Ginsberg.

Kerouac and Ginsberg arrived in Tangier to see for themselves. Kerouac typed up Burroughs' work and Ginsberg came up with the title (a misreading of 'naked lust'). The book was published in Paris in 1959 and immediately courted controversy, but it became an international success. Its cut-up prose, surrealism, sadism, comic-book portrayals of insanity and themes of body invasion were deemed depraved by the authorities, but the book was a signifier of its own vagrancy and became the password to the *cognoscenti*. Burroughs' work was never to receive the same level of attention again, but his influence on writers such as J.G. Ballard, Angela Carter, Don DeLillo, William Gibson, Bret Easton Ellis and Kathy Acker would subsequently become apparent.

Burroughs left Morocco and, after 20 years of living in Paris, London and New York, settled in Lawrence, Kansas until his death in 1997. He kicked his habit once and for all, and admitted that there wasn't 'much left to do' in terms of writing. He took up painting and had several solo exhibitions. There were several musical collaborations, including ones with Laurie Anderson, Bill Laswell, Tom Waits and Kurt Cobain. Despite surviving all the abuse and a triple heart bypass operation, Burroughs died suddenly of a heart attack, four months after his closest friend, Ginsberg, had also died. Taken together, these two books capture more of the spirit of the man and his writing than any straight biography ever could.

Originally published in the Financial Times, August 1998.

On Shakespeare's *The Tempest*

On Hallowmass, or All Saints' Day (November 1st) 1611, *The Tempest* was first performed, by the King's Majesty's Servants at the Banqueting House in Whitehall. A new production, starring Ralph Fiennes as Prospero, was staged in September 2011, thus marking the 400th anniversary of the play's first performance. *The Tempest* is amongst the last and shortest plays Shakespeare ever wrote, and what marks it out from all the others is its magical quality. It is as if all the magical elements in the rest of his work are collected and distilled in this final piece, one that contains some of Shakespeare's most entrancing and profound language. Prospero's island is famously 'full of noises / Sounds, and sweet airs, that give delight and hurt not', and the text abounds with music, song, incantations, spells, curses, lucid dreams, moments of suspension, somnambulism and mesmerism. An other-worldly atmosphere pervades the entire play, creating a heavy-lidded, hazy experience; but from where did Shakespeare get this tremendous knowledge of and interest in magic?

The early 17th century was the Golden Age of Alchemy and its most famous exponent was John Dee. An enigmatic and controversial figure, Dee was favoured by Elizabeth, who employed him as court astrologer (he predicted the most auspicious day for her coronation), but he was also a mathematician of importance, an expert geographer and engineer and a consultant on problems of navigation. He was a teacher to the upper echelons of English society (his pupils included Philip Sydney) and he exerted influence over the development in scientific thinking of the day. It is not proven that Shakespeare knew Dee, but even if he didn't, he almost certainly would have heard of him and been aware of his opinions and teachings.

Today, the abiding image we have of an alchemist is of a deluded crackpot locking themselves away in a laboratory trying to convert base lead into gold, but at that time there were others, like Dee, for whom alchemy was something entirely different. It was the serious pursuit of the transmutation of a person's *prima materia,* their basic nature, into the pure gold of selfhood. Alchemy wasn't the manipulation of materials in the interest of personal wealth or power, but was aimed at 'soul-making'.

In order for this to happen, the personality had to undergo a transformation of some kind. In myth and legend, that transformation might involve a journey into the underworld, as in Orpheus' case, or it commonly leads to a journey through water, as in Odysseus'. *The Tempest* is the story of such a transformation. At the beginning of the play, Prospero's voyage is only halfway complete and *The Tempest* as a whole is a depiction of Prospero's inner journey and how he comes finally to achieve his personal transformation. It is the tale of a soul in its making.

Prospero has been overthrown and banished by his brother from his dukedom in Milan, put to sea with his infant daughter in a leaky boat and is eventually marooned on a small island. The play begins many years after this event with a terrifying storm at sea. A boat caught up in the storm carries Prospero's brother, among others. This storm is a *grand mal* seizure, an enormous unleashing of psychic energy, created by Prospero in order to draw his brother to the island and wreak his revenge. During the course of the play, the culprits are exposed, old conflicts are resolved, Prospero becomes Duke of Milan again and a suitor is found for Miranda, but this denouement of the plot expresses only a thin layer of the play's richness. Much more revealing is what is going on between the characters already present on the island before these men were spirited there by Prospero.

The Tempest, like all of Shakespeare's best work, is an open text, inviting us to fill in the blanks. The play has been studied from the perspective of its dramatic structure, its politics and its language, but a more revealing way of looking at the play is from a psychological point of view. Looking at the play as we would a dream or a fairytale, we see that the characters are all closely related in a highly internal way. Through the rather superficial action, the characters already on the island can be seen as manifestations of aspects of a single psyche, the dominant centre of the play: Prospero.

The first of these manifestations is Ariel, the 'airy' spirit. He is impish, volatile, hermaphroditic. He is identified as male but he is asexual and all the roles he plays at Prospero's command are female: sea nymph, harpy, Ceres. Ariel is associated with mercury (*hydra argyrum*) or quicksilver, and one of Ariel's attributes is this ability to 'shape-shift'. He can also arrest movement and cast spells, through music and magic. He tells Prospero that he has 'stow'd' the crew of the ship 'all under hatches', dispersed the others ''bout the isle' and has hidden the ship in a 'deep nook' of the island.

When Prospero first arrived on the island, Ariel had been trapped for 12 years in a cloven pine, put there by the witch Sycorax. Prospero used his own magic to release him and Ariel is thereafter captured in unwilling servitude, kept in bondage by a mixture of promises, threats and appeals. Prospero uses Ariel to carry out all his plans and stratagems, anything that is the product of his intellect and imagination. Prospero constantly refers to Ariel as his 'spirit' and he represents everything in Prospero that is airy, fiery, rational, logical, verbal.

Prospero's attitude towards Caliban could not be more different. Caliban makes his first appearance by erupting from a rock, and his first words are a curse on Prospero, in answer to which Prospero assures Caliban that he will bestow upon him 'cramps / Side-stitches that shall pen thy breath up'. The offspring of Sycorax and Satan, Caliban is a 'salvage and deformed slave', 'a strange fish' 'not honour'd with a human shape'. The cruelty Prospero shows towards Caliban is reminiscent of that found in Mary Shelley's *Frankenstein*. Once brought to life, the creature in Shelley's book is exposed to

Frankenstein's cruelty and ill-treatment, and the plot of the book is driven by the creature's desire for revenge and justice. Caliban, too, is forced to revolt against his controller, saying to his master, 'You taught me language; and my profit on't / Is, I know how to curse'.

Their relationship is one of loathing and mutual mistrust. Caliban says at one point that, given the chance, he would even force himself on Miranda in order to inflict pain on Prospero. He is bitter, envious, filled with lust, alive with feeling, hateful and hurting, but Prospero cannot do without him. Caliban knows where crabs hide, where jays nest and where springs and pig nuts can be found. 'This island's mine', he says. He lives close to nature, but Prospero, with his books and his Art, 'neglects worldly ends' and lives exclusively through his intellect. Caliban—the 'moon-calf'—is Prospero's link with the elements of water and earth and represents everything within Prospero's own self that he represses and dislikes. This is finally achieved at the play's end, when Prospero says, 'this thing of darkness I / Acknowledge mine'.

But perhaps the most intriguing presence of all is, in fact, an absence: Sycorax. Derived from the Greek 'sy' meaning sow and 'corax' meaning raven, the witch Sycorax is the progenitor of monsters, lover of the devil and the island's original inhabitant. The witch is an archetypal figure, a neglected mother goddess of the earth, and the ghostly presence of Sycorax on the island acts on the islanders as a collective unconscious. Unseen and invisible, she brings a dark power and depth to the play.

The similarities between Sycorax and Prospero are striking. Like Prospero, she came to the island with an infant. They have similar powers and both are driven by the same emotion—anger. She is black to his white, Sol & Luna. In his flight upwards into 'spirit', Sycorax represents everything that Prospero has left unattended to in his psyche. She is all that relates to the body and feeling, earthiness, uncertainty, ambiguity and multiplicity, and she is Prospero's unconscious twin.

Throughout the centuries, Prospero has been depicted in a variety of ways. In Hogarth's 1728 painting, he is shown as a Rembrandt-like rabbi, and Fuseli's idea of Prospero in a later painting is as a god-like polymath, a representation based on Leonardo da Vinci's autobiographical sketches. He has also been seen as a tyrant, a civiliser and a colonialist. In this shamanic reading of the play, however, Prospero is the perfect example of the fully-fledged Renaissance magus.

In the play's final scene, Prospero dons his 'magic robes' and traces a circle with his staff. Within this magic circle, he forgives his usurpers, gives his blessing to his daughter's union with Ferdinand and, most significantly, frees Ariel and Caliban. Ariel, the spirit who represents the elements that rise in the air, and Caliban, the monster who embodies those that fall to earth, are the two aspects of Prospero's split personality. The play is about how Prospero finds the right balance between above and below. At last, his right hand knows what his left is doing. Only now can he leave the island and return to the land of the living.

The entire time Prospero spends on the island can be viewed as an altered state of consciousness, an out-of-body experience from the mainland. Its uncertain geographical location and the 'sweet airs' on the island add to this sense that it is only a state of mind. When we are lost or confused, we say we are 'at sea', and all the time that passes in *The Tempest* is a trance, a dream, but time eventually returns everything to its true owner and, by the play's end, Prospero has finally 'come to his senses'. Prospero breaks his staff and drowns his book, renouncing his magic, for he has no further need of it; his personal transformation has been achieved, he is whole again. He relinquishes control over Ariel and Caliban, releasing them to the elements so that he can return to Milan the rightful duke and a man in harmony with himself once more.

On *Sir Gawain and the Green Knight*

During 1987–88, I was a TEFL teacher in a small village in northern Italy called Magenta. The town was so-named after the decisive battle fought there in 1859 and won by a French-Sardinian army led by Napoleon III against the Austrians. According to local legend, so many lost their lives that day and so much blood ran in the streets that they named the colour of so much blood after the town. When you exit Magenta railway station, the first thing you still see is a villa peppered with bullet holes.

The school I taught in was owned by local priests and one of them would arrive every Friday evening and take away a bag of cash with him. The classes were organised and taught by myself and one other teacher, Chris, and we were left pretty much to our own devices. I taught evening classes twice a week as well as some one-to-one lessons with local businessmen who had to learn English for their jobs. These hour-long one-to-one sessions were tortuous as the businessmen were often there against their will and were always dog-tired after a day at work. I remember one very overweight man falling asleep in front of me every time we tackled the present perfect.

One day, however, in walked a student with a strange request. His name was Bruno and he was 16 years old. He said that, at his local *gymnasium*, they were going to read the 14th-century Middle-English alliterative romance, *Sir Gawain and the Green Knight*, and he wanted someone at our school to help him tackle the text. I had, and still have, no idea why an Italian secondary school would put their 16-year old pupils through such an ordeal, but I was intrigued and so agreed. From then on, we met at the school once a week for three months or so, each time going through line-by-line a section of the text I had photocopied for him the week before. I was as much a newcomer to the text as

Bruno and learned just as much as him about the intricacies of Middle-English verse—the way the alliterations come in threes, the way the stresses produce the four-beat pulse of each line, the turning of the shorter 'bob and wheel' sections. It was one of the most unusual and rewarding teaching experiences I've ever had.

Sir Gawain and the Green Knight is a test of courage and a tale of the limitations of personal integrity. The story opens with a giant Green Knight arriving on horseback at Camelot and issuing a challenge—any of King Arthur's knights may cut off his head with a single blow of an axe on the condition that the Green Knight may return the blow in one year's time. Gawain, Arthur's nephew and famous as the most noble of his knights, immediately stands up and accepts the challenge. He makes his strike and cuts off the Green Knight's head, but the Green Knight merely picks it up and rides off, telling Gawain that he must seek him out and fulfil his part of the bargain. The text follows Gawain as he rides out the following winter to find the Green Knight and face certain death.

Not just a story of chivalry under duress, *Sir Gawain and the Green Knight* is also a nature poem, a ghost story, a thriller, a romance, an adventure story, a 2,500-line tongue twister, a myth and a morality tale. The imagery is unforgettable. As Gawain rides along the borderlands of Chesire, Staffordshire and Derbyshire, we see the turning of the seasons; the hills, vales and forests gripped in winter's clutches. Gawain sleeps in his armour, taking shelter under waterfalls, and the pages of the poem seem tinged with frost.

Four years later, I was doing an English degree at Sussex and came across Gawain again, this time in a course on Semiotics. The tutor for that course, Jacqueline Rose, was looking at *Sir Gawain and the Green Knight* in light of an essay entitled "Morphology of the Folktale", written in the 1920s by Russian theorist Vladimir Propp. The essay is still one of the most fascinating and convincing demonstrations of the underlying homogenous nature of all plots. For his essay, Propp looked at more than a hundred folktales and drew up a chart, or 'morphology', of their basic elements. He first of all noted that there were only seven basic character roles: Hero, Villain, Donor/Provider, Dispatcher, Helper, Princess and False hero. He then made a list of the thirty-one basic 'functions', as he called them. Not all the folktales included every single function, but the overall shape of all the tales remained the same. The functions are:

1. A member of the family leaves home or is absent.
2. A restriction of some kind is placed on the hero.
3. The hero violates that restriction.
4. The villain tries to find the hero.
5. The villain secures information about the hero.
6. The villain tries to trick the hero into trusting him.
7. The hero falls for it.
8. The villain hurts the hero's family or one of the family desperately lacks something.
9. This injury or lack comes to light and the hero must act.
10. The hero decides upon a course of action against the villain.
11. The hero leaves home.
12. The hero is tested in some way and, as a result, receives a magical agent or helper.
13. The hero reacts to the actions of the future donor.
14. The hero uses the magical agent or the helper aids him.
15. The hero is led to what he is looking for.
16. The hero fights the villain.
17. The hero is wounded or marked in some way.
18. The villain is defeated.
19. The injury or lack [in #8] is put right.
20. The hero returns.
21. The hero is pursued.
22. The hero is saved from this pursuit [Propp notes that

many of the folktales ended here].
23. The hero returns home, unrecognised.
24. A false hero makes false claims.
25. A difficult task is set for the hero.
26. The task is accomplished.
27. The hero is recognised.
28. The false hero or villain is exposed.
29. The hero is transformed in some way.
30. The villain is punished.
31. The hero is married and/or crowned.

What's remarkable about Propp's morphology is how well it can be applied to all kinds of story, from any period, including *Sir Gawain and the Green Knight*. Here is a synopsis of its plot in 'Proppian' terms:

On New Year's Day in Camelot, King Arthur's court is feasting and exchanging gifts. A large Green Knight armed with an axe enters the hall and proposes a game. He asks for someone in the court to strike him once with his axe, on condition that the Green Knight will return the blow one year and one day later (4). Sir Gawain, the youngest of Arthur's knights and nephew to the king, accepts the challenge (5) (6) (7). He severs the giant's head in one stroke, expecting him to die. The Green Knight, however, picks up his own head, reminds Gawain to meet him at the Green Chapel in a year and a day (New Year's Day the next year) and rides away (8) (9) (10).

As the date approaches, Sir Gawain sets off to find the Green Chapel and complete his bargain with the Green Knight (11). His long journey leads him to a beautiful castle where he meets Bertilak de Hautdesert, the lord of the castle, and his beautiful wife (12); both are pleased to have such a renowned guest. Gawain tells them of his New Year's appointment at the Green Chapel and says that he must continue his search as he only has a few days remaining. Bertilak laughs and explains that the

Green Chapel is less than two miles away and proposes that Gawain stay at the castle (13).

Before going hunting the next day, Bertilak proposes a bargain to Gawain: he will give Gawain whatever he catches, on condition that Gawain give him whatever he might gain during the day. Gawain accepts. After Bertilak leaves, the lady of the castle, Lady Bertilak, visits Gawain's bedroom to seduce him. Despite her best efforts, however, he yields nothing but a single kiss. When Bertilak returns and gives Gawain the deer he has killed, his guest responds by returning the lady's kiss to Bertilak, without divulging its source. The next day, the lady comes again, Gawain dodges her advances, and there is a similar exchange of a hunted boar for two kisses. She comes once more on the third morning, and Gawain accepts from her a green silk girdle, which the lady promises will keep him from all physical harm. They exchange three kisses. That evening, Bertilak returns with a fox, which he exchanges with Gawain for the three kisses. Gawain keeps the girdle, however (14).

The next day, Gawain leaves for the Green Chapel with the girdle. He finds the Green Knight at the chapel sharpening an axe (15), and, as arranged, bends over to receive his blow (16). The Green Knight swings to behead Gawain, but holds back twice, only striking softly on the third swing, causing a small nick on his neck (17). The Green Knight then reveals himself to be the lord of the castle, Bertilak de Hautdesert (18), and explains that the entire game was arranged by Morgan le Fay, Arthur's enemy. Gawain is at first ashamed and upset, but the two men part on cordial terms (19) and Gawain returns to Camelot (20), wearing the girdle in shame as a token of his failure to keep his promise with Bertilak (21). Arthur decrees that all his knights should henceforth wear a green sash in recognition of Gawain's adventure (22).

Of course, I'm not suggesting that anyone should slavishly follow Propp's morphology, but it is a brilliant, illuminating way to see how a plot works in practice, from the inside-out, as it were. Reading Propp's morphology in tandem with *Sir Gawain and the Green Knight* showed how well its author had laid the traps and sprung the surprises. The beauty of the tale is that, while the story initially seems to be about one thing—the beheading game—it turns out actually to be about something else entirely—temptation.

Ultimately, every story has its own personality. Plot may be the genetic code of a text, but, just as human beings who share the same DNA are obviously and wildly different from each other, so books that show their common lineage are also peculiarly and stubbornly individual. Thank goodness for that! There are very many stories that follow, more or less, the same plot, but it is the writer's task to create stories, not copy plots. Stories these days might not be original, but they can still be authentic.

Michelangelo Antonioni—"Auteur of eerie angst"

Nothing happens, nobody comes, nobody goes, it is terrible', said Jean Anouilh after seeing *Waiting for Godot* in 1952. Michelangelo Antonioni is 80 today, and much the same was said of his film *L'Avventura,* when it was shown at Cannes for the first time in 1960. The audience shouted 'Cut! Cut!' during the long tracking shots and openly laughed at the film's ending. Yet it began to pick up awards and, 10 years after its release, was voted one of the 10 best films ever made. Like Anouilh before him, Roberto Rossellini knew he had seen something different that night: what he had seen was one of the staging posts of modern cinema.

To be fair to the film's critics, nothing much does happen in *L'Avventura.* A group of friends go sailing and one disappears. The others start searching for her, but it gradually becomes apparent that she won't be found, so the friends return home one by one. Eventually, only the missing girl's lover and her best friend remain, and by the film's close, they have begun an affair. Antonioni rejected all notions of drama, saying that 'stories are what they are, with neither a beginning nor an end necessarily, without key scenes, without catharsis'. The girl's disappearance, like Janet Leigh's in *Psycho,* is replaced as the main theme of the film by what happens afterwards. Indeed, as the lovers come together at the end, her disappearance is all but forgotten.

It took Antonioni 10 years and five films to perfect the method seen in *L'Avventura,* and he went on to make a further three films about similar angst-ridden themes: urban alienation; non-communication and moral laxity. But it is for *Blow-Up* that he is, perhaps, best remembered in Britain. The film was a sea-change for Antonioni: his first in English for an international studio and his first made abroad. And it is his only film that has anything vaguely resembling a plot. Set in sixties London, the film is about a photographer who may or may not have photographed a murder. As with *L'Avventura*, however, events take a back seat to the underlying themes: this time, the nature of reality. 'I want to recreate reality in an abstract form', he said. 'One of its chief themes is about seeing properly, or not, the true nature of things.' Behind its cool façade, *Blow-Up* has some very serious concerns. We see everything the photographer sees and, like him, we learn not to trust what we see. Or rather, we learn to trust what we don't see. It's a mental minefield but if you're not interested in the angst, just sit back and watch Verushka doing one of her photo-sessions, or The Yardbirds circa Jeff Beck.

This was the height of Antonioni's commercial success; the combination of his ideas, blended with a specific time and place, and he had an unexpected hit on his hands. On the strength of this, MGM hired him to make a film about the counter-culture in the US. What they got was a beautifully measured study of space and colour. Not surprisingly, *Zabriskie Point* flopped at the box-office, and Antonioni entered a wilderness, taking on a documentary project abroad.

His career was saved by the unlikeliest of people, Jack Nicholson, whose meteoric rise since *Easy Rider* meant he could afford a risk. Nicholson was scouting for a suitable European project, a move that many of his generation were then making: Donald Sutherland worked with Federico Fellini and both Marlon Brando and Robert de Niro worked with Bernado Bertolucci. Antonioni was preparing a project, for which he was only able to secure financial backing once Nicholson signed his name to it.

In the film that resulted, *The Passenger*, Nicholson plays David Locke, a TV journalist who is trying to set up a meeting with the leader of a guerrilla group in some unnamed African country. The opening desert scenes are pure Antonioni: Locke travels further and further into the desert on a series of slender promises.

The further he travels, the more powerless he becomes, until, in a moment of fury and frustration, he starts to beat up his Land Rover. The idea of using the desert as a symbol of barrenness or futility is not new but rarely is it used to such stunning effect. On returning to his hotel, Locke finds that another guest, who bears a remarkable resemblance to him, has suddenly died. He decides to fill the dead man's shoes and live out his life. What follows is a long, looping journey across Europe.

Nicholson has talked admiringly of Antonioni's method: 'I found working with Antonioni a tremendous discipline. And Antonioni is always very much the master. With him, what is in the film is exactly what he meant to put there.' Gone are the hysterics that Nicholson uses so often elsewhere; his performance is so subdued, you have to keep reminding yourself he's acting. 'Antonioni's basic approach to acting is "Don't act, just say the lines and make the movements"', says Nicholson. 'He doesn't make dramatic constructions, he makes configurations.' The great Japanese director Ysujiro Ozu once said, 'I want to make people feel, without resorting to melodrama', and this seems to be Antonioni's approach too. As is the case with both *L'Avventura* and *Blow-Up, The Passenger* ends with an unsolved mystery. Does Locke die at the end? Is he murdered? If so, by whom? While the film is a road movie, it is something more: a road movie with a brain. Themes of identity and destiny are ruminated over by the film's characters. But again, if you're not an existentialist, just enjoy the story of a gun-runner on the run.

Antonioni's sense of locale is impeccable: the empty town in *L'Avventura*, sixties London and the magical park in *Blow-Up*, the highways and byways of Europe in *The Passenger*. As a child in Ferrara, Antonioni was fascinated by buildings. He would make models and place people inside them, making up stories as to why they were there. This interest in space, and the relationship between people and space, runs through all his work. *The Passenger* is almost exclusively about people moving in, through or between buildings. In one scene, Locke and the Girl (Maria Schneider) see each other at the Gaudi buildings in Barcelona but are kept separated by the baffling system of walkways, fences and exits. This interest in architecture seems to have found contemporary sympathies, most notably from American director Paul Schrader, for whom *The Eclipse* was an influence for his film *American Gigolo* and who, while making his most recent film, *Light Sleeper*, would retire to his trailer to watch *Red Desert* for inspiration.

But on the whole, Antonioni has fallen from favour, since not telling a story is tantamount to treason these days. In the past, Antonioni's directorial style may have seemed a bit flat, compared to the visual riches of, say, Fellini or Luchino Visconti, but that excess can date, while Antonioni's films retain a certain freshness. Where other modernist films, like *Last Year in Marienbad*, wore their cerebral conundrums very much on their sleeves, Antonioni's films hide them somewhere deep inside. As Antonioni says: 'Some believe I make films with my head; others think they come from the heart; for my part, I feel as though I make them with my stomach'.

Originally published in the Guardian, September 1992.

Jean Vigo—"Film-maker who saw the angel in man"

Whenever he is in London and takes a taxi, the film-maker Bernado Bertolucci insists on travelling via Vigo Street, regardless of whether it's on the way. He says he knows the street probably wasn't named after Jean Vigo, but that that's not the point. Such is the devotion with which this French film-maker is remembered and revered.

His reputation is made all the more remarkable with the knowledge that in his brief life, he produced only three short films and one feature before he died at the age of 29. With the news of a filmed biography on the way and a reissue of P.E. Salles Gomes' 1957 biography, Vigo's work has been given a new lease of life.

Vigo was born in a Parisian garret full of cats in April 1905. His father, Eugene Bonaventura Vigo, was better known as Miguel Almereyda, a militant anarchist who spent his life organising political rallies and editing magazines and newspapers. Almereyda was imprisoned several times for his political beliefs and, during one of these spells in prison, he was found dead in his cell.

An official statement claimed that Almereyda had hanged himself with his shoelaces, but the details are murky and the suspicion of murder is strong. Jean was 12 years old. Much later, Vigo cruelly discovered that the shoelaces he had bought for his father that morning were the ones used to kill him.

Vigo's mother was too unwell to look after him and so he grew up with relatives in the south, where he attended local boarding schools under the pseudonym Jean Salles. While at the Sorbonne, the tuberculosis that was eventually to kill him forced Vigo to spend some months at the Font-Romeu sanatorium, where he met Elisabeth Lozinska, or Lydou. When each was well enough, they settled in Nice and married in 1929.

As a wedding present, Lydou's father gave them a sum of money which enabled Vigo to buy a second-hand film camera. With it, he made his short films—a satirical documentary on Nice's bourgeoisie, a poetic film about France's champion swimmer and the subversive, free-wheeling *Zéro de Conduite,* which drew heavily on Vigo's years at boarding school.

All were learning exercises and Vigo's influences were apparent. He was a great admirer of René Clair, von Stroheim and Soviet Kino-eye techniques, and this led reviewers to categorise Vigo primarily as an avant-garde auteur. Vigo himself knew of this formalism, but was no pedant. He stated that if a film 'does not commit us as artists, it does commit us as men. And that's worth at least as much.'

He made good on his word in *L'Atalante,* a profoundly humane look at *les petits gens* filmed along the dreary canals of northern France during the bitter winter of 1934. The story is simplicity itself—a young barge captain, Jean, marries a village girl, Juliette, and takes her away with him to live on the barge. She longs for the city and runs away, but they are re-united when she returns.

By this time, Vigo had seen and championed Buñuel's *Un Chien Andalou* and integrated into *L'Atalante* the importance the Surrealists placed on the near-sacredness of everyday objects and mental processes. The film is a tale of *erotika pathemata* punctuated by a series of epiphanic moments. When Juliette has run away, Jean is so overcome by desire that he licks ice and swims underwater to 'find' his love.

But Vigo was once again ill, sometimes directing scenes from a stretcher. He organised a screening for his financiers, who hated it, claiming it was non-commercial. They insisted on a radical re-cut and added a sentimental ballad that was popular at the time. Vigo was exhausted—the exertions of the long shoot and the cold weather proved too much and he died before a final version of the film could be agreed upon.

Salles Gomes' biography is a beautiful exploration of Vigo's life and work, marred only by the occasional lapse into dryness of tone. It includes a comprehensive account of his father's life, so important when understanding the forces that drove Vigo. By amassing a dossier of testimonials and evidence, Vigo always hoped to clear his father's name, but he never managed to.

During his life, he placed the greatest emphasis on relationships—*L'Atalante* was made and acted by his band of followers and friends. Many people attest to his love of comedy, dressing up and playing pranks, but he could also be distant and haughty. Crucially, Vigo fell out with his mother and Salles pinpoints a pattern in Vigo's life whereby he is drawn to people and subjects, from which he then unconsciously withdraws.

By the end of the book, the sense of lives repeating themselves is tangible. Like his father, Vigo displayed a healthy disregard for authority, but the price he paid was marginalisation and poverty. *L'Atalante* was mutilated by its distributor and sank without trace but a pristine print, deposited in the National Film Archive during the blitz, was discovered in 1989 and the film was re-released to universal acclaim the following year.

Another of Vigo's heroes was the film-maker Jean Epstein, one of whose comments on film Vigo particularly loved and quoted. It could easily serve as an epitaph to Vigo's life and work—'This form of photography in depth sees the angel in man, as one might see the butterfly in a cocoon'.

Originally published in the Financial Times, August 1998.

Krzysztof Kieślowski—An Interview

There's a scene in *The Double Life of Veronique*, Krzysztof Kieślowski's luminous film of 1991, in which the eponymous heroine is playing with a shoelace when she pulls it taut, mimicking a flatliner on an ECG. The moment is poignant within the context of the film because Veronique's 'twin' has died suddenly of a heart attack, cut down in the prime of her career as a singer. In reality, much the same happened to Kieślowski himself: on 13th March 1996, Kieślowski checked himself into a Warsaw hospital where he was due to undergo a heart bypass operation, had the operation, and never woke up. At just 54 years old, his sudden death seemed terribly premature, but it seemed doubly cruel because he, too, was in his prime as a filmmaker.

I had the good fortune to meet Kieślowski, not once, but twice. The first occasion was in 1990, after the success of his film *A Short Film about Killing*, but before he became famous. I met him in the dining room of his Brighton B&B, where we talked one-to-one for an hour. He was courteous, but wary, professing not to like watching films much, or doing anything else, for that matter. He claimed that his favourite film was *Dead Poets' Society*, but I never knew whether or not he was being disingenuous. The second time I met him was at the Venice Film Festival in 1993. By then, Kieślowski was a fully-fledged star and *Blue* had just astounded everyone at the festival. In the press conference afterwards, I started by asking if he remembered our conversation three years earlier. He nodded that he did and it struck me then that the man had not been, and would never be, changed by all the praise heaped upon him.

Krzysztof Kieślowski was born in Warsaw in 1941 and graduated from the famous film school in Lodz in 1969. He started making documentaries—about factories, bricklayers, copper mines, films that subtly and covertly prompted criticism of the state. 'We were in a luxurious position', Kieślowski explained. 'The state funded us, and with the state's money we made films opposing it.' But the authorities gradually took notice and things came to a head when, in 1980, the authorities seized footage that Kieślowski had shot for a documentary about the main railway station. They explained their seizure by claiming they were looking for a murder suspect, but Kieślowski knew better and he realised that his role as filmmaker was helping, not hindering, the state in their surveillance operations.

When martial law was declared in December 1981, life became even harder. The military clamped down on any remaining political support for the now defunct Solidarity movement. Writing graffiti, for instance, or organising a strike, was punishable by up to three years imprisonment. Kieślowski became interested in making a documentary of the various trials taking place at that time. He approached one of the defence lawyers for permission to film and, after initial caution (Kieślowski could, after all, be working for the authorities), the lawyer, Krzysztof Piesiewicz, agreed.

While filming in the courtrooms, Kieślowski noticed something strange—when it came to passing sentence on the accused, the judges often failed to do so. Initially baffled, Kieślowski slowly realised that the judges were nervous in front of the camera. 'The judges knew that some time in the future, after three, ten or twenty years, somebody would find this film.' When other defence lawyers picked up on what was happening, they all begged Kieślowski to attend their trials and so Kieślowski set up a second, dummy, camera in more than fifty trials in order to ensure that the charges were dismissed.

The tables had been turned and, although the documentary never materialised, Kieślowski and Piesiewicz got on famously. 'Piesiewicz doesn't know how to write. But he can talk. He can talk and not only can he talk but he can think.' Kieślowski decided to make a feature about martial law and asked

Piesiewicz to collaborate on the script, bringing to it his legal experience and expertise. It marked the beginning of a collaboration that was to last for the remainder of Kieślowski's life.

The resultant film, *No End*, is a curious hybrid of the personal and political. A woman, Ula, grieves over the recent death of her husband, a defence lawyer, and gradually becomes involved in the cases her husband was working on. In doing so, she discovers that she loved her husband more than she realised and increasingly longs to rejoin him. When the film was released, Kieślowski once again ran into trouble with the authorities—they hated its pro-Solidarity stance and suppressed it, and it remained unseen in the West for several years. In retrospect, the film's slightly awkward mix of the moral and metaphysical was perhaps a dry run for the much more successful project the two men next wrote together—*The Decalogue*.

Kieślowski described how the project came about: 'I happened to bump into my co-scriptwriter in the street. It was cold. It was raining. I'd lost one of my gloves. "Somebody should make a film about the Ten Commandments," Piesiewicz told me. "You should do it." A terrible idea, of course.' Thankfully not, since the subsequent series of ten films made for television is one of the absolute gems of post-war European cinema.

Set in and around a housing estate in Warsaw, each hour-long film loosely takes one of the commandments and dramatises it. Kieślowski chose early on to steer clear of politics altogether, concentrating instead on 'our essential, fundamental, human and humanistic questions'. By setting the films in one place, apparently the most beautiful housing estate in Warsaw ('It looks pretty awful so you can imagine what the others are like'), Kieślowski emphasises the communal nature of the films. Characters from one film appear in another and the series is linked as a whole by a young man who appears at crucial moments to watch over the action without comment.

In *Decalogue 2*—'Thou shalt not take the name of the Lord thy

God in vain'—a woman asks her neighbour, a doctor who is treating her seriously ill husband, what his chances of survival are. She explains that she is pregnant, but not by her husband. If he lives, she will have an abortion, but if he is going to die, she wants to keep the baby. Thus, the doctor is asked to play God with the child's life. What should he do? Kieślowski presents this moral maze in a typically clear-eyed manner, describing these people in their everyday surroundings without praise or condemnation.

Decalogue 5, perhaps the best of the lot, was lengthened into a feature, simply entitled *A Short Film About Killing*. The film follows a disaffected youth who, for no apparent reason, murders a taxi driver. He is tried, found guilty and the state executes him. Shot in a sickly green, the film contains some of the most brutal depictions of violence—whether inflicted by a single person or the state—ever committed to film and its blistering indictment of capital punishment was at least partly responsible for bringing about its abolishment in Poland.

The film won the first ever European Oscar for Best Film and it, as well as *A Short Film About Love*, which followed soon after, brought Kieślowski to the attention of critics and audiences around the world. Following quickly on the heels of these films came the fall of communism and with that came the opportunity to work abroad. But while he enjoyed his new-found artistic freedom, Kieślowski grew weary of the responsibilities fame thrust upon him and he missed his homeland badly. His next project, *The Double Life of Veronique*, a film about two identical young women, one French and one Polish, was in some sense an embodiment of this split.

In Poland, Weronika is a promising singer, suffering from a heart condition that endangers her life. Despite knowing that she should give it up, she continues and, during a concert, collapses and dies of a heart attack. At exactly that moment in France, Veronique—also a singer with a heart defect—suddenly senses something missing from her life. Worried that her heart will give out, she gives up her singing career and becomes a teacher, only learning of Weronika's existence later on through a series of signs and signals.

The Double Life of Veronique is an enigmatic film whose geographical split is mirrored in its stylistic differences. Weronika's story is told more or less realistically, but Veronique's story is much more esoteric and abstract. For this section, Kieślowski used extreme close-ups in an attempt to go beyond the concrete, beyond the physical. 'The film is about sensibility, presentiments and relationships which are difficult to name', Kieślowski said and revealed that he had difficulty getting the film's sense of mystery right: 'If I show too much the mystery disappears; I can't show too little because then nobody will understand anything'.

Some critics tended to agree with the latter, complaining that the film, photographed using a golden yellow filter, was little more than an extended Chanel ad. For them, Kieślowski's new-found fame had heralded a shift away from the 'grit' of his Polish films towards the 'gloss' of his French ones. Kieślowski disagreed. 'A lot of people don't understand the direction in which I'm going. They think I'm going the wrong way, that I've betrayed my way of looking at the world. The goal is to capture what lies within us, but there's no way of filming it. You can only get nearer to it. I really don't have any sense of having betrayed my own point of view.'

Audiences agreed with Kieślowski and he received hundreds of letters from people who had been greatly moved by the film. A young girl in Paris approached Kieślowski in the street one day and told him that, after having seen the film three times, she realised that there was such a thing as a soul. 'There's something very beautiful in that', Kieślowski said. 'It was worth making Veronique for that girl.'

Despite some criticism from the press, the film did well on the festival circuit, with Irene Jacob eventually being named Best Actress at Cannes for her 'indelible' performance. Realising that they had stumbled on a winning formula, Kieślowski and Piesiewicz decided to do another series of linked films, this time a trilogy: *Three Colours: Blue, White, Red*. Named after the colours of the French flag, the films were loosely based on the ideals of liberty, equality and fraternity, though Kieślowski hated attaching tags or labels to his work. *Blue* is actually much more about melancholy, or the immaterial, than liberty. By privileging colours over concepts in this way, Kieślowski hoped that viewers in the new, post-ideological Europe would draw their own conclusions about what, if anything, the films 'meant'. He believed this very strongly, saying, 'The moment something is named, the possibility of free interpretation is cut off'.

Whatever they were about, the films resonated once again with audiences around the world. They were showered with prizes and acclaim, but Kieślowski himself was exhausted. At one point during production, he was editing *Blue*, filming *White* and writing the script for *Red* at the same time. After the completion of the trilogy, he announced his retirement, much to everyone's surprise. All he wanted to do, he said was smoke and read at his country home in his beloved Poland. As ever, that wasn't entirely true and, by the time of his death, Kieślowski had embarked on a new project with Piesiewicz, another trilogy, entitled *Heaven, Purgatory & Hell*. A screenplay for the first instalment had been written and was eventually filmed by the German director Tom Tykwer and released in 2001. The other parts might yet see the light of day.

Kieślowski was the last in a long line of classic European 'auteurs', a deeply unfashionable word in our interactive, reality-TV-besotted times. While Kieślowski's work deals with such lofty notions as 'the human condition' and 'the divine', he wears these themes lightly. He is less pessimistic than Bergman, less ponderous than Tarkovsky and remained a total pragmatist to the end. Increasingly, his work concerned itself with coincidence and chance, freedom and fate—the workings of God, some would say—but Kieślowski refused to believe in a state-sanctioned God, preferring his own, private deity. He was a sceptic, yet he had a visionary streak.

I can't help thinking that the drastic decline of the role of formal religion in the life of Western Europeans goes quite some way towards explaining the chord that Kieślowski's films have struck in people around the world. In the role of metaphysician that Kieślowski assumed, albeit reluctantly, audiences turned to his films for some kind of comfort or guidance in our post-moral world. His films map the marginal difference between what is inexplicable and what is merely left unexplained. People looked to his films for answers, but he smiled his wry smile and showed them that there were no answers and, even if there were, he certainly wasn't telling.

Chinatown—"Hard-boiled nostalgia"

Next to the western, the hard-boiled detective story is America's most distinctive contribution to the history of cinema and the world of storytelling. In 1929, ex-Pinkerton agent Dashiell Hammett published *Red Harvest*, the first ever hard-boiled detective novel. He followed this with three more novels—*The Maltese Falcon* (1930), *The Glass Key* (1931) and *The Thin Man* (1934)—which kickstarted and virtually defined the genre. Hollywood was quick to use these novels as source material for a style of black and white films called *film noir*, the classic period of which is generally regarded as beginning with *The Maltese Falcon* (directed by John Huston) in 1941 and ending with Orson Welles' *Touch of Evil* in 1958.

The narrative blueprint of *film noir* has as its protagonist a private investigator who occupies a marginal position with respect to the official social institutions of criminal justice. His position on the edge of the law is important because one of the central themes of the hard-boiled story is the ambiguity between institutionalised law enforcement and true justice. Only the individual of integrity who exists on the margins of society can solve the crime and bring about true justice. Our hero's marginal status is crucial to the story, but it is also central to his character. The private eye is usually presented as a failure. He is a relatively poor man who operates out of a seedy office and hardly ever makes much money and, when he does, he loses it.

The classic detective story begins when the hero is given a case by a client, someone who is almost always duplicitous. Mary Astor as Brigid in *The Maltese Falcon* is the villain of the piece and the person who shows up in Sam Spade's office to start the story. Often, the detective is being used as a pawn in some larger plot of the client and he soon finds himself enmeshed in a very complex conspiracy involving a number of people from different spheres of society. The detective investigates through movement and encounter, coming up against a linked series of criminal acts and responsibilities. He eventually discovers not a single guilty individual but a corrupt society in which wealthy and respectable people are linked with gangsters and crooked politicians. Because it is society and not just a single individual that is corrupt, the official machinery of law enforcement is unable to bring the guilty to justice.

Another essential ingredient in the hard-boiled detective story is the *femme fatale*. In almost every case, during the course of his investigation, the hero encounters a beautiful but dangerous woman, to whom he finds himself drawn, even to the point of falling in love. Sometimes the woman is his client, sometimes a figure in the conspiracy. In some cases (eg *The Maltese Falcon*) the woman turns out to be the murderess, but even if she doesn't turn out to be the murderess, she has a deeply negative impact on the hero's life and he is forced to return to his marginal status at the end of the story.

In many ways, and up to a certain point, the storyline of *Chinatown* follows this formula very closely. Its setting—Los Angeles in the 1930s—is very much the archetypal 'hard-boiled' setting, the same place and time of Hammett's and Chandler's novels. The dramatic lighting, period furnishings, costumes, make-up and gesture in *Chinatown* are all strong signifiers of *film noir*, but *Chinatown* diverges crucially from the classic *film noir* formula in a number of ways. Firstly, and obviously, although Roman Polanski carefully controls the visual motifs of *film noir* throughout *Chinatown*, it is not strictly speaking a *film noir* because the film was shot in colour. In addition, many of its scenes are shot outside in broad daylight, contrasting sharply with *film noir*'s tendency to be shot indoors and at night.

Secondly, the name of Jack Nicholson's character, JJ Gittes, carries with it very different connotations to the standard *film noir* hero. The name Sam Spade implies hardness, a digging beneath the surface to get at the truth; Philip Marlowe has an aura of knightliness and chivalry. Gittes, on the other hand (or 'Gits' as Noah Cross ironically keeps pronouncing it), connates a self-serving, grasping character. Moreover, he is not a poor man living on the margins of society but actually a flourishing small businessman who has made a successful career out of catching his clients' spouses in flagrante delicto. Faye Dunaway's character, Mrs Mulwray, also diverges from the usual *femme fatale* archetype. In *The Maltese Falcon* the character of Brigid Shaughnessy, although deceitful, is nevertheless a strong character, an active generator of incident rather than the usual submissive, passive victim of circumstance. Mrs Mulwray, however, has a neurotic fragility, an underlying quality of desperation and the impression is that she is never in control of, or determining, her own fate.

But the strongest difference between *Chinatown* and a classic *film noir* like *The Maltese Falcon* is in its tone and the extremely downbeat nature of its ending. Like the traditional hard-boiled detective, Gittes gradually finds himself becoming a moral agent with a mission. However, instead of demonstrating his ability to expose and punish the guilty, as is the case with Sam Spade or Philip Marlowe, Gittes steadily finds himself confronting a depth of evil and chaos so great that he is unable to control it. In the classic detective movie, the hero, like Oedipus, to some extent shares the responsibility for the crime by either a failure to see it or by hubris that he can solve the problem. In attempting to solve it, he becomes part of the problem, and this is the case in *Chinatown*. In the classic detective story, the detective is involved in the investigation, but he is really investigating his own limits to act in a way that is meaningful and positive. Unlike Sam Spade or Philip Marlowe, Gittes ultimately fails to solve the problem and fails even to see it.

This theme of 'seeing' or not seeing is a recurrent motif in *Chinatown*. Again and again, we see cameras, spectacles and binoculars pop up in the film's storyline. When the spectacles do appear, however, they are smashed, just like the watches and headlamps we see in the film. And then there is also the recurrent motif of the flaw in Faye Dunaway's eye. The other running symbol throughout *Chinatown* is, of course, water. Water, or the lack of it, is everywhere in the film, its presence or absence somehow implied in almost every scene. The story, and these motifs running through it, reach an apogee in the pond scene. As the Chinese gardener is removing weeds from it ('bad for the glass'), Gittes sees something shiny in the water. He bends down, about to retrieve the object, when the door opens and Evelyn Mulwray comes out. The solution to the crime is right there in front of him—some broken glasses glinting in the salt-water pond—but he fails to see it.

Robert Towne has said that he got the idea for *Chinatown* from a book called *Southern California Country*, in which there was a chapter called "Water, Water, Water" about the destruction of the Owens Valley and how water was siphoned from there to the San Fernando Valley 225 miles away, completely bypassing Los Angeles. The San Fernando Valley was arid sheep-farming country which land speculators had secretly bought up and then caused a panic in Los Angeles by instigating a drought. They made millions and millions of dollars as a result of this speculation and the Owens Valley was destroyed.

Towne says:

> I hoped to dramatize the formation of the city on a basis which was deeply destructive both for the city that was destroyed and the city that would gradually grow like a cancer ... I thought I would couch it as a detective story because I didn't feel that a polemic on water and power would sell very well. I thought that a mystery just following water—you turn on a water faucet and water comes out—wasn't very mysterious but you could make it into a mystery, and it would be a real

> crime, although not a crime as in most detective stories where it involves something more ostensibly exotic like a jewel-encrusted bird. Whatever it was, I wanted a real crime … It may seem strange, but one of the basic structural problems that I had to deal with was what scandal do you deal with first, the water-and-power scandal or the incest? The more serious one in the water-and-power but the more dramatic one is the incest. I got it right finally because one led rather nicely into the other.

At the end of the film, Gittes fails to act meaningfully and positively and Noah Cross is free to continue his rapacious destruction of the land, the city and the body of his own daughter/granddaughter. The result is not heroic confrontation and the triumph of justice but tragic catastrophe and the destruction of the innocent. The name/place 'Chinatown' thus becomes a locus for darkness, a symbol of life's deeper moral enigmas, those consequences of actions that are past understanding and beyond control.

The extremely downbeat nature of this ending was almost certainly an echo of the strong sense of disillusionment in America following the Vietnam War and the Watergate scandal. *Chinatown* was one of many films made in the 1970s and early 80s that reflected this sense of moral ambiguity and social uncertainty. George Lucas' *American Graffiti* (1973) set out to recapture the lost innocence of the Eisenhower era. Robert Altman's *The Long Goodbye* (1973) was ironic and foulmouthed in a way that the original story never was. Lawrence Kasdan's neo-*noir Body Heat* (1981), which borrowed some elements of its plot from *Double Indemnity* (1944), was much more sexually explicit. Arthur Penn's *Night Moves* (1975) was a highly ambiguous portrayal of a reluctant quest for the truth about a series of crimes. As the detective (played by Gene Hackman) approaches the solution to the crimes, he becomes (like Gittes) morally and emotionally involved in the quest, making it more and more difficult for him to integrate truth, feeling and morality. In the end, the detective (like Gittes) is totally disillusioned by the catastrophe his investigation has brought about.

With its carefully-constructed and beautifully-controlled evocation of *film noir, Chinatown* displays a profound self-consciousness for the historical past. But in the permissive 1970s, it could no longer set out to represent that past, it could only represent our ideas and stereotypes about that past. The action in the film is updated to reflect the realities of contemporary life and the result is a mythic, nostalgic reincarnation of the hard-boiled, laced with the uncertainties of post-Vietnam America.

"Flickers"

Edith Scob's night-time walk, strange birds whooping, in George Franju's *Les Yeux sans visage*. The white horse running, its mane on fire, in Franju's *Thomas l'Imposteur*. Robert de Niro stirring his cup of coffee for an inordinate amount of time in *Once Upon a Time in America*. The barge captain looking for his love in the underwater sequence in *L'Atalante*. The barge captain licking ice to cool his ardour in *L'Atalante*. The woman licking the toe of a statue in Buñuel's *L'Age d'Or*. Buñuel's fear of the clergy. The whole of Luis Buñuel's output. Michael Powell's comment that he wanted the nuns' habits in *Black Narcissus* to look like oatmeal. Ray Durgnat's comment that *Black Narcissus* is 'A Bresson film, with rainbows'. *Un Cœur en hiver* as the greatest film Bresson never made. *In the City of Sylvia*—Eric Rohmer shooting Andy Warhol's screen tests with a soundtrack by Luc Ferrari. The determination of the women bombers in *The Battle of Algiers*. The colour red in *Don't Look Now*—a bloodstain that refuses to be scrubbed out. The white paint marks on the quinces in *The Quince Tree Sun*. The fact that Victor Erice has only made three films since 1973. The scene in *32 Short Films about Glenn Gould* in which Colm Feore plays his recording of a Beethoven Piano Sonata to a bemused German chambermaid, after which she says 'Danke schön'. Julie Christie staring into the marble egg at the end of *McCabe and Mrs Miller*. *Apocalypse Now* versus *The Deerhunter*; expressionism versus realism. The pin-sharp monochrome photography of *Ice Cold in Alex*. Clocks & counters, intercoms & phones, bells & locks in Truffaut's *La Peau douce*. Truffaut's idea that a single word can encapsulate an entire film—his word for *Last Year in Marienbad* is 'persuasion'. The play on the words double vie to mean 'double life' and 'W' in *Double Life of Véronique*. *Véronique* following the concrète tape in *Double Life of Véronique*. Jan Hann's gradual humiliation in *The*

Sign of Leo. The smile of the Polish soldier in *The Eagle Has Landed* when Larry Hagman asks if he is making fun of him. Robert Duvall preparing himself to be executed in *The Eagle Has Landed*. Birds in *Psycho*. The bird in the cage in Jean-Pierre Melville's *Le Samouraï*. Alain Delon as the most handsome man in cinema. Sandrine Bonnaire's performance in Agnes Varda's *Vagabonde*. Alida Valli's expression of sadness throughout *The Third Man*. Orson Welles' hands (actually Carol Reed's) gripping the grille at the end of *The Third Man*. The symphony of close-ups of Falconetti's face in Dreyer's *The Passion of Joan of Arc*. The cut to the charred stake in Bresson's *The Trial of Joan of Arc*. The cut from the lit match to the sun in *Lawrence of Arabia*. The cut from the bone to the spaceship in *2001: A Space Odyssey*. The footprints in the sand in Satyarjit Ray's *The World of Apu*. Pointing the camera into the sun in Kurosawa's *Rashomon*. The weirdness of the scene in which the dead man talks through a medium in Kurosawa's *Rashomon*. The scene in Kurosawa's *Dersu Uzala* in which Dersu saves the captain's life by building a shelter made from marsh reeds just as a storm descends. The dolly shot onto Al Pacino at the end of *Godfather Part II*. The blind narrator in *Black Sun* telling a story about being robbed in Delhi only for the thieves to return his belongings because they saw he was worse off than them. Shirley Winters' hair flowing like underwater weed in *Night of the Hunter*. The skiff ride downstream in *Night of the Hunter*. The suffering of the donkey in Bresson's *Au Hasard, Balthazar*. The fact that Godard married Anne Wiazemsky after seeing her performance in *Au Hasard, Balthazar*. Roland Barthes' idea of punctum. The films Jack Nicholson made between *Easy Rider* and *The Passenger*. The role of architecture in Antonioni's movies. Antonioni's comment that he made his films, not with his head or heart, but with his stomach. The opening credits—blue lettering on black and white film—for Bertolucci's *The Sheltering Sky*. The orb in *Burnt by the Sun*. Harvey Kietel's hubris in *The Duellists*. Dogs barking in Tarkovsky's movies. The cow in *La Haine*. The deer in *Mad Dog and Glory*. The streetcar ride in *Sunrise*. The red glass vase in David Lean's *Summertime*. The white china vase in Ozu's *Late Spring*. The fact that Claire Denis' *35 Shots of Rum* is a 'remake' of Ozu's *Late Spring*. Denis Lavant freaking out in the disco at the end of Denis' *Beau Travail*. The line 'Who are those guys?' in *Butch Cassidy and the Sundance Kid*. The sepia freeze frame at the end of *Butch Cassidy and the Sundance Kid*. The freeze frame at the end of *The 400 Blows*. The fact that Truffaut named his daughters after films by Joseph Losey and Otto Preminger (*Eve* and *Laura*). The trilogy of films that Losey made (*The Servant, Accident, The Go-Between*) that captures Englishness better than any English director. The trilogy of open-ended films that Antonioni made with *L'Avventura, Blow-Up and The Passenger*. Aperture versus closure. Harry Dean Stanton's nod of recognition to his brother in *Paris, Texas*. Peter Lorre's eyes in Fritz Lang's *M*. The carnation in *La Grande Illusion*. The line 'Blaue Augen' in *La Grande Illusion*. The final line of *I Am a Fugitive from a Chain Gang*, in which, when asked how he survives, Paul Muni replies 'I steal'. The song at the end of *Juno*. Chris Petit's *Flight to Berlin* as the greatest film Wim Wenders never made. The metronome and dartboard in David Fincher's *Se7en*. The shoot-out in Michael Mann's *Heat*. The idea of heaven in a radiator in David Lynch's *Eraserhead*. Mel Brooks' comment that David Lynch is 'Jimmy Stewart from Mars'. The giant photograph and the folded pieces of greaseproof paper at the end of Louis Malle's *Damage*. Peter Woollen's comment that 'whereas Godard is Godard, and Truffaut is Truffaut, Louis Malle is the Nouvelle Vague'. Blank expressions in the films of Robert Bresson. The Bressonian heroine. The tank in Bergman's *The Silence*. The fact that Anthony Mann made *film noir* in the 40s, westerns in the 50s and epics in the 60s. The baroque beauty of Anthony Harvey's *Eagle's Wing*. Carl Orff's music in *Badlands*. The glass in the river in Terence Malick's *Days of Heaven*. Men waving flags in fields in *Days of Heaven*. Godard versus Pasolini.

Ennio Morricone's score for *Once Upon a Time in America*. John Barry's score for *Out of Africa*. Abandoned David Lean projects: *Out of Africa, Gandhi* and *The Bounty*. Colour and design in Vera Chytilová's *Daises*. The uncompromising career of Dusan Makavejev. The camera dollying through the trees at the end of Tarkovsky's *Mirror*. The 'key' to Mirror—that the woman with her hair up is the mother, with her hair down is the wife. Hitchcock's reply 'Send her to the cleaners' when he received a letter from a woman complaining that her daughter would no longer take a shower after seeing *Psycho*. People running in Miklós Janscó's *The Round-Up*. People running in Melville's *L'Armeé des Ombres*. The irony of Jean Martin metering out torture in *The Battle of Algiers* only to be the victim of torture himself in *The Day of the Jackal*. The soldier saying 'Fuck it' while drinking whisky in *The Deerhunter*. The lit glasses of vodka, one for each dead comrade, in Andrzej Wajda's *Ashes and Diamonds*. The kisses in *Cinema Paradiso*. Paul Bettany's scream in *Gangster No. 1*. Blowing out the lights in Wim Wenders' *Alice in the Cities*. Mise-en-scène versus montage. Henri Alekin's silky monochrome photography in *Wings of Desire*. The girl's jump from the windowsill at the end of *The Dream Life of Angels*. The father's slip from the wooden tower in *The Return*. The hardness of Ralph Fiennes' stare in *The English Patient* (another film Lean could have made). The story about the woman with the white parasol in *Citizen Kane*. The story about Cary Grant sneezing while hiding in the nostril of one of Mount Rushmore's presidents in Hitchcock's *North by Northwest*. The subliminal skull in *Psycho*. Opera in *Diva*. The haunting, mystifying images on the video tape in Hideo Nakata's *Ring*. Takashi Miike's *Audition*—never has a film seemed so like one thing only to end up being another thing entirely. The red buoys sinking in the soup cauldron, only to resurface in the Hudson River in *Once Upon a Time in America*. Hal Hartley's comment that there is no such thing as adventure and romance, there's only trouble and desire. Jean-Luc Godard: 'All you need to make a movie is a girl and a gun'. Bergman's *Cries and Whispers* as adult *verité*. The whole of Ingmar Bergman's output. Scorsese is to Michael Powell as Spielberg is to David Lean. Cameras, watches, headlamps, spectacles and binoculars in *Chinatown*. The flaw in Faye Dunaway's eye in *Chinatown*. The essential question in *The Draughtsman's Contract*—should an artist draw what he sees or what he knows? Hitchcock's films of the 30s as realist; his films of the 40s as modernist; and the 50s as postmodernist. Bernado Bertolucci describing his early films as being like 'sea urchins—very closed, very difficult to handle for an audience'. Isabelle Huppert's comment that *The Piano Teacher* is really about 'the soul of Schubert and the soul of Bach'. Sprites, driads, nymphs, knights, divas, servants, satyrs and statues in Matthew Barney's *Cremaster* series. The conscience of the main character in *Young Adam* is pricked, but fails to bleed. The manner in which Emily Mortimer falls into the canal in *Young Adam*. George Sluizer's *The Vanishing* as the greatest film Krzysztof Kieślowski never made. The idea that *Lost in Translation* is made up of the bits of film that other filmmakers would have left on the cutting room floor. The apartment in *Uzak*. The jump cuts and upside-down shots in *Elizabeth*. Temps mort in Antonioni's films. Barthes' comment that Antonioni's films are 'matte'. The 'exchange of guilt' at the end of Chabrol's *Le Boucher*. The careers of Sally Potter and Paul Cox. The first seven minutes of Kieślowski's *Blue*. Sigourney Weaver's loneliness in *The Ice Storm*. The beginning of *Le Mepris*. The otherworldliness of Michael Powell's *I Know Where I'm Going*. Steve McQueen's coldness in Peckinpah's *The Getaway*. Steve McQueen as the coolest actor in cinema. The fact that the people have shadows in *Last Year in Marienbad*, but not the topiaried shrubs. The match game in *Last Year in Marienbad*. The directness of treatment in Resnais' *Night and Fog*. Frederic Forrest's performance in *Hammett* versus Jason Robard's in *Julia*. The ending of *Les Diaboliques*—the best twist ever? The line 'Match me, Sidney', in Alexander Mackendrick's *Sweet Smell of Success*. Miles Davis' score for Louis Malle's *Lift to the Scaffold*. Erik Satie's "Gymnopédies" in Malle's *Le Feu follet*. Malle's comment that his best films are *Au revoir les enfants, Lacombe, Lucien* and *Le Feu follet*, but that his favourite films are *Zazie dans le Métro, Le Souffle au coeur* and *Atlantic City*. The candy-coloured photography in Harmony Korine's *Gummo*. The tilted video camera in *Henry: Portrait of a Serial Killer*. The dialogue between father-in-law and daughter-in-law in Bergman's *Wild Strawberries*. The medieval world portrayed in Bergman's *The Seventh Seal*. The future world portrayed in *Blade Runner*. The chilling opening kidnapping sequence in Sidney Lumet's *Murder on the Orient Express*. The taut, spiralling plot of *No Way Out*. Although it's full of holes, the ingenious plotting for *Memento*. Jack Lemmon's performance in *Missing*. Klaus Maria Brandeur's performance in *Mephisto*. The glowing glass of milk in *Suspicion*. The cut from the scream to the train whistle in Hitchcock's *The 39 Steps*. The missing half-finger in *The 39 Steps*. The car chase in *French Connection*—even better than the one in *Bullitt*? Gene Hackman chasing the boat at the end of *French Connection II*. Gene Hackman playing sax in his wrecked apartment in Coppola's *The Conversation*. Warren Beatty's final run to the open door in *The Parallax View*. The way the paths of Jeff Bridges and Stacy Keach keep crossing in *Fat City*. The money in Addie's hat in *Paper Moon*. The rococo dialogue in Abraham Polonsky's *Force of Evil*. The windscreen wipers and fade to white at the end of *The Unbearable Lightness of Being*.

Originally published in Staple 73, summer 2010.

"Dub: Red Hot vs Ice Cold"

For J

> *'The first Dub I heard was* King Tubby Meets Rockers Uptown. *I couldn't make head nor tail of it. I didn't know what was going on, it sounded like a series of mistakes.'*
> Lol Bell-Brown

Growing up in Trinidad in the late 60s and early 70s, as I did, was a magical experience. My first memories are of the sea, white beaches, palms, caimans, scarlet ibis and the hot tropical sun. And music was everywhere, too, on the radio, in the towns and on the beaches, but it wasn't reggae I remember hearing, it was steel bands playing calypso music. Reggae was predominantly a Jamaican music and Jamaica was far away from Trinidad, especially in those days. No, the songs I remember clearest from my childhood aren't reggae songs, but "Drunk and Disorderly" by Mighty Sparrow, "Midnight at the Oasis" by Maria Muldaur and "Lucy in the Sky with Diamonds" by The Beatles, which I remember singing with my sister in the back seat of our car.

When I was at secondary school back in England in the late 70s, reggae was at the height of its popularity in the UK and, on his death, Bob Marley was mourned at my school at least as much as, if not more than, John Lennon. Then along came bands like Human League and Heaven 17 and everyone forgot all about reggae. I remember buying the 7-inch single of "Messages", by OMD, and being struck by the B-side, which I couldn't stop playing. It was a strange echoey instrumental version of the A-side, called "Taking Sides Again", which was a snippet from the lyrics. Little did I know it at the time, but I was hearing my first Dub version, but this was not reggae, it was a cold but beautiful, precisely-programmed synth-pop song by a couple of white guys from the Wirral.

Years later, in 1995, I heard an album entitled *You Love Chinese Food*, a kind of 'Fourth World' record full of ambient soundscapes and spoken-word stories. The album was by a group calling themselves Pablo's Eye, an international collective of musicians headed by producer Axel Libeert and based in Brussels. I loved their album so much that I was compelled to get in touch to tell them. I did, and Axel and I became friends. For their next album, he invited me to write the texts for the 'voice' of Pablo's Eye, Marie Mandi, to speak on the record. Our collaboration was entitled *all she wants grows blue* (the name of one of the texts) and was conceived as the 'Invisible Soundtrack' to an imagined film. Under/behind the late-night tales of travel, time and lost connections, Axel used the mixing desk to build his languid, libidinous Dub rhythms, allowing them to pulse in and around the stories. The energy of Dub was channelled and funnelled into dark hollow grooves, creating a gloomy landscape lit only by the flickering glow of cinema screens. I was mesmerised by the music he made, but I didn't know how he did it. A lot of reviews of *all she wants grows blue* made reference to the album's roots in Dub, but at the time, I wasn't sure I knew exactly what the term 'Dub' meant. I was curious, and my collaboration with Pablo's Eye led me into a lifelong passion for this style of music.

So what is Dub? Dub is the science of studio pressure, when engineer becomes artist. Appropriating left and right as well as front and back, the engineer uses the mixing desk to examine and exhaust the possibilities of moments. Dub is a record of that examination and exhaustion, but it is also a record of your own inner space. By means of depth placement, psychoacoustics and spatial fug, Dub is experienced in the deeper reaches of the body, as an explosion in the cortex and a detonation in the solar plexus, bypassing the conscious part of the mind entirely. The tools of Dub are drums and bass, which are set at odds with each other to satisfy both hemispheres of the brain: dread bass versus slack time. Drums are Dub's heart, its heartbeat, but Dub's heart has a murmur, always on the verge of cardiac arrest and collapse. Bass is maternal, it is Dub's spine—fluid, sinuous, reptilian, a great lumbering of low-end vibration. Dub is the turning of recorded music inside out to show its seams. It interrogates a song, stripping down the body of the song to reveal its bones. Dub is in the interstices of music, it plugs the gaps, fills the holes. Dub seeks out the concealed mechanisms, it is a song's hidden agenda. Dub is the ghost in the machine, a voice coming through the Gates of Horn and Ivory, an infection, a virus, corrupting and altering everything it invades.

> *'Anything that malfunction we use it and make it sound great.'*
> Sly Dunbar

In Jamaica during the 60s, big open-air, night-time dances were common in the Spanish Town area of Kingston, hosted by massive sound systems, or 'sets', and held in enclosed pieces of land that had been flattened and cleared for dancing. In order to attract the largest audiences to these dances, each sound-system owner had to make certain they had the latest exclusive tunes, so each of them started putting together cramped studios the size of matchboxes and hiring engineers to cut 'specials'—one-off acetates, made especially for a particular set and not commercially available. In order to ensure exclusivity, the label on these acetates was scratched off and their source kept secret. These specials were designed to keep the people faithful to a particular sound system, to make them want to come back again and again and pay their entry fee. The high end—the horns and cymbals—was turned right up so that they could be heard for miles in the night air, drawing people in from all around, while the low end—the drums and bass—was turned right down, ensuring that people who had come to the set experienced huge bodily pleasure, close to sexual.

Filling the other side of these acetates was the 'version', an edition of the song re-using the rhythm track. These B-sides were more commonly called 'Dubs', short for 'double', a copy. One night in 1967, Rudolph 'Ruddy' Redwood, owner and deejay of Ruddy's The Supreme Ruler Of Sound (SRS), started his midnight set. He says: 'I put on [The Paragons'] "On the Beach" an' I switch over from the singin' part to the version part, cut down the sound and man, you could hear the dance floor rail an' I was getting the vibes'. Unbeknown to him, the engineer had forgotten to add the vocal track to this particular B-side but, to his amazement, the audience went wild for this unintentional instrumental version. For future releases, he instructed his engineers to record the A-side vocal version as usual, with voice and guitar high up in the mix, but to make the Dub version on the B-side by taking snippets of the original and splicing them together to create something new, paying particular attention to accentuate the low end. He spent more of his set playing these very heavy one-off Dubs, sometimes playing them ten or twenty times over because the crowd couldn't get enough of them. By the mid-70s, every single 45-rpm record released in Kingston contained the standard vocal version on the A-side, but also a new bass-heavy instrumental version on the flipside. Among the crowd at Ruddy's deejay set that night was an engineer called Osbourne 'Tubby' Ruddock, who liked what he heard. A lot.

> '*At a Tubby's session, they might play five, ten version of the same riddim, all with a different mix. In fact they didn't call it* version, *they called it* chapter. *And each chapter opened your mind in a different way.*'
> Bobby Vicious

Tubby, who became known as 'King' Tubby, took the principles and practices of the 70s' Dub version to its apogee. He took the instrumental B-side and played around with it to a degree that no one had before or, arguably, has ever since. His sound was unique because he would strip pieces of recording equipment, including his Fisher Reverb Unit imported from the US, and rebuild them, adding his own faders and echo unit. With these alterations, he would feed echoes via a revox or phaser into the mixing desk, which would then be fed into the Dub. His signature was to strip a vocal completely from its backing track and then manipulate the version with a spellbinding array of techniques and effects such as drop-out, delay and space echo, often hitting the spring reverb unit in order to create whipcrack highs and thunderclap lows. Tubby's Dubs were long echoplex delays, displacing time and suspending moments, an endless series of interlocking circles that sometimes ran together but then ran out of synch, turning a song into a cavernous groove and stretching it out into a vast mental landscape of peaks and troughs, looping and extending beats to vanishing point, creating new psycho-systems.

In the way that Tubby spliced together bits of tape in the studio, Dub bears a certain similarity to the way in which *musique concrète* was composed. The out-of-phaseness of some Dubs resembles Steve Reich's vocal pieces, "It's Gonna Rain" and "Come Out", which use two tape machines running at slightly different speeds, as well as his composition "Drumming", which Reich wrote after a trip to Ghana in 1970 to study drumming with the drummer-master Gideon Alorwoyie. Indeed, with its emphasis on rhythm and repetition, and its transparent structure, which makes the sounds themselves the goal of the piece, Dub is not so far away from Minimalism in general; Terry Riley's *Poppy Nogood and the Phantom Band's All Night Flight*, recorded live in 1968, with its incredible use of a time-lag accumulator, might very well be the heaviest Dub ever made and recorded.

For his experiments, innovations and achievements in the studio, King Tubby needs to be placed alongside these wonderful composers. By the mid-70s, Tubby had become the top sound in Kingston, but his life was cruelly cut short when he was shot and killed outside his home in 1989 by persons unknown. But Tubby was a pioneer, and his legacy lives on, forging the way ahead for those that followed. The classic period of Dub is the 70s, but the lineaments of Dub can be tracked from those original productions, through the digidub of the 80s and up to the explosion in dance culture that ran into the 90s and beyond. The features of Dub can be traced in this way because, although it was born out of roots reggae, Dub isn't just a genre of music, it's also a *style,* and its principles and aesthetics can be applied to all manner of musical forms. The generation that grew up in the west infected with the Dub rhythms of the 70s and 80s turned Dub away in the 90s from its origins in the red-hot weather of Jamaica and redirected it toward the icy climates of Europe and North America. Jamaica's 'JA' style is all echo, delay, sustain and reverb, whereas this new style of Dub makes use of 'trace', 'merge', 'push' and 'filter'. Ice-cold terms replace red-hot ones. Matters 'irie' become 'eerie'. Dub's viral nature spreads and seeps into new soil, embracing alien forms of music to create new hybrids, but the palimpsest of Dub is always there, the faint echoes of previous records can still be heard, plaintive cries from the past.

> *'I realised as a teenager that people like King Tubby were probably more innovative than, say George Martin, in using the studio as an experimental tool, abusing delay units, deconstructing mixes and the rest.'*
> Guy Fixsen

Laika were one such band that took Jamaican Dub production techniques and used them, in their particular case, in conjunction with the motorik of Krautrock, as well as with vibes and marimbas, to create their lush, textured, unclassifiable sound. Founded by American writer and vocalist Margaret Fiedler and

British engineer/producer Guy Fixsen, the group's spacey sound is earthed and driven by bass energy and rhythmic complexity—John Frenett's resonant reggae basslines and Lou Ciccotelli's proto-African beats—but has a quietness and dark expansiveness all its own. The titles of their 90s releases—*Silver Apples of the Moon* and *Sounds of the Satellites*—reflect this spatial approach, sounding like Sun Ra releases.

Düsseldorf's Mouse on Mars, comprising Jan St. Werner and Andi Toma, are another. During the 90s, Mouse on Mars pulled Jamaican Dub away from conventional reggae towards the distressed textures and digital cut-and-paste of IDM. The surface of their digital Dub is notched, punctured and chinked, revealing the Dub effects hidden deep inside them, sloshing around like soup. "Stereomission", which kicks off their 1995 album *Iaora Tahiti*, has a stifling bassline as the undertow, hooking and pulling us through the candy-coloured pop. The flecks and flurries of digital interference in their Double Mix of "Schlektron" sound like a planet on fire. The stray whips and cracks of sound in "Subnubus" are the perfect embodiment of Deleuze's 'rhizomes', strands of sound that grow in an organic, vegetal way, finding growth and renewal in, and through, the gaps of a song.

Another new Dub maestro is Stuart Matthewman, the main songwriter and producer for Sade ever since her debut album, *Diamond Life*, in 1984. During the 90s, Matthewman assumed an alter ego, Cottonbelly, under which he recorded and released his Dub productions and remixes. He has taken soul and R'n'B tunes by artists such as Maxwell, Seek and Sade herself, and transformed them into highly distinctive freeze-dried, vacuum-packed Dubs. No other contemporary Dub producer is as dry, or tight, as Cottonbelly. His remix of Gregory Isaacs' hit "Night Nurse", a founding stone of 70s Jamaican reggae, is in itself a masterclass in neo-dub production techniques.

'Sabotage is the only thing you can do if you want to display a critical position—it's the only thing that's left.'
Markus Popp

But it is not just Imaginary Soundtracks, post-rock, IDM and soul and R'n'B that have been reshaped and remodelled using Dub's practices and principles. During the 90s, not many musical genres and subgenres of electronic music were spared the Dub virus. In the black communities of Bristol, Birmingham and London, a major strain of Dub to be born, grow and flourish was Jungle, which took the tradition of 'toasting' from Jamaican dancehall culture and overlaid it with impossibly hectic drum patterning and subsonic bass frequencies. Early Jungle releases, such as More Rockers' *Dub Plate Selection Volume 1* (1995), were a peculiarly English concoction of Hip Hop 'cubed' multiplied by the square root of Dub. But the red heat of Jungle quickly transmuted into another strain, called Drum 'n' Bass, a much colder form of Jungle, one which slowed the beats down, making them more precisely programmed, taking on aspects of Jazz and Ambient. Tracks by Photek such as "KJZ" and "Rings Around Saturn" use samples of jazz licks and Sun Ra, while his tracks "The Seven Samurai" and "The Water Margin" spin off into the realms of Zen culture with their clashes of swords and the slamming of dungeon gates.

Other forms using the principles of Dub proliferated as well. Bandulu and Leftfield, for instance, also took Jamaican dancehall culture, but this time melded it with the highly identifiable 4/4 beats of English techno to produce Techno Dub. The post-Techno, industrial soundscapes of Scorn, Ice, Spectre, Germ and Coil are rendered colder and darker by the addition of booming, clanging Dub. Back in Germany, the cool, minimalist releases from Berlin's Chain Reaction imprint during the 90s produced hypnotic 4/4 'waveform' Dub, best represented by Porter Ricks' "Nautical Dub", which sounds like a whale's heartbeat recorded using contact mics. Dub crops up again in another subgenre of German electronica, the so-called 'clicks & cuts' aesthetic of Pole, To Rococo Rot and Microstoria (one half of Mouse on Mars). Taking radio frequencies, ambient washes and the sounds of machines operating themselves, these Dubs are 'conceptual', more a comment on what Dub is rather than aiming to make people dance. To Rococo Rot's *Paris 25* EP (1997) is a supremely elegant example.

At the same time as all these English and German musicians and programmers were using Dub style as the mother lode for their productions, the atavistic nature of Dub also reared its head in New York, as 'Illbient', a marriage of blunted Hip Hop beats and the blasted urban landscapes of Brooklyn. Among the many groups producing these new sounds were Sub Dub and We, both collectives of DJs, sound manipulators and musicians. Sub Dub's John 'Dubs' Ward is a DJ whose weekly Dub nights in New York are legendary. Perhaps the most typical exponent of Illbient is DJ Spooky, whose tracks "Soon Forward" and "Why Patterns" are asphodelic soundscapes of dead dreams, propped up by Hip Hop beats and organised by the principles of Dub.

During the 90s, there were also many musicians who applied Dub techniques to varieties of World music. The other half of Sub Dub, Raz Mesinai, is an Israeli who spent much of his childhood living with the Bedouins in the Sinai desert. At seven years old, he learned about Middle-Eastern drumming in a Palestinian refugee camp and went on to master the bendir, zarb and darbukka. Under the moniker Badawi, he played these instruments on an album entitled *Bedouin Sound Clash* (1996), drenching the tracks in echo and reverb, and creating a rich mix of World beats and Dub effects. From a small house in Manchester, Bryn Jones spent the 90s releasing highly-politicised, pro-Palestinian music under the name Muslimgauze. These delicate, luminous Dubs, using found sound and field recordings of Middle-Eastern percussion, are all the more extraordinary as Jones never set foot in the Middle East. At just 37 years old, Jones contracted a rare fungal infection and died in 1999. He was so prolific that, ever since his death, several Muslimgauze albums are still being released every year. And in the US, Bill Laswell collaborated with Ethiopian singer Ejigayehu 'Gigi' Shibabaw and several Ethiopian master musicians in a project named Abyssinia Infinite, releasing *Zion Roots* (2003), an album of harps, flutes, accordions and percussive instruments, all treated by Laswell's pounding, thunderous Dub production.

> *'Switch on, switch off self preservation, a flashback from way back … they label me insane …'*
> Tricky

But perhaps the most complete and utterly compelling embodiment of 70s Dub in the 90s is Tricky, who released his stunning debut record, *Maxinquaye,* in 1995. Named after his mother, who committed suicide when he was just a young boy, *Maxinquaye* is a startling release from the leftfield, one that none saw coming and which remains as innovative and fresh today as ever. The songs on the album are opaque, discordant mumblings, scribbles and smudges of urban life, cryptic and elliptical. Numbed, concussed tracks such as "Aftermath", "Overcome", "Suffocated Love" and "Feed Me" are gaping soundscapes of disintegrating states of mind, susurrations of loss and trouble, confusion and paranoia, using Dub's sub-sonic echo as a form of the supernatural. These fluctuations of air waves remain imperceptible to the ear but shake the bowels, making the characters in the songs vanish, leaving only their trace, their ghost, their outline, including his own. *Maxinquaye* is a disappearing Trick, his duppy leaving nothing but murmurs and whisperings from the other side. With his release, Tricky is reborn as an African Gnostic, a magical seer, spellcaster, shapeshifter, the physical and spiritual reincarnation of Obeah man Lee 'Scratch' Perry.

'I am the ghost captain.'
Lee 'Scratch' Perry

Tricky was famously part of the Massive Attack crew, appearing as 'Tricky Kid' on *Blue Lines* and *Protection* as a rapper and co-writer. When *Blue Lines* appeared in 1991, Massive Attack were approached to do a Dub remix of Nusrat Fateh Ali Khan's "Mustt Mustt". This remix, which they named "Duck Pond Dub", predates the whole Trip Hop scene by about four years and has never been bettered. The initial Sufi devotional song is stripped down and remade using double drum loops, one playing off the other, a boom of low-end frequency, echo and delay on the harmonium, with the original vocals now only existing as ghostly residues swirling and dying in the mix. Submitting "Mustt Mustt" to Dub's machinery, Massive Attack produced an alchemic, shamanic version every bit as hallucinatory as the original, remarkable for revealing something hidden on each play.

'Every object have a shadow, you have to find your shadow. Every song could be Dub, you have to find the Dub.'
Mad Professor

Not only were Massive Attack consummate remixers themselves, but they in turn gladly handed out their own work to be stripped down and remade. In 1994, they commissioned Neil Fraser, aka Mad Professor, to remix *Protection* in its entirety. The result is another absolute apogee of Dub in the 90s. The Mad Professor's remixes are mighty assaults on the senses, towers of Dub that shimmer and shake, that rattle the body's core and restructure the brain. They destroy the original song's chord progression and melody, instead emphasising timbre, spatiality and texture. To indicate that these Dub remixes grasp the 'shadow', not the substance, of the originals, the album was named *No Protection.*

An integral part of *No Protection,* and indeed of Dub remixes in general, is the renaming of the original tracks. The vocal versions on the original release are restructured to such a degree that their initial titles no longer have any relevance, and a new name is selected to reflect this transformation. "Protection" becomes "Radiation Ruling The Nation"; "Karmacoma" (itself the older sister of Tricky's "Overcome") is reborn twice, once as the "Bumper Ball Dub" and again as the "Ventom Dub Special"; "Three" morphs into the "Trinity Dub"; and "Weather Storm" is calmed and tamed into a "Cool Monsoon".

In Dub mixes, songs are separated from the signifiers of their titles, leading to a multiplicity of titles for the same material. In 1997, Bristolians Smith & Mighty released the "Dread City Mix" of a tune known as "Demolition City", first performed and recorded in the 80s by Sly & Robbie. But that song was itself a version of a much earlier tune, a song by The Tamlins released in the 70s entitled "Baltimore". In the Smith & Mighty remix, the vocals have been reduced to nothing more than cries and whispers lingering in the ether. One of the most immediately recognisable sonic features of the Dub mix is the way song lyrics are omitted and/or fragmented, leaving just snippets and traces of original voices. This manipulation removes the comprehension of lyrics and transforms them into political calls-to-arms, shouts, spiritual moans and exaltations. Another remix of "Demolition City" was also released in 1997, this one by LA producer Tom Chasteen, who renamed his version "Graveyard City—The Skull Valley Remix". This version, too, has wisps of the original vocal held in limbo in the reel-to-reel, the groans and wheezes of the long dead.

With remixing comes a new language of taxonomy: Black-Nosed Buddha Dub, Black Orpheus Dub, Tien Clan Dub, Alsema Dub, Azmari Dub, Abyssinian Dub, Arctic Dub, Loisaida Dub, London Dub, Catacomb Dub, Couchie Dub, Chinatown Dub, Nyambie Dub, Salmonella Dub, Solomon's Dub, Spiral Dub,

Suspicious Dub, Indicator Dub, Cellphone Dub, Cuttlefish Dub, Nihilismus Dub, Numbskull Dub, Duck Pond Dub, Traurige Tropen Dub, Muzique Mechanique Dub, Java Dub, Mystery Dub, Future Dub and Vanishing Dub. All these are names of Dubs suggested, realised and treated by Dub producers from the 70s to the 90s and beyond. The names of these Dub tracks recall the black arts, magic, murk and mental disintegration. They allude to ancient peoples, Rastafari and Biblical references. Dub takes us back to the primal instruments—the handclap and the drum, instruments that are still heard today in the Nyahbinghi, Tuareg and Samburu tribes. It's all about rhythm and repetition, a looped beat extending infinitely. As is the case with all good Dub tracks, it's about what's left out, not what's put in. Dub does the impossible—it maps the invisible, and the better the Dub, the more invisible it is as it moves inside us and becomes indivisible from our bodily rhythms and energy. It is a negative—it isn't there. It defies logic and evades definition. Whatever you think Dub is, it isn't. Dub's viral nature continues to spread into new music currents, dragging all types of music in its wake. Grime, Garage, Twostep, Dubstep, the Zeds Dead remix of "Eyes On Fire" by Blue Foundation, Boards of Canada's "Orange Romeda", the Dub-Jazz of Nuspirit Helsinki, the electronica of Christian Fennesz, the dub tango of the Gotan project, Plaid as remixers, FOKN Bois, Burial… The incubation continues.

> *'People get warped by Dub and they never recover.'*
> Ian Penman

Originally published as an ebook by NOCH, July 2013.

Plug—*Back on Time*

In a 2004 interview, Luke Vibert (aka Plug) insisted that he hadn't released the best tracks that made up his 1996 album, *Drum 'n' Bass for Papa*. 'I really like Plug 1 and Plug 2, Plug 3 is OK and the album was pretty good too, but I don't think I compiled the best tracks.' This is an astounding admission, not least because the album was one of the seminal releases of the flourishing and divergent dance music scene in the mid-90s. He has admitted, too, that he can no longer create any new Plug tracks. 'Y'know I just can't,' he says, 'it's hilarious. I still try every so often to do a Plug track and I just can't do it—I don't know why. It just ends up sounding like an Amen Andrews track which is why I came up with that stupid name in the first place. I think the Plug stuff was how it was because I was just getting into jungle and I wanted to have a bash and it went slightly wrong in a way.' So, if Vibert thinks he got it wrong on *Drum 'n' Bass for Papa*, did he get it right on these 15-year-old Plug tracks, finally gathered together onto a recently-released album entitled *Back on Time* (Ninja Tune, 2012)?

Proceedings kick off with "Scar City", and 'kick off' is the right expression. The bass drum kicks in straight away and we are immediately back on familiar territory. The track is a stunning mix of sampladelic vocals and a melodic, metronomic bassline, all driven by an off-kilter yet highly infectious rhythm track. "A Quick Plug for a New Slot" is equally impressive and could have easily sat anywhere on *Drum 'n' Bass for Papa*. Its beats are so propulsive and catchy that the whole thing just leaves you breathless with its energy and enthusiasm. Perhaps the album's best track is the title track, which has the same monster bass and sprangy, time-stretched beats as the title track of *Drum 'n' Bass for Papa*. The album closes with another highlight, "Flight 78", which has the same tight, ersatz-jazz feel as "Delicious".

One of the most amazing things about *Drum 'n' Bass for Papa* was that no track was under seven minutes long. The vocals on the brilliant early Plug EPs were goofy and the beats choppy, but *Papa* showed more attention to the development and flow of each track as it was built up steadily to a head-crunching climax and was then given a slow, long outro. That's not the case on *Back on Time*—only two tracks exceed seven minutes and a couple hover around the three-minute mark. "Come on My Skeleton" is a bit ravey while "No Reality" and "Mind Bending" would fit better on one of his Wagon Christ releases, but these are mere quibbles when faced with such killer tracks.

As with previous Plug releases, Vibert's trademark humour is evident all over these tracks, but don't be fooled—behind the apparent tomfoolery is a master producer, whose productions are tightly arranged, beautifully programmed and sequenced. *Drum 'n' Bass for Papa* was a showcase for Vibert's extraordinary production skills and techniques. He is a master of making a track that, while seemingly cut'n'thrash and throwaway, moves you forward in unexpected, compelling and clever ways and the tracks on *Back on Time* are no exception and equally good. Luke Vibert might think that the output released under his Plug moniker 'went slightly wrong' but *Back on Time* shows how wrong *he* was. It brings him right back to the future and bang on track.

Beach Boys— "Life was a beach"

The Beach Boys played Wembley Arena two weeks ago and got a reception like I've never heard before. Delirious, they were. The band themselves seemed relaxed and easy. But there was one member missing, the oldest Wilson brother—compositional genius and drug-addled rock star. Indeed, his absence was the most notable thing about that night, since the Beach Boys are nothing without him, nothing but a crass nostalgia trip, California-style. Since 1982, when Wilson was fired by the others, contact between them has only taken place through lawyers.

The most depressing thought of all is that for many people, the sight of Wilson's cousin, Mike Love, shuffling his weight around the stage to "California Girls" will sum up everything the group have become. Now seems an opportune time to take stock of their career, which is exactly what Capitol Records is allowing with the release of the *Good Vibrations* box-set—five CDs of tracks spanning the band's output from 1961–91.

For the first 10 years, when Brian was with them, they made some of the most heavenly pop music ever recorded. They took twangy Chuck Berry-like riffs and sang sweet falsetto melodies over the top to make a 'white spiritual sound'. To this, they added sleighbells, chimes, tambourines and other percussive sounds. Later they did their Tamla Motown record (*Wild Honey*), their TM album (*Friends*), their misunderstood masterpiece (*Sunflower*) and their early 1970s 'anything goes' album (*Holland*). Along the way, they did loads of drugs, reflected the times, and dug deep graves for their personalities.

Nowadays, their influence remains, perhaps surprisingly, widely felt. Mike Mills, bassist with REM, calls *Pet Sounds* 'probably the greatest pop album ever made'. For today's indie scene, the Beach Boys are a prime source of inspiration. The Jesus And Mary Chain, Sonic Youth and Frank Black have all acknowledged this influence by doing cover versions.

Brian, Dennis and Carl Wilson grew up in Hawthorne, a suburb of Los Angeles. Their father, Murry, was a mean-spirited disciplinarian who regularly thrashed them with anything he could lay his hands on. But Murry had a hidden, kinder side and encouraged his sons to play instruments and vocalise together in their special music room. Together with Love and their friend, Al Jardine, the Wilsons played school hops and Carl and the Passions, doing a set that drew on Johnny Otis and the vocal harmonies of the Four Freshmen.

To the others, it was a hoot and a great way of earning money, but Brian took it much more seriously. While Dennis was playing hooky, Brian studied music theory. He would listen endlessly to the radio and complain that he could do at least as well. Dennis finally suggested that Brian try to write something instead of just talking about it. So he wrote a song about surfing called "Surfin"—their first big hit, in 1961, and an ironic start since Dennis was the only one who could surf at all (Brian hated the sea).

Over the next few years, the band toured all over America performing the steady flow of songs Brian was writing. He dissected Phil Spector's "Be My Baby" and learned how to write and produce with more sophistication—compare "Surfin" with "I Get Around" to see how much he had improved in just three years. But he hated touring and Murry, who was managing them, constantly interrupted his work in the studio. Something had to give.

On a plane during a tour in early 1965, Brian 'freaked' and began to run up and down the aisle screaming and crying. It was the beginning of a full-scale nervous breakdown. He told the rest of the band that he could no longer tour, but would mastermind their success from behind a mixing desk. So began his long artistic drift from the band. He had started experimenting with soft drugs and professed to be 'hearing music' in his head all day long. Later that year, he spent an evening with his drug buddies listening to the newly released *Rubber Soul* by the Beatles. It represented everything he wanted to achieve. That night, he told his wife he was going to make 'the greatest rock album ever made'. He was 23 years old.

He wanted to fill the album with his favourite 'feels', his 'pet sounds'. During recording, he would conduct an orchestra in the studio, building each instrument's part from scratch. To these gorgeous backing tracks he would add soulful vibes and organs and sounds such as washboards, toothcombs, bicycle bells and clippety-clop percussion. The result was a mix of the sublime and ridiculous, which sums up Brian's personality pretty well. Paul McCartney recalls, '*Pet Sounds* flipped me. I just thought, "Oh dear me. This is the album of all time. What are we gonna do?"'

But the album flopped and Capitol was only slightly pacified by the enormous success of "Good Vibrations", Wilson's first 'pocket symphony', created out of 72 hours of recordings. Brian was hearing music faster than he could record it and went straight back into the studio to start work on what would be his most enigmatic project, *Smile*.

These legendary recordings became one of rock's 'greatest albums never made' and, even in their present, half-finished form, remain a remarkable achievement. He spent a year working on tracks in the studio, but the project was beleaguered with problems. His relations with the band, who wanted more commercial material, were strained. Acid had had a bad effect on Wilson and some of the studio experiments he was trying were truly bizarre (at one point he started a fire in the studio and asked the orchestra to 'play what they felt'). Then came the bombshell—*Sgt Pepper*. Apparently he listened to it on headphones for six months. Realising he could never better it, he went to bed for the best part of 10 years.

At this point, the family started to implode. In 1969, Murry persuaded a bombed-out Brian to sell the rights to his songs to him for a pittance, a move which alienated him from his sons until his death soon afterwards. Love began to emerge as the band's leader, insisting they go on tour. But the group were running on empty without Brian's input, which only amounted to the odd Smile song being dusted down and tagged on to the end of an album. Songs such as "Cool, Cool Water", "Cabinessence" and "Surf's Up" showed just how good *Smile* would have been.

Things reached a low point in 1983 when Dennis fell drunk into the bay in LA and drowned. By this time, Brian's wife had fixed him up with Dr Eugene Landy, whose controversial techniques at least got him up and running again. But Carl, Love and Jardine felt Landy was sucking him dry and a court order got Landy removed. Brian decided to sue the publishing company to whom Murry had sold the rights to his songs. He won, but now Love is suing Brian for royalties to songs Love claims he contributed to but wasn't paid for. The case still goes on; hence no Wilson at the concerts.

Still, at least we can hear them all performing together on the Capitol box-set. Starting with a glorious solo demo of Brian singing "Surfin USA" and finishing with the ubiquitous "Kokomo", the selections are comprehensive but understandably top-heavy towards the *Pet Sounds–Smile* era. The *Smile* tracks, in particular, are quite something—the baroque "Wonderful" and the mellow "Wind Chimes" give off the flavour of the times.

The critical success of Brian's 1988 solo album must have scared the boys but the truth is that he never really needed them. Spector described the Beach Boys as 'Brian Wilson and his background singers'. Perhaps too much has now passed between Wilson and the band for him ever to rejoin—perhaps he wouldn't want to—but he does say he's hopeful of a reconciliation. Some day.

Originally published in the Sunday Times, July 1993.

Steely Dan—A Lexicon

A is for *Aja* (1977), possibly Steely Dan's finest hour and certainly their most commercially successful record. *Aja* made Steely Dan as famous as Fleetwood Mac and the Eagles. Using more than 30 musicians, mostly jazz musicians (including sax legend Wayne Shorter), the album is brimming with complex jazz chord changes. Its gatefold sleeve, featuring Blue Note-style liner notes, added to the impression that the roots of *Aja* lay in the 50s jazz scene. But the subjects of the songs were still those down-and-out characters living on the fringes of society that so fascinated Fagen. "Deacon Blues", arguably Steely Dan's greatest character study, is a song about an aspiring musician dying drunk in an after-midnight car crash. It is the closest Becker and Fagen ever came to autobiography. Fagen says, 'It was a kind of socio-cultural explanation of how we grew up and some of the reasons that people became musicians.'

B is for "Barrytown", one of Becker and Fagen's oldest compositions, which finally saw the light of day on the band's third album, *Pretzel Logic* (1974). The song is named after a hamlet near Bard College in Annandale-on-Hudson, New York, where Fagen and Becker first met in 1967. The sci-fi writer William Gibson is a huge Dan fan and references to their songs litter his work, including his novel, *Count Zero*, in which the futuristic settlement is named Barrytown.

C is for "Charlie Freak", the eponymous character in a song (from *Pretzel Logic*) about the effects of drugs and the levels to which people are taken advantage of in their pursuit of them. On a par with those other classic drug songs, Bert Jansch's "The Needle of Death" and Neil Young's "The Needle and the Damage Done", it is beautiful but chilling… 'And while he sighed his body died in fifteen ways.' Don't do it, kids, just say no!

D is for "Doctor Wu" (from *Katy Lied*, 1975), one of the many

Asian-Americans to inhabit the Dan's songs. A song about loss, illusions and how the image we have of certain people fades in our minds. Or does it? The narrator goes searching in the Biscayne Bay, 'where the Cuban gentlemen sleep all day', for the song that Doctor Wu used to sing. But he finds nothing, only the shadow of a man he once knew.

E is for "East St. Louis Toodle-Oo", the cover of the Duke Ellington track that appears on *Pretzel Logic*. Becker and Fagen got hold of all the available versions of the song and combined elements of them for their 'cover'. It amused them that a wah-wah guitar could sound so similar to a muted trumpet. The song was originally recorded in 1926 and is an early example of what Ellington called his 'jungle music' (See also the line in "Babylon Sisters"—'turn that jungle music down, just until we're out of town').

F is for "FM", the best Steely Dan track never to make it onto an original album. The track's propulsion was built up entirely from a click track (metronome) in the studio. Becker did the guitar bits and Johnny Mandel did the string arrangement but, brilliant as both are, they are upstaged by Fagen's fanstastically sneering vocal. Lovely sax, too.

G is for "Green Earrings", one of my favourite Steely Dan songs, taken from my favourite Steely Dan album *The Royal Scam* (1976). Its upbeat, infectious shuffle masks a very seedy story of the mysterious Greek man (a pimp? sugar daddy?) who is eyeing up a much younger woman. What catches the narrator's eye is the rather fetching jewellery she wears, which he remembers because of its 'rare design'. Lovely.

H is for Hoops McCann (who features in "Glamour Profession" from *Gaucho*)—another fantastic Steely Dan hipster. Apparently a 'crowd-pleasing man' with 'brut and charisma', but just who is Hoops McCann? What's he doing lurking in the shadows, accepting packages outside a basketball court? Is he fixing a tournament? And why is he going to Barbados?

I is for Influences. Becker and Fagen were passionate devotees of jazz, obviously, but in the mix there is also some blues and numerous songs that would fit perfectly into the Great American Songbook, plus smaller amounts of rock, bossa, reggae, etc. Contrary to popular belief, Steely Dan are NOT predominantly a rock group. In the 70s, *Rolling Stone* magazine opined that 'Steely Dan are the only group around with no conceptual antecedent from the 60s.'

J is for the swampy R'n'B groove of "Josie" (from *Aja*), one of the many women who appear in the Dan's songs, the others being Peg, Aja, Ruthie, Rose (Darling), Snake Mary, Rikki, Katy (who lied), Lucy, Babs (in love with Clean Willy), Lady Bayside, Cathy Berberian, Louise (the pearl of the quarter), the Broadway Duchess and the Queen of Spain. Fagen has said the name Aja came from a schoolmate whose soldier brother had returned from Korea newly wedded to a woman named Aja.

K is for "Kid Charlemagne" (from *The Royal Scam*), yet another druggy Steely Dan lowlife, dressed up (I imagine) just like the Harvey Keitel character in *Taxi Driver*—tight stripy pants, white vest and a trilby with a feather. Cooking up dope in his hotel room, Kid Charlemagne has to go to 'LA on a dare and go it alone'. His cover is soon blown and he has to do a runner. Is there gas in the car? Yes, there's gas in the car.

L is for Lhasa, which pops up in the song "Time Out Of Mind", from *Gaucho* (1980): 'I am holding the mystical sphere / It's direct from Lhasa'. Seemingly continuing Fagen's fascination with the Far East, the song was actually yet another song about taking drugs. Becker's heroin addiction was getting out of hand around this time, culminating in him breaking his leg in a traffic accident. The song features a guitar solo from Mark Knopfler, who later explained how exasperating an experience his guest appearance was. Becker and Fagen insisted on take-upon-take but, as he couldn't read music, Knopfler had to take a tape of the song back to his hotel room and work on it through the night.

M is for Mizar, a star in the constellation Ursa Major (better known as the Plough), approximately 88 light years from Earth. In fact, Mizar is not just a single star, but a 'quadruple' star—consisting of two binary stars orbiting each other. A reference to 'Mizar Five' crops up on "Sign in Stranger", from *The Royal Scam*, and is typical of Fagen's interest in sci-fi, more fully explored in his solo album *Kamakiriad*.

N is for Napoleon, who is name-checked in the song "Pretzel Logic". The narrator says he's never met him, but plans to find the time. "Pretzel Logic" is one of the Dan's three 12-bar blues songs, the other two being "Bodhisattva" (from *Countdown to Ecstasy*, 1973) and "Chain Lightning" (from *Katy Lied*).

O is for oleanders (*Nerium oleander*), a poisonous evergreen shrub with fragrant white-to-red flowers and narrow, leathery leaves. Originating in the Mediterranean, it is now in common use as an ornamental plant in gardens around the world. The plant appears in "My Old School" from *Countdown to Ecstasy* another song about Bard College: 'Oleanders / Growing outside her door / Soon they're gonna be in bloom / Up in Annandale.'

P is for "Parker's Band", a track from *Pretzel Logic*, the Parker in question being Charlie 'Bird' Parker, born 29th August 1920 in Kansas City. Renowned as probably the best and most influential jazz saxophonist of all time, he died aged 34 after a life of serious excess. In Ken Burns' magnificent documentary, *Jazz*, Winton Marsalis described Charlie Parker as a man 'who could never outrun his appetites; his appetites always outran him'.

Q is for ... Nope, couldn't think of anything for Q.

R is for Rikki. Whatever you do, Rikki, don't lose that number because it's the only one you want.

S is for Steely Dan, a type of (fictional) Japanese dildo featured in William Burroughs' 1959 novel *Naked Lunch*: 'Mary is strapping on a rubber penis. "Steely Dan III from Yokohama," she says, caressing the shaft. Milk spurts across the room. "Be sure that milk is pasteurized. Don't go giving me some kinda awful cow disease like anthrax or glanders or aftosa."'

T is for "Third World Man", the melancholy story of demented youthful idealism gone psychotic. It was originally recorded at the *Aja* sessions but, when they needed a song to finish *Gaucho*, Becker and Fagen pulled it from the vaults, re-wrote the lyrics, kept Larry Carlton's gorgeous guitar solo and built up a whole new song about a Rambo-like youth. Beautiful and silky smooth.

U is for Ulysses, whose story is retold in "Home at Last" (from *Aja*), another of the Dan's most beautiful and accomplished songs: 'I know this superhighway, this bright, familiar sun'. The song is filled with natural imagery—sky, sun, sea, shore, rocks. Although it is not technically a blues, it nevertheless has a firm bluesy shuffle (named the 'Purdie shuffle' after legendary drummer Bernie Purdie), lulling like waves. The sirens serve the road-weary narrator smooth retsina, they keep him safe and warm, but it's just the calm before the storm.

V is for Las Vegas, where all the "Show Biz Kids" (from *Countdown to Ecstasy*) live in their corner houses with their booze, Steely Dan T shirts and all that money can buy. They've been all around the world, and they've even been to Washington Zoo. They try, they really do, but they just make movies about themselves and don't give a fuck about anyone else.

W is for whores, or, more precisely, the "Babylon Sisters" (from *Gaucho*)—so fine, so young. 'Tell me I'm the only one.' A song full of lust and longing and the dust of the Santa Ana winds. The sisters are like a Sunday in TJ—cheap, but not free, and they will make you realise that you are not what you used to be.

X is for … Nope, couldn't think of anything for X, either.

Y is for "Your Gold Teeth", a title so good they used it, not once, but twice. "Your Gold Teeth" appears on their second album, *Countdown to Ecstasy* and is as much about the tobacco they grow in Peking as anything else. "Your Gold Teeth II", which appears on their fourth album, *Katy Lied*, is in a jazzy 6/8 time. The drummer on part II was a young Jeff Porcaro, who described the track as 'pure bebop'. In both songs, Donald Fagen implores their owners to 'throw out your gold teeth and see how they roll'. The answer they reveal? Life is unreal.

Z is for drinking a 'Zombie from a coco shell' ("Haitian Divorce"). The Dan's songs are filled with their favourite tipples—beer in "Here at the Western World", retsina in "Home at Last", coke and rum in "Daddy Don't Live in that New York City No More", piña coladas in "Bad Sneakers", Scotch whisky in "Deacon Blues", Cuervo Gold in "Hey Nineteen", cherry wine in "Time out of Mind", grapefruit wine in "FM", kirschwasser in "Babylon Sisters" and a black cow in "Black Cow".

Elliott Smith—An Introduction

'There are two big enemies: bitterness and style. If I can escape them both, then I'll be happy.'
Elliott Smith

My two favourite American singer-songwriters are Mark Eitzel and Elliott Smith. Both are *poètes maudits* who look at life from the gutter and sing about what they see. But whereas Mark Eitzel has an occasional tendency towards melodrama and solipsism, Smith never wavers or slips into self-pity. Not once. I don't know of any other 'confessional' artist whose work is as personal, honest and coherent as his. That is why he is so revered and why his body of work will endure.

In his lifetime, Smith recorded six albums, the last of which was released posthumously. His first release, *Roman Candle* (1994), was recorded in his bedroom on a four-track and was a 'lo-fi' classic—just his fingerpicking, occasional brushes and his whispery, spiderweb-thin delivery, which he always double-tracked because he felt his vocals were 'weedy'. He honed his style and songwriting on another two albums, *Elliott Smith* (1995) and *Either/Or* (1997), while expanding his sound to include drums and electric guitar, all of which he played himself.

From the beginning, Smith's songs were peopled with dissolutes, dopers and dropouts. These early albums contain some of his most harrowing songs—"No Name #3", "Angeles" and "Between the Bars". Whenever he hears Smith's "Needle in the Hay", the usually stoic Pixies-frontman Frank Black admits openly to weeping at its sadness. And what tunes! Smith's melodies are soft and gossamer-like. He hardly ever riffs, preferring instead to move through very intricate chord changes, which are emotional and direct. It is this knack of setting such sour words to the sweetest tunes that makes his songs so affecting.

Gus van Sant used some of these early songs on the soundtrack to his film, *Good Will Hunting*, and the song Smith wrote for the film's closing credits—"Miss Misery"—went on to earn him an Oscar nomination and a whole new audience. With this success came the chance to expand his sound even further. His next album, *XO* (1998), sounded fuller, more baroque, with songs featuring a horn section, Chamberlins and string arrangements, although his double-tracked vocal and acoustic guitar style remained intact. Even better was his next release which is, arguably, his masterpiece—*Figure 8* (2000). There isn't a duff song on the album, which revels in its power pop songs and complex arrangements. It's a kaleidoscopic album which wears its heavy Beatles influence very lightly. From the piano-led "Everything Means Nothing to Me", which outros with swirling, echo-drenched drums, to the aching and razor-sharp "Everything Reminds Me of Her", the album is note perfect.

This is when Smith was at his most confident as a songwriter and musician. In six short years, he had moved from playing guitar in his bedroom to performing as a multi-instrumentalist in expensive LA studios. For *Figure 8*, he even went to Abbey Road studios in London and played on the piano used by his beloved Beatles on "Penny Lane". Things went very rapidly downhill from here. He toured with *Figure 8* and, sometime during this period, Smith started using large amounts of heroin. Friendships were broken, studio deadlines for the follow-up album came and went, as did the money. Smith was soon a fully-blown addict, paranoid and alone. He recorded dozens of songs in a borrowed basement, once again playing everything himself. He was back where he started.

But he finally managed to seek help and, by 2003, he was clean. He sought help to finish his album, which he told everyone was going to be his 'White Album'. But, just as things were looking bright again for Smith, news came on 21st October of his death. Although the circumstances surrounding it are unclear (his then girlfriend was in the house at the time), Smith died of two stab wounds to his heart. Smith had tried several times to take his own life, so it was almost certainly suicide.

The following year, his family allowed his final album, *From a Basement on a Hill* (2004), to be released. Recorded during the depths of his addiction, it is by far Smith's bleakest album. Never before had he recorded songs as noisy and dark as "Strung Out Again", "Don't Go Down" or "King's Crossing" (sample lyric: 'It's Christmas time and the needle's on the tree / A skinny Santa is bringing something to me'.) Smith wanted *From a Basement on a Hill* to be a double album but, while going through the tapes, his family chose not to release some of the tracks because of their extreme bleakness. And yet, it also contains two acoustic songs—"Twilight" and "The Last Hour"—that are absolutely stunning in the lightness and beauty of their melodies. Even to the last, he was setting his sour words to the sweetest tunes.

Erik Satie—"The Velvet Gentleman"

Erik Satie was an iconoclast, a visionary and a pioneer. He was an iconoclast because, throughout his life, he refused all conventional teaching. As he said himself, he was a man who was happier using 13 letters of the alphabet to evolve his own language than using 26 letters like everyone else. He was a visionary because the music he composed broke so firmly with the past, particularly with Wagner. No one had written music like his before, nor have they ever since. His limpid, languorous style has often been imitated but never bettered. Finally, he was a pioneer because his music and ideas were the forerunners to a great deal of music that we take for granted today—furniture music, ambient music and repetitive (or minimal) music. Without Satie, we would have had a very different kind of John Cage, and without John Cage, we would have no Brian Eno.

Satie was born in Honfleur in 1866 and, apart from one trip to Brussels, lived in Paris the whole of his adult life. And, besides one disastrous six-month affair with an artist and acrobat called Suzanne Valadon, he remained single and celibate all his life. More than anything or anyone, he loved children and animals. For 27 years, he let no one into his room except stray dogs. He said, 'The more I know about men, the more I admire dogs'. But Satie did have one great friend in Claude Debussy, who was the composer Satie most admired in his life and with whom he maintained one of the greatest ever friendships between musicians. Satie claimed to have only ever cried twice in his life—once at the death of Debussy and once at the death of Lenin.

One of the keys to understanding Satie's life and music was the idea of Immobility. He said that, for him, it was richer to 'imagine' life than to experience it. For him, experience was a form of paralysis and so he withdrew into himself. I think one of the reasons the act of withdrawing was so important to him was because he wanted to live many different lives in one place rather than the same life in many different places. Immobility allowed him to stay in one place and grow, change and shed skins, and this was symbolised by the various 'uniforms' he adopted throughout his life. He started out dressing in a priestly, floor-length 'smock', then, for seven years, he wore nothing but seven identical velvet suits, and then, in the last stages of his life, he wore the black suit and bowler hat of a minor civil servant.

Another key to Satie was the idea of The Miniature. Jean Cocteau said of him that 'The smallest work by Satie is small in the way a keyhole is small. Everything changes when you put your eye to it.' He made countless drawings of tiny houses, manors and châteaux, the production of which would absorb him for hours and days. These imaginary worlds were, for him, every bit as real as the 'real' world and he felt more at home in them. For Satie, The Miniature was a refuge of greatness.

The final key to Satie's work is the idea of Repetition. In 1949, John Cage went to Paris to find out more about Satie's music (apart from a few *cognoscenti*, Satie's work was unknown at that time) and one of the pieces he discovered was entitled "Vexations". Played through once, this rather innocuous piece made up of 36 diminished and augmented chords lasts no more than 2–3 minutes, but Satie had set a trap for the performer by saying that the piece should be played 840 times in succession. To do this, he said, 'it would be advisable to prepare oneself beforehand, in the deepest silence, by serious immobilities'. If you follow Satie's instructions, the average time it takes to perform the piece is about 24 hours, which is longer than it would take to perform all his other pieces of music put together.

It might seem like a joke, but Satie was deadly serious and the repetitive nature of all his pieces raises interesting questions about the function of boredom in art. Satie said that 'boredom is deep and mysterious'. Of "Vexations", Cage said, 'The music first becomes so familiar that it seems extremely offensive and objectionable. But after a while the mind slowly becomes incapable of taking further offence, and a very strange euphoric acceptance and enjoyment begins to set in … It is only boring at first. After a while the euphoria begins to intensify.'

In May 2007, I was in the audience in the Turbine Hall of Tate Modern for a performance of "Vexations", performed according to Satie's instructions. One of the pianists for the event was Gavin Bryars, who talked about its difficulties for a pianist. He said that, even after performing it many times over, pianists have great difficulty committing it to memory because of the baffling complexity of its construction and notation, and the piece requires tremendous concentration to play precisely because you return to zero 840 times. It is only *in* time that the piece works. For both performer and listener, "Vexations" is a test of the limits of endurance and patience—it is a maze, a koan, an inner journey as well as a spiritual vexation.

Satie was never rich or famous in his lifetime; indeed he was a pauper by choice for the whole of his life, but he was greatly admired by many musicians and artists who would go on to become famous. At his funeral were, among others, Picasso, Cocteau, Brancusi, Man Ray and Georges Braque. Satie's favourite book was *Alice in Wonderland* and he often said that, because he was half Scottish, he was the only Frenchman who could fully understand English humour. He approached life humorously and was by nature an absurdist, so when Dadaism and Surrealism came along, despite being much older than others in those groups, he fitted in quite naturally with their ethos. His younger friends called him 'Le Mâitre' ('The Boss') and he sat in on their meetings as chairman, but was also their mascot.

Satie always maintained that he was a bad composer and an even worse pianist. He was indeed a very bad pianist, but of course, we now know that he was, in fact, a very good composer.

The most famous of his pieces for piano are the "Trois Gymnopédies", written when he was 21 and ill in bed during his military service. They were three versions of the same theme and Satie likened them to walking round a piece of sculpture and viewing it from three different angles. Based on ideas of purity, antiquity and tranquillity, the pieces remain amongst the best-known and most famous ever written for the piano.

But of all Satie's creations, I think the most magnificent was his own life. I've always admired his refusal to conform, his dedication to his art, the singularity with which he pursued his dreams. Just as he was receiving some small recognition for his work, Satie fell gravely ill with pleurisy brought on by cirrhosis of the liver. He was moved to the St Joseph Hospital and was given a private room paid for by the fabulously wealthy Comte de Beaumont. It was there that he died in 1925. It is hard to sum up any life in a single line, particularly one as willful and eccentric as Satie's, but his contemporary Louis Durey came closest in his description of Satie as 'one of those capricious plants which produces a strange unique flower in some solitary and inaccessible place'.

Originally posted on Faber's Thought Fox blog, January 2014.

Iannis Xenakis—"Making music out of mathematics"

'I am a classical Greek living in the 20th century.'
Iannis Xenakis

In his Parisian atelier, Xenakis—Greek composer of some of the most thrilling and disturbing music of the last 100 years—always had to hand a slide rule, an electronic metronome, a stop-watch and at least one book by Plato in the original. His workspace looked more like a factory than a studio. Being without attachment to a particular style, school or movement, Xenakis personified the political and social struggles of post-war Europe more intensely than any other composer. His music actually has no content at all—it is pure sonic energy, a revelation of the deep mathematical structure of the world and the universe. His music is governed by geometric shapes, statistical laws and the forces of nature—the patterns found in tree branches, clouds and coast-lines. Although his artistic thinking had its roots in Greek philosophy, architecture and literature, his imagination was as daring as any science-fiction writer. He is a complete one-off, without any antecedents at all and we will probably never see his like again.

Iannis Xenakis was born on 29th May 1922 in the Romanian port of Braïla on the Black Sea. Although born in Romania, all his family were Greek. His paternal grandfather came from the island of Euboea; his mother's father from Limnos, in the northern part of the Aegean. When Xenakis was 10 years old, his father sent him to boarding school on the Greek island of Spetse. He was lonely and miserable there, his heavily-accented Greek separating him from the other boys. He loved the sea and taught himself to swim, winning first prize in many swimming competitions. He naturally veered towards maths and physics but he also studied music. Although he found the music lessons 'boring', he realised that music could affect him very strongly. 'I remember once passing one of the common rooms and suddenly, through the open doors, hearing Beethoven's *Fifth Symphony*. I had no idea, of course, what it was, but the effect the music had on me was unexpected and very powerful.'

He left Spetse in 1938 and set off for Athens, where he enrolled at a prep school in order to prepare for the engineering course at Athens Polytechnic. In his spare time, he also studied harmony and counterpoint privately with Aristotle Koundourov. It was at this time in his life, aged 16, that Xenakis fully engaged in his Greek heritage. 'I felt I was born too late—I had missed two millenia. I didn't know what there was for me to do in the 20th century. But of course there was music and the natural sciences. They were a link between ancient times and the present, because both had been an organic part of ancient thinking.' He immersed himself in the writings of Plato, Thucydides and Xenophon. He adored the Greek poets, particularly Sappho, whom he read in the original Aeolian dialect.

He visited the sites of ancient events, including several trips to Marathon, where he 'projected' himself into that age. He would cycle to these places and camp out at night, listening to the wind, the crickets and the sound of the rain on his tent. At the same time that he was engaging with ancient Greek civilisation, Xenakis was also falling in love with nature, and if anything could sum up his musical vision it would be this dual love of this Greek heritage and the natural world. He once described being caught in a storm out at sea in a small rowing boat. The waves, rain, thunder and lightning. The experience left a deep impression on him and he said that he wanted to make those who listened to his music feel the same sense of awe and terror.

This idyll was shattered in October 1940 with the Italian invasion of Greece. The Germans followed six months later. The Resistance in Athens began to organise itself, which Xenakis joined and stayed with for three years, helping to organise demonstrations, making speeches and mobilising public opinion. In July 1943, Italy capitulated and retreated, followed by the Germans in October 1944. When, three days later, Churchill sent in British troops to quell the Communist uprising amongst the Greek youth, Xenakis then found himself unthinkably fighting the British.

During the ensuing street battles in January 1945, Xenakis was inside a building when a shell of a Sherman tank hit it. The explosion caused a huge splinter to enter and destroy his left cheekbone. His left eye burst out of its socket. His palate was pierced and his jawbone broke. He started choking on his own blood and vomiting. He only survived due to the help of a woman named Mâkhi (after whom he named his only daughter). His father, who was searching for him everywhere, bribed a police officer to help him and together they found him and moved him to a hospital.

He had an operation to remove a piece of shrapnel lodged in his cheek and had three further operations to reconstruct the left side of his face. For months afterwards he was unable to stand up straight. The distance of objects kept on changing and he kept tipping and falling over. His hearing was irreparably damaged too. He was unable to hear high pitches and there was a constant buzz in his inner ear for the rest of his life. The results of these injuries left him feeling as though he lived 'in a well', intensifying the sense of solitude he had always carried with him. But even in the midst of battle, Xenakis was listening. 'I discovered things about sound that I was not taught, that no one had told me. People shouting in waves, the bullets in the night, whistling, and explosions here and there. It was a large scale spectacle that was very interesting.'

After the British withdrawal, a fascist military junta was put in power and death sentences were issued against those who had been involved with the Communists, including Xenakis. He immediately fled the country under an assumed name—Konstatin Kastrounis—and arrived in Paris, via Rome and Turin, on 11th November 1947. He was helped at first by a refugee organisation. He sought work and, because some acquaintances of his worked there, he was eventually employed by Le Corbusier's firm of architects.

In these early years in Paris, Xenakis made his first forays into composition. In 1951, Xenakis introduced himself to Olivier Messiaen and showed him some of his first attempts. Messiaen said to him, 'You are very talented but you compose in a naïve fashion'. Xenakis was shocked and dismayed at Messiaen's frankness, but Messiaen went on to explain himself: 'You have the good fortune of being Greek, of being an architect and having studied special mathematics. Take advantage of these things. Do them in your music.' Later on in life, Xenakis said that this encounter with Messiaen was the most astounding interview of his life. Xenakis found himself returning to the sounds of his lonely childhood—flocks of birds, bees swarming in groves—and the sounds of his years in the Resistance—mass phenomena, chaos and violence—and vowed to transcribe these masses and swells of sound into his music.

His first piece, named *Metastasis*, after the Greek *Meta* (after or beyond) and *stasis* (immobility) is an exploration of the dialectical contrast between movement and immobility. This problem fascinated the ancient Greek philosophers, beginning with Parmenides and continuing with Zeno, and is illustrated in the fable of Achilles and the tortoise. In *Metastasis*, Xenakis transferred the radiating lines on his drawing board into criss-cross *glissandi* for the strings. Superimposed string slides, each with a different gradient, create huge sweeps of sound that expand and contract asymmetrically, producing continuous and discontinuous change. This is his famous 'stochastic' method of composition, a system based on the 'calculus of probabilities' whereby notes are assigned randomly in the manner of Brownian motion of gas molecules or massed blood cells, which create a form resulting not from the movement of the individual but the aggregate. Music is no longer visualised as a one-directional process moving through various stages to a logical conclusion but rather a distribution of vast numbers of sound events. The piece was premiered at the Festival of Donaueschingen in 1955 but the performance was met largely with miscomprehension and indifference. Xenakis, however, knew he had found his way as a composer.

'[Xenakis is] the prophet of insensitivity.'
Milan Kundera

At the same time that he was breaking new ground as a composer, Xenakis was working full-time for Le Corbusier. Xenakis was always keen to point out that he was never an architect. He trained as a civil engineer and, at first, he only did stress computations but, more and more, he took part in the actual design work. He contributed to the design of the Couvent de la Tourette but his major collaboration with Le Corbusier was the Philips pavilion made for the Brussels World Expo in 1958.

The structure of the building is extraordinary and difficult to explain. It has been described as a three-peaked nomadic tent, or like the interior of a cow's stomach, but it is in fact ruled concrete surfaces arranged in a series of dramatic airborne spirals, called 'hyperbolic paraboloids', or saddle shapes. With his design, Xenakis was trying to replicate in architecture what he was doing in his music and the Philips pavilion is really just *glissandi* in space. 'In the Philips pavilion I realized the basic idea of *Metastasis*: as in the music, here too I was interested in the question of whether it is possible to get from one point to another without breaking the continuity. In *Metastasis* this problem led to *glissandi,* while in the pavilion it resulted in the hyperbolic parabola shapes.'

Like Messiaen, Le Corbusier appreciated Xenakis' singularness and the two had developed a friendship. They also had something very particular in common—they both had only one eye, and neither could therefore judge distance very well. There is a lovely story about how, whenever they shared a meal at a restaurant, Le Corbusier would aim the bottle of wine at Xenakis' glass, pour and say, 'Am I in or out?', to which Xenakis would reply, 'In, I think'. But the pair fell out when Le Corbusier claimed all credit for designing the Philips pavilion and gave the younger man no credit at all.

At around this time, Xenakis became interested in early computing and the idea of generating music using machines rather than orchestras. In order to explore this further, he made use of the famous GRM studio in Paris, then run by Pierre Schaeffer, inventor of the term *musique concrète*. Xenakis made four electroacoustic pieces here: *Diamorphoses* (1957), *Concret PH* (1958), *Orient-Occident* (1960) and *Bohor* (1962). For the apocalyptic *Diamorphoses*, Xenakis' sound sources were earthquakes, wind, bells, doors slamming, railroad cars crashing and aeroplanes taking off. He said his project was 'to mix timbres in order to arrive at a body of sound like white noise; to study the evolution of timbres, dynamics and register; to make unisons with attacks; to make chromosomes of attacks'.

For *Concret PH*, Xenakis recorded crackling embers from which he extracted very brief sound elements and assembled them in huge quantities, varying their density each time. The resultant two minutes of glistening, granular work is a sound continuum without a single break. *Concret PH* was originally composed to be played in the Philips pavilion (the PH stands for 'hyperbolic parabola'). Inside the pavilion, more than 400 speakers fitted into the walls and ceilings played Edgard Varèse's *Poème Electronique* to the millions of visitors to the pavilion. As the tape of the eight-minute piece was being wound back, *Concret PH* was played. Both pieces were played 30 times every day.

Xenakis defined the term 'density' in music as the number of sound events per second and these tape pieces are studies in white noise and its graduations through the process of densification. He would record sounds on one tape, copy it, edit the copy so that any repetition was avoided and then mix the copy with the first tape. He carried out the same operation with three tapes, then he re-recorded those three tapes on three tape recorders, thus increasing the sound events per second by a magnitude of nine. For this reason, these superdense electroacoustic pieces are absolutely (and intentionally) overwhelming to listen to. Xenakis' electronic music forms only one-ninth of his total output but his status in the field as a pioneer (along with that of John Cage's work in the same field) is unmatched.

> *'I do lack lyricism. Maybe life killed it in me—but it's also possible that I was born without it. I don't know.'*
> Iannis Xenakis

In the late 60s and into the 70s, Xenakis developed his electroacoustic tape pieces on a much grander scale, creating massive alliances between sound, architecture and light. He called these multimedia events 'Polytopes'. The first of these, the *Polytope de Montréal* (1967), was a performance of a tape piece accompanied by 1,200 sources of light fixed to steel cables so that a kind of transparent sculpture was formed. In 1971, in the Roman baths of Cluny, Xenakis created another Polytope, a multimedia spectacle of 600 strobe lights, 400 mirrors and three lasers. But the most ambitious and dramatic of all of Xenakis' Polytopes is *La Légende d'Eer* (1977), written to be played in a special architectural construction accompanied by laser lights and composed for the opening of the Pompidou Centre in Paris, where it was performed for three months in 1978 and seen by thousands of people.

The work is projected over seven separate tape tracks, each

made up of a mix of electronically generated sounds, noises and instrumental sounds. Although it is a continuous 46-minute piece, there are discernible sections which suggest the voyage of a mythic hero through underworlds filled with demons and Furies of both the ancient world and the world to come. The music is ritual without religion. It assumes there is a man and there is a cosmos. Nothing else. It invites us to inspect the cosmos with fascination, awe, terror even, but without piety. The experience it unleashes in us is the product of our own minds and cultures, with no intervention at all from a God-like presence.

The title comes from the final pages of Plato's *The Republic* and the legend links back to Xenakis' wartime experiences—the mass movements of people and machines in the darkness and the play of searchlights over cities under bombardment. It is hard not to link the fate of Er, whose body returns to life after ten days, and that of Xenakis himself, whose wartime wounds were so severe that he was initially deemed unsaveable. It is the most pitiless and brutal of all of Xenakis' work, the purest embodiment of his musical aesthetic.

By now, Xenakis was established as a composer and received endless commissions for new pieces. He continued to work solidly, producing numerous substantial works until he died peacefully in his sleep on 4 February 2001. He was cremated at Père Lachaise cemetery, with a wooden oar by his side and his favourite copy of Plato. His ashes were scattered over his beloved Aegean, homeland of his forefathers.

'The music of Xenakis is an alien shard, glimmering in the heart of the West.'
Ben Watson

Luc Ferrari—"Inaccurate Autobiography #15"

'I am light with meditation, religiose / And mystic with a day of solitude.'
Douglas Dunn

Sunday 7th February 2010, 10.15am. I am sitting in Place des Abbesses situated halfway up Montmartre in Paris. The thin houses in the square are grey with white shutters and sloped leaden roofs. There is a tall church made of red brick, its bells ringing. Tourists are taking photos of each other in front of the Art Nouveau metro sign. Three Arabic men are gathered in one corner, sharing a joke. One of them repeatedly touches the shoulders of other two. Whenever someone walks across the square, pigeons take flight and whirl around the square for a few moments before landing and regrouping again.

While I am sitting in Place des Abbesses, I am listening to "Place des Abbesses" (24'31") by Luc Ferrari, an electroacoustic piece for tape. Ferrari was one of the co-founders of GRM but quickly began to incorporate pieces of 'real' taped sounds into his *musique concrète*. "Place des Abbesses" mingles fragments of taped voices, street sounds and natural sounds and places them in a collage, taking the idea of Cage's 'imaginary landscapes' literally.

Listening to the piece while sitting in the actual square is bewildering. I put the voices I am hearing into the mouths of the Arabs, making them say what I hear. The sudden entry of the woozy bongos causes the pigeons to take flight. What is inside and what is outside? I have always thought of Ferrari's piece as a spiral—whorls of sounds, ascending, fading, repeating, becoming tighter and tighter, yet more and more distanced. The piece that I'm listening to is a highly-compressed simulacrum of what I am seeing, and the line between inside and outside is blurred. Which is true? Which do I follow? To make what is inside concrete and keep the vastness of what is outside is the first task of the imagination.

> *'With the early experiments in musique concrète, we would take sounds from the studios—piano, bits of metal, etc.—and treat them as if they were notes. As soon as I walked out of the studio with the microphone and the tape recorder, the sounds I would capture came from another reality. I listened to all these elements that I had collected outdoors and I thought these sounds developed a discourse that had something to do with narration. There was no name for this kind of music so I said: "that's 'anecdotal' music."'*
> Luc Ferrari

Ferrari's music relies heavily on narrative principles. There is the 'time of the telling'—24'31"—and the 'time of the thing told'—days and days of recording. The sounds on these environmental tapes are all natural but, as in cinema, 'real' time is compressed into 'narrative' time, on a scale that focuses our perception on small details but keeps the vastness of the landscape intact. Ferrari's montage is executed with such subtlety that it recalls the Zen story of the master who painted a landscape so perfect that he walked into it and disappeared.

The white shutters of the tall buildings stand out in the winter light, the bells continue to ring, more tourists take photographs. The Art Nouveau metro sign remains the same. The Arab who touches the shoulders of the others still looks them directly in the eye. The pigeons take flight, making frenzied undulations around the square before sinking downwards again on extended wings.

> *'In searching out the truth, be ready for the unexpected, for it is difficult to find and puzzling when you find it.'*
> Paul Auster

This text was commissioned and published as part of the Writing Sound 2 exhibition held at Lydgalleriet in Bergen in November 2014.

Christian Patracchini—A Monograph

The audience is waiting. Around 50 people are gathered into a small gallery, lining the white walls, waiting in silence, tense and uncomfortable. There is nothing else in the gallery except a glass of milk on the floor. The date is November 2008 and the location is the Nolia Gallery, just off the Blackfriars Road, London. We are waiting for a performance to be given by Christian Patracchini. Eventually, he makes an entrance into the gallery space, wearing nothing but a pair of off-white long johns. He is walking backwards, holding a piece of tripe. He stops and turns around, facing the glass of milk. He puts the tripe down and picks up the glass. Putting the glass to his lips, he drinks, but also lets the milk cascade down his front, his long johns and onto the floor. When the glass is empty, he puts it down and walks to a corner of the gallery. We don't know what's going to happen next but, unbeknownst to us, he has already placed a small square mirror there. He picks up the mirror and we notice that it has holes drilled into it for a pair of eyes. Christian puts the mirror to his face, and approaches a member of the audience very slowly, looking at them through the holes. I try to picture what it must be like to be approached like this. As he does so, you must be seeing yourself becoming larger and larger in the mirror, but with Christian's eyes looking at you, not your own. The effect must be very unsettling. I am hoping he won't approach me and, luckily, he doesn't. He gestures that another member should study their neighbour through the mirror and then pass it on for their neighbour to do the same. As they do this, they do so with a sense of bewilderment, and Christian slowly makes his way out of the gallery. After he has disappeared for a few minutes, it becomes obvious that he is not returning. Nervous clapping starts, then stops, and we all disperse, not sure of what we have just witnessed or been a part of.

I have known Christian since 1999, which is when he first arrived in London from Italy. Since then, we have become very close friends, meeting on a regular basis to touch base, exchange ideas and to assess where we are with our work. Our meetings have become a necessary part of our lives. In our discussions, a few issues have repeatedly cropped up, issues that strike at the heart of what it means, for Christian and for myself, to be an artist.

Perhaps the most central of these is the degree to which he feels he should or shouldn't ingratiate himself for his work. Christian hasn't shunned opportunities that have come his way, but he has been careful to select only those invitations that he feels will develop and advance his work and his connection to it. Of course, as any artist, he wants people to see his work, but he has never striven for great recognition or financial reward. Quite the opposite, in fact. In this sense, Christian is the best embodiment I know of a person whose life and work are inextricably bound.

And then there are the issues of art itself. 'Maximalism' or minimalism? Showman or observer? This is an area where he and I agree more often than not. On the whole, we share the same sensibilities in our attitudes and approaches to art. We both feel a strong sense that art should be pure. It has to come from the right place, a place deep inside oneself. If you make art to make money, you're finished; your reasons for producing work have to be more personally risky than that. The more you dedicate yourself to your work, regardless of the reward, the greater the chance of success. If there is no risk on those terms, there is no reward, and what you risk reveals what you value.

Christian and I share many of the same preferences for other artists: Marcel Duchamp, Yves Klein, Iannis Xenakis, John Cage, Fernando Pessoa. Still, silent, simple. The work should, we agree, be as simple as possible—much better to use simple images to convey complex ideas than vice versa. Always looking for ways to reduce, not expand. Finding the essence. Christian's work is simplicity itself, which may sound easy to achieve, but it is not. I have seen how much thought, preparation and analysis have gone into a piece by Christian before it is performed. He is a perfectionist and sees no reason to do things differently, and I entirely agree. Of course, this presents problems. Occasionally, Christian has reached an impasse when developing an idea for a piece and has had to change radically or even abandon his original idea. But that is all part of the process. A quotation of Erik Satie's has always resonated very strongly with both of us: 'Boredom is deep and mysterious'. Impasses are thresholds, they are just invitations for you to do better, they are doorways which, when passed through, change utterly the landscape, usually for the better.

As dedicated as he is to his work, however, I wouldn't be at all surprised if Christian suddenly announced one day that he was going to give up art for good. It is not a given that he will pursue this line of enquiry for the rest of his life, and part of our discussions is to assess continually where we are and how we wish to proceed. Christian is a very organic artist, prone to choices that others would find quixotic, bloody-minded even, but always right, in the end. Of course they are right; he is his own man. I admire and respect him enormously because such diffidence in the face of our corporate culture takes great courage and commitment. He is unwavering in his determination to find ways of enriching his life and discovering new forms of expression and, regardless of its outcome, that alone should be applauded.

Originally published in REM magazine, October 2011.

In Conversation with Maria Fusco

RS: In your collection of short stories, *The Mechanical Copula,* you played a great deal with ideas of perception, simulation and the authenticity of experience. I'm thinking in particular of your interest in Federico Fellini's 1976 film *Casanova,* in which this is a central idea. Do you think these issues also play a part in your novel, *Sailor*?

MF: *Sailor* sprang from a scar. A little monkey bit my mother's leg sometime in the mid 1930s in Belfast. The bite mark is still visible today, not quite angry but definitely agitated. The novel's monkey is not the same one who marked my mother, my Sailor, the eponymous narrator of the novel, is the 'providential machine', as Kant might have it, who embodies and extends my current social, theoretical and creative pre-occupations: without this monkey I would be mute. So, in direct relation to this, authenticity of experience is central to how I begin to write but not to how I carry on writing. This novel has been necessarily extremely research-heavy, demanding a thorough processing of oral and historical archives to get the right voice; I've had to mine my own Belfast demotic, (now inevitably diluted as I've been living outside of Northern Ireland for twenty years), and rely upon my family and archives to return my own voice to me. I keep coming back to the same quote, 'The human word is midway between the muteness of animals and the silence of God', borrowed from Louis Lavelle's *La Parole et l'Écriture,* I'm somewhere in between.

RS: The other day, I came across the term *dinnshenchas,* which, as I'm sure you're aware, is the Irish word for the way in which the land/landscape is translated into story, a kind of 'toponymic lore', so that every place-name bears a story. As well as being an archive of your demotic, how important is this sense of place in your novel?

MF: The local as the universal interests me, it seems such a practical, sensible proposition, speaking to the limits of what can and cannot be remembered by an exile. The sense of place in *Sailor* is an intricate one, the monkey is very happy to be in Belfast, which might seem odd, but this is the emotional complexity at the core of the work. John McGahern has written 'everything interesting begins with one person in one place', whilst I'm slightly sceptical of the totality of this, I am convinced by the precision of subjective knowledge. *Dinnshenchas* then may be about the distribution of such knowledge rather than the production of it (even though as a term it blushes specificity), its most tangible value is to let you know you can leave.

RS: I know that you are interested in literacy and orality—the power of utterance—and the space that lies between them. How have you approached the performative aspect of *Sailor*? What effects have you tried to engage with in your thinking and preparation for its iteration in a gallery space?

MF: I don't have an expectation visitors to my sound work in Whitechapel Gallery will 'hear' an entire novel, I think the temporal compression that that would demand would be unfeasible, or at the very least undesirable, in a gallery context. With this work, I am concerned with precision of delivery through textual method; to that end I've made extractions from *Sailor* that can stand alone from the novel as a whole, and which require close listening, but which at the same time may be heard. Perhaps this seems quite a simple proposition, but when part of the process of reading the novel *Sailor* is, to a certain degree, to learn how to read like a monkey talking in thick North Belfast 1940s vernacular, calibrated around the syllabic meter of monkey vocalisations, it's not so direct. Aural deceleration is a key process here, as is the live editing that the four Northern Irish actors make when applying their own distinct accents, breaths, speeds and pitches to the text. This sound work then may be a trail, *Sailor*'s time in the gallery merely a tenancy.

RS: It seems to me that there is always a problem with authenticity when you repeat a performance many times over. Repetition denies the linearity of time and often leads to spatial, trance-like states of being. I imagine the performers could get 'lost' in this repetition by necessarily bringing into it a growing reliance on automatic prompts, responses and recitals, but perhaps that's the idea? What are your thoughts on this?

MF: I wonder if it's useful to reflect upon the score here, in terms of its iterative functionality, rather than the textual script... To consider the *Sailor* readings as score for the actors to find their way through, to find their voice as that one particular time of recording, working organically outwards from the open structure of the score, its open-ended potential, so there can be no definitive version in the speaking of it. This leads me to wonder if then the novel form of *Sailor* is the 'definitive version', what do you think, are novels the final word?

RS: Yes and no. I think novels are the final word of the creative process but the beginning of their life in the world. You do the best job that you can when you're writing, but a book will never be perfect. A book is never finished, only ever abandoned, and you have to make your peace with that. Once they are out of your hands, there is very little you can do to determine their fate. For me, it is rather like rearing children—they gain an autonomy.

Originally published on the occasion of Maria Fusco's Writer-in-Residence exhibition at Whitechapel Gallery, London, 19th April–10th June 2012.

For HARK magazine, November 2014

HARK: You write both poetry and prose. How do they relate to one another in your own work?

RS: A lot of people ask me that question and I'm not sure I know the answer. Increasingly, I feel that poetry is my first and foremost 'calling'—I started out writing poetry and I know I'll end my days sitting in a bath chair wrapped in a blanket trying to finish a poem… In my late twenties, I hit some kind of brick wall with my poetry and I didn't know how to break through to the other side. That was when I turned to prose and I got an immediate response with my prose in a way that I never had with my poetry, so I went on that tangent from then on. Novels are big, baggy beasts with a lot of room for error. Not so with a poem. For me, a poem needs to be the striking of a tuning fork. It is fleeting and elusive. Novels need to be built from the foundations up and they take years and years to evolve, like a planet massing. I guess the one thing for me that's vital in both poetry and prose is an exactness and concision of language. I have never been able to write long novels—my editor at Faber jokes that I am the only writer of his that he has to send away to write more—because I am always looking for fewer, better words and sentences. But, during all the time I was writing novels, I never entirely gave up on poetry. I would write about one poem a year and put it away. I felt out of the loop with poetry. Then, in 2008, I taught the General Workshop on the Creative Writing MA at Goldsmiths, where I was a tutor, and I had three poets in my class—Aviva Dautch, Matthew Gregory and Abi Parry—who were an absolute revelation to me. They were so young and, as writers, already fully committed to poetry. They were so knowledgeable and yet so hungry and I became very inspired by their attitude and approach towards poetry. I began to write poems with a new vigour and some of the poems written since then appear in my pamphlet, *Terrace*, published in 2015. Of the two, I would say that writing a good poem is a much harder task than writing prose. The task itself is never very clear with poetry; but with a novel you have a journey to embark on and the sense of time passing. A poem is capturing a moment. I have written four novels and am now writing my fifth and, in all that time, nothing has been more satisfying for me than finishing a poem and feeling that feeling that there might be something good about it. It's a hard feeling to describe but it's what we're all after.

HARK: Your Vanguard Readings in London are very popular events. What are your thoughts on the spoken word and poetry reading scene, of its possibilities and potential?

RS: I set up Vanguard Readings in 2011 because there were so many brilliant writers coming through Faber Academy who couldn't get a reading gig because they were unpublished and I wanted to give them a platform to share their work. It now has a large, dedicated audience and doubles up as a thriving community where writers can meet each other and share their experiences. I cannot think of anything negative about Vanguard; it's a totally positive thing for so many people. I have just started a publishing arm of Vanguard Readings, fetchingly called Vanguard Editions, the inaugural publication of which is *#1PoetryAnthology*, an anthology of more than 40 poems written by poets, both published and previously unpublished, who have read at Vanguard. All these Vanguard activities are run as not-for-profit ventures. There are dozens of similarly run events around the country, which is a tremendously positive thing, I think. It gives new writers such a confidence boost. Time and again, I've seen their nervousness before their reading and their total joy afterwards and it's great to be able to use whatever profile I may have in order to provide that for the next group of writers coming through.

HARK: How would you respond to the recent statements made by Nobel judge Horace Engdahl, that grants for writers and creative writing courses are having a detrimental impact upon contemporary western literature?

RS: I'm very tired and bored of this debate. I have no time for writers who feel compelled to tell other writers what they should or should not be doing. His comments were patronising and arrogant. No one raises an eyebrow at music or painting academies so why should writing be any different? I could give you a list of 50 novels right now that were written by people who took creative writing courses and whose books have made an impact on contemporary western literature. The debate is an outdated one and the argument in favour of writing schools was won a long time ago.

HARK: What are you working on at the moment?

RS: I'm currently writing a crime novel, entitled *Blood Work*. It's about a father and son on holiday in France, during which time the father is brutally murdered. As he was the only person present at the murder, the French police arrest the son and put him on trial. He is found not guilty due to lack of evidence and released, but if the son didn't kill him, who did? And why? The son conducts his own investigation into his dead father's past and finds there a very different man from the one he knew...

HARK: You've talked before about your interest in point of view—of the narrator, of characters and other voices. For us, *The Red Dancer* was a very intricate way of handling these differing perspectives, while also, it seemed, never fully revealing Mata Hari herself. She remained an enigma at the heart of the book. Was this your intention—to reveal but also to hide these 'selves'?

RS: Yes, that was exactly my intention. Well spotted! I started researching *The Red Dancer* by reading the various biographies of her life and, as I read them, I found that they all contradicted each other, and so I thought I couldn't trust any of them. But they all had one thing in common—that there seemed to be two keys to understanding her life: personal reinvention and self-delusion. How strongly we identity with historic figures depends on principles of singleness and consistency—the more singular and consistent they are, the more 'knowable' they become (think of Einstein, Churchill or Gandhi)—but the life of Mata Hari was neither singular nor consistent; quite the contrary! Rather than let that stop me from writing the book, though, I decided to structure of *The Red Dancer* around this problem of who exactly Mata Hari was. I quickly arrived at the idea that the narrative could be a series of multiple and inconsistent points of view, made up of eye witness accounts, by people both real and imagined, letters, newspaper cuttings, documents, quotations, interviews both real and imagined, as well as fiction. In the book, there are multiple narrators who, taken together, make up a kaleidoscopic portrayal of Mata Hari. The only character who doesn't have a voice in the book is her. Living in the public eye as she did, and in such a male-dominated world, Mata Hari's life wasn't entirely her own to control or keep. I think this is the real sadness in the story. But she was also her own worst enemy. Ultimately, my aim was not to take up a position either for or against Mata Hari; rather, I wanted to present enough material for the reader to judge for themselves. History itself is made up of contesting stories and the differing stories surrounding the myth of Mata Hari lie at the centre of the narrative.

HARK: Historical fiction is very dominant at the moment in terms of awards, prizes, publicity. Why do you think this is, and why now?

RS: I think historical fiction has always been popular in the UK. It's one of the most widely read genres in the UK marketplace.

HARK: What advice would you give to aspiring, younger writers?

RS: I think the most important thing I could say to someone just starting to write is to be true to yourself. For me, writing (and creativity in general) is all about finding that very true place within yourself and letting the writing flow out from there. Be patient, remain 'empty'. The best ideas are those that are received rather than sought. Don't write what you think other people want you to write, or what you think other people will like to read, write because it's a need you have to satisfy. The 'necessity' of writing comes way before its 'beauty'. I would even go so far as to say that new writers should write the story they think no one will publish. It's your best hope of writing something really good.

For Pieced Work Samples, July 2013

'Prose adds. A poem multiplies.'
David Burnett

For me, poetry is the highest, deepest form of expression in the English language and so the most difficult form of writing to do well. In the right circumstances, a poem can be read once and never forgotten. A lot of people find poetry difficult but I have come to realise that a poem isn't something to be 'understood', as though it were a code to be 'cracked', only after which it gives up its meaning, but rather something to be felt. It is much more fruitful to experience a poem than to hanker after its meaning. I revisit *The Wasteland* all the time but still have no idea what some bits of it mean.

Short poems work best for me. I love the super-condensation of a short lyric or imagist poem. The density pulls you in but there is too little of it to direct you along a particular path towards a definite meaning. It's clear to most what the meaning of TS Eliot's "The Journey of the Magi" is, but the 'meaning' of William Empson's "Let It Go" is much less certain. Short, dense poems can expand your mind in every direction and the shorter the poem is, the more expansive it is. For me, that's what David Burnett was getting at in the above quotation.

Of course, we're lucky to have such an enormous and varied vocabulary in English. The ancient Britons, Romans, Anglo-Saxons and then the French have all contributed uniquely to make English the mongrel language that it is. Just as Leonard Cohen is described as one-third Lorca, one-third Yeats and one-third Elijah, so English is one-third German, one-third Latin and one-third French. It is this sponge-like quality that gives English its vibrancy and variation. If language doesn't grow and change, it must die.

'Experience passes through you and you have to try to digest it in some way, assimilate it—and then let it pass.'
Helen Chadwick

The spelling of plants in English is a fascinating record of change within the language. In 1420, 'daffodil' was spelt 'affadille'. It then became 'daffadilly' and 'daffadowndilly' before the version we have today. I wonder what it will be in 200 years' time? In 1265, 'hollyhock' was 'holihoc', then became 'holiyhokke', 'hollyoak' and finally 'holyoke'. In 1000, 'cowslip' was 'cu slyppan' (source 'cow slobber'); 'parsley' was 'petersilie'; 'pea' was 'pyse' and 'leek' was 'leac'. In 1356, 'onion' was 'unyonn', then 'uniowns', 'oynyons', 'hunyn' and finally 'ingyon'.

Not only is the development of a single word in one language a fascinating story, but so is the way the same word changes across several languages. Our word 'dandelion' in English is taken from the French 'dents-de-lion', which means 'lion's teeth'. The French word for 'dandelion', however, is 'pissenlit', which translates as 'wet the bed', a reference to the plant's diuretic qualities. In Norwegian, 'dandelion' is 'løvetann', which also translates as 'lion's teeth', but in Swedish the word is 'maskros', which means 'worm rose'. In Latin, the plant is called 'Taraxacum Officinale'.

Language is a record of its own change and development, but it is also a record of its invasion and occupation by others. With the Norman invasion of England, the French brought their cultured words for meat, so the animal was a 'cow' but the meat became known in English as 'beef' after the French 'bœuf'. Ditto 'mutton' from 'mouton' and 'pork' from 'porc'. In Norman times, the vast majority of the conquered English couldn't understand French and so, to ensure the whole population could understand key concepts, phrases were coined that had an English part and a French part, hence expressions such as 'law and order' and 'peace and quiet'.

'Don't write about anything you can point at.'
Leontia Flynn

A poem is a watermark of perception. The world around us is visible and tangible but poetry is speaking about what's invisible and intangible. A poem can be anything, from a recipe, or a shopping list, to an epic. I once wrote a poem that was comprised solely of the chemicals found in Liquorice Allsorts. A few years ago, I wrote this poem after my grandmother died.

My Grandmother's things

A brown bakelite telephone
with separate handpiece, Leicester 58803.
Her mother's newspaper
cuttings, a wooden letter rack.
Wooden mushroom, needles—darners & sharps.
Royal Worcester milk jug
shaped out of fronds, a bone-
handled knife.
A wind-up cheese grater, a colander, egg
poacher and steamer pan.

'Du musst dein Leben ändern.'
(What the torso of Apollo said to Rilke in Paris, 1908)

I've never been a huge fan of reading poetry in translation. Someone once described reading a poem in translation as like kissing someone through a veil. It doesn't completely satisfy. Poets have got round this by doing very 'free' translations, as Pound did from the Chinese and Don Paterson did with Rilke's *Sonnets to Orpheus*. I lived in Italy for a few years in my early twenties and read a lot of Italian prose and poetry but never felt I had mastered the language well enough to pick up on all the nuances. One line that has stayed with me, though: 'Quando si scrive delle donne, si deve intingere la penna nell'arcobaleno'. Diderot, I think.

German is a fascinating language because individual words have enormous power. I once had a long discussion with a German friend as we tried to translate into English the term 'Einsatz leitung', which we had seen written on a car at the scene of a traffic accident. The word 'Satz' in German has multiple meanings: clause, principle, setting, rate, leap. 'Einsatz' is impossible to translate directly into English but it has the connotation of one of these things becoming important in a moment, something that achieves importance over other things. 'Leitung' is another German word that has many meanings and it is impossible to find a direct English equivalent. It can mean cord, circuit, wire, pipeline, duct, mains. The name for 'tapwater' in German is 'leitungswasser', or 'piped' water. Eventually, after talking on and off for days, we arrived at the conclusion that the closest translation of 'Einsatz leitung' was 'Operation Leader'.

I have always found Wallace Stevens' work fascinating—his poem "Tea at the Palaz of Hoon" is a favourite of mine—and I would say that I have favourite poems rather than poets. When I was living in Italy, I used the British Council library a lot and came across a wonderful short poem there by Lotte Kramer called "White Morning", which left an indelible impression on me. Yeats' "The Wild Swans at Coole" made a similarly big impression, as did Geoffrey Hill's "A Song from Armenia" and Anne Stevenson's "Utah". Some of Donald Davie's early poems I like a lot, including his "Ezra Pound in Pisa". That leads me on to Pound, whose Imagist Manifesto is still meaningful to me. Wallace Stevens' "Thirteen Ways of Looking at a Blackbird" is the very embodiment of Imagism and a wonderfully alive poem. Stevens' poem "The Dwarf" is one of the weirdest and most wonderful poems I've ever read. Stevens' poem "The Snow Man". Sylvia Plath, Ian Hamilton, Paul Muldoon, Keith Douglas.

And, whichever way you turn, there is always TS Eliot.

Titles of poems not yet—nor possibly ever—written:

Vale, Parsley Sidings, Moth Cull, Yews, The Innocence Manoeuvre, Oiseaux 96-98, Flemish, Jean & the Found Things, Oxblood, Lontano, Stretch (You Are All Right), Triolet, A Polished Solid, Sooki's Lullaby, Enchanted Looms.

Wanhope

My favourite word ever might very well be 'wanhope', the Old English word for despair.

Vade Mecum

A *vade mecum* is a guide or handbook, kept close at all times and used for instruction. An early 17th-century term from modern Latin, it means, literally, 'go with me'.

Contemporary culture has eliminated both the concept of the public and the figure of the intellectual. Former public spaces – both physical and cultural – are now either derelict or colonized by advertising. A cretinous anti-intellectualism presides, cheerled by expensively educated hacks in the pay of multinational corporations who reassure their bored readers that there is no need to rouse themselves from their interpassive stupor. The informal censorship internalized and propagated by the cultural workers of late capitalism generates a banal conformity that the propaganda chiefs of Stalinism could only ever have dreamt of imposing. Zer0 Books knows that another kind of discourse – intellectual without being academic, popular without being populist – is not only possible: it is already flourishing, in the regions beyond the striplit malls of so-called mass media and the neurotically bureaucratic halls of the academy. Zer0 is committed to the idea of publishing as a making public of the intellectual. It is convinced that in the unthinking, blandly consensual culture in which we live, critical and engaged theoretical reflection is more important than ever before.

Don't Joke on the Stairs

How I learnt to navigate China by breaking most of the rules

Cecilie Gamst Berg

BLACKSMITH BOOKS

To Ellen, with thanks

Don't Joke on the Stairs
ISBN 978-988-19002-0-3

Published by Blacksmith Books
5th Floor, 24 Hollywood Road, Central, Hong Kong
Tel: (+852) 2877 7899
www.blacksmithbooks.com

Front cover photo by Liz Hemmings
Back cover photo by Steve Harvey

Contents

Don't Joke on the Stairs

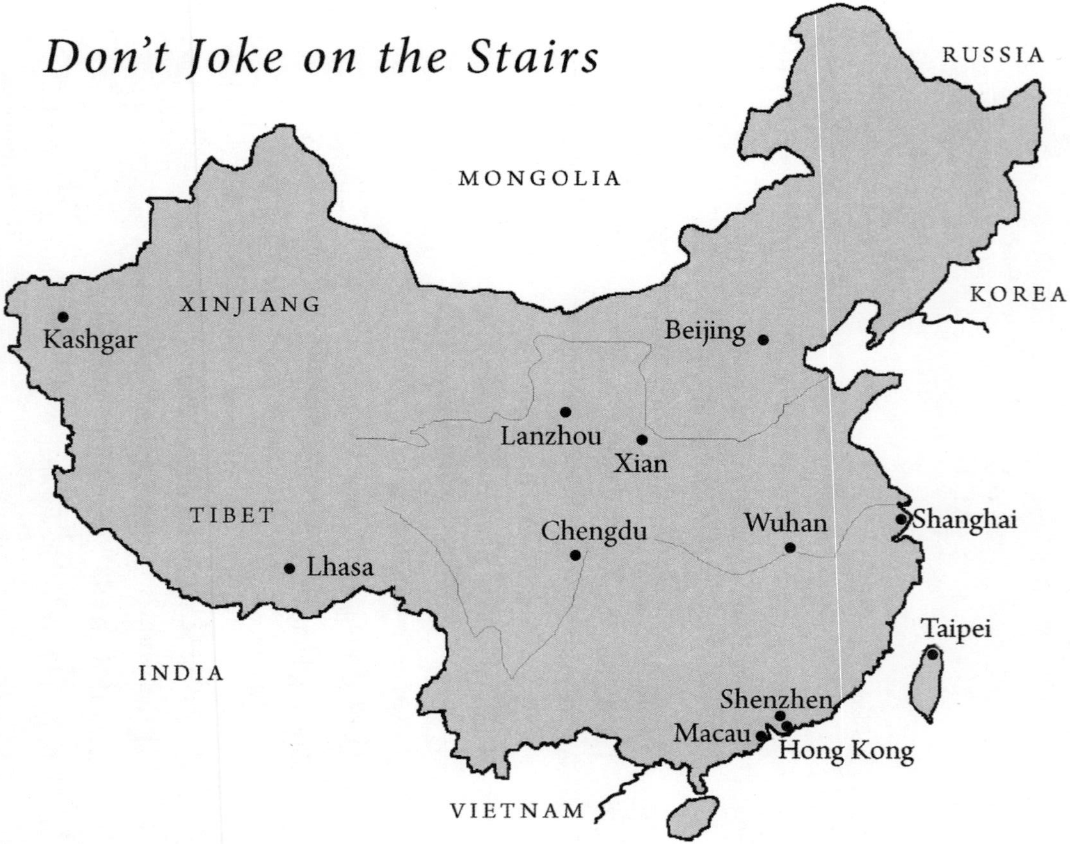

I

A Nadir Country

"This is possibly the lowest point of my life," I thought as I stood outside a hotel in the middle of Central Asia at 3:50 in the morning, fighting with a hotel security guard.

You think I mean fighting as in 'arguing with'? No, I mean fighting. Fisticuffs. Hitting and kicking. And twisting and pulling.

Well, maybe it wasn't the absolute lowest point of my life – if it was, I wouldn't have had much of a life, nadir-wise. But it was certainly among the top, or rather bottom, five.

"Let go!" I shouted, trying to pull my wheelie bag out of his grip. (I think I even added "You bastard.") "I want to leave!"

"You're not going anywhere!" shouted the guard, twisting my wrist. I gave him a good kick on the thigh and he relented a little, then tightened his grip again. He tried to pull me into the hotel but I stood my ground.

In the middle of this I couldn't help noticing that hey – I can hold my own physically in a fight against a man in his early twenties! That's something. But then again I was stuffed to bursting point with adrenalin, and he wasn't what you'd call strapping.

Not for the first time on this dismal trip, I thought: "Damn you, George. Damn you to hell."

It hadn't been a good day.

In fact it hadn't been a good ten days; ten days of travelling during which I had frequently cursed George. George, yeah, good old George, whose idea this trip to Xinjiang, the most remote of China's many remote provinces ("remote" meaning "far from Beijing") it had been. My good and fun friend George, who had pulled out of the trip at the last minute; five days before take-off in fact.

*

Four months earlier, he had called me early one morning, tearing me out of sleep.

"They're knocking down the old city of Kashgar!"

"What... who... where?" As if I didn't know who and where. It was just that I was still in a dream about a choir weirdly singing the same tune as the ring-tone of my mobile.

"The Chinese are going to tear down the old city of Kashgar!"

"Bloody hell. No. Not even they can do that."

"I'm emailing you the article now!"

Two minutes later I was staring at a news item from the *Daily Telegraph* confirming what George had said.

To enhance tourism in Kashgar, the Chinese government was going to eradicate the very thing that tourists from all over the world had been coming to see: The medieval Old Town. Largely untouched for the last 400 years, it was one of the few parts of China, and certainly the only city, that hadn't been razed to the ground to be reborn as a high-rise, pink-tiled urban nightmare.

Oh, and as well as attracting more tourists, this development would help the Uyghurs of Kashgar to live in "civilized" homes, far, far above the nasty ground floor where they had hitherto spent their miserable lives; away from the primitive courtyards exhibiting all sorts of backwardness such as being covered in cooling grapevines.

George called again: "We must go to see it before it's too late!"

"I'm in."

"This summer! After I've been to the States."

"Dude, you do realise that when the Chinese government say they're going to tear something down, they don't exactly hang about?"

"I know, I know... let's see... now it's April... how about we go in August? I just have to sort some things out first."

"All right."

"We must take photos!"

"Oh, I know! Let's make a documentary!"

"Yes! That's what I thought too! With your Mandarin and my Arabic we've got it all covered. And maybe buy some carpets!"

"Let's go by train!"

"Oh God, I can't wait! This is going to be legendary!"

That's what I thought too. Maybe not as legendary as my trip to Xinjiang the year before with Richard – oh, Richard, too painful to even think about – but then again very few trips could be as legendary as those with Richard had been before he platumped (platonically dumped) me when he found the love of his life. And also I had never reached Kashgar during my trip with Richard.

No, travelling with George would be fun; super fun. He was adventurous, intellectual, he understood my jokes... Being an archaeologist, he even knew about the history of the place we were going to. This meant that I'd probably have to accompany him to not a few museums but that was okay – I'd just wait outside. Yes, I was looking forward to this trip. And as the months went by, I was starting to look forward to it with a kind of China fever; the kind of exaltation one feels when one knows one will be inside the motherland for weeks on end, eating excellent food and looking at – even talking to – beautiful guys every day.

I suppose I had been looking forward to it a little too much. How else to explain that I had become extremely irate when George told me, in an offhand manner a week before we were supposed to leave, that he couldn't go to Xinjiang after all because his boyfriend had arranged something else – a *weekend in Tokyo.* Three weeks in China thrown over in favour of two days in Tokyo, to which, let's face it, they could go every weekend of the year if they wanted to?

This, more than anything, told me that during the four months we had been planning this trip, he had never really meant to go at all.

So yes, I had been vexed. More vexed than a vexed vex can possibly be, and cursing George. And nobody else I knew could go to Xinjiang at six days' notice, it seemed. Vexed!

And now I was angry again, here in deepest Central Asia all by myself and fighting with a hotel guard, instead of doing what I should have been doing: namely being asleep somewhere after a nice evening of drinking beer with George, possibly including Chinese poker-playing with dudes. Not fair! But was the persistent lack of justice in this world an acceptable reason for fist-fights with strangers?

All right, so I shouldn't have kicked that desk.

It was a childish and unbecoming thing to do for anyone over the age of twelve, let alone a middle-aged woman who was supposed to be a seasoned and sophisticated traveller with 20 years of traversing China under her belt. Yes, I was so ashamed of having kicked that desk that I didn't tell anybody about it after I came back to Hong Kong; not even in a blog entry.

It was just... I was so frustrated and so tired; so pissed off with the whole province and everything in it, that I did it without thinking. At the time I justified it by blaming the receptionist who wouldn't let me stay in this 1.5- to 2-star hotel when I had turned up at 3:30 in the morning desperate for a bed. But even in mid-blame I knew it wasn't her fault.

It hadn't been the fault of the receptionists who had refused to let me stay in the three other hotels I'd tried that morning either.

Since I had arrived in the smallish town of Kuche at two in the morning after what's known as a "gruelling" 12-hour journey by local bus from Kashgar and then on from Akesu by means of what we could call "compensated hitch-hiking," squashed together with four other people in the back of a small private car with a maniac driver, I had done nothing but try to get a roof over my head for the night.

I had thought it would be a cinch; waving my Hong Kong permanent resident ID card and saying I was a Hong Kong compatriot – it had always worked before, so why not now? But no – "It's not suitable for you."

"It's more suitable for Chinese people" and "You'll be better off staying at the Lido" was all I'd heard at hotel after grimy hotel.

One receptionist had almost given in. "Well, I suppose... if you don't mind not having your own bathroom..." she had started, over my relieved cries of "Anything! I'll do anything!" at which point a hotel security guard had come in, gesticulating wildly. She immediately backed down and started bleating about the Lido being more suitable.

So I went to check out this Lido. Aha – 900 yuan a night! Now I saw clearly. Not one receptionist had had the guts to tell me it was a government edict: Foreigners can only stay in the most expensive joint in town, for "security reasons." Because all foreigners are terrorists. Or all the locals in Xinjiang are terrorists. I forget which.

*

Yes, the awfulness of this particular sojourn into the hinterland of China had been exacerbated, a few weeks before I left Hong Kong, by the Chinese government having shut down the entire province. I had read about it in the paper but not paid much attention; I had been used to shutdowns of this and that, and a huge presence of paramilitary police in China ever since the sacred Olympic Games the year before. To enhance that event, Beijing had suddenly stopped issuing visas to any foreigners, including in many cases those who had tickets to the Games, four months before the Games.

Then there was the trouble in Tibet, with a closing of that province to foreigners – really, it was always something, somewhere. More stuff about crackdowns, shutdowns and nail-downs came pouring in from China every day. Shutting down a province meant for me that I couldn't get into it physically, but I had my three-year visa so had nothing to worry about. Yes, that's what I thought.

Oh, the restiveness of a people occupied. It had all started with a rumour put out on the Internet that June by a Chinese worker who had been fired from his job at a factory in Shaoguan in Guangdong province.

He claimed that two Chinese women at the factory had been raped by "six Uyghur boys," also workers at the factory, in their dormitory.

Although this rumour was immediately quelled by the government as well as by the women in question, furious Chinese workers who "wanted to teach these Uyghurs a lesson" stormed the factory and at least two Uyghurs were killed, with hundreds of people injured. In July, local Uyghurs marched through Urumqi, the provincial capital of Xinjiang, protesting what they saw as yet another transgression against a people who have consistently been marginalized, suspected and looked down upon as backward and stupid since their "liberation" in 1949.

Angry Chinese settlers armed with pickaxes, spades and other implements attacked the (allegedly) peaceful demonstration, and fights between Han Chinese and Uyghurs broke out in Urumqi and other major cities such as Kashgar.

The Chinese government, after having allowed the Chinese to beat up a lot of Uyghurs for a while, reacted with the usual method: Sending in thousands of troops and shutting the whole province down – that is to say, cutting off all kinds of communication with the place.

This was the fact that I had somehow chosen to ignore.

It was only when I crossed the border from Gansu that I realised what the shutdown meant: No internet. And no telephone. There was no access to email, no phoning, landline or mobile, out of the province, and no texting within it. I was effectively closed off from the outside world. I couldn't even have called Hong Kong from a five-star hotel, or a post office, or... anywhere.

Now, if I had been with George, this wouldn't have been much of a problem. Being middle-aged, as I mentioned earlier, I had after all lived a whole life without internet and mobile phones. But by myself it was a whole different ballgame of kettle-fish. When I realised I was to spend the next two weeks effectively cut off from all contact with the outside world I had even, for a couple of seconds, considered going back to Gansu and just spending the rest of my holiday cruising around the northern provinces; visiting Tibetan strongholds in the wilderness of northern

Sichuan and Qinghai perhaps, taking photos and putting them on my blog and generally enjoying what now, compared to Xinjiang, seemed like extreme civilization.

Then I reminded myself that I was on a mission, and the mission was to document the destruction of the old city of Kashgar before it was too late. With or without George, texting, blogging and email – damn it, I was going to go through with it even though that bastard had chickened out.

In a strange way I also think I wanted to punish George's cravenness by putting myself through what I now knew would be not a little suffering. When I was killed by insurgents or trampled to death by bloodthirsty camels, for example, *then* he would understand what he'd done to me! Yes, then he would be sorry.

So on I pushed. I could have a fantastic, vindictive holiday by myself, see if I couldn't! It would be character-building.

But that didn't mean I couldn't get angry with the government's cavalier treatment of tourists. Some violence-loving young hotheads get into a fight, and three months later I can't stay in whatever hotel I want? Unacceptable.

During the taxi ride to the overpriced Lido I had seen a sign in English saying "International Tourist Hotel" and thought that would be fair go, so I directed the taxi down the main drag of Kuche.

I was cross-eyed with fatigue but thought I could save at least 500 yuan by not staying at the Lido and, more importantly, I didn't want to be told where to stay by some jumped-up government agent. The reception of the Precious Lake International Tourist Hotel looked promising: It was filled with huge banners in Chinese and English praising the hotel for its tourist-worthiness.

Here, at last, I would get some sleep. And, by the looks of things, my own bathroom. Unfortunately, the receptionist had other ideas. "It's not suitable for you, you should stay at the Lido..." she started up the usual spiel.

I tried reasoning, I tried pleading. I tried "I'm a Hong Kong compatriot." Nothing. "It's more suitable for you to stay at the Lido..." "This place isn't suitable for foreigners..." On and on the argument went.

But I mean, really! If you're going to lie anyway, can't you just lie and say the hotel is full? But no. After 20 minutes of argument, she closed the deal with that age-old Chinese (and, I'm embarrassed to say, increasingly Hong Kong and worldwide) excuse: "It's for your own safety."

Really? So sending me out into the street by myself in a strange city at 3:45 in the morning is safer than letting me take the lift two floors up and sleep in a hotel room?

So yes: I lost it. I lost my temper and dignity. And on the way out of that bastard reception, in my anger and frustration I kicked at an object and the object was a desk. Not hard, a mere touch of the foot it was, and I was aiming for the leg. But I hit the wooden panel between the table legs instead.

Outside on the pavement I suddenly felt something holding my wheelie bag back and heard an angry voice shouting about criminal damage. What the...? I went back into reception, and yes there it was: A tiny indentation, a little bending of the plywood. Shit.

The reception guard was beside himself with anger, shouting about compensation (400 yuan), about his boss, my craziness. I told him to piss off and walked back out. And that's when the fight started. He pulled my bag, I pushed him, he grabbed my wrist, I kicked him – oh how fun it would have been talking about it afterwards safe in my hotel room with George... but of course if George had been there it would never have happened in the first place.

The receptionist and the other hotel security guard stood by, speechless, while we fought grimly on. After a few minutes I realized I couldn't beat him off and so went back into the reception to wait it out. At this point I was so angry and tired I didn't care what happened, and laughed scornfully as they called first their boss, then the police.

A definite nadir, I thought, but nothing I couldn't handle. I could speak Chinese. I had money. And I was a Hong Kong compatriot.

After half an hour the police called back: They couldn't be arsed to come. How I laughed! How scornfully (again) and with how much venom! I threw a hundred-yuan note on the floor – after all, I *had* kicked the desk – and got into a taxi conveniently waiting outside. That's when the boss of the hotel turned up, drunk, clearly having been torn away from a night of debauchery on taxpayers' money.

Through the rolled-down taxi window he gave me a lecture on how to behave in China and I think the Chinese version of "when in Rome, do as the Romans" was mentioned more than once.

Yes, it wasn't my proudest moment, that's for sure. But when he started on "It's for your own safety" I had really had enough.

"Go to the damned Lido, just go."

And thus endeth my nadir, that is to say, my nadir-est nadir, in Xinjiang province. The whole trip was pretty much a disaster but this was without doubt the lowest point. My wrist was bruised and I had another bruise on my arm, but nothing was broken. My dignity, however, was in tatters.

Damn you, George, I thought as I lay in the 900-yuan bed (or rather *on* it as Chinese hotel beds are hard as tombstones), unable to sleep. Again I had failed to listen to what locals had told me about the situation where they lived: It was really true that foreigners could only stay at the Lido! Why couldn't I just have accepted it? Was it because my inexplicable need for justice was greater than my need to sleep? Was it stingy of me not to want to spend 900 yuan on a few hours' sleep, just because I knew that normal hotels in the area went for about 120 yuan a night?

I tried to think about what I could learn from this nadir. Do you think I thought I should learn to control my temper? Of course not! I thought about how I shouldn't put so much faith in other people, believing what they said and stuff. I had to remind myself that just because someone suggested going somewhere, spending weeks and months talking about it, didn't necessarily mean they had for a second actually meant they would go.

I also thought about how I mustn't in any way let this minor setback influence my love for China. My love for China was supposed to be of the same nature as that of Xinjiang according to the Chinese government, namely that it is, has always been and will always be part of China. I love China, have loved it since 1988 and will always love it. And, unlike the Chinese government, I don't think Xinjiang is part of China at all.

2

Smile Comes Before A Fall

So what's with the love? What is it about China that enthralls me so, to the point where I love her, or rather, him, for richer, for poorer, in sickness, in health and in tainted food scandals, forsaking all others? Why this monogamous and almost unconditional love (I say almost, for there are a couple of things about China that even a mother couldn't love) which began at exactly 09:02 on September 31st 1988, the moment I first set foot on Chinese soil?

People often asked and still sometimes ask me, with increasing incredulousness year by year, what it is about China I love so much. For ages I couldn't pinpoint the reason, apart from the dull and hackneyed "Oh, I suppose the people, the food and the language, the music and the beauty of traditional Chinese architecture... and because it's huge and not Norway."

Well, these reasons still hold true. (By "people," by the way, I mean "men," by "food", "Sichuan food" and by "language," Cantonese). But the real reason for my Sinophilia eluded me until I went to Lanzhou in 2002.

It was there I saw *the sign* which finally told me exactly why I am such a slavering, unconditional lover of China who must have my regular fix of it every month.

I saw the sign.

Now at last I knew why I am happier squatting over the stinking cesspit latrine of some two-table restaurant in Sichuan while three pigs look on, than sitting daintily – well, just sitting – on the gleaming seat of a deep-carpeted, perfume-wafting "rest room" of a five-star Hong Kong hotel.

I realised why I'd rather sit up all night on a train thundering through Inner Mongolia with only three peasants for a pillow than fly business class to some golf resort in Thailand. And I finally understood why I'd rather sit and drink beer and play cards with three geezers on a street corner in Guangzhou than swan around a cocktail party with suave men in dinner jackets, being handed sparkling flutes of champagne by starched waiters.

It was the sign.

I was coming down by train from another, marginally happier trip to Xinjiang province; that furthest upper-left corner, the jaunty tail feathers of the chicken-like map of China, on my way home to Hong Kong, the chicken's arsehole as it were. That particular train journey had been something of an epiphany in many ways. It was on it that I discovered my real identity; not a normal, day-to-day *lao wai* (Caucasian) closed off from Chinese things like shitty hotels, but a true-blue Hong Kong compatriot. That was also the trip I spent 31 hours on a wooden bench, resting my head on wood. After this harrowing but edifying two-day journey I stopped over in Lanzhou, the provincial capital of Gansu. The city clings to the banks of the Yellow River which is the "cradle of Chinese civilization" and is known as "China's Sorrow" due to its terrible floods.

About the "cradle of civilization" thing: Just like I've been to Xian probably seven times without ever bothering to see the famous Terracotta Warriors, I don't know how many times I've been to Lanzhou without even once checking out the famous cradle. I knew it was on the banks of the Yellow River somewhere, but it was only after my ill-fated, nadir-rich trip to Xinjiang in 2009, coming screaming into the city gagging for an internet connection and someone to text, that after a serious bout of online reunion I thought of going to see the cradle.

I crossed the famous river on a footbridge and started asking people: "Where is the cradle of civilization? Is it here? Or here?" No one could or would really tell me, but in the end I found a unassuming spot covered in brush which looked promising.

It felt good having finally found the spot whence we all sprang.

That's when I saw the pig.

No, hang on, it wasn't a pig at all, it was a *human corpse.*

A big, fat, pink, swollen river corpse washed up after I don't know how many days in the water. This was by no means the first corpse I've seen in China (but the second) so I thought nothing of it, just kept going, thinking: They could have put a blanket over it.

But that probably only happens in detective stories. The real thing, corpse-wise, probably looks like the scene I beheld: A bored policeman taking notes, another irritating upset to his largely peaceful day; a police boat put ashore, some spectators talking among themselves and, a few metres away, people drinking and having fun on anchored river boats.

I looked at the sexless, lifeless thing washed up, thinking: There's really nothing more still than a corpse. Not even concrete. A corpse is the most immovable thing there is.

Murder, suicide, accident? Who knows? I didn't care to ask.

I bought a newspaper the next day, as I felt a certain attachment to my corpse, but there was nothing. What was mentioned, though, was that a woman enjoying a Sichuan hotpot meal had felt a movement under her armpit only to see a "big, hairy, shiny fellow" (a rat) running away and promptly diving into one of the hotpots to be not only boiled alive but also beaten to death by diners. The screams of the woman, the article said, quickly taken up by fellow female diners although they knew not why, had "put diners at the high-class dining establishment off their appetite." I'd say! Rat on the loose in China, that is big news.

Several hours after seeing the thing-like thing, I had no appetite either, and suddenly felt the need to text friends in Hong Kong: Guess what – I've just seen a corpse!

"Wah, bloody hell, where, how?" came the immediate answers, which made me feel a lot better. I hadn't been so unperturbed after all, it turned out.

I sat down to have a soothing beer, and right next to me I saw a matronly woman knitting comfortably away outside a SEX SHOP. Well, the sign in Chinese (on the curtain pretending to be a door) said "Maintain Health-Products" but it really was a sex shop full of dildos and other sex paraphernalia.

Death, sex. They are one.

And seeing death in all its, well, mundane-ness, really, made me feel so alive and to-be-or-not-to-be. It certainly made the pain of being all alone in the world go away. It could have been so much worse. I could have been the one lying there washed up on some riverbank with all my clothes torn off by the currents.

Morbid though it may seem, things like finding a corpse on a riverbank while looking for the cradle of civilization are what I love about China. But I was going to tell you about the one reason: The sign.

*

Lanzhou bears the dubious distinction of being the most polluted city in China (and believe me, that takes some doing), windless and nestling among high hills, and with perhaps more than the usual number of smoke-belching factories. But I have always loved it for its rough-and-readiness combined with that old-world charm – "we're the cradle of civilization and we know it" attitude, its weirdly coloured hills, festooned with temples clawing on to the sheer cliff-face, that rise straight up just behind the train station.

Oh, and the train station itself, yeah, I'd go there just for that. It's beautifully designed, has a lovely statue of a leaping horse in front and those rust-, green- and brown-striped hills rearing up right behind it. About a third of the population of China are invariably milling around this station in ordered chaos at any given time of day; everybody going anywhere in the north has to pass through it. The place is such a hub that you have to wait for up to six days to get a train ticket out, so even I, a big anti-flyer, have had to fly out of the city more than once, instead of travelling the civilized way: by train.

*

Lanzhou, far away from the eastern provinces and Beijing, hasn't been completely thrashed by "progress." You can still find winding streets with old geezers sitting outside their one-storey brick houses, shooting the breeze or playing board games, while other old geezers stand around them, commenting on the game.

In trees and on window sills nearby are clusters of bird cages, for the excuse the geezers use to go out every day and meet their mates is that the birds need to be taken for a walk. The birds look as if they're bored senseless if you ask me, but maybe they secretly appreciate the outdoors and the opportunity to pick up the latest gossip from their feathered pals, too.

Of all the cities in China I've been to, Lanzhou probably has the highest percentage of people openly not working and proud of it. At least half the city's population, day and night, are engaged in sitting down, chatting or playing some kind of board or card game.

Those who are standing seem mostly to be spiky-haired, impossibly thin young people (men) grouped around pool tables, fags parked permanently in corners of mouths. They look like youth everywhere; bored, indifferent and cocky. But even a middle-aged *lao wai* like me will make them break out in the most delightful smiles and they will come up, wanting to chat.

That's one of the many things I love about China, and which separates it from western countries. If I were walking down the street in, oh, let's say South London, or maybe inner-city Washington DC, and I saw a group of spiky haired, no, hooded, thin and saggy-trousered young men, I'd feel... if not exactly worried, at least decidedly middle-aged and terribly bourgeois. Perhaps I'd clutch my handbag a little harder, avoiding eye contact – what do I know?

But in China! Not only can I talk to these guys with impunity, more often than not they will invite me to actually socialize with them. Where else does that happen, I wonder?

Wherever it is, it has to be pretty good to beat China and its young men. They are so unthreatening. And so beautiful. Lovely skin, no facial hair... My oh my. And there are so incredibly many of them! With China's one-child policy, most girls have been eradicated, so the country is fast becoming the paradise known as "a world without women."

*

The Yellow River is, despite its sad nickname, Lanzhou's pride and joy. Like most famous and touristy places of modern China, its northern banks have been "beautified," that is to say stripped of any distinction and anything reminding one that the thing came into being more than five years ago. The new concrete steps, the paved promenade with multi-coloured tiles, the scattered concrete benches without any kind of shade, the plastic sculptures – it looks very much like any riverbank in any Chinese city that's come into a bit of money of late.

But disneyfied or not, it's still the mythical Yellow River, a brown mass of turgid goo coming down from the red and barren hills, and I like the feeling of standing on her banks, knowing that this is the well from which all sprang.

Anyway, on this visit to the city, I had been doing what I enjoy most wherever I go in China, which is just walking around, talking to everybody I meet (in China everybody is approachable for *lao wai*) and taking photographs.

I had been out of the English-speaking world for several weeks and had no idea what was going on in the world; being stared at and mumbled about by Uyghurs who thought I was American having been my only contact with world news.

I nipped into an English language school to see if they had a *China Daily* (an English-language Communist Party mouthpiece) from at least the same month.

That's where I saw the sign.

On a large poster stuck on the wall at the bottom of the stairs, it said in English:

> **Avoid exchange of jokes while using the stairs and don't concentrate on stairs that cause trip and fall.**

I can tell you I forgot all about *China Daily* as I perused this sign which, as well as warning people about the danger of joking, also featured an additional three well-intentioned tips (rules) about how to traverse two flights of stairs unharmed.

As I sat in my hotel room that night, still laughing as I looked at the photo I'd taken of the poster, I had an epiphany. Of course! That was it. Of all the things I love about China, that poster summed it up neatly.

It's the surrealism.

Surrealism was the word I'd been looking for all these years. Yes, more than anything, on every trip great and small I've undertaken in the Middle Kingdom, surrealism has unfailingly been at the forefront. Surrealism, strangeness, weirdness, outlandishness, drollness, kookiness... but most of all, surrealism. One could argue that what I call surrealism is just realism or reality for 1.3 (and counting) billion Chinese, and everyday, humdrum, boring, painful and often dangerous reality at that, especially that which is controlled by the government. Which is, let's face it, most of the reality in China.

So in the following pages I have set out to describe the surreal reality that I have met in China for better and for worse; run of the mill, ordinary stuff for all the Chinese with whom I've come in contact, but surreal for me, a westerner with western sensibilities.

Yes, after 21 years in China I find I still have western sensibilities, so bearing in mind that many people think all cultures are equal and nobody has the right to pass judgement on another culture, the stuff I will go on to describe is what I and I personally, only me, solo, find surreal; whether it's Mao's curious hold on the Chinese 30 years after his death, or the habit of China's government to imprison people who try to help others who have had their homes taken away to make way for an Olympic-themed flowerbed, or simply alert the authorities to the fact that the blood peasants have been selling for money has been infected with AIDS... That's right, that's the kind of thing I find weird. Yes, surreal. I don't set out to engage in what many liberals call "China bashing," nor am I making fun of individuals. I just relate the stories as they happened to me.

I remember once I was cycling around Denmark with a friend, and we happened by accident upon a place called "Hamlet's Grave". A group of Americans were there and we, being young and silly, started spinning a tale about being Shakespeare addicts and having sold all our belongings to be able to achieve our lives' goal: Camping out on Hamlet's Grave.

The oldest American looked at us for a long time. Then he said: "That's bullshit. But it's a good story anyway!"

That's the thing about China too. No matter what happens, it's a good story anyway, and with the added bonus that unlike my youthful lying escapade, it's all true.

China is surreal. At least for me. And that's the main reason I love it.

For a lullophobe like me (a lullophobe is a person who abhors a lull, and it was indeed the over-abundance of lulls which made me leave my homeland, Norway, forever in 1988), being in China, anywhere, any time, has always been a guarantee of a lull-less time.

And I don't mean sightseeing, shopping or even playing cards, or more, with men. Just by being there, there is simply so much surrealism to be had, seen, heard and consumed on every corner and in every spot, that even the boring things are somehow fun.

China has got to be the most happening place on earth, and it's not for nothing that the place is storming forth as the Country of the New Millennium or Two. But rather than quoting the normal reasons – "economic miracle", "fastest-growing economy", "fastest changing" anything – I say it's the surrealism that makes China what it is for me: The country of my life. And it starts as soon as I cross the border from Hong Kong into the fabled mecca of whore-mongery and fake goods: Shenzhen.

But before we go to Shenzhen, I want to tell you how I went from being a *gwei po* ('devil hag', foreigner) to a real Hong Kong compatriot.

*

"You have blue eyes and I have grey eyes. We must talk," says the huge bloke in a hoarse and broken Putonghua and immediately sits down at my table in the train restaurant car. He starts talking away at once while gulping down beer straight from the bottle. A large bottle.

The train staff look at him with badly concealed disgust. He is, to put it diplomatically, shitfaced. Everybody working on the train is Chinese and he is so obviously not one of them: Tall and burly with brown hair and watered-down grey eyes. He looks like a Russian athlete who hasn't yet run to fat. He drinks like a Russian too: gulping down a big bottle of beer for every small glass I can manage (and I'm no mean drinker), and becomes more and more melancholic, not to say maudlin.

He's a Kazakh, one of the ethnic minorities the Chinese are so proud of and whom they are fond of trotting out on a national day or other celebrations to perform in charming folk costume. He staggers through the sentences as if wading in mud, and I can just make out that he's complaining about how crap it is to be a Kazakh in modern China, while the restaurant car staff hover with their ears sticking further and further out of their heads.

My Putonghua, which was always of the "speak better than understand" kind, is really put to the test during the three hours he holds me hostage at the table, for he belongs to a generation which, although born in China, was forced to learn Putonghua at a fairly mature age and with great unwillingness. And the Putonghua he does know is becoming more and more muddled.

"Why have they taken my country?" he exclaims several times while gripping my arm with giant strength.

I signal "help" with my eyes in the direction of the train staff, but no help is forthcoming. They probably think we two foreigners should be together. Oh dear, this is not good. It is evening and I'm already knackered after having spent 30 hours on the train without a berth. I'm travelling through Xinjiang province, the biggest in China, and it really takes a fair bit of time to get out of it.

My plan had been to have a light dinner and a bottle of beer in the restaurant car and then go back to my awful seat (I seldom call anything on a Chinese train "awful," but after 30 hours in, or rather on it, my seat had taken on distinctly terrible properties) and maybe catch a couple of winks before getting off the train at 1:00am. Instead I'm being "forced" to drink one glass of beer after another while listening to a quacking, drawling litany about the old cottage back home, the wife, the horse and the dogs that he had to leave to find work in enemy land, which is actually his own land where he was born.

Like the inhabitants of so many liberated countries, the people of Xinjiang, which would have been a country called East Turkestan if the Chinese hadn't discovered its rich natural resources, have discovered the true meaning of the word liberation.

It is the freedom to be poor, to be second- or third-rate citizens in one's own country. It's the freedom to be hauled into prison even for thinking that one's country is a country. What heresy – everybody knows that Xinjiang is a province which has "always" belonged to China – much in the same way as Tibet.

Looking at the drunk and distraught man, I wonder if China is the only place in the world where large parts of the population can't use the country's name as their nationality. Although the different minorities of China – the Uyghurs, Kazakhs, Tibetans, Mongols, Koreans and so on – are technically Chinese, they can't call themselves Chinese. Only the ethnic majority, the Han, can. Every person living inside the vast entity called China carries an identity card on which their ethnicity is clearly stated. He was born in China and should therefore be Chinese, but: Kazakh.

Thus a third-generation Han Chinese born in the US who has never been to China and doesn't know a word of Chinese is more Chinese than, for example, a Kazakh, Uyghur or Mongolian born and bred in China and with fluent Putonghua. It's a question of looks. Or "blood," as they call it.

The official name of Xinjiang province is Xinjiang Uyghur Autonomous Region. That sounds fair and reasonable, but not surprisingly, the Uyghurs (and Kazakhs, Uzbeks, Kirghiz and Tatars, forced into a common nationality under Chinese suppression) have no more autonomy than the donkey has from the farmer.

Before the Communist Party came to power in 1949 it was part of its political platform to liberate the ethnic minorities of China from the "Han hegemony" they suffered under the Nationalist Kuomintang party. The pre-revolution Communists tempted the Uyghurs with autonomy or even independence if they would only support Mao and his band of merry liberators.

The Party had planned that cadres from the ethnic minorities, groomed by 10,000 Han Chinese sent into the hinterland, were to administer Xinjiang after the province had been liberated.

After the revolution, however, Mao had a change of heart. Why let this gigantic area, filled to the brim with oil, minerals (a third of China's total) and other resources, just sit there for the sake of some minorities who didn't have the wherewithal to take advantage of it anyway?

He started a big operation to build roads and railway links to the provincial capital Urumqi and beyond, putting Han Chinese in all key positions, ostensibly to assist Uyghur and other minority leaders temporarily in their quest to bring communism to the hinterland. In reality, of course, they came to rule, and they came to stay. Today Han Chinese make up more than 41% of Xinjiang's population, not counting military personnel and their families.

My drinking captor is not happy with this situation. I get the impression that he thinks of little else than the Chinese invasion of his country, at least when drunk. When he eventually starts abusing the Communist Party in a rather thunderous manner, the train staff get their fingers out at last. He is brusquely half-carried, half-pushed out of the restaurant car, but the damage is already done: I am drunk. Not hammering, screaming drunk like the Kazakh, but drunk enough to start thinking that this is truly a miserable train journey and where am I, who am I and how much is it?

I might as well stay in the restaurant car – going back to the seat doesn't bear thinking about.

After a month's travel in Xinjiang I had got on this train without securing a sleeper ticket, confident that it would turn out all right somehow. I was counting on the train staff taking mercy on me; after all, I was a foreigner and not as hardy as the Chinese. But two and three in the morning came and went, no sleeper was available and the staff stubbornly refused to throw anyone off the train so I could take their place. I had to resign myself to my fate.

At least I had a seat, that was something, and by the window at that, so I could rest my weary head on the window sill with the cool night air from the Gobi Desert caressing my troubled brow. I was privileged compared to many of the other passengers thronging the aisle, sitting wherever there was a scrap of space on their sacks and inevitable red, white and blue striped plastic bags. Many of them had been on the train for more than two days already, and were staring hungrily/compellingly at my luxurious bed arrangement, namely a wooden seat with a ninety-degree back and a rolled-up towel to put my head on. I didn't budge an inch. Here it was every man for himself. A trip to the toilet could result in extensive arguments to get my seat back, with the seat-thief uttering absurdities like: "I thought you had got off."

Yeah right, from a moving train in the middle of the Gobi Desert!

That's the thing about the Chinese; they really appreciate a good *opportunism*. Let's say you catch a *baozi* (steamed bun) seller cheating you by charging two yuan instead of one. He feels it is his right, as all foreigners are loaded. And of course, two yuan is not a lot of money, but it's still a 100% mark-up. If you then point out that *baozi* cost one yuan and that you in addition paid only one yuan for a *baozi* from this very stall the day before, he won't be embarrassed at all. No, it's thumbs up and braying laughs from the scoundrel himself as well as from the large congregation that has inevitably assembled hoping to catch an entertaining argument between *lao wai* and *lao bai xing* ('Old Hundred Surnames' – the ordinary Chinese).

When a corrupt cadre is caught embezzling 20 million yuan, people shake their heads and tut-tut. But not necessarily because he stole money from his company or from the people he was supposed to help, such as the hundreds of thousands displaced every year by the government's many ambitious infrastructural projects; no, they disapprove of the fact that he became *too* greedy. Couldn't he just have taken a few hundred thousand here and there, like normal cadres? Just enough to build the three-storey house, send the kid abroad to university and buy the mistress some furs and baubles? But no. Trust old Wang to let his avarice run away with him. Oh well, he'll have time to ponder that in the labour camp. (Or, as in some unfortunates' cases, in front of the barrel of a gun.) Pity he dragged so many of his underlings down with him though...

But everybody can appreciate someone who goes for it.

Because of this national (or indeed global) trait, I can't get much sleep on the train even with the luxury of a window seat, because every time I find a relatively comfortable position on my rolled-up towel on the one spot on the window sill without nails sticking up, some conductor or other always comes up and tells me to look after my stuff so it won't be permanently removed by opportunists.

Therefore I'm more than ready to go to bed when I finally, at one o'clock in the morning, reach my destination, a small desert town. (By "small town" I mean "not even two million people".)

I'm stiff and aching and with a head swirling with beer and hoarse Kazakh mutterings and cries as I stumble from the train down onto dry land, my feet uncertain of how to deal with a surface with no movement.

As usual when I get to a new place, I saunter, or in this case stagger lightly, over to the nearest hotel, just across the road from the station.

But for the first time I experience the unthinkable: The station hotel is full. Not even the luxury super suite, for which I would have gladly forked out the additional 50 yuan, thereby pushing the room price up to a stratospheric 250 yuan per night, is vacant.

The situation is the same in the next hotel, and the next. Is it a cadre conference? The receptionist says something about a meeting. The only meeting I care about, however, is my imminent meeting with death if I can't go to bed right now.

I'm too old to stay up two nights in a row, and not sleeping is just out of the question and also undignified. So I get into a taxi and ask the driver to take me anywhere at all. We go here and we go there as the warm August night (morning) deepens, but there isn't a vacant cupboard to be had anywhere. The driver insists on going into each hotel to enquire for me so I can rest, but every time he gets back to the car he looks more despondent. The town is stuffed like a *baozi*.

Then the driver has an idea and we drive to a small hotel, more like a pension without even a neon sign, huddled down some back street. He takes both me and the luggage inside. The reception is as simple as simple can be: A woman behind a desk, one staircase going up. Up, up to clean sheets and a horizontal placement of the body! And rejoicing glory to eternity, there are vacancies. Except for one little detail: Foreigners are not allowed.

What the...?

It's not the first time I have encountered this curious phenomenon, which in many other countries would be called "racial discrimination" but in China is labelled "protection against substandard or unsuitable accommodation for foreign nationals." Or something.

No, it's not the first time I've encountered it, but it's the first time it's made me so full of despair. The other times I had, after all, had the opportunity to swing around the corner and into another hotel with a more global outlook.

The driver is now frantic with worry, a sense of responsibility and eagerness to please. He tries to talk some sense into the receptionist but that is of course impossible, rule-bound as she is. Foreigners are not allowed and that's that.

So we're back in the car.

The driver is taking this rather personally, it seems. He is almost whimpering with discomfort, while shaking his head and uttering: "aiaaa" a lot. This expression has a lot of different meanings but in this case it's probably "By Jove, this is a nasty mess and now I feel responsible."

Then he is hit by a huge idea, an epiphany really, which turns out to be the greatest idea an inhabitant of the lovely China has had on my behalf since... possibly ever. The taxi driver says:

"Didn't you say you live in Hong Kong?"

Snore. "What? Yes, yes, I did!"

"But then of course you're a *Hong Kong compatriot!* You have an ID card, right?"

"Of course! I'm a permanent resident." And proud of it, damn it!

The driver is also beaming with pride as he marches back into the reception with my suitcase in one hand and my hard-earned Hong Kong ID card in the other.

"*Xianggang tongbao* (Hong Kong compatriot)!" I hear him shout triumphantly by the desk as I follow a little hesitantly, so tired I'm staggering.

A group of people – what are they doing up at 2:30 in the morning? – stand looking at my ID card, discussing it loudly. The receptionist can't get a word in, but that's not necessary. As a *Xianggang tongbao* I have the same rights as a normal (in other words, Chinese) person from Hong Kong.

With my Chinese name, which with some presence of mind in 1991 I made sure got onto my ID card, I can pass for a normal Chinese person. How will the officials going through the guest registration records of the hotel (or as it turns out, "building containing some rooms with beds") know that the number and lettering on my ID card identify me clearly as a non-Chinese and not a normal Hong Kong person at all, without as much as one star? (Hong Kong Chinese have three stars on their ID cards; foreigners, even when born in Hong Kong, none.) As far as they are concerned, everything is fine as long as there is no passport palaver.

Yes, it's not really racial discrimination. No, no. It's just that some hotels have the right forms to deal with *passports*, while others do not.

For the first time I feel I'm officially a real human being in China, and not just some foreigner to be given preferential treatment as some kind of strangely patronizing gesture, or even inverted racism. The Chinese are actually more likely to discriminate against their own people than against foreigners. I feel I have broken through a kind of barrier and I have broken out of my foreigner pigeon-hole, despite my un-Chinese appearance.

Wei-hey, I'm no longer *Lao Wai* (Old Outside) but *Lao Nei* (Old Inside)!

Hong Kong is also not above discriminating against her own people. When I acquired the said ID card in 1991 it was by virtue of having married a Hong Kong man. I think I had to wait three days after the wedding to be issued the card, without any questions asked. Fair and square you may say, but a little not-so-fair when you consider the fact that if a Hong Kong person marries a mainlander, that spouse must wait ten years or more to achieve the coveted status of a Hong Kong person. Even if they have children.

As a Norwegian I'm certainly not used to that kind of discrimination. In Norway, as in every European country I've come across, it's the foreigners who need to be kept firmly at bay, not the country's own people.

And so, as a *Xianggang tongbao* and no longer a mere foreign devil, I can finally get some sleep. It is with a new-found and, I think, well deserved sense of identity that I slip laughing under the covers.

Since this momentous day I have often been denied access to certain hotels with the words "this hotel isn't suitable for Foreign Friends." "Foreign Friends" is the official name for us foreigners which the Chinese use when they want to keep us from doing something.

But whenever this happens, I take out my ID card with a smile: "You may not be aware of the fact that you're dealing with a *Xianggang tongbao?* Write me into the guest register post-haste!"

Thank you, O wonderful taxi driver by the name of Wang! Had I met you sooner I could have saved thousands of yuan throughout the years I'd been staying in over-priced (in Chinese reckoning) hotels. If I had wanted to live in pensions for normal Chinese, that is. But I suppose I will continue to seek out hotels where the rooms come equipped with bathrooms and so on. And from now on I will always make sure I get a sleeper on the train. And nowadays, with modernization and all that, surprisingly many long train journeys start in Shenzhen.

3

So Near and Yet so Feared

"Shenzhen? No bloody way! That dirty shithole – it's dangerous! And the toilets? Don't get me started on the toilets." Astonishingly often this is the reaction I get from both local Hong Kong people and foreigners – who, more often than not, have never set foot across the border – when I ask them if they fancy a swing around Shenzhen.

Considering that Hong Kong is now politically part of China and geographically has always been, it's amazing how many people I know have never been across the stinking cesspit of a river separating Hong Kong and China proper, and would rather let themselves be lowered into a vat of boiling snot than spend a night in a normal five-star hotel in Shenzhen. Although it has to be said, the town's name does mean "Deep Drain".

"You'll get killed! Robbed! And more!" these people bleat on in that exclamation mark-filled way of theirs.

"They're all crooks! They kidnap white people! And the toilets! Don't get me started!" they exclaim, seeking instead the safe haven of Lan Kwai Fong, the main bar area of Hong Kong Island where foreigners often outnumber Chinese, and its overwhelming absence of surrealism and most other -isms except consumerism.

*

When I first came to Hong Kong in 1989, that fair city of Chinese immigrants and Westerners on the make (FILTH was an acronym much bandied about in those days: *Failed In London, Try Hong Kong*) had its share of surrealism too. Sadly, with each successive administration the innate surrealism of Hong Kong has gone the way of the rabid colonialists, and the place has now been sanitised down to your normal post-modern Asian city full of skyscrapers, rife with McDonald's and Starbucks and all the other trappings of whitey-hood or what people think is "gracious European living," i.e. down-market Las Vegas sprinkled liberally with Liberace's and Michael Jackson's bastard child.

And I have to say, Hong Kong is perfect for expatriates sent here by their company with everything paid for and with an extra "hardship posting" bonus. It's safe (this is how safe it is: In 2005 the Hong Kong government closed down all beaches on the south side of Hong Kong Island for five weeks because – wait for it – they had found a 40-centimetre-long shark *skeleton.*) It's clean (the buttons in lifts come with the message "disinfected every hour") and you can live there your whole life without ever having to do the dishes, look after your own children or learn a word of the local language. In fact, locals will do anything to keep you from learning the language, but more about that later.

Yes, Hong Kong is a home away from home at the chicken's arsehole of China; you can get Marmite and a real steak, the bread is almost good and you can watch the cricket in any of the vast number of sports bars scattered all over the tolerable-for-whitey parts of the city. It's like home but with better weather and the locals are still subservient enough for you to feel great.

China, on the other hand! So near, but light years away for some.

The border between Hong Kong and Shenzhen, still in place with passport control, barbed wire and everything border-like despite Hong Kong having been returned to the welcoming claws of the motherland more than ten years ago, is only about 50 minutes' comfortable train ride from Central, downtown Hong Kong. Yet many people choose to be cooped up on planes to Thailand, Malaysia or Indonesia for hours every time they have a couple of days to spare, and that with the oil prices rising as they are.

But hang on, maybe it's not China or even Shenzhen itself that makes people freak out so when I tell them I'm off on one of my mainland trips again, but the fact that I always travel by train? Could it be that these middle-class people, who never stop writing in to the *South China Morning Post* about how the government should do something about the terrible air pollution, don't think a trip is really a trip unless it involves air travel?

Is it some kind of travel snobbishness (must go by plane and then with Thai Airways as the lowest-priced airline acceptable) – a feeling that without excessive carbon footprint it's just not a real holiday? Is there a minimum price under which one can't go? Or is it just – well, a train full of *Chinese;* not really our ilk? After all, they don't even *speak English...*

Or perhaps it is simply this: They have listened to Hong Kong people telling them to avoid China at all costs.

Every time I take foreigners, my British, American or Australian friends, into the mainland, this is what I hear: "My colleagues told me I was crazy! They said I would never come back! That I would be murdered and kidnapped, not necessarily in that order, and that the toilets..." (etc, see above.)

It must be mentioned that the local people doling out such sage advice are invariably people who have never been to the mainland themselves or, if they have, have deemed it okay for themselves, but "not suitable for foreigners."

My friends then go on to tell me how delighted and amazed they are at not having been murdered at all but on the contrary treated like some kind of rare royalty by everyone they meet on the mainland.

And really, if I told you that whatever you do, don't ever go to, for example, Switzerland, wouldn't your first question be: Have you been there? And if I said no (as at least 80% of the people giving my friends the stern advice about the mainland do) would you then believe me?

After all, the Hong Kong people who tell foreigners that they will be killed as soon as they cross the border from Hong Kong are the same people who advise foreigners (again Caucasians from Western countries) never to attempt to learn the local language in the place where they live.

If a foreigner wanted to settle in Paris, would the Parisians spend untold amounts of energy explaining that he should under no circumstance attempt to learn French? With the added, incredibly patronising reason "because it's too difficult for you"?

When I arrived in Hong Kong in 1989 with some basic Mandarin after a few months in China, I found to my surprise that Mando might as well be Swahili as far as Hongkongers were concerned. When I started with my Beijing-accented Mandarin, where every vowel and most other letters is an "r", people just looked at me strangely and hurried away. At the time I was deeply in love with everything Mando, and thought the local language of Hong Kong, Cantonese, sounded like three cats fighting on a blackboard.

(Now I think Cantonese is the delightful song of angels, angels dancing on a harp, while Mandarin sounds like two cockroaches fighting in an arse.)

In those days, being an extra in the incessant stream of Canto-movies that were churned out every day was a respectable job for the poorer end of the expatriate strata living eight to a room in notorious hell-hole Chungking Mansions. Never one to shun the limelight, of course I also extra'd away with the worst of them. One day I got a speaking part in Cantonese where I was to play the nurse in a vampire movie called *One Bite OK.*

That line, "Mister Wu, your illness has no cure. No matter how much blood we give you, it's no use" set me on the path to a lifetime of Cantonese.

Through playing cards with workers on the ferry from Lantau Island where I eventually moved, initially writing down every conversation in Chinese characters and then slowly moving into spoken Cantonese, I picked up the worst swearwords in the language. I quickly caught on to the fact that "fuck your mother's smelly cunt" didn't mean "hello" as I first thought (they looked so cheerful, slapping each other on the back and shouting out these words that I thought they were happily greeting each other) and after a few months I could have a lewd and terrible conversation.

It didn't take long before I was a total convert to Cantonese, realising it was far superior in every way to staid, stick-in-the-mud, Communist speech-language Mandarin. Cantonese was so much more suitable for me. It was the Glaswegian of Asia: A great fighting language, straight to the point and with excellent swearwords, not all of which concerned your mother.

It must have been in 1995 that a friend of mine asked me to teach him Cantonese *for money!* Two of his friends quickly followed suit and before I knew it I was teaching Cantonese full time and able to call myself the only Norwegian Cantonese teacher in my village. Sure, there was still the odd Englishman who accused me of "going native" (for the record, only English people – I'll say that again, English *men* – have ever said that) but on the whole I found people admiring me no end for something so simple: Being able to communicate in the local language in the place where you live.

*

Before I start a course (whose slogan is 'Learn Cantonese the Natural Way – From a Norwegian,') I always tell people that they don't really need to take lessons from me, as there are seven million people in Hong Kong who will teach you Cantonese for free.

But they insist.

Over the years I have come to realise that my students, whom I call 'victims' as they give me shitloads of money for something they could easily have got for nothing, don't come to me because I'm such a great teacher, but because they are terrified of talking to Chinese people. They prefer to learn Cantonese their way: By speaking English. When I try to tell them that this would be like learning the violin by playing the piano, they just laugh, safe in the knowledge that their method is the best.

Sometimes I wonder if tutors of other skills meet with the same intransigence in their victims. Do people who teach judo have their students saying: "I know you know a lot about judo, but I have found this great CD-rom about arm-wrestling, so I'm going to watch that until I know judo."

Do swimming teachers, who insist on their clients actually going in the water in order to learn how to swim, frequently have to contend with being told: "Well, this going in the water thing is all well and good, but that's just *your* view. I'm going to watch a video about a man crossing the Antarctic on water skis. That will teach me all I need to know about swimming, I reckon."

No? Well, that is what I get from many of my students. They simply will not accept the fact that in order to learn a language, you have to *speak it with speakers of that language*.

However, some of them actually make the effort, and within a couple of months of learning Cantonese the natural way, they really do acquire a quite impressive vocabulary and syntax.

That's when Shenzhen rears its not exactly beautiful head.

That's right: I encourage my victims to boldly/borderline timidly go into the wild hinterland of even more Las Vegas/Liberace-land than Hong Kong, to practice their new-found skill.

This is often met with a strange reluctance.

After having spent all that time and money, one would think that they would use every opportunity to hone their language skills, but no. "Dirty, dangerous, kidnapped in the toilets!" they exclaim. I then know that they have been listening to the local Chinese people in their office; the same people who only a couple of months earlier told them that they could never learn Cantonese because it was "too difficult – for you."

Well, they should know. Who better to tell you how difficult a language is than the people who have been speaking it from birth? I'm sure they put up a great fight there on their grandmother's knee (Hong Kong women go back to work four days after giving birth) arguing about grammar and syntax, complaining about how difficult it is.

I'm not being entirely fair when I say that none of the 'hardship-posting' expatriates go to Shenzhen. Of course they do. Every weekend they stream across the border in their hundreds to descend upon that Mecca of counterfeit goods, foot massage and ear cleaning that is the Lo Wu Shopping Centre just across the border.

But even they say: "Of course, Shenzhen's not really China."

Oh but it is! Just a few metres away from the Lo Wu Shopping Paradise is a China as real as any. Once, just next to Shenzhen's main drag Jianshe Lu, I saw a man being beaten to a pulp, possibly to death, by three policemen for having tried to push aside a heap of mattresses that was blocking his shop. If being beaten up by police for trying to protect your livelihood isn't vintage China, I don't know what is. And take the advanced begging methods. Although the area has since been cleaned up, a few years ago there were child beggars in rags all along Jianshe Lu. They would cling to you (foreigners are more gullible) and look at you with those big, child-y eyes: Hungry! And will be beaten by my handlers if you don't cough up!

There were adult beggars too of course. Advanced ones. The first time I saw one, I was almost taken in. I was striding down the aforementioned Lu (road), looking for a cash point. Outside a hotel I noticed a woman sitting on the pavement, legs outstretched, open-mouthed baby hanging from the crook of her arm like a casually clasped handbag. She was eating out of a dustbin.

Touched as well as slightly rattled in my middle-class sensibilities I reached into my wallet. I wanted to reward her for being too dignified to beg. Eating out of dustbins – what a life! Now where did I put that one-yuan note? Looking around to see if anyone had noticed how benevolent I was being, I spotted another woman a few dustbins further up the road, in an almost identical position. Sleeping baby slung over arm, hand full of rice going from dustbin to mouth.

Ouch! They almost had me. Now I noticed that the women looked remarkably well fed to the point of plumpness compared to other citizens milling around the streets. They should be – they were the only beggars in China constantly eating.

The dustbins were empty and clean apart from the rice; the women, by choice or force, working of course for crime syndicates. The babies, probably sedated, had been provided by the unscrupulous gangs for added pathos.

Wasn't this a kind of irony of China, I wondered. Millions and millions live in abject poverty and misery, and yet the beggars who rake in the money are fake, and could do with losing some weight.

But of course, most beggars in China are real and, unlike the beggars in Hong Kong who (as every Hongkie will tell you when they tire of telling you not to learn Cantonese) are invariably multi-millionaires of the kind whose mattresses are bursting with Hong Kong dollars to the degree that they can't sleep at all but must spend their days sitting around in the streets begging for fun, the beggars in China really could do with the cash.

*

Shenzhen is primarily a service centre. The kind of service you can get there is: Everything you want. Everything.

Over the last couple of years it seems like the city has gone through a certain gentrification; at least everything is twice the price of other similar-sized cities in China. There are even shops with real, not counterfeit, goods. But I think Shenzhen will, at least for Hong Kong people, always primarily be known for its fake... everything.

I'm not a fan of shopping, but I know many who are. And in the same way as he who is tired of London is tired of life, she who can't be arsed to shop in Shenzhen is tired of shopping. And therefore, apparently, tired of life. Here you can get false nails, fake Gucci bags, fake watches and fake DVDs, fake shoes, fake jewellery and fake electronic goods, all at a fraction of the price in Hong Kong and the world at large.

There are two kinds of people: Those who feel that a handbag should be manufactured in, for example, the Prada factory and cost HK$3,000 to be worth carrying around, and those who think a copy is good enough as long as it looks and acts like the original. I, of course, belong in the latter category. I think the important thing is not what it is, but what it looks like.

When you consider that most of the "real" goods available in the world today, in Milan, New York or Oslo, are normally made in China anyway, what the hell is the difference? The fake goods are more often than not produced in the same factory that makes the real goods, with the blessing of the foreman and management, and the quality is superb.

And really, does it matter so much if the DVD player is called JVT, Banasonic or Sonyc, as long as it functions?

Shenzhen was built on fake goods, but one thing is real: Massage. There's a massage institute about every three metres, and the best head, body and foot masseurs flock here from all over China. Yes, foot massage is the only reason I need to scuttle across the border several times a month. If Shenzhen didn't have tailors, excellent restaurants, 10-yuan DVDs (which reach the shops in Shenzhen before the films have even opened in the USA), I would still go to Shenzhen to have my feet expertly handled by beautiful, sometimes even ugly, men.

*

Now, you may be under the impression that I think Shenzhen is some kind of paradise, and yes it is. I don't understand what people are afraid of. It is indeed true that because the city works as a big and powerful magnet for all Chinese who want to make money, many crooks gather here. But it's possible to be a bit sensible when on holiday, isn't it?

Personally I've only been robbed twice in my life and both times were in Oslo. In Shenzhen, like the rest of China, I have never been robbed or mugged. I have probably been cheated many times, but everybody agrees that cheating is clean and honest – the cheatee has only himself to blame. But robbed? No.

I think it's all about being a little bit careful, not walking around brandishing the Rolex under people's noses, and perhaps not stapling wads of money to your lapel but rather carrying it in a pocket in your handbag. A pocket with a zipper.

No. Shenzhen is a holiday destination as good as any.

And even if I hadn't liked it, I would have liked it for one reason: It has a railway station, from which you can reach all other stations in huge, wonderful, thrilling mainland China.

But beautiful it is definitely not.

Only 20 years ago, Shenzhen was something that's normally referred to as a 'sleepy backwater' with some farms, some duck ponds and a couple of geese. Now it's a mega metropolis and the prototype of what the Chinese government wants the whole country to look like when they have finished their life's work: The total destruction of China.

4

Your Home is Your Cast-Off

"Destroying China, and by "destroying" I mean totally obliterating it, razing it to the ground and, if there's anything left, annihilating it with a flame thrower, is a national sport that has taken on gigantic proportions.

One moment you'll be sitting guile-and-worriless in a meadow or paddy field, humming a cheerful melody while you scratch a water buffalo distractedly behind the ears; the next you'll be flat as a pancake or *shaobing* (flat fried bun with or without sweet or savoury stuffing), buried beneath an eight-lane super highway. It will be empty of cars and going nowhere, but it's there and it's infrastructure so it must be good.

Most articles recently written about China begin like this: "During the last decades, China has undergone an explosive development..." or words to that effect. Mark the word explosive. It seems that to explode, obliterate and annihilate everything older than two and a half years, five to be generous, is the main objective. To build something on top of the ruins and debris seems to be but an afterthought. But that afterthought arrives fast, it has to be said, and with devastating effect.

Make no mistake: The fact that the well-maintained 300-year-old house you live in belongs to you and indeed has belonged to your family for five generations is of no consequence to the developers or indeed the local or central government which gives them free rein. Let's say your house is the former home of, oh, China's Shakespeare, declared a national monument by the People's Number 1 Democratic Antiques Bureau.

They have given you a plaque, decorated with Mickey Mouse and Hello Kitty, stating in flowery terms how wonderful and unique your house is, and how it should be treasured for the millennia to come. You clutch this plaque as the police drag you kicking and screaming out of your house, while the wreckers stand around, tapping their fingers, the saliva of destructive ecstasy running down their chins.

You should have known this would happen when you turned down the developer's offer of 500 yuan to relocate to the 36th floor of a tenement block 90 miles outside the Third Ring Road. When the window-breaking, paint-splashing vandals turn up the very next day, their trousers looking remarkably similar to those of The People's Democratic Police Force, you should have called it a day and got out. But would you take a hint? No.

So it's off to prison you go for "obstruction and vandalism" and the very same night there's just a debris-strewn moonscape where your house and indeed the whole neighbourhood was. But not for long. Two weeks later a new shopping centre stands proudly on the site, 300 metres tall and covering the whole block. A small sacrifice to make for the motherland, no?

Or picture this: One June morning you may be sitting in a little pavilion built in the Ming Dynasty, gazing dreamily at the green lake constructed especially because the emperor's favourite concubine was so fond of boating. The tender, transparent leaves of the weeping willows gently caress the water's mirror-like surface, spreading delicate rings and ripples over the sun-flecked lake, while a row of swans sail majestically past.

"Verily, here is good," you think, while the cheongsam-clad waitress cracks open another bottle of Tsingtao with a practised hand. The sound of flutes comes wafting out from the bamboo thicket, and you almost expect to see a gang of scholars dressed in silken gowns come gliding out of the woods, all long-sleeved splendour and inscrutability.

You feel transported back in time as you gaze and gaze, feeling the serenity of millennia wash over you. China's beauty is timeless, you think as you drain the last golden droplets, staggering merrily away.

Then, perhaps three weeks later, you fancy going back to the pavilion by the lake to enjoy the calming effect that Chinese scenery, albeit man-made, has on your soul. You want to sip another dewy Tsingtao on the edge of the lake where poets have sat gazing deeply (shit-faced) at the moon and written about it, since the time Europeans were still living in caves or at least starting to wipe their mouths with their sleeves after eating wild boar.

First you think you've made a wrong turn. Wasn't there a wooden gate with intricate carvings, weren't there weeping willows and pavilions? Wasn't there, in fact, a big and dreamy lake? Now there is a residential complex with high-rise buildings of 80 floors. The entrances are decorated with columns in the Dorian, Ionian and rococo styles – on the same column – and white statues of Napoleon on his steed, Santa Claus and half-naked Greek goddesses are scattered around the neon green grass cut with nail scissors by cheap labour.

The lake is now so criss-crossed with concrete walkways that you can hardly see it, the concrete and heavy rosewood banisters decorated with lanterns shaped like Donald Duck and Doraemon. All this you can behold through the grille of the tall, wrought-iron gates in fake Nazi-Gothic style, before you are chased off by servants wearing 17th-century livery, brandishing AK-47s.

As if that wasn't enough; as you stagger backwards in shock, you are crushed beneath the wheels of a sixty-ton truck thundering past on the ten-lane highway they built while you were looking in through the gate.

The Chinese are proud of their recent "development", especially because it has all happened at such breakneck speed and has been so all-encompassing. Now China can at last compete with the US in lack of taste! Now it's the Chinese people's turn to spend several hours a day in traffic jams! What a lovely modern life, just like on TV."

This was the first draft of my article "China's Relentless Development" – for some reason I thought I should modify it a little before submitting it to the interestingly named *Elite Reference*, a Beijing newspaper. That paper, the four characters of whose Chinese name really do mean "Elite" and "Reference", had called me up a few months earlier.

They were starting a weekly column called something like "China seen through the eyes of *Lao Wai*," and needed foreigners with some China experience to write for them. I suspected the editor had envisaged a row of blond, big-nosed, blue-eyed ones turning out grovelling pieces entitled "China, the country I would most like to have been born in", "Why China should rule the world" and "What we foreigners can and should learn from Chinese culture."

Believing that people shouldn't be mollycoddled and have all sorts of illusions reconfirmed by others just for the sake of, well, grovelling, I just wrote what I wanted. And amazingly, *Elite Reference* printed it all.

Since the Communists took power in 1949, or probably during the entire history of China, Chinese citizens have been at the mercy of a personal freedom pendulum effect. As soon as the government *du jour* thinks things are getting a little out of hand with the freedom stuff, it swings right back to "Nothing is allowed any more. Ever." During the infamous "Hundred Flowers" campaign in 1956, Mao encouraged people to speak out freely against the Communist Party, and they did, saying things like: "I thought the Party was a bit unfair in 1932 when they beat my grandfather to death with shovels and took all his livestock." He took a terrible revenge, killing and imprisoning more than 550,000 people deemed to be intellectuals and "rightists," not to mention counter-revolutionaries.

Ah, Mao. Mao, Mao, Mao. The wily fiend, the evil genius. Let me just say something about him right now:

When writing about China, indeed when spending five minutes in China, it's difficult, nay impossible, to avoid Mao, possibly the most surreal of history's rulers. For a start, his glaring mug is everywhere. Yes, still. From the front view mirrors in taxis his portrait dangles, framed in red plastic with silk tassels like a Buddha figure, staring fatly out at driver and passengers.

In toy shops, giant posters of his inscrutable face lord it over remote control cars, Hello Kitty and Pokemon. In little beer-and-snacks shops, a staple feature of the back streets of China's cities big and small (or "enormous" and "not quite as enormous"), his face hangs, staring phlegmatically like a hovering blob of lard with eyes and a mole.

And if you decide not to go anywhere by cab or buy a single thing but stay in your hotel room and live off room service, the Chinese, in a strange deviation from Deng Xiaoping's policy of banishing personality worship, have put the geezer on every denomination of their money.

Only a few years ago, Chinese paper money down to one fen (about a millionth of a US dollar) bore the noble and beautiful miens of various ethnic minorities. A few years before that again, when I first arrived in China, the notes were decorated with heroic peasants and stalwart soldiers with guns, sitting purposefully on tractors while smiling their way dazzlingly toward a great socialist future. Now we have the picture of the most successful mass-murderer in the history of the world.

What happened there, really?

At some point the Chinese have decided that what Mao did, for example "allegedly" being directly responsible for 70 million of his beloved countrymen meeting an untimely death, was "70% good and 30% bad."

Considering the Chinese people's propensity for numbers, these are apparently percentages they can live with. Now that a number of years have passed since the geezer buggered off to the big struggle-session in the sky, decidedly long in the tooth and in his own bed like most evil dictators, one would think that at last the Chinese would be able to look at him with rational, if not cynical, detachment.

Not so.

Even today, not even those who survived torture, persecution and prison as well as losing most of their family members to starvation only to see the few remaining ones commit suicide or "shoot themselves in the back while jumping handcuffed from the fifth floor while trying to escape", can bring themselves to express the truth:

The guy was 100% bad. And if percentages by their very nature hadn't ended at 100, we could safely say that he was 1000% bad, and more.

During my travels in China I have had many discussions, debates and not a few blistering arguments about Mao. One of the results of Deng Xiaoping's "open door policy" is fortunately that it is possible to sit for example in a packed compartment on a train and discuss Mao at great decibel expenditure without risking a trip to the slammer. At least not for me.

And things are moving forward in people's minds too, because some people have actually started to think, or rather been allowed to think aloud, that Mao perhaps wasn't all he's cracked up to be and not all good – in fact I'm sure some wildly dissenting heads are even willing to toy with the idea of the "not good" being *32%*.

It's certainly easier to get your average Chinese to say that Mao wasn't a saint and that it is possible that he didn't single-handedly create a socialist paradise, than to entertain the idea of Taiwan as an independent country.

Actually, in about 20 years of arguments and discussions, always ending in "You don't understand these things because you're not Chinese," I've only met one Chinese who agreed with me about the Taiwan question, and he was a Mongolian. "Free Taiwan, death to the bastard Chinese government," he wrote on the piece of paper where we were scoring the cards, before falling into another comatose beer intoxication. Yes, the ethnic minorities drink perhaps even more than the Han Chinese themselves.

But back to Mao. How can it be that the Chinese, in retrospect and with all the facts on the table about the unfathomable suffering he set in motion, still worship him as the very inventor of China – while at the same time banging on about their 5,000 years of culture? Isn't it, well, a little bit surreal?

A wild little theory I have is that such an incredible number of people – for Mao's various insane antics, after all, touched every single person in China born in the last century and onwards – can't admit to themselves or others that all their sacrifices and all their incessant toil, all the death, suffering and privations were in vain. And that they were, in fact, victims of a lunatic who at one stage suggested that all Chinese should have numbers instead of names; a deranged psychopath who mercilessly and without scruples made a whole nation into his personal worker ants and slaves.

Yes, how can they admit that they were led so completely down the garden path and into the garden shed where they willingly nailed their own tongues to the work-bench, and that by the man who elevated himself to be their very saviour? All that trouble of killing rich landowners and dividing up the land, only to find themselves owning not even the little they had owned under the feudal system?

Not to mention all the melting down of doorknobs and pots and pans and working round the clock stoking backyard furnaces while the grain rotted in the fields. Yes, I can see how they must strive with all their might to keep up the illusion that it was all for a good cause. To even suggest anything else would be to take away the very foundation of their lives.

At the time when the worst chaos was going on, of course, anyone who complained would have been killed or worse, but one would think that in these enlightened and liberal times it should be allowed to let loose a little rant or litany.

No. It is still the norm in China that anyone who speaks the truth gets punished by the authorities and vilified by his peers. After 60 years of communism, people can't easily shake the habit of self-censorship and suppression of critical thought – it's just so much easier that way. And one can hardly blame them.

Another explanation is that today's Communist Party needs Mao as a rallying point for the nationalism they have been relentlessly pushing as China's new religion for the last few years. People need something to believe in, and if 1.3 billion people by means of worshipping the idol of Mao will also glorify the party in some way, it's beneficial to everybody. Especially the party. Because to be honest, the party hasn't of late been subject to the reverence and open-mouthed saliva-dribbling awe from the masses that it feels is its due.

For years there have been rumblings, mutterings and sometimes veritable outbursts ostensibly directed at unscrupulous factory owners who don't pay wages, property developers who just move in and take people's homes and mine owners who calculate it's cheaper to pay compensation to the families of killed miners than actually improve work safety.

But, as always in China, mutterings against one thing can easily lead to mutterings against the thing that should be muttered against and whose existence is the true basis for a system in which the above transgressions and worse can take place, namely the Holy Communist Party itself.

And that is something that can't be tolerated. Although the Party knows it's always correct, glorious and righteous and that the mumblings come from a lunatic fringe which just needs help to see the light, it can't help having a sneaking suspicion that its fan base isn't as solid as it once was. So a new theocracy has sprung up with Mao as the father, China ("the People") as the son and the Communist Party as the Holy Ghost – indefinable, invisible and omnipresent.

Therefore, if people within the Party suddenly turned around and admitted that Mao, father of the Communist Party and thereby China, actually was an evil bastard with not a few psychopathic characteristics, it would be the same as saying that the Party had no reason to exist.

In remote parts of China you can still see big banners, the Big Character Posters that covered China wall to wall during the Cultural Revolution, encouraging people to "Follow Chairman Mao's thought." One of his thoughts was that China could afford to lose 300-400 million people in an atomic war. Another was if you planted seeds nine feet deep and closely together, they would grow into really tall and strong plants.

Recently, more developed areas have exchanged these banners with slogans penned by former president Jiang Zemin, asking people to follow "the three represents." These apparently mean something like the Party "always has to represent the development tendencies of China's advanced productive forces, the orientation of China's advanced culture and the basic interests of the vast majority of the Chinese people." Er, right.

Old Jiang probably wouldn't have minded creating a tiny little personality cult for himself when he came to power; his publishing of "Jiang Zemin's thought" would lead even the least cynical to that conclusion. But after Deng Xiaoping's pragmatic rule, where the short and "peppery" power plug from Sichuan province didn't allow as much as his finger to be immortalised in a statue, the Chinese could finally relax from dictator worship. Jiang's attempts at self-elevation died a quiet death, probably from boredom.

Mao, though, didn't have a problem with a little adulation.

A funny thing about today's China is how the geezer, who ought to be loathed like Hitler and Stalin, has somehow managed to stay cool, almost like Che Guevara but having died too old to become sexy. Mao posters, Mao paintings ("ironic"), Mao's Little Red Book, Mao T-shirts and other Mao paraphernalia are selling like never before, especially to foreigners who may or may not know that the porcine red face they sport on their neon green t-shirt is the world's biggest mass murderer without compare.

Having said that; in my bedroom I have an original poster from the 1960s of Mao visiting a coastal village somewhere, being welcomed by identical-looking strong, brown peasants of matinee idol beauty and with sub-atomic white teeth. I know I shouldn't have it but… the artwork is just so damned attractive!

So how do modern Chinese look at Mao? No matter whom I ask, I normally get the same knee-jerk reaction: He-is-China's-saviour-he-is-the-father-of-China-he-saved-China-from-the-Japanese-devils and so on and so forth until it occasionally quite frankly makes me puke. Even well-educated people hang on for dear life to the idea that he wanted what was best for the Chinese people until he was mysteriously misled by leftists in the sixties.

The Mao of the thirties, forties and fifties was kindness itself. Like a Chinese Jesus he walked around and did good deeds, and if China perhaps didn't reach a Nirvana of socialism right away, and especially during the Great Leap Forward, it was only because the evil brown-nosers surrounding Mao wouldn't tell him what a state the nation was really in.

They have a point there – the brown-nosing sycophants surrounding Mao didn't tell him what kind of death and decay was really going on in the country because they knew very well that any negative report would lead to ostracism from the party followed by torture and execution. Or, as has been the norm in all of China's dynasties, the choice to save face by committing suicide.

In this there was no difference between the modern, liberated China and that of bound feet, billowing sleeves and the white silken cord and delicately painted beam tactfully presented to those who transgressed. Except that in Mao's empire, not even suicide was good enough; like untold emperors before him, he would annihilate the transgressor's entire family one way or another.

Fallen leaves return to their roots. If you had a grandfather who for example pointed out to party leaders that the local peasants were starving to death while officials wallowed in luxury, it is obvious you must be viewed with suspicion, a suspicion confirmed by your shooting yourself in the back while jumping out the window from the seventh floor, handcuffed, during an escape. In that respect things have perhaps improved a little in that the families of suicides are nowadays left alone, at least by the authorities. But the fine old tradition of shooting the messenger lives proudly on, and China has more journalists in jail than any other nation.

Of all the surreal aspects of China today, one of the most surreal is undoubtedly this: Many Chinese still worship Mao, if no longer as a god, at least as a demi-god. And if you should happen to meet a Chinese who looks at him not as a god but as a human being of lard and blood, he will probably say that Mao, well, he wasn't a saint, but he did invent modern China, and what he did was only 30% bad. The rest was good! The numbers don't lie.

So I thought I probably shouldn't mention Mao much in my writings for *Elite Reference*.

During my years in Hong Kong I had seen periods of relative relaxation of the mainland media wax and wane – if you can call a sudden cut-off of all opinions and numbers of editors and journalists thrown in prison "waning."

So, although this *Lao Wai* thing of *Elite Reference* happened at a time during which the iron grip of authority wasn't choking China's press but merely holding it by the neck and slapping it around a little, I was surprised to the point of having to lie down when the paper printed every word I wrote.

I wrote about the death penalty, corruption, the over-dependence on cars; indeed I questioned the Chinese love of absolutely everything American. Weren't the Americans supposed to be the enemy? The piece that got the biggest applause was one where I criticised Chinese youth (and thereby, the government) for running wild in the streets of Beijing attacking Japanese shops and cars during one of the many spats between China and Japan, this time over Japan's membership of the Security Council of the United Nations. I likened the two countries to five-year-olds fighting over a toy in a sandpit, and I was praised for it.

The only time a piece was questioned was when I wrote on the topic "Why I love Chinese men." The editor felt that instead of praising their beauty, cleanliness and ability to cook, I should have written about how family-minded Chinese men are, how they love and obey their mother and seldom roam far from her steely gaze. Exactly the things I *don't* like about Chinese men...

For these outpourings of opinions I received the staggering sum of 400 yuan a pop, which meant I would have had to write about 3000 words a month to equal the pay of a Chinese teacher. This state of paradise-like living lasted about two years, until the Chinese media-openness pendulum swung back with a mighty thud.

*

One day my editor, whom I had met a couple of times in Beijing and got on well with, called me, sounding almost in tears. "We have to talk about your writing."

Oh, no! Was it what I wrote about the Doric columns? (I had printed a watered-down version of "China's Relentless Development" only a few days earlier.)

"No, it's... we have a new leader in the office."

"Leader, do you mean editor?"

"No, just... this woman who is in the office all the time."

"Ah, let me guess. Around 50, glasses, thick-set, shrill voice, doesn't know anything about publishing or writing but reads through all the articles, killing them?"

"... how did you know?"

Yes, how *did* I know? I just did. Probably it was having spent my adult life studying China up-close with my own eyes, and through reading books. The party had panicked over something someone had written somewhere, and quickly installed one of these former Red Guard middle-aged people in each department to keep an eye on things.

"So how do you want me to write now?"

"Just like before, it's just..."

"Just?"

"Just that we're now only paying freelancers 100 yuan per article."

Aha. So that was how the wily former book-burning, art-smashing torture-monger wanted to play it. More often than not almost illiterate after never having gone to school, the adult Red Guards had to be smart to survive in a changing world. Of course it helped that none of these criminals had ever had to face charges or even criticism, as that would have been tantamount to criticising Mao himself. They were left to flounder in a world without any iron rice bowl or cradle-to-death security, safe in the knowledge that they'd only followed orders and had a great time.

What, free train travel, no school and as many teachers as you can kill – who could wish for a better youth? And then, in middle age, be allowed to tell people, in every sense your superior, what to do, what to write and say and how to act (with the big swinging dangling prize maybe being allowed to fire an editor, or better, to send him to prison) – oh what a lovely life.

Yes, I'm sure it was with great pleasure that the new leader of *Elite Reference's* features section killed off all the foreigners with one mighty blow of the pen – so much mightier than the sword, as we all know.

So the gig was up with *Elite Reference*, but the destruction of Hong Kong and all mainland cities and villages continues relentlessly; in Hong Kong even gathering pace because so many people are speaking out against it. Nobody can tell this administration what to do – except the property tycoons, naturally. And the central government. But those two entities are becoming inseparable anyway.

At least Hong Kong is already as built up as it can be, with lots of country park whose sacredness is set in stone – until the government decides to "develop" it of course. But China – all that space just left to rot! Or, in the case of Guangdong province, build factories on!

Guangdong, without exception the most fertile province in China, is now a province with only a third of the arable land per person of the rest of the country. Most people in this huge land could easily live off what this one province could produce in the way of rice, vegetables and poultry. But that's the very province the progress-blasters needed to cover in concrete, to build millions of factories with Hong Kong and foreign money in order to satisfy the western world's (and increasingly China's own) insatiable craving for useless crap.

I had to laugh the other day when I was in Guangzhou in a taxi on my way to Guangzhou East Railway Station. I was thinking about a day, it must have been 13 years ago, when I was on my way to the same station, also in a taxi.

Well, not exactly the same station. In those days it was called Tian He ('Milky Way') station and consisted of a couple of train tracks held together with chewing gum and elastic bands, with some rickety sheds shivering nearby. It was a typical rural train station, without luxuries like hotel service, restaurants or flushing toilets. There were toilets of course, but they were of the good old-fashioned kind: A trough without doors or walls. Or water.

I was in Guangzhou with twelve Norwegians, members of an avant-garde theatre troupe, who were looking for props for their next show *Good Good Very Good*. I thought Chinese police uniforms and military equipment, easy to get hold of in China, would go down well on the Norwegian alternative arts scene, and I wasn't wrong.

The troupe members were in a frenzy. They were especially fascinated by the trousers of the police uniforms; green, shapeless and with two yellow stripes down the trouser leg.

(In the year 2000, China's police force, as with so much else in the country, changed from funky to depressingly ordinary. Their uniforms used to be of a jaunty green hue, like that of the People's Liberation Army; it was in fact, for the untrained eye, difficult to tell which was which. The garments were three sizes too big, and with moss-green shirts with worn collars where you could see T-shirts of different colours peeping out at the throat. The uniforms were accessorised with plastic sandals or cloth shoes. Now the police wear black uniforms which reminds one not a little of those of the SS. Yes, black, razor-sharp uniforms are what they are wearing now, with dark grey shirts and silver insignia. It's almost as if one should start to be afraid of cops.)

I wanted these Norwegian innocents abroad to see as much as they could of the "real" China, having so far only savoured downtown Guangzhou, and thought it would be a good learning experience for them to travel back to Hong Kong from little Milky Way station with its charming rural atmosphere. I therefore forced two times four troupe members into two taxis at Shamian Island, a little sand spit in the Pearl River which used to be the only place foreigners were allowed to live in Imperial China. (The place is still full of charming colonial buildings, strangely enough.) I told the taxi drivers where to go and, with the remaining three members, jumped into a third taxi.

When we arrived at Milky Way and after having negotiated various planks and rocks, thoughtfully put down by people who didn't want our shoes to be sullied by the mud from what seemed to be hastily covered vegetable fields, we sat down to wait for the others at a nearby outside restaurant with a good view of the station area. Well, not exactly a restaurant – it was a shed with some stools outside.

We thought it was strange that the taxis which left five minutes before us still hadn't got there, but there was no way eight foreigners could blend in with the waiting public. I looked and asked around and even checked the stinking privy, but there was no sign of anoraks or rucksacks – or even green police trousers with yellow stripes.

I started to feel very worried about these eight people who, although they were adults and used to getting around by themselves, were after all my responsibility and who didn't have a word of Chinese between them. After four hours of waiting we had to admit defeat and realise they were never going to turn up. It was with a terrible angst I wended my way home; the terrible angst of having lost no less than eight people in China. People who have never lost eight people in China, or any people for that matter, probably can't imagine that feeling, but believe me, it is terrible.

Back in Hong Kong, happy and drunken messages awaited me on my answerphone (we didn't have mobiles in those days): "Hello, hello! We're in Hong Kong! What happened to you lot?"

In two different taxis, two times four people had decided that no train station could be situated *that* far into the countryside. They had driven on and on, but all they had seen was fields and more fields. One troupe member had even been desperate enough to pee in an empty beer bottle while another discreetly held a newspaper between him and the incredulous driver.

Independently of each other, the two groups of passengers had tried to argue with their driver claiming he was cheating them, yes, that the driver in his cunning Chinese way had tried to take them to a completely different place than the station to somewhere deep into the countryside where fifteen strong members of his family stood waiting to rob, rape and kill them.

So naturally they had forced their respective drivers to go back to the main station in Guangzhou where they had somehow managed to find each other among the two million people sitting outside the station waiting for work or for a ticket home, and gone back to Hong Kong together. When we finally caught up with them, they were shouting and calling us "damned slowpokes."

Yes, I had to laugh thinking about that in the taxi the other day, on my way to the same Milky Way station, which is now called Guangzhou East and is one of the biggest train stations in China.

The journey which in those days took an hour and something, through rural fields and wasteland, is now a brisk ten-minute ride on a highway on stilts lined with high-rises. The station, formerly situated far into the countryside, is now more or less downtown Guangzhou. This is how fast China is changing.

On that day, I laughed, or rather, chuckled. However, my personal opinion is that the aforementioned explosive development is a reason to cry, nay, howl, more than anything. "Development" takes on a new and more poignant meaning when I look at the new China.

Take Beijing for example. When I first arrived unsuspecting in that city in 1988, the last thing I expected was to fall screamingly, helplessly in love with it because of its beauty. But that's what happened.

I had visited Stockholm and Paris and actually lived in London, and felt these venerable cities were more than up to par in the beauty stakes, in fact they were my yardsticks for urban perfection. But after two days' cycling around Beijing I realised I had been wrong, and that it was in fact Beijing which was the most beautiful city in the world. It was car-less. Billboard-less. Neon light-less. And free of loud colours.

Right behind the endless, Stalinesque main streets was a warren of labyrinthine back streets where people seemed to do everything outside: Have their hair cut. Do their homework. Play cards. Sit and read. Sit and eat. Sit and talk; or just sit.

This city of nine or ten million was like a giant village with its one-storey grey brick houses mysteriously beckoning behind grey courtyard walls. Everything was grey, harmonious and without disturbing elements like McDonald's, shopping malls and all the other things in modern society that hurt the eyes and, well, soul of the discerning aesthete. It was like a sepia photo from the past that I was sucked into, shrieking with joy and with all senses open.

But now – now everything's gone. Everything. The Forbidden City (or Palace Museum as it's called in Chinese) is still there of course, with the portrait of inscrutable fatso Mao still incongruously suspended above the main gate, but apart from that, Beijing is now a normal anti-human city where the car is king.

Everything is made to accommodate The Sacred Car, and there are so many six- and eight-lane highways that it's hard to find room for all the supermarkets and mega shopping malls... but that problem is partially solved by building higher and higher. And, weirdly, more and more widely. Now every building which doesn't in itself take up an entire block isn't worth the concrete.

When I lived in Beijing I knew the city well, doing almost nothing but cycling around gazing and gazing, for five months. When after ten years of absence I finally saw my beloved city again, as the last stop on an appalling guided nightmare on the Silk Road – a trip I'll return to with exquisite pain later in the book – I arrived in an alien land on an alien planet: The planet Naff.

And not only was everything now ugly; I didn't recognise a single thing. Had the Forbidden City and Tiananmen Square with its many monuments to Communist superiority not still been around, I would have thought it was a completely different city; a ghastly parody of Houston, Texas with a huge dash of Shenzhen and not a little Disneyland.

The destruction of Beijing started in earnest in 1999 and took a terrifying turn for the worse when China was granted the Summer Olympics of 2008. Furious at having been pipped at the post for the 2000 games (the symbolism!) Chinese authorities had gone all out to get the coveted games, with their promise of the chance to flush billions and billions of yuan down the toilet.

Now no stone must be left uncrushed. To show those foreigners that China has cast off everything smacking of feudalism, superstition and any lingering memory of the past, Beijing was laid to ruin and not a single building older than ten years was allowed to escape. To make way for flowerbeds with garish flowers spelling out the words "China Rules The World" and "We Will Win Everything" (or whatever) houses were, even two weeks before the games, still being torn down, their inhabitants dragged out in their pyjamas.

Flowers need water, but unfortunately Beijing, like the entire north of China, suffers from a severe water shortage and has done for years. But no sacrifice is too big for the sacred Olympics, so Beijing naturally had no qualms about taking water from neighbouring provinces, leaving the inhabitants digging far below the water-mark for ground water, with a clap on the shoulder: Your babies will die of thirst but foreigners will go home from the Olympics safe in the knowledge that China can put on a good flowerbed.

Readers of this book may get the impression that I'm against all development; or "progress," as wrecking-ball wielders call it.

That is correct.

I'm against everything that lets grass be replaced with concrete, woodwork with plastic and any form of beauty with eye-tearing ugliness. I'm against people being thrown out of their homes to make way for projects they'll never benefit from in any way. And I'm against turning cities and towns, formerly suitable for human life, into mere backdrops for mega motorways where people must spend 15 minutes navigating through underground shopping malls just to get to the other side of the road.

I thought for a long time that the reason Chinese cities were able to change from the world's most beautiful to the ugliest in just twenty short years was that the Chinese had had anything resembling taste whacked out of them during the Cultural Revolution, when being in the possession of anything deemed decadent and imperialistic, like a flower in a glass of water, could lead to imprisonment or even death.

But now I'm not so sure. The thing about China is that everything goes around in circles. Everything that happens has happened before. This is not my opinion, OK? It's what the Chinese themselves keep telling me.

To say something about the present or future, Chinese people frequently choose to look into the past, a past maybe three or four thousand years ago, quoting old Chinese proverbs or invoking historical characters. Whenever I ask someone "So, how do you feel about tearing up real trees to replace them with plastic ones?" he will answer: "In the Tang dynasty there was a merchant named Huang. One day he saw a horse..." etc.

"Yes, but how do *you* feel?"

"We Chinese have 5,000 years of culture. One day in the Zhou dynasty..."

"I just asked you about your personal opinion. I would like to know what you think about these plastic trees here."

"I don't know. But the famous poet Du Fu in the Tang dynasty..."

"Let's have another beer."

So here's why I think China and, especially under the latest administration, that of intolerable gnat Donald "Bow-Tie" Tsang, Hong Kong, are so hell-bent on destroying everything more than ten years old:

In the past, when a new dynasty came to power, it was the custom to raze whatever had gone before it to the ground and try to obliterate every sign that it ever existed.

Palaces were burnt, scrolls and books torched, scholars buried alive. But the difference between now and then is that in the past they had to rely on manual labour – admittedly the labour of thousands, but there were still limitations as to what they could achieve in terms of destruction in a dynastic period seldom lasting more than a couple of centuries before sinking into decadence and licentiousness, overpowered by muscular, hard-riding hordes of northern nomads.

In addition, the new dynasties were built with an eye to beauty and visual harmony, using only exceptionally skilled craftsmen.

Now ugliness rules, handiwork is sloppy, there is visual chaos and everything is judged by how short a time it can be erected in and how much money made from it (and how much can be saved by cutting corners), with all principles of beauty and harmony gone the way of foot binding and hair queues.

Yes, it is true that during the Cultural Revolution people were so starved of impulses in art, beauty and design that they now think Japanese cartoon characters are the ultimate in pattern-making for furniture and curtains. But communism, built directly upon and carrying forward the principle of dynastic rule, has done much more than that to destroy the last remnants of the old and beautiful China.

It is in the very nature of the Communist ideology, which is mediocrity put into system. It is the rise and victory of the busybody.

Just like communism can't let people do or even think what they want, so the whole country has become one that can't leave anything as it is. A tree with a mighty crown, where birds and insects (those scourges of civilisation) can live, must be hacked down until only the trunk is left and painted white. Around it there must be a concrete ring bearing a plaque: "This is a tree. You can sit under it, enjoying beautiful nature and take a photo."

A forest path can't be left in peace; it must be "improved" and widened into a concrete road, lined with metal railings and arrows pointing: Walk here!

There must be reinforced concrete steps and plastic statues of animals to liven up the sad and boring nature with its endless trees, rocks and little else to look at.

Least of all can old urban neighbourhoods be allowed to stay and be renovated for the sake of new generations and tourists: Everything must go. New dynasty, new everything.

When Mao ordered workers to tear down the old city walls of Beijing, saying that he wanted to see the city as a forest of factory chimneys, he was only doing what scores of emperors had done before him.

But the destruction this particular emperor set in motion was without doubt on the largest scale in Chinese history, and it's been gathering momentum ever since, until today it is an insane dinosaur run amok.

What Mao, and "emperors" after him, have been seeing is in fact nothing less than Le Corbusier's wettest dream taken to completion. This Swiss-born Belgian architect who wanted to get rid of all the fripperies of the Victorian age certainly did that, and more. It is his vision of a landscape criss-crossed with high-flying motorways weaving in and out of concrete "living-machine" tower blocks and with satellites flying around – think the Jetsons of the 60s and you will see the ideal of China today.

Highways, cars, high-rises, no people... a scene from innumerable sci-fi movies. And in China, the decoration on the gates of every school in the country – like the middle school in tiny Chuanxing in Sichuan province where I suddenly found myself one day in 2002...

5

West is Best

"Go West!" In 1851 the good old US of A reverberated to this cry, and in the year 2000 the Chinese government started to sound the same clarion call. Everybody always has to imitate the Americans, and none more so than the Chinese.

Of course, Beijing had at this stage been sending people westwards incessantly for a number of years; for various reasons but mostly out of kindness. For one thing, they couldn't bear the thought of the poor helpless ethnic minorities sitting there all alone without being properly liberated like the rest of China.

There was just one thing: a lot of those ordered to go west during the first years of the establishment of the New China were... if not exactly negative, at least a little apprehensive about the thought of going. A little sceptical. They probably had an inkling that they would never be able to come back, and they were right. But as Mao said, power comes from the barrel of a gun, and not only power but enthusiasm, it turned out. Thus millions of happy volunteers went west to be at one with the peasants.

In the year 2000 on the other hand, people were tempted with *fat salaries* to go west and *develop* the distant provinces Sichuan, Qinghai, Yunnan, Xinjiang, and of course Tibet. The latter two aren't just provinces, but Autonomous Regions which the Uyghurs and Tibetans are allowed to rule all by themselves, with only the odd piece of well-meaning advice from the politically more experienced cadres of Beijing. Well, perhaps a little bit more than that, occasionally, but it's for their own benefit and they have all reason to be thankful; if it wasn't for the help of selfless Beijing officials they wouldn't even have McDonald's, let alone eight-lane highways.

One day in 2002 I stumbled upon an article that said this 'Go West' campaign was looking for volunteer experts to go into the hinterland and train the population – in what? Anything, really, was the impression I got. It was more or less an imperial edict, but this time roping in the people of Hong Kong as well. We were to share our wisdom and skills with the poor, backward and unsophisticated masses of China, and for this purpose a Hong Kong body had started its own Go West campaign.

Train the population, eh? Experts, eh?

As I read, I was filled with a huge need for adventure. I suddenly simply had to go to those western provinces where my people so clearly needed me. I called the journalist and got the number of... what was it again? The Hong Kong People's Democratic Bureau For Development Of The Western Provinces Of The Motherland. Something like that.

The woman on the other end of the line seemed to be quite taken aback when I told her I was from Norway. "But... but you speak Cantonese?"

"Yes, I'm a Chinese teacher."

"But... how can you teach Chinese? You're a foreigner!"

And so on and so on, for ages.

It's always like that. Hong Kong people can teach English, but I can't teach Chinese. It seems to be against the very laws of nature. Hong Kong people, in general, refuse to believe me when I tell them I teach Cantonese, not only to Caucasians but also to Overseas Chinese who choose me as a teacher. The latter choose me because they can't stand the constant ridicule of Hong Kong people, taunting them, sixth-generation immigrants to Texas or wherever, for not *genetically* knowing fluent Cantonese the moment they touch down in Hong Kong.

In the end she gave up from sheer exhaustion and maybe because of the fact that we'd just had a 15-minute phone conversation about whether I could teach Cantonese – in Cantonese. I also eventually managed to convince her that my English, although I wasn't an English *person,* was good enough to be passed on to the poor unsuspecting population of the less privileged provinces as the real thing: A native speaker of English.

I went to the introduction/training meeting, which consisted of a geezer with a comb-over, that least enchanting of all male hairstyles (and which the Japanese so aptly have coined "bar code hair") standing in a beige room in a dubious-looking block of flats in Kowloon, talking about the motherland and how we as Hong Kong people ought to feel a responsibility towards building up the poorest provinces. Pretty much a verbatim rendition of the newspaper article.

I was ready. Very, very ready. When given the choice between six poor, undeveloped and desperate provinces, I chose Sichuan because I'd never been there before and from reading about it, I figured they had the best food. I was on my way.

The people from the bureau couldn't really believe I'd rather go by train than plane, but after much discussion I managed to convince them that the train was cheaper (save money for the motherland) and I was off.

I was to go to a middle school in a village in the southern part of Sichuan province, by hard sleeper and via Chengdu, the provincial capital which is rather north in the province. After two lovely days on the train I reached Chengdu and nipped into the station hotel to shower and get ready for the next stretch: The night train south to Xichang, China's centre for satellites, the same evening.

Outside the hotel was a sandwich board I felt was talking directly to me in English:

Welcome bedraggled
Forgive we
Cannot reception

Bedraggled! But how did they know? Yes, after two days without a shower and with only a metal (enamel) cup with boiled water in which to brush my teeth – I couldn't get more bedraggled, I thought. So I was a little disappointed to find, when I read the Chinese characters, that it actually meant "Welcome. We apologise for being unable to accept guests with improper clothing."

Welcome bedraggled! Beautiful.

Unfortunately I couldn't say the same about Chengdu, a city of about 11 million people who own two cars each and drive them both at the same time. Here the Development Devil had not only arrived a long time ago, but settled for good with his extended family. Even the parks (normally calm and beautiful oases in the screaming building sites that are modern Chinese cities) had somehow become Disneyfied. Yes, tacky.

Perhaps it's difficult to imagine *grass* being tacky, but here it was. Not to mention the flowers: ghastly, orange, ball-like flowers standing in rows of fascist precision or forced into patterns to make out the words 'Welcome to our gloriously beautiful, natural, singular and wonderful park'.

This was as far from My China as it is possible to get, but OK, tomorrow I would be in a village. A village in the furthermost of the innermost, three days' train journey from Hong Kong. Good enough for me.

In Xichang a delegation from the school was waiting – at 6:00am! They were smiling so hard their heads were about to split in the middle. Me too, of course. We shook and shook hands for ages, as if I was some pop star or Nelson Mandela visiting. Cool! So much better than being ignored. There were three headmasters (!), three teachers of English and a couple of other people whose function was unclear, plus the driver.

One of the teachers, a thin girl whose height just exceeded that of my navel, spoke the best English. I would have preferred to practise my Putonghua of course, but wanted to seem accommodating on the first day at least.

"Now we will going to have breakfast," the girl declared and into the noodle shop we went. As usual when I eat with Chinese people, I was asked if I was "able to" eat "our Chinese food". Yes, it's just open my mouth, push the stuff in and chew, I answered, as usual. They laughed a little but exchanged looks.

When the steaming bowls of noodles arrived at the table I could understand their doubtfulness. This was chillies in chilli sauce with a sprinkling of chilli powder. With sweat and tears (and, I have to admit, not a little snot) running down my face, I sat chewing away, enjoying the feeling of having my mouth flayed from the inside by a small but insane combine harvester.

Afterwards it was off to the school, fifteen minutes' drive away from the ugly and nondescript town of Xichang. The teachers seemed very proud of its status as China's satellite centre number one, however, so I ooh'd and aah'd in the right places. I wondered what kind of satellites. Perhaps they were sending them up to spy on Norway, to lure her oil-finding secrets away from her. Probably not.

The car wove through quite narrow streets; unusually narrow for the New China.

So this was Deng Xiaoping's home province.

In articles he is often described as "peppery." Until I came here, I thought perhaps it meant "a man who makes people sneeze," but now I knew. Deng Xiaoping was a man who could make you cry and tear you apart from the inside.

Apart from the chilli peppers, which act pretty much like chilli peppers anywhere and more viciously the smaller they are, Sichuan also sported a speciality called "Sichuan peppercorn" which was very mild, fragrant and un-sneeze-inducing... and made your mouth go completely numb, the English-speaking girl told me while we were driving. I couldn't wait.

Xichang wasn't a prosperous city, by the looks of it. People were short (not as short as Deng Xiaoping, but short) and dressed in the kind of clothes that have been washed so many times by rubbing them on a hard surface that they have taken on the same colour. Most people's faces were dark brown, a big no-no and dead give-away in China: Poor! Many women were carrying a kind of open cylindrical basket on their backs like a rucksack, out of which farm produce and children peeked.

"Those are the Yi minority," the English teacher, Wang Rong, said.

"China has many minorities. They are: Yi, Zhuang, Hui, Miao, Dong, Yao..." followed by a stream of words I'd heard dozens of times before. The phrases "let them..." and "give them..." featured frequently.

We drove along a narrow, unpaved and extremely bumpy road lined with sunflowers. Behind the tall and sturdy flowers I could glimpse iridescent paddy fields. It all looked exhilarating beyond words. All too soon we swung through the tiled school gates, decorated with pictures of rockets (missiles?), satellites, high-rises and motorways, the futuristic dream mapped out by Le Corbusier, as well as a quotation by Deng Xiaoping about how education leads to all good things. Like missiles, apparently.

Inside the school gates was a little room where a number of geezers in uniform sat smoking. Those would be the turnkeys.

Students walked to and fro, stopping dead in their tracks when they saw me, giggling long and hard. They remained rooted to the spot, staring, as I walked across the school yard with a tail of eight people behind me, minus the driver.

There were 1,200 pupils at the school, Wang Rong informed me. And one toilet. An outhouse to be exact, with three... not exactly cubicles, but *places*. Holes, rather.

Have I mentioned Chinese toilets before?

Chinese toilets are one of the reasons, or maybe *the* reason, why so many inhabitants of Hong Kong, both Chinese and foreign, refuse to set foot on the other side of the border. "Dirty!" they wail. "Disgusting! Smelly!"

But I don't know. Why does a toilet have to be so clean and fragrant, really? What you do in the toilet isn't exactly something you'd do in mixed company. And also – how long do you really spend in the toilet each day, compared to outside?

No, those who are afraid of Chinese toilets must have another, deeper and more sinister reason than dirt and smell. They are probably psychopaths.

Now China has become as much of a "use and chuck" society as other countries, but it's not so long ago that everything was used and nothing thrown away of that which we politely call "human waste". In the countryside they had, and still have, outhouses: a depression in the earthen floor with two rocks to put your feet on, normally in a corner of the pigsty. Simple and convenient and straight out onto the fields shortly after deposit.

In the cities, in a time when few people had running water, let alone any indoor sanitary system, "night soil" collectors used to come and pick the stuff up from public toilets. The collectors came early in the morning with their overflowing barrels carried on yokes, and were of course despised intensely, like most people doing life-important work.

Now China has for many years been active in modernising the urban public toilets, which can be found in most streets, as it is only in the last few years that most people have had indoor plumbing.

When I first came to China in 1988, many if not most citizens had one communal toilet per street, and you never had to ask for directions – the fragrance led the way. Practical and time-saving.

These toilets consist of one or more troughs in the floor, over which one squats. Some of them have water cascading through at intervals, others don't. In any case it's useful to be good at squatting, and to have the ability to squat while looking upwards or a little sideways, not down. No, you wouldn't want to look down. And if one isn't good at squatting, one soon gets the hang of it, for it is not always very tempting to use one's hands to support oneself on the wall. If there is one.

If there is a wall, it'll be a low dividing wall without a door, but mostly toilets are just rooms where you can do stuff that people in the street can't see. Apart from that, privacy is pretty much an unknown phenomenon in China.

For me, when it comes to this, I'm a little bit fussy. I prefer to be alone – completely – when I'm in the toilet. So it was a bit difficult in the beginning when I was cycling around Beijing and had to visit the neighbourhood's Fragrant House and everybody who was there, or came in, started staring at me. Staring thoroughly.

It was probably the giggling that I found most disconcerting.

So here I was standing in Chuanxing Middle School's privy, the olfactory properties of which were of such awesome power that I was almost thrown backwards out of the room. There was no trough, no water, just three shallow holes separated by knee-high walls made up of three scrawny planks. Someone must have come to scoop up the stuff at regular intervals, judging by the lack of height of the three heaps, because the place served more than 500 female students.

Oh, and teachers too, Wang Rong told me. I felt myself blanching a little bit inside. And outside. What if I had to get up in the middle of the night? There was a kind of lightbulb hanging by the door but it was so weak that it could just be glimpsed as a yellow blur in the blessedly dark room.

"But no matter, you have a toilet in your apartment," she continued. Thank God! The word "relief" took on a new dimension.

The flat was big, especially by Hong Kong standards. There were actually eight rooms, if I included the bathroom and the clothes-drying room inside the kitchen. There was no furniture apart from a sofa in beige and piss-brown plush with a kind of cartoon pattern, a fake oak table with a glass top, also with a cartoon pattern, and a bed with a plastic upholstered headboard.

"Everything is new, bought especially for you," the headmaster, Mr. Ma, beamed through his interpreter Wang Rong. Although I had been stressing the fact that I did understand Chinese and would like to practise, it was like whispering in a hurricane. Wang Rong was the designated interpreter and she would interpret. End of story.

"There's hot water in the shower, from solar panel," they told me proudly. Wow! That was more than we have in Hong Kong, where most of the energy comes from burning coal. Progressive, environment-loving China.

The headmasters begged me again and again to forgive them for not providing me with a TV set and a fridge, but assured me they would get hold of both items as soon as possible. After ten minutes of much exchange of looks between the various leaders and interpreters I more or less managed to convince them that I hated TV and didn't intend to waste one second of my time looking at it.

And fridges... although I don't exactly hate them, they are far from crucial to my life. I wasn't going to cook in the flat anyway as I never cooked, and I was used to drinking warm beer after many years in pre-industrial China. No, there was no reason to put oneself out for my sake. But I did intimate that I wouldn't mind a lamp by the bed. And a desk. Two headmasters left at once to procure these items. Should I feel bad? No, it was a school for Christ's sake. They were bound to have desks.

Well. Oh, but the view! From the kitchen, bedroom and what would be the library when I got a desk and some books, I could see the most enchanting scenery through tall windows with iron grilles. Wildly green rice paddies stretching into eternity, one behind the other, bordered by clusters of traditional houses made of red clay and with black Chinese roof tiles. Behind were green hills, turning more and more blue and pale grey as they went on and on into the distance. This was a China I thought existed only in pictures. Touched-up pictures.

Not one modern or ugly thing ruined this vista, which could have been of any time or dynasty, if it hadn't been for some electric cables outside the window. O joy. The houses! Now I only needed a bicycle, and then I would...

I didn't want to seem too demanding on the first day, or possibly any day, but before I could stop myself I had asked Wang Rong if somebody could possibly lend me a bicycle. She looked at me oddly, but translated to the headmasters.

"Bicycle?" a headmaster, Mr. Li, asked, as if I'd said I needed a bucket of slime to wash myself in.

"No, that's not necessary. If you need to go anywhere we will drive you."

"But I would like to ride a bicycle. I like to ride bicycles."

"It's too dangerous. You'll get hurt."

"But I've been cycling my whole life without an accident. (Not exactly true). And there is no traffic here."

They all exchanged looks – again! – and looked decidedly uncomfortable. I thought I could understand what was going on. To ride a bicycle is low status, almost as bad as walking, and they couldn't let a teacher at their school, a foreigner into the bargain, cycle around like a peasant or worse. On the other hand they couldn't refuse me anything. I was a foreign expert and must be treated well.

Here was a typical unsolvable situation, and teachers and headmasters, all of smoke-stained teeth and really bad haircuts, stood around, hands clenched behind their backs, rocking from heel to toe, sucking their teeth. A feeble "ai ya" escaped from a teacher before he was quickly brought to silence by a stern look from Headmaster Li.

Hmm. To save everybody's face I used my own method from Western culture, namely to cut through a Gordian knot with a lame attempt at humour and flattery.

"I have to cycle every day because I'm afraid of getting fat from the fantastic food you have here." Ha ha.

This way we had reached a kind of status quo, and they left me alone in the flat to shower and "rest" after the long journey which had consisted of sitting and lying down. I wasn't to start work until the next day.

Wang Rong had given me a schedule which suggested I was to work three hours every day; one in the morning and two after lunch.

A shower at last! Fortunately it wasn't as hot here as in Hong Kong, only 20-something degrees, but a night on the train is a night on the train and I had been well on the way to becoming re-bedraggled.

The solar-powered water was freezing. That's okay if it's 35 degrees, but not when it's 22. So that was how the solar panels worked – they only heated up the water when it was sunny; on a cool and overcast day the water remained ice cold.

But I could do cold water. I had swum (well, submerged myself in) the Trondheim Fiord in February (it was a bet) and also spent a winter in a Beijing hotel where the water was only hot from 6:30 to 7:30 in the morning and most of the windows in the bathroom were broken. The way to take this kind of shower is to shout as loudly as possible and shower one toe at a time.

Clean and fragrant, I stepped outside to take a look at the village and surrounding attractions, but was intercepted at the gate by a couple of headmasters (or whatever they were) saying I couldn't go out because it was too dangerous. Oh no, not that old story again! What was it this time – were they afraid geriatrics would point at me with their walking sticks?

I was now frustrated and not a little pissed off. A situation had arisen which no joking could solve. Wang Rong was sent for, but I was not exactly mollified by being told I would "occasionally" be given permission to go outside the gate – with her as a bodyguard. Well, that was reassuring! She was half my height and weighed about 35 kilos.

I tried to explain that I was 42 years old and had been travelling in China for 14 of those years, without as much as a quarter of a bodyguard to defend me at any time. But it was no use – the village was a seething quagmire of untold dangers and they, the various headmasters, were responsible for me. If I wanted to go anywhere I would be driven, and if I absolutely had to walk, it would be under the protection of Wang Rong, who looked extremely unenthusiastic at the thought of ferrying me around in addition to her normal job.

Desperate, I played my last card: If I couldn't get around by myself I might as well leave at once. I immediately realised that this was the worst thing I could have said. I should of course have suggested signing a piece of paper saying I would take responsibility for my own safety.

This wasn't the first time I'd acted undiplomatically in China and it would by no means be the last.

It's always like this when they try to get me to do something that is for their benefit, while trying to pretend it's for mine.

"Hey, let's go and watch that outdoor performance with happy smiling people of Turkish descent dancing in colourful costumes!"

"Oh no, that's not suitable... for you."

"Hey, let's go to that party with the really cool and handsome guys we met last night!"

"Oh no, it will be too boring... for you."

"Hey, let's play cards and drink beer all night!"

"Oh no, that will be too tiresome. For you."

It's seldom a good idea to push the Chinese up against the wall without giving them a chance to save face for themselves and everyone involved. Conflicts must be solved before they reach crisis point, and preferably through a middleman. The exception is street fighting, where a throw-away comment like "I think this head of cabbage is somewhat overpriced" or an action like trying to push a heap of mattresses away from a door can lead to an explosive, frothing-at-the-mouth argument which goes from nothing to fully-fledged hurricane in a few seconds. It's fun to watch but not so much fun to participate in.

Now the glances they were incessantly exchanging were ricocheting around the gatekeeper's office and I didn't like it. Although I feel at home in China and think I've got a good handle on what's going on, it is also very easy to feel ostracised and start wondering if it isn't they who are right after all. The 5,000 years of culture... acupuncture... the invention of gunpowder... and foot binding! This situation must have direct roots to the foot binding tradition, I decided. Refusing to let grown people outside a gate? Give me a break!

After some mumbling in the Sichuan dialect the headmasters arrived at a face-saving solution.

"You can go around by yourself if you sign a paper saying you take full responsibility for your own safety."

I tried desperately to hide the smile forcing its way out. Wang Rong almost winked at me while giving a soft moan of relief, for I had told her that I was addicted to exercise and in Hong Kong walked my dog at least two hours per day. Two hours was something her extremely hectic working day just couldn't spare, and besides, she hated exercise.

Well, that was easy. Now I had a document saying I was allowed to do what I've been doing for most of my life, with varying results, namely taking care of my own safety.

Outside the school gate the sun had popped out and the endless paddy fields were so green they were almost white. The road was made of packed dirt. The sunflowers were yellow explosions. I was filled with a wild, bubbling China Joy. There were no cars!

Everybody stared, and I was used to that, but here people stared not only as if they'd never seen a foreigner before, but as if they'd never seen *anyone* before.

This must be the main road of the village, I thought; it was slightly wider and more evenly packed than the road outside the school. The right-hand half of the road was used for drying chillies and corn, stretching for what seemed like miles, like a very long curtain lying on the road. The screaming yellow corn and the fire-red chillies competed with the rice plants for the loudest colour. Peasants sat outside their houses, binding baskets and shoes. They were binding shoes! But they put down their work in disbelief as I walked past.

The little clusters of houses soon gave way to open farmland. The road was straight for hundreds of metres, and in the distance I could see two geezers in their usual peasant's uniform: once-blue suits from the 1970s. They started staring at me from about 300 metres. They stared and stared as I approached. They stared as I passed. When I had finally passed them by a few steps, one of them said, in an explanatory way: "Lao Wai."

"Yep. Lao Wai," the other one agreed.

At night Mr. Yang, who wasn't a headmaster at all it turned out, but what Wang Rong called a "leader" (which can mean anything in China) took me out for dinner with some English teachers and headmasters. The restaurant was situated in possibly Sichuan's most beautiful beauty spot: By a huge and shimmering lake, silver purple and blue in the approaching night.

The staff gave Mr. Yang a lot of face by chasing away some customers from the best table, right on the edge of the water under a colossal tree, so we super-important people could sit down. Dish after steaming dish arrived and there were five toasts a minute. I got sucked into the festivities and everything was jovial – all "misunderstandings" from earlier in the day were eradicated as the table reverberated to the sound of China: *He! He!* (Drink, drink.)

There was a big dish with some black things that looked like pebbles on a beach after an oil spill. They were water chestnuts, a local speciality. They didn't taste of anything much, certainly not of anything good, but everybody looked at me so expectantly that I had to pretend it was the best food since... the invention of gunpowder.

Why can I never, ever learn not to pretend to like things I don't like? As I staggered away from the table at nine o'clock, the staff came running with a big bag of black stuff that they handed me with many excuses about it being "not enough." The bag contained two kilos of water chestnuts that the staff had personally extracted from the lake.

When I was just about to go to bed (21:43), there was a knock on the door. It was Wang Rong handing me the *revised* timetable. Instead of three hours, I now suddenly had to work five hours a day, spread between 08:00 and 20:30, when I would be teaching the teachers. This way I would have no time to mill around outside the school gates by myself.

They'd got me.

The next day arrived in glorious sunshine. I had been given six classes, of which the smallest – the least numerously populated, that is – consisted of 79 students. The biggest one had 97.

As I entered the first classroom, the students, all 83 of them or whatever, stood to applaud... before I had time to say anything.

This boded not well.

The classroom was of the size I remembered from my schooldays so long ago, only with five times as many students – most of whom I couldn't even see, because they were hidden behind mountains of books towering over the poor mites' heads on the tiny sliver of desk space each had at their disposal.

Here there were no modern fripperies like slide projectors, computers – or curtains. The room was rather bedraggled, threadbare, really; just some walls where the paint had given up, and a platform on which the teacher's desk perched precariously. I felt transported to my first year at school, anno 1967, where my big fear was getting to the 7th grade because I'd heard maths was so difficult in that advanced grade.

A maths class had recently taken place in this classroom too. I found fresh traces of equations on the blackboard, a good old-fashioned black blackboard with real, dusty chalk. A ripple of nervous giggles ran through the room when I picked up a long piece of chalk (pink) and promptly broke it. It had been a long time since 83 teenagers laughed at me. If at all.

I wrote my name in Chinese on the blackboard and told them that although I may look like a *lao wai* and they had been told I was going to teach them English, I was actually a Hong Kong compatriot (here I wrote "Hong Kong compatriot" in big characters) come to teach them Cantonese. In the rather shocked silence that followed, I taught them some mild slang from Hong Kong, the arbiter of Chinese style, gaining a little respect. Maybe. If hysterical giggling means respect.

One thing was for sure: although they were no less fond of giggling hard, long and often than other teenagers, mainland teenagers attend school in order to study. Study, study, until flames are coming out of their ears. These students were 17 and 18 years old and in their last year at middle school before trying to enter university. And enter university they must, or else... or else it's straight back to the farm.

The entire family's honour hinges on them, and because they are the result of China's one-child policy, which has turned the structure of society upside-down in a way the Cultural Revolution could only wetly dream about, it's not only the parents who depend on being able to say that their offspring has bagged a place at university, but two sets of grandparents and probably a slew of uncles and aunts too. Everybody has chipped in to ensure that the miserable wretch will make them proud, get a good job and spend the rest of his life acting as the cash-cow of the family. And it's not any old university that will do; no, it's got to be Beijing, Shanghai or Nanjing (at a pinch), otherwise they might as well forget it.

The problem is that these sons and daughters of the soil must do so much better than their counterparts from the capital and the eastern provinces to keep up.

Many of the students I saw before me – thin, badly dressed and wearing glasses held together with sticky tape – just hadn't had the same start in life as youth from the big cities. For one thing they had been raised on farms where they'd had to work after school and in the holidays, whereas the city youths had spent their upbringing at their desks, fed and waited upon hand and foot by adoring parents and grandparents.

Secondly, these students' parents were often illiterate or, if they could read and write, didn't have the time or ability to help with the homework. Many of the parents themselves had their education cut short by the Cultural Revolution and were products of Mao's insane idea to send all China's young people to the countryside to learn from the peasants.

Their textbooks were bad and dated and they'd had a different curriculum from the richer provinces as well as having teachers with less education. From this starting point, they still had to take the same exams as students from more privileged backgrounds. To compete with their peers from Beijing or Shanghai was for them to run a hurdle race with an anvil attached to their leg, and in which their competitors' hurdles were lying on the ground.

They studied from 06:00 until 23:00, with a two-hour lunch break. On top of this they had homework. And this was supposed to be their summer holiday.

All this, however, I found out later from their teachers, in what would come to be known as "teachers' psycho hour."

For the moment I was just impressed at how un-teenage-like these 83 (or was it 92?) students behaved, and how much they were on the ball. They hung on my words as if I was a sports star extolling the benefits of doping, and were touchingly "spontaneously eager" to find out about Norway and Europe. Hands up for questions for *lao wai*.

"And we are been told that you come from the Norway. Norway is famous seafaring nation. Can you tell we, us, something about Norway... (frantic shuffling through papers)... naval history?"

"Er... no. Sorry. Next question."

"Do you ever have meet Mister David Beckham?"

"What do you think?"

"... maybe... no?"

"That is correct. Next."

This was going brilliantly. We talked about football, Hong Kong, Norway and China. Everybody wanted to know how I felt about China (especially the food) and that question I could at least answer in a satisfactory manner. When I told them that I thought Chinese men were the most handsome in the world, a veritable storm of giggles broke out.

I told them about the party at the lake the night before and my shock upon going to the toilet and finding three grown sows in it. But at this, they looked at me uncomprehendingly. Doesn't everybody have pigs in the toilet?

The day galloped forth in a whirlwind of black heads, blackheads and thin arms. I had to lay me down backwards for the English these people had acquired in only three years, taught by people whose own English was somewhat quavering. Some spoke with great authority, others were so shy they didn't even dare to look at me. But they were all burning to learn, to study and to get ahead. Not for their own sake, they all told me, but for the family and, most of all, for China. Or so they said in front of the others...

*

The time is 20:30 and it's time for the teachers' psycho hour, also known as "Teachers' Study Group with Foreign Expert." All the English teachers at the school, 10 or 12, turn up. The younger ones like Wang Rong, her husband Ma Fu Qiang and Miss Xie, are full of beans and expectations, while those of 40 and upwards look more resigned. Another study group – and they still have 300 exam papers to mark!

One of the mature ones, Mr. Li, however, has a very positive attitude. His English name is, inexplicably, Pold Well Li, a moniker he insists was given to him by a Frenchman. He laughs and talks incessantly in a braying but passable Advanced American – a kind of English that's gaining ground in China and to a certain degree Hong Kong: Every consonant (and some vowels) is the letter R.

"Hello'r an'r'd plearesed to'r mee'r't you. R."

He is, I realise after a while, shitfaced.

As a foreign expert it is expected that I know everything about pedagogy, as well as not a little about magic.

"How can we spend more time on each individual student when there are 95 pupils in the classroom?"

"How can we teach them modern English when we don't speak very good English ourselves?"

"How can we get hold of modern teaching equipment when we don't have any funds?"

"How can we compete with Shanghai when our students have been raised among pigs and chickens?"

"How can we have some fun with the students without them losing respect for us?"

"Yes! How can we make the students laugh?"

I'm afraid I couldn't help them as much as they had expected, or at all, during those psycho hours, which quickly turned into complaint fests. The teachers told me how corrupt the school was and how the parents bribed the headmasters, indeed how they had no choice but to turn to bribery to even get their children into the school. Meanwhile the teachers received the same measly salary no matter how many students the leaders managed to squeeze into the classrooms, already packed to the point of exploding.

They told me how they each were in charge of four to five hundred students, all requiring personal follow-up and having their homework and tests marked. They told me how they had to go to meetings and sit for hours applauding some headmaster or leader who didn't know the first thing about education, whose views they totally disagreed with but weren't allowed to express it, and who were "idiots." (It was normally Pold Well Li, who turned up at our meetings more or less drunk out of his skull every day, who used expressions like that.)

We all agreed it was just as well that neither the headmasters nor any of the other leaders, Communist Party cadres as they all were, understood a word of English.

No, it would probably take a magician to help the teachers at Chuanxing Middle School. Either that, or a complete overhaul of China's educational system. But the complaint sessions at least brought them closer to each other and to me.

On the third day there was a meeting happening in the headmasters' meeting room and the meeting was about me, a flustered Wang Rong told me as she dragged me away from a class just as we were discussing the merits of Sichuan peppercorns.

Outside the meeting room were several journalists and a TV crew. I posed for photographs, playing the role of the Foreign Expert – happy but dignified – before Wang Rong intervened like some kind of personal assistant to the stars. "Move along, we are busy people here."

The first thing I saw in the meeting room was something I hadn't seen in many years, in fact not since my first day in China in Tiananmen Square on National Day, 1988: Pictures of Marx, Lenin and Stalin.

Mao was up on the wall as well, that went without saying, as were Zhou Enlai and Deng Xiaoping. But Marx? I knew that Chuanxing was a place reasonably far away from civilisation, but... Stalin?!?

The meeting room was soon filled with middle-aged men stinking "Communist cadre" to high heaven. Communist cadres in China – and especially in Sichuan Province, where most people are poor and therefore enjoy an extremely good and healthy diet of fresh vegetables – are known by these signs:

They are taller than average. They are fat. They walk with their stomachs in front of them and a slew of sycophants behind them. They sport comb-overs and big, square sunglasses. They drive (or rather, are driven in) big, black cars with darkened windows, preferably on the pavement. They are King of the Hill and they know it. Female cadres are the same, only with stiffly permed curls or intricately combed quiffs instead of comb-overs; marginally slimmer but with shriller voices.

In the meeting room, all the leaders of the educational committee of Xichang's Communist Party are present, as well as the chief of the local Security Bureau and some newspaper journalists and, bugger me, the local TV station.

Yes indeed, this is big news. The meeting is about me, but nobody looks at me or talks to me. One by one the fatties stand up to pontificate at length in the Sichuan dialect – of which I can pick up only a few words – but they seem to be telling each other who I am, where I am from, how I feel and what I will do (i.e. magic.)

Everybody smiles and applauds wildly after each long-winded speaker, but during the soporific monologues many of them seem to be nodding off. The headmasters and leaders nod and nod, smiling stiffly. This is probably not far removed from the endless study sessions people were forced to suffer through during the Cultural Revolution or from as far back as the early 1930s, since Mao took charge – Mao was a man pathologically unable to stand (other) people having a moment of leisure or fun.

Hours pass in unspeakable boredom. Presently there is a kind of movement. The committee has decided it will go and inspect my flat to see if it is good enough. I am torn from sleep and manage to pipe up: "It is more than good enough."

They stare at me as if I have uttered that China's Communist Party consists of mortals who can occasionally make mistakes. Oh no, here we go again. But I'm sick to death of being bulldozed and ignored.

"If you want to look at my apartment, why don't you ask me? I am very satisfied with my apartment and I'm very satisfied with all the things that Mr. Yang has arranged for me. ALL," I quack forth in my kind of Mandarin, looking hard at Mr. Yang who, with a movement of his eyebrow, lets me understand that he is thankful for the intrusion.

Even I know that as soon as these gits, dizzy with their own power, clap eyes on my – even with its abundance of rooms – very simple flat, they will come up with all sorts of crap about the lack of TV, fridge and whatnot, which the school will then have to cough up. They are here to find fault and probably find some way of pocketing the money allocated for my use; nothing's too good for our foreign friend, and after all, they have to justify their corrupt little lives one way or another.

A long and embarrassed pause descends, and some face-giving is clearly called for. And yes, the chief of the Security Bureau dissolves the tension by laughing loudly with horse teeth.

"Yes, yes, it is good, it is good," he says, pushing the leader of the Education Committee out of the door. They probably want to relax with a long lunch of *bai jiu* and fags before going whoring on taxpayers' money.

Outside it's time to be hounded by the media, but it's all in a day's work for Foreign Expert. The question everybody asks is: "How can you work *for no money*?"

They seem to have forgotten the spirit of Lei Feng, the revolutionary hero/soldier who was so self-sacrificing he couldn't rest until every soldier in his squad had clean clothes, socks in particular, which he would unfailingly scoop up and wash in the sweat of his own brow, so to speak, preferably at four in the morning. (His speciality was actually *darning* socks.) Change tyres, do the dishes, tie people's shoelaces – this "rust-free screw in the socialist machine" would help people before they even knew they needed help, and every time he did an amazing good deed, a photographer would miraculously be on the spot to chronicle Lei's latest self-sacrifice.

(In fact, Chuanxing Middle School had a whole concrete wall over by the basketball court dedicated solely to Lei Feng's noble acts and thoughts).

Lei is regularly trotted out by the authorities when they want to remind the people that although it is glorious to get rich, a little selflessness wouldn't go amiss.

So I answer the journalists that I'm following the example of Lei Feng, and also that I want to do something for the motherland. And I love Sichuan food. They snigger at the first reasons and scribble furiously at the last. The next day's article is all about food, not a word about Lei Feng and also nothing about a sentiment I think I expressed quite beautifully: That China was my mother and the Communist Party my father.

The next evening we can watch ourselves on TV, in a karaoke bar in the throbbing metropolis of Xichang, after the Teachers' Psycho Hour. If you think it's terrible listening to your own voice on tape, imagine what it's like to see yourself on TV talking a language you can't speak.

That night I selflessly teach *Choh Dai Di* (Chinese Poker) to the entire teaching staff at Chuanxing Middle School. At least seven minutes pass before they start tearing me to shreds. I wonder if Lei Feng's selfless altruism would have extended to letting me win at cards?

*

It was a couple of days after this that I saw the first corpse of my life (the second being the river-corpse in Lanzhou.) I was on one of my frequent outings away from the school; with my bicycle I could fit in one hour here, two there, and this time I had made it into Xichang city, a mere 15 minutes of hard pedalling away from Chuanxing village. I was planning to go to the local internet café and afterwards have lunch with myself and a book, only looked at by sophisticated city people who only stared at me from a distance and didn't come up to loudly discuss what I was eating while sitting down at my table and going through my handbag.

On a bridge I saw a larger-than-normal crowd and instinctively knew it was something bad – there was none of the animated chatter and excitement so typical of normal mainland crowd-gatherings. On the riverbank below lay the corpse of a young man in a dark blue suit; the uniform of the Chinese peasant.

I asked a nearby restaurant-keeper if he knew how the man had died, and he shrugged: "From hunger." I thought this sounded strange. Does anybody die of hunger in today's China? Around the restaurant stood large rubbish containers filled to the brim with discarded food. Couldn't the guy just have eaten out of dustbins like the plump beggars of Shenzhen? Then again, why did I assume that just because the restaurant owner was a local, that he should automatically know why any random stranger had died?

Cycling rather slowly back to the school without having been to either internet café or lunch, the image stayed with me: The curiously silent crowd, the man (So young! What a waste!) lying on the ground with knees bent, the gruff police arriving on motorbikes. The total absence of noise, which was the strangest of all.

I thought about how, if it were only 30 years earlier, the sight of a corpse on any given riverbank on the mainland would have been the order of the day and not even worth stopping for by anybody.

I thought of a photo I'd seen a few years earlier in a Hong Kong newspaper, taken at Guangzhou's main railway station, at a time when on average 100,000 people arrived by train each day to look for work. In that photo a man lay dead in a heap of rubbish while three people were squatting right next to him on the ground, eating out of lunch boxes and smiling. Why let a corpse stand between them and a good lunch?

When I saw the corpse, quite near me, I was surprised at my own non-reaction. "Corpse. Dead. OK. Move along, nothing to see here."

But when I got back to the school I felt quite... not exactly excited, but as if something monumental had happened to me that I wanted to share. So I told a couple of my fellow English teachers, fellow sufferers at the psycho hour. Instead of asking "where, when, how?" however, they just shrugged indifferently. Death is not big news in China and they had other things to worry about, like keeping themselves and their families alive on US$65 a month.

I stayed a month in the rural paradise of Chuanxing, spreading the word of my not having ever met David Beckham and, I hope, a little bit more, to about 900 students. Or maybe I just confused them and made their lives even worse by insisting that they didn't have to stand up just to talk to me and could call me by my Christian name. Who knows?

I visited the school the next year, and a couple of times after that. Each time, things were like before, except that I had to stay in a hotel in Xichang and not my own eight-room flat. But, a short walk from the town, there it would all be. The Chinese countryside at its best. Forever.

Yes, although China's relentless destruction continues night and day without let-up, I somehow thought that this place would always be the same as before. All the horrific buildings and roads in Beijing and the other big cities have been allowed to obliterate all things of beauty because China is now a rich country and the Chinese, despite the 5,000 years of civilisation they're always harping on about, think everything old is ugly. But where there is poverty, beauty must still exist, I thought... like a moron.

In 2008 I went back to good old Chuanxing in Sichuan province to visit the school and my old friends, and to let the tired eye rest on endless stretches of iridescent green paddy fields and rust-red houses made of packed earth and straw. I wanted to saunter along the winding country road to see the mighty water buffalo behind the plough; to sit on the edge of the shimmering lake and play cards, and maybe even try to rent an old farmhouse this time. Oh, the farmhouses with their drying corn and chillies hanging from the rafters – the sun shining on the ancient wooden beams surrounding the courtyards.

How naive is it possible to be? When I had been there only two years earlier, everything had been like before, except that the rice fields were grey and black seeing as it was Christmas time. But even in winter Chuanxing was beautiful, serene; a place of soothing lines and two-tone harmony. However, that was before the "Go West" campaign had come to town. Or, should I say, stuck its greedy and annihilating tentacles into my lovely village.

The rice fields were buried under six-lane highways, black and glistening, as straight as the crease in police uniform trousers and completely empty. The traditional rust-red clay houses had, if still standing, been given a coat of grey concrete, and the black roof tiles had given way to sheets of corrugated iron. But most of the old houses had been pulled down and, in their place, three-storey monster houses now lorded it over all they surveyed, all multi-coloured, shiny tiles, metal-framed windows and blue window glass. And the inevitable fake columns, wrought iron railings and white "Greek" statues in the garden.

Mr. Yang, Wang Rong and several of the headmasters (or leaders) gave me a proud tour of the school, which now had 6,000 students instead of 1,200. A slew of new, shiny, white-tiled buildings had sprung up and the outhouses had been replaced with normal flushing toilets. That was good. But when I asked if the nice new classrooms now had fewer students so that the teachers' workload could decrease, I was told that – on the contrary! – now each class had an average of 120 students. But the teachers had been given *microphones.*

The beautiful blue lake, on the edge of which I had been forced to eat so many water chestnuts and where I had played so many noisy games of cards, was still blue, grey, purple and dreamy. But on its banks a revolution had taken place. Where I not long ago had sat at a simple wooden table under a big tree, gazing at the shimmering ripples and perhaps thinking about life, there was now a long jetty made of fake wood, with white plastic banisters decorated with plastic flowers in plastic baskets. The ground was covered in multi-coloured flagstones laid out in various screaming patterns, and two-foot-high plastic picket fences kept most of the ground out of bounds to walkers – of which there were none. The restaurant was closed because nobody came any more.

Sic transit gloria mundi.

*

But my very first, and by far most wonderful, sojourn in Sichuan had an unexpected, quite bizarre aftermath. Back in Hong Kong after a month of culinary perfection, I was desperate for Sichuan food. As soon as I stepped off the train, I rushed to the nearest restaurant to ask if they served 'fish-fragrant aubergines', so named because the sauce – sweet, sour, spicy, salty, pungent, wonderful and all other flavours known to man – is normally connected with fish.

"Of course, and *wah!* You can even say *fish-fragrant* in Chinese!" beamed the waiter.

The dish arrived and I died. It was greyish-brown slop instead of the Sichuanese red, green and purple. It was full of small, over-salty fish.

When I called the waiter over and said there must be some mistake, he got stroppy and showed me the menu. It said *fish fragrant,* therefore it must contain fish, right? *Right?*

A famous Sichuan dish, made into slop by Hong Kong so-called chefs (who make about HK$25 an hour so we can't criticise them too much). Whereas in other countries destitute, dispossessed guys are drawn into the military, in Hong Kong they become either hairdressers or cooks. Bad cooks. But if hairdressers, not gay. In fact Hong Kong must have the highest percentage of non-gay hairdressers in the world: About 99%.

Anyway, instead of having to suffer through another inferior meal at the hands of the ignorant (but persistent), I decided to learn how to cook Sichuan food myself. How hard could it be? A quick trip to Chengdu for a three-hour introduction to the art – followed by the purchase of Fuchsia (whose name *isn't* pronounced Fuck-see-ah, I quickly found out) Dunlop's excellent tome *Sichuan Cookery* – soon got me up to speed. How hard it could be turned out to be about 2 on a scale of 1 to 10.

I really only dudded out once, when old friends and travel mates Jacq and Hap Tsai (an Englishman whose surname is Box, so he's known in Cantonese as Hap Tsai, Box-Boy) came to dinner on my roof. I had travelled to China with Jacq on several occasions, the most memorable of which was a trip up the Yangtze before the Three Gorges Dam spurted into action. (The murky secrets of that trip will be revealed in a later chapter). I had met her when she took Cantonese lessons from me, as had Hap Tsai, another excellent travel companion on trips to Norway and Australia. When I introduced them to each other at a Cantonese film-viewing party at Hap Tsai's, they quickly fell in love and moved to Singapore, so that was another example of how an act of kindness never goes unpunished: I lost two friends and travel companions in one go.

At least here they were on my roof, ready to taste my first public outing of my new-found cooking skills; my first foray into cooking in my whole life, in fact.

I made my favourite dish from the local restaurant near the school, *Gan Bian Tudou Si*, dry-fried potato slivers, sprinkling it liberally with Sichuan peppercorns which I had picked up in Chengdu.

Hap Tsai, being a British public school boy, kept that famous upper lip stiff – he had no choice anyway because his entire face had gone numb. Oh yes, those peppercorns were numbing all right. Jacq, being Australian, had no qualms about pretending to like the food. "I can't feel my face! My face has disappeared!" she kept complaining.

So had mine. Decades in Hong Kong and China have taught me a thing or two about face; I feel the loss of it almost as keenly as Chinese people. Nowadays any pain I may feel in my face is largely phantom pain, like the pain in a leg long amputated, seeing as I lost the last shreds of what little face I ever had ages ago.

After the face-numbing fiasco, however, it seemed I could actually cook. By following Fuchsia and doubling any amount of garlic, ginger and the white parts of the spring onion she recommended for each dish, I suddenly had people if not flocking to my house, at least turning up occasionally when there was Sichuan food to be had.

Unfortunately, soon after I came back from Sichuan, my house became unsuitable for receiving guests. Was it an irony of fate or just some kind of divine punishment for all that slagging off of the school's one, quite unbearable, toilet, that made me lose all use of my own toilet in my little village house in Tai Tei Tong?

One day I tried to flush it only to find that instead of going down, the stuff came up. Subsequent attempts at flushing only made it worse. It seemed that the village septic tank had given up the ghost. Weeks went by where I had to use the common village toilet and it really wasn't fun. At all. I could sympathise even more with poor Wang Rong and the other teachers for whom trekking out to an awful cesspit in the middle of the night was the only reality they knew.

When the weeks turned into months I had no choice but to move, but where to?

I wrote down my requirements for a house, trying to visualise my ideal dwelling so it would come into being. I had learnt the art of creative visualisation from a guy called Napoleon Hill in his book *Think And Grow Rich*, written in 1920.

My requirements for the ideal house were: Must have a working toilet. That ruled out every single house in my village, but I was open to new places.

A few weeks later I was walking my dog Piles (a pain in the arse) in Pui O, an hour's walk away from where I now spent my increasingly put-upon, constipated days.

A woman of South-East Asian appearance came running up to me: "Do you speak English?"

"Well, a little," I said, trying not to sound too proud.

"I need to visit my husband in Ma Po Ping prison but I don't know where it is! Please help me."

Wah! Everyday drama! Of course I must help. Having played cards with the wardens in that particular prison I actually did know where it was, and tore out the back page of the book I was reading (I have to read while I walk Piles because I have no inner life and therefore can't stand just thinking) so I could draw her a map. (I bet the Hong Kong government gnashes their teeth every day over the British colonialists' insistence in building *prisons* everywhere on Lantau Island in places where a more commercially-minded government would have knocked up huge holiday resorts).

Oh dear, no pen. And the woman didn't have a pen either. I nipped into a nearby *si-do* (Cantonese for 'store' which means a little convenience shop where you can buy beer, soft drinks and various paraphernalia for overnight stays in the countryside, as well as instant noodles).

An old couple ran the shop and they were happy to lend me a pen. They also asked if I wanted a house, as they happened to have one for rent. Serendipity? I think not! As soon as I had finished drawing a detailed map of the road leading to Ma Po Ping prison I went with the sprightly old geezer, Mister Wu, to see the house.

The house: Oh. My. God.

Yes, that Napoleon Hill had known what he was talking about. Not only did the place have a fantastic flushing toilet, it also had a sea view, a five-metre-high ceiling in the living room, and a 700-square-foot roof terrace. And many, many rooms. Three bedrooms, for example.

It looked like shit, of course, with an awful brown kitchen ensemble with yellow walls, concrete floors and a fridge which looked like it hadn't been cleaned since Mao was still idealistic, but nothing that a coat of paint and some hard cash couldn't fix.

"Oh, I don't know," I said, trying to hide the huge excitement that threatened to make me jump up and down. "Will you put in a new fridge?"

"Sure," the old geezer said. "The place has been empty for a year. The woman who lived here before moved out because it was too big."

Too big!!! Moron!

"How much?"

"Four thousand Hong Kong dollars a month. We've just put in new windows."

Scream! Try not to scream!

Thus endeth my days of hauling myself off to the public toilet. While my old landlord had put the price of my current house down to two thousand dollars a month after the toilet facilities disappeared, I was happy to pay double just to hear the most wonderful sound in the world: That of a modern toilet flushing and flushing.

An interesting added benefit of having a toilet *and* a 700-square-feet roof terrace soon presented itself. Having become a relentless maker of Sichuan food, I could now invite people to my house without shame. Although the new place was much further away from 'civilisation' (Central in Hong Kong) than my old house, people actually wanted to go there to eat. For anyone not currently residing in Hong Kong, I can't tell you what a huge compliment it is to anyone's cooking or party-throwing skills when people are willing to leave the safe cocoon of Central and actually get on a ferry to go to an island more than half an hour away. Huge! I mean, when Kowloon, seven minutes from Central by the (formerly) venerable Star Ferry, is known as "the dark side," you can imagine how people feel about the outlying islands. "Mars is closer", "I would rather die", "Is that in Asia?" etc.

So I started throwing one dinner party after another, but ended up slightly disillusioned.

People were partying on my roof while I was downstairs in the kitchen cooking all night. Through the open kitchen window I could hear peals, sometimes screams of laughter, as my friends were having a great time without me.

How could it turn into this?

An article about 'private kitchens' (illegal, non-licenced) restaurants, the latest rage in Hong Kong, finally made me see the light.

With little fanfare I opened the Lo Uk Tsuen Country Club Democratic Personal Sichuan Kitchen, and started cooking for money.

Now, the peals of laughter I hear from the roof while I rustle up dish after steaming dish of Sichuan food don't fill me with envy but with joy. They are happy customers having a good time. And when they leave, they leave money. It's a nice little earner for me, and allows me to cook and eat the best food in the world, that of Sichuan, while making people happy and spreading the gospel of parties Chinese-style; which I'll tell you all about in the next chapter.

6

Let Steeping Dogs Die

The Chinese used to be quite sensible when it came to partying, especially compared to Norwegians. And English, Germans and Danes. And Australians.

At the time I discovered Chinese parties, however, around 1988, sensibility was the last thing on my mind. Yes, I was both disappointed and not a little confused when the first party I went to in China, starting at 6:30pm at the factory of Gillette shaving equipment, finished at 9pm on the dot.

But… but... where *was* everybody? One moment they were there, a hundred or so people sedately swinging around on the concrete factory floor under fluorescent lights; the next they were gone. Gone!

There was nothing to do but start shivering on my Flying Pigeon bicycle and zigzag painstakingly through the sideways-pummelling snow in the empty streets, parsimoniously lit by gas lamp-style street lights. All the way I cursed the Chinese party etiquette that had forced me to spend three hours cycling for only one-and-a-half hours of party (the first hour was taken up by speeches, naturally).

But in retrospect I've come to understand how sensible this type of partying is. Start early and finish early, and never drink other than in connection with food. That's the healthy way. No pre- or post-dinner visits to bars, no boozing far into the early hours with consequent embarrassing scenes in front of bosses, children or worse.

Let me tell you about the Chinese party style of yore: Ten (or twelve or whatever) people seated at a round table. One thousand bottles of beer and a couple of bottles of *bai jiu* ('white wine'.) *Bai jiu* is the stuff we foreigners call *maotai*, but Mao Tai is actually just a brand of *bai jiu*. When the Chinese invite you to drink *bai jiu*, beware! It looks innocent and can sometimes be curiously drinkable, but gives you a hangover so colossal it will make you wish you'd never been born.

Last time (or, I hope, *the* last time) I drank it, I wisely had only two or three sips. It was orchid wine which had been buried in the ground for 14 years, the proud restaurant proprietor told me. The guy I was travelling with, a Norwegian, was more face-giving and chucked back two or three glasses on top of the five bottles of beer we'd already drunk.

Five 750ml bottles of Chinese beer is nothing, but because of a thimble-full of orchid wine I felt like death the next day. However, although my walking skills were not impressive, I could still make a show of standing upright without a walking stick as early as 11am. My poor friend on the other hand, polite and with a 'when in Rome' attitude, could only manage to seep greyish-brownly out of the hotel room in the early evening. He looked like a worm stuck under a stone for so long that it had become fossilized, and claimed to have been haunted by fever dreams where *he* was the one who had been buried for 14 years. Three days later he was still complaining about the *bai jiu* fumes emanating from the pores of his skin.

Yes, all foreigners in China will sooner or later be invited to drink *bai jiu*, whether made from rice, wheat or orchids. They should all be on the alert. Although the little glasses may look inoffensive, make no mistake: They are mortal danger in a liquid shape, and death and destruction follow in their wake.

Back at the Chinese banquet, the food arrives. Everybody eats as much and as fast as they can and toast people as often as they can, but seldom more than twelve times per minute.

Because so many Chinese people lack the enzyme that breaks down alcohol in the body, most banquet participants quickly turn red in the face, then purple, with the whites of their eyes going yellow. This is called *Mian Hong*, Face Red, and is apparently not dangerous. Still, it can come as a surprise for the casual foreign observer. One minute you're sitting there with a normal, beige person, the next it looks like his body has suddenly been invaded by a giant aubergine.

The time is nine or half past. One person (the 'leader') looks at his watch and then everybody stands, raising a last glass in a braying toast. The bill arrives and everybody fights over it. It's a carefully choreographed fight because everybody already knows who's going to pay. The leader.

However, to an outsider it can look like a fight to the death between tigers over a particularly tasty morsel; it's the kind of fight that looks like each fighter is trying to *get hold* of money, not *get rid* of it.

There is shouting, pulling of arms and legs, sometimes of hair. One participant may temporarily win possession of the bill before he's kneed in the groin and tackled to the floor by the one for whom the bill was intended all along, who surfaces red-faced and victorious from a sea of thrashing limbs.

The winner (leader) then triumphantly counts out the right amount of notes from a great wad extracted from his inner pocket and everybody disappears, leaving a table which looks like food debris and empty bottles have been dropped onto it from a great height. From the moon, say.

This is what it was like during my first years in China, in a time when most people were poor. Most parties took place in restaurants of various standards, and bars were only to be found in five-star hotels.

But now! Now there are bars on every corner and parties last all night. There is heavy drinking without eating, and if one should feel peckish and the bars are closed, the country is now crawling with outdoor restaurants which don't close before the last reveller has staggered away.

Drinking etiquette: As a foreigner in China you pretty much have *carte blanche* to do whatever you like, and people seem to get disappointed if you don't do anything a little bit strange. If you don't drink alcohol, for example, well, that's certainly a little bit strange, but OK. Have a beer!

Yes, but I don't drink alcohol, you protest, politely but firmly. Yes, but beer isn't alcohol, is it? Have a beer!

Beer is drunk in small glasses and you should only drink when somebody wants to toast you, which happens with such breathless frequency that you won't have much time to do anything *but* drink, even when nimbly handling the chopsticks. And you can't just take a sip, no, it's bottoms-up every damned time.

Chinese beer, I think, ought to be good enough reason for anybody to go to China.

When the Germans started China's first brewery in Qingdao (Tsingtao) in 1903, they laid the groundwork for an industry that surely must be China's largest, at least after prostitution and tobacco. Beer is now everywhere, it is drunk all the time and at all meals with the possible exception of breakfast, when many hard men prefer *bai jiu*.

When the Chinese were first given a taste of this strange brew, a yellow wine with bubbles (which turned out to complement Chinese food better than any other drink), they asked the Germans what this might be. *Bier*, came the answer. All right, we'll call it *Pi Jiu*, the Chinese decided: 'bier wine'. It quickly became the country's most popular thirst-quencher, right up there with tea. And even the most rabidly anti-linguistic foreigners in China seem to have no problem learning these particular words: *Pi. Jiu*.

*

Four hours' train ride north-west of Hong Kong is Siu Heng (Zhaoqing in Putonghua), one of the best party towns in China. Nestling among lakes and scraggy crags reminiscent of the area around Guilin, it has a tranquillity unusual in Chinese cities.

In the daytime, that is. At night it's a roaring, honking, screaming party with the whole long road running along the lakeside dedicated solely to dozens of bars. Small and welcoming, they suck you in and don't spit you out before you're finished.

One night in Siu Heng it's the birthday of the owner of a Sichuan restaurant I like to frequent. He leaves work early, giving the reins of the restaurant to his wife, and tells me to come to his birthday party in a karaoke bar near the lake. I don't get to the bar until midnight and I have a few beers inside me already, so I decide to take it easy. Every time someone wants to toast me, which is every four seconds or so, I therefore take only a small sip while the guy (women are rare guests at parties in China unless they are 'hostesses') sucks the whole glass down in one go.

"Why the hell don't you drink up when you drink?" the birthday boy shouts, peeved.

"I don't want to get drunk. I am a woman and we women can't drink as much as you men," I lie, to give him face.

"What kind of bullshit is that? You're in China now! You have to *Ru Xiang Sui Su* (follow the village custom)!" he roars and the poor guy standing next to him, trying to belt out a Canto-song, almost drops the microphone.

"Drink! Drink! Drink up! It's my birthday and you're only taking a sip at a time?"

I get the impression that he takes this very personally. It is one of the very few times I have been criticised directly by a Chinese (another was a guy furious with me for touching somebody's baby "because I would give it AIDS") so I understand it is serious. The birthday boy's face is on the line here, so I have to swallow down, and fast.

The next day, when I can see straight again, I swing around the market with my laptop to show my Sichuan friends the photos I took the night before. I feel quite kind and thoughtful, to be honest. But where is the birthday boy? Only the wife is holding the fort, again, and she tells me grimly that her husband is too ill to go to work.

So this is the new party standard in China: drink, drink so you can't even go to work the next day. But what are wives for, eh?

The guests of that particular birthday party were 30-something-year-olds, but it is again in Siu Heng that I come to experience the party mores of the younger generation. I'm there with a couple of students, the lovely Ali and Jan, on a "language seminar" – a euphemism for drinking yourself into the ground while playing cards and talking Cantonese with local people.

The bars are closed already at only 2:30 in the morning, and we're walking around looking for more fun when we find ourselves on a construction site from which loud drum'n'bass music issues. We follow the sound and suddenly there's somehow a karaoke bar among the tarpaulin and sawdust, with private rooms laid out in rows down an unfinished corridor. The accommodating staff show us into a room where a party is in full swing.

The revellers are all people in their twenties and they seem very happy to see us.

I think, as I have so many, many times before during my expeditions in China, that my god, it should have been Norway. Or any other western country. In how many countries but China can one just gatecrash a private youth party, aided and abetted by the staff, AND be welcomed with open arms?

It's obvious that this is a different generation from what I'm used to in China, however, for there are several girls there; not whores ('hostesses') but members of the gang.

But looking at them I think they seem a little un-energetic for 20-something-year-olds and the reason soon becomes obvious: When we've sluiced down the first couple of beers, a thin... no, scrawny, young man appears with a small tray with some white stuff and a straw. It's *Lao K*, Ketamine.

As Ketamine is actually a horse tranquillizer and our drug-taking days are long since over, we decline politely (fortunately the younger generation is more tolerant of people's different habits for intoxication) and just stay on the beer – which, of course, we're not allowed to pay for, being total strangers who have gatecrashed their party.

Meanwhile the young people keep sniffing up the K, becoming more and more lethargic. They lay drawling incoherently around the sofas, neither dancing nor singing. You'd think they were in 1978, smoking pot and listening to Pink Floyd...

After my first encounter with *Lao K*, I seemed to come across it time and time again. At every karaoke bar there was *Lao K*, presented more or less surreptitiously. A wink, a slight inclination of the head, a hand-signal for the Western man (never me, of course) to follow whoever into the bathroom or to the darkest corner of the room; there it was, the white stripe of some washing-powder-like substance with a straw.

Even a few weeks ago, when calling up an old friend who wasn't even in his twenties or thirties but forties, with the subsequent invitation to karaoke, I was intrigued to see the *Lao K* laid out in heaps straight on the glass-topped table. This particular friend's friends weren't happy about having foreigners in the room while they snorted up the drugs through a *bent* straw, so we quickly left. Or maybe it was the fact that I was taking photos.

Still, it puzzled me why a horse tranquillizer should gain such a foothold among a people who, to put it mildly, need more energy and wildness at parties, not less. Then a drug-savvy friend in Hong Kong enlightened me: *Lao K* may be a tranquillizer, but what it does is separate the mind from the body. The mind is working overtime while the body is rendered completely immovable. Therefore (and I'm quoting this) – the brain tries desperately to fill the space where the normal action of the body is no longer, leaving the owner of the head with wildly fluctuating dreams and visions, going into a kind of trance.

So – magic mushrooms while paralysed?

Naw, it's not for me. Chinese beer is more than enough. And if beer is a bit boring and middle-aged, there is always snake wine. You know, the big vat with a couple of snakes submerged in it for a few years, with the scales starting to come off.

*

The first time I try this special-tasting drink is in a snake restaurant in Guangzhou, where I'm showing around 12 Norwegians, members of the avant-garde theatre group mentioned earlier. At the sight of the mesh cages where hundreds of snakes slither around, and the colossal glass jars with thick pythons rotting away in *bai jiu*, the enthusiasm among some members is huge. Among others: Non-existent. But: Snake restaurant? It's too good a story to pass up.

Since that day, probably 1995 or thereabouts, the snake has become an endangered species, so I have given up this delicacy too. But on that day with the theatre group I was ready to eat, and also intrigued to see how the snake's gall bladder was revered.

The restaurant owner takes us into the kitchen where we get to see how a fresh, live snake first has its head cut off with a pair of scissors, and then is sliced open from the neck (if snakes indeed have necks; perhaps they are just one long neck) to the end of the tail. The gall bladder is then torn out and crushed into a glass of *bai jiu*.

Drink, drink, urge the cook, the waiters and a number of people who have wandered in from the street to behold this great spectacle, "*Lao Wai* eats snake."

Snake gall bladder wine is said to be good for the throat, and the meat of the poor bugger, like that of dog, is supposed to be "warming." Both are therefore mostly eaten in winter, although you can get wine with pickled snakes all year round.

So the evening ends with us quaffing snake gall bladder wine as if we all have laryngitis, and eating snake meat which, even the culinarily most pusillanimous (me) must admit, tastes excellent. Yes, more or less like chicken.

However, the snake is about to go the way of the dodo so for geo-political reasons I can't recommend it. Nor shark fin soup, a staple of big and important banquets throughout the country, especially in the south of China and in Hong Kong. What they do, allegedly, is scoop up the shark from where it goes about its business in its capacity of Dustbin Collector of the Sea, slice off its dorsal fin and throw it back in again to die a slow death from drowning. You wouldn't think a fish could drown, but without its dorsal fin it's finished.

Of course the shark is a fish and not a mammal like, for example, the whale, which, if Chinese gourmets and gourmands found out how delicious it tastes, would be extinct *tomorrow,* but I think we ought to feel sorry enough for drowning sharks to stop hunting them down. The sea needs the shark, did you hear that, wedding guests? And let's be honest here: shark fin soup tastes of almost nothing. Certainly not chicken.

And talking of sharks – I think it will be about as difficult to stop the Chinese ordering shark fins when they want to show off as it is to make Cantonese a world language. One day, I think it was in 2003, I got a new group of students. After eight years of teaching Cantonese, I had learnt to spot more or less immediately the ones who would make it and the ones who wouldn't.

Most wouldn't.

There were many reasons for this. Number one, my ludicrous illusion that everybody is like me. At least deep down.

Yes, I really thought that armed with a list of words and after a couple of hours of practising simple food-and-drinks ordering conversation with me, my students would run out, speaking Cantonese with everyone they met. That was, after all, how I had learnt Cantonese.

It turned out that the opposite was true. As mentioned earlier, most of my students chose me because they had no real interest in learning Cantonese, or rather they wanted to know how to speak it without having to go through the tedious process of learning it – much the same as fat people who want to be slim but don't want to eat less or exercise: They just want to take a pill or have their stomach stapled.

These were the same people who asked me if I didn't have a DVD or a CD-rom they could learn Cantonese from in the safety of their windowless rooms and who, when I *did* make a beginners' DVD (everything you need to know in 90 minutes), never watched it.

I realised that it was a personality thing. Extrovert people learn languages the natural way, the way they learnt their first language as children, by osmosis.

Introverts, with their varying degrees of terror of other people, have to rely on other tricks. Rote learning is one. But no matter how much they want to avoid it, the day will come when they actually have to talk to a

Chinese in his/her language (or feel they have to because I'm standing right next to them with a large mallet – metaphorically).

And that's when the second reason for not winning in the war that is mastery of the Cantonese language kicks in: Chinese, in particular Hong Kong, people's reactions to a foreigner speaking Cantonese. These reactions come in four different variations:

1. *The eyes are stronger than the ears.* A Chinese person hears Cantonese, but because it's spoken by somebody who could never in a million years be speaking Cantonese, thinks it's English that he can now miraculously understand perfectly – and so he answers in 'English.'

2. *A dog that can ride a bicycle.* A CAUCASIAN is actually attempting CANTONESE, which *everybody* knows is the *most difficult language in the world* (so difficult, in fact, that only Chinese and some selected types of South-East Asians can learn it)!? – ha ha, that's too hilarious! Chinese person goes into a paroxysm of laughter and starts applauding like a sea lion at Ocean Park, then proceeds to answer in 'English.'

3. *My English is far superior.* The Chinese don't have a word for "patronising" (talking down at a person perceived to be inferior in a fatherly, supercilious way) in probably the same way as the English language doesn't have a word for *Schadenfreude* (joy at other people's misfortune) – it's too close to the national psyche to need a word. I have sometimes asked Hong Kong people why they break into applause and shout "Wah! You're so *intelligent!!!*" when I say something incredibly difficult like "Good morning." Without being able to use the word, as it doesn't exist in Chinese, I have then gone on to try to explain how some people could find this reaction *patronising*.

I use examples to explain this, saying for example: "When people treat me like a two-year-old and applaud me when I say something really simple like "Good morning!" in a way that I feel is looking down on me – what do you call that in Chinese?"

"Happy?"

No, not happy.

"Surprised?"

Certainly not that. More like... angry at being treated like a stupid baby.

"Oh, I know: Very happy and surprised?" is what I get.

Yes, being patronising is seen as a good thing in Chinese culture. And so, after they've finished screaming with joy, applauding and telling you how good your Chinese is – in English, naturally – your interlocutor then goes on the show you how it's really done: In 'English.' Because, although you may be able to speak a few words of Cantonese, such as explaining what "patronising" means *in Cantonese,* you couldn't possibly be able to understand the answer in anything but English.

4. *Cantonese is useless and inferior and I will fight to the death anyone who says otherwise.* Some people, again mostly in Hong Kong, react with anger and resentment when Cauca-geezer tries to speak to them in the local language in the place where they were born and raised. For it is set in stone: Cantonese is *not* a language, it's merely a dialect (if that) of superior Mandarin, and should never be spoken by anyone not born in Sham Shui Po (pronounced *Sam Seui Poh*) or currently eking out a living as a Hong Kong taxi driver.

"Don't learn Cantonese! It's useless! You should learn Mandarin instead!" these proud defenders of Hong Kong's honour will snarl as they hurtle down a one-way street at 110 km/hour, overtaking a school bus. When asked if they themselves can speak Mandarin, they answer no. And then they proceed to talk to you in 'English.' ("Yoo wan' see-top heeeah?" *You want to stop here*? "Yoo pay ho' machee?" *You pay how much*? "Tong why heeah?" *Turn right here*?)

No fluency in Cantonese in their passenger will divert them from their original plan: To speak English to the white person because no whitey can ever speak Cantonese – even when he can.

So, facing these obstacles, fighting against seven million people who actively try to stop them from learning Cantonese in every way, it's small wonder that many of my victims indeed give up.

Persistence, bloody-mindedness and a keen competitive spirit is the order of the day in the war between the Canto-learners and the people who will thwart them at every turn, and sadly over the years I have been made to realise that not everybody has or indeed wants to have these qualities.

And in the new group starting on that particular day, I knew that two people would drop out almost immediately; especially the one who said that she had no interest in Cantonese and only came along because her girlfriend wanted her to. Of the five people starting that day, only one lasted longer than three months: Richard.

A tall, slim and extremely attractive Englishman 14 years my junior, he wasted no time in acquiring Cantonese in the same way I had. He quickly became a kind of protégé of mine, sucking up the Cantonese at double speed and using all my methods to get Hong Kong people to answer in Cantonese instead of the English they keep quacking forth – like saying "O m sek gong yingman" (I don't speak English) or "Ha? Lei m sek gong gongdungwah meh?" (What? You don't speak Cantonese?) or just repeating "Ha? Ha? Ha?" in a Canto accent until they break down (four times is normally the penny-dropping moment) – as well as using all my standard jokes.

Soon he had shed his original study mates like so much unnecessary snake-skin and was taking private lessons from me, once a week without fail, and with plenty of linguistic progress evident from one week to the next. It was a joy to hear about his arguing with taxi drivers, standing up to shop-girls who laughed at him and ignoring the horrified bleatings of the mainland Mandarin teachers at the international school where he taught: "You mustn't learn Cantonese! It's not a language! It's just a gutter dialect for plebs, blah blah blah..."

"You're just jealous because I understand Cantonese and you don't," Richard told them. He was like a mini-me.

After a few months I arranged a 'language seminar' in Guangzhou and only Richard turned up. That's when he discovered mainland guys. Still, instead of ogling these outer-worldly wonders of male beauty, we found ourselves talking to each other all night, telling each other stuff.

He told me mostly about his female friends – of whom he seemed to have hundreds – all about what they did and how annoying they were with their clingy neediness and propensity to call him up "every five minutes" to complain about guy trouble. I thought if this was the way he talked about his friends, I'd better watch out. But it was so deliciously bitchy and entertaining, and he looked me in the eyes and asked interested questions about me, actually listening to the answers instead of only waiting for his turn to talk about himself. He got all my jokes and, unlike most British people, didn't correct me when I said on purpose "Bob's your oyster" and "The world is my uncle." Oh yeah, make no mistake, most of them do. Because I'm Norwegian, it's impossible that I should make sport with the English language. Oh well, at least they understand me when I say "Don't patronise me, you bastard." At least they *have* a word for patronise.

But here was Richard, so young and beautiful and charming, getting all my literary references and more outlandish jokes; being totally on my wavelength and making me laugh and laugh. That night I seemed to be pulsing to a different beat and our conversation seemed more like 'duelling stand-up comedy' than 'shared intimacies between fag and fag-hag.' And he fell for China, immediately and without condition. That night, although I didn't talk to a single straight guy or any straight single guys and didn't play as much as one hand of cards, was the best night I'd had in ages. Months.

I knew what it was. As I lurched ever deeper into middle age, the one thing from my youth I had been missing more and more was carefree and meaningless conversation just for the sake of it. Friendly banter. Jokes related to, or puns taken from, the works of Shakespeare. Discreet but waspish remarks about the appearance of total strangers as they hove into view.

This may sound as if I didn't like my other friends. I did. But, just like when I got married and realised that it wasn't being married in itself that made the difference between being boy/girlfriend and suddenly married so huge, it was the different treatment from other people: The semi-sniggering remarks like "but you can't do that now you're married" and "you probably have to go home now – you're married" and "now that you're married I probably shouldn't tell you this..." in the same way it wasn't being middle-aged in itself that made life more boring, it was other middle-aged people.

When I wasn't married any more but suddenly edging into what they call 'a certain age' – again it was my contemporaries that were the problem, I felt. Now they were all paired off with a comfortable 1.8 or 2.3 children, suddenly no conversation seemed to be complete without: Complaints about domestic helpers. Wallpaper and other interior decorating. Property prices. Intense conversations about how long someone had been in Hong Kong and where they lived. (Not as small-talk icebreaker but as the main topic of conversation of the evening.)

Nothing about personal stuff. Nothing about feelings. Nothing philosophical. No politics. No playful banter. My contemporaries had become a group of people (couples) who acted as if they were in a boardroom with a particularly dreary and demanding boss – even when they were drunk.

Is it any wonder Richard fell like torrential rain upon the parched desert of my intellect?

And so began our friendship; I kept teaching him everything I knew about the language and culture, we met for drinks where we made the other laugh at what had happened to us in the week, and as often as we could we slipped across the border to be with 'our people.' Chinese men.

We had amazingly similar tastes in what constituted a good weekend away in the mainland. In the daytime: Walk around old neighbourhoods with good 'hovelage' as I called it; places that many people would describe as hovels but which we thought were just beautiful, picturesque and 'the real China.' At night, we gatecrashed parties.

And now I'm going to share my gatecrashing secrets with you. This is how you gatecrash any party in China:

1. Be a foreigner who can speak a little bit of Chinese, preferably Cantonese.

That's it.

If you're on a trip in China and you're feeling a little bored, you can just approach a table in or outside a restaurant. Mainland Chinese, for some reason, love foreigners, and you will be welcomed like an old and dear friend. A chair will be pulled up, a new glass called for, and you're away.

You can also hover outside private rooms in karaoke bars. The first person to come out to go to the toilet, for example, or go in search of *Lao K*, will inevitably pull you into the room where you will be pushed down onto the sofa and given a drink and a microphone.

Offering to pay is out of the question, no, you are the guest and now we're going to party until dawn. Sometimes you can spend up to 16 hours with total strangers, staggering away from the table at six in the morning realising you never found out the names of any of them.

The Chinese ask how old you are and how much you earn, and they don't mind taking a good old look at what's in your handbag. But asking your name? No. That's too personal.

But who cares? Socialising is the important thing, and it's good to be able to count on being taken in, poor foreigners as we are.

*

One Siu Heng morning at about 3:00am, Richard and I find ourselves walking aimlessly around, not wanting the evening to end. There is a table with three guys (geezers but in a good way) outside a restaurant waving at us to join them. Despite the staff pointedly cleaning and carrying away empty tables, a game of cards (*Choh Dai Di*) with copious amounts of beer is soon underway.

It's "drink, drink" and more bottles all round. Dawn arrives but we don't care. Around seven we finally gather the last iota of sense and drag ourselves to a standing position.

"I'll get a taxi," the heaviest drinker, ah-Keung, says.

"No, no, we'll walk. It's very close."

"No, no, I'll get you a taxi," he insists.

I look at my friend, the gay Richard who always complains about mainland guys, despite being beautiful and touching him a lot, never seeming to be quite out of the closet or any other piece of furniture. Is ah-Keung implying that he wants to come back to the room(s)? There has been no flirtation to speak of.

"No, really, we can walk."

But as usual, Chinese hospitality is something to which one cannot say no.

"I'll get you a TAXI! All right?"

All right, all right. We had been planning to walk it off but… fine. When in Rome you must *Ru Xiang* the old *Sui Su*. The guy leaves the table and two seconds later a taxi pulls up – with ah-Keung behind the wheel.

The taxi he was going to get was of course *his* taxi. And it has to be said, shitfaced as he seemed to be when he was just ah-Keung the geezer playing cards, his driving, all 230 metres of it, is immaculate. Then again, he'd only, as far as we knew, been drinking beer. And beer isn't really alcohol now is it? At least not in China.

And in much the same way as beer isn't considered to be alcohol, so chicken, ham, beef and mutton aren't regarded as being meat. Or at least, they aren't *called* meat.

Earlier on the night of the taxi incident we go to a Sichuan restaurant (incidentally my first meeting with the When in Rome-insisting drunk birthday boy) in the excellent *Lat Chiu* (chili pepper) Market, open all night. Feeling culinarily adventurous, we let the staff choose the food, but point out that we don't want meat. No problem! Ten minutes later a strange, oddly spiky, concoction appears before us.

"But we said we didn't want meat?"

"That's right! I know! That's why I'm serving you this."

It was ducks' heads.

Vegetarians, you are hereby forewarned. Most dishes, even desserts and cakes, come with a sprinkling of meat of some sort. Things that look innocent on the menu, like 'boiled cabbage' or 'stir-fried seasonal vegetables,' will have that little extra meat without which mainlanders nowadays cannot live.

And it's no good saying you don't eat meat, as only pork is considered 'meat'; you have to say you are *Sou sek* – pure (vegetarian.) But even then, the stock that the vegetables are fried or boiled in will have been made from chicken and pig bones anyway, so you might as well eat meat. And if you find yourself in Hong Kong and in a REAL vegetarian restaurant – the 'fake beef' and 'fake chicken' contain so much sugar and other crappy flavour-enhancing chemicals that if it's health you're concerned about, you'd be much better off in a normal carnivorous restaurant.

Most of my strict vegetarian or vegan friends have been happily munching through stuff enhanced with taste extracted from animal products for years; they just don't know it. And – I know I'm wading with loudspeakers and big metal bra-enhancers into a huge vat of wasps here – has that chicken stock really harmed them?

I'm just saying! Yes, we can easily get our protein needs covered by tofu. But do you know where most of the tofu we consume in Asia really comes from? No? Chopped-down rainforest in Brazil, that's where. Those farmers in Brazil are killing off more acres of rainforest per day than you've had hot lattes, so that we can feel good about not eating meat.

*

Although drinking in bars is now *de rigeur* and drinking without food perfectly acceptable, food is still the centre of Chinese people's lives. *Chi le mei you* (have you eaten yet?) is still a common greeting in China, meaning 'How are you?' If you've eaten, everything must be okay. And where in English you're supposed to say "I'm fine" even when you're not, so in Chinese you're supposed to say you've eaten even if you're a rattling skeleton of hunger. A lesser person could certainly be forgiven for asking "So why then ask?" But hey. Etiquette. And it is true that Chinese take a deep, passionate interest in discussing meals already eaten and still to come. And meals, especially in the southern provinces, must happen at least every four hours, and a two-hour lunch break is still common in many parts of the country, notably among government officials.

According to an old Chinese proverb the Chinese eat everything with legs except the table. Everything on the animal can (and must) be eaten, including the head, claws, eyes and ears. As well as the innards and the skin.

For the newcomer to China, perhaps used to buying meat in the supermarket in dainty little packages where everything that reminds one of the animal's origin has been removed, it may be a little disconcerting when chicken arrives at the table in its entirety with the head, including staring eyes, and claws intact. But you'll get used to it.

Chicken feet is still one of the biggest delicacies in China, but to be honest I can't quite see the charm in eating feet that have been plodding around in shit. They are also almost devoid of meat.

Heads of all persuasions have also never quite cut it with me. I think it's so sad looking at the opaque, staring eyes: "Why did you take my life? Quack, quack. Why... why..."

No, I don't like my food either looking at or talking to me, no matter how mutely.

A common joke among foreigners in China when something unknown appears on the table is that "this is probably the cook's dog (or cat, wife or daughter), ha, ha... (uneasy laughter)"

To these people I will categorically say: You're wrong. Cooks in China normally work from 04:00 till midnight, and that for a pittance, and can't afford the luxury of having a wife, let alone a dog.

Also, the restaurant would be proud of serving dog meat and would advertise it with big sandwich boards on the pavement showing smiling puppies cavorting in the sun.

That the consumption of dog takes place in China is indisputable. It also seems to be increasing as people make more money. And actually, disregarding the fact that the meat is full of bones and tendons, dog meat doesn't taste so bad in itself and I think it's quite hypocritical of people to sit stuffing their faces with beef or shark fin soup while getting up in arms at the thought of eating Fido. I have a dog myself and wouldn't hesitate to eat him if I was starving. It's not as if dogs are an endangered species or anything.

But the thing about dog meat is that the dogs are killed in such an unappetising way; in a way that makes every petit-bourgeois person with a sense of what is fair and what isn't, throw down their chopsticks and join the RSPCA or more.

In short, because the Chinese believe that adrenaline tenderises the meat, dogs – preferably young ones – are hung upside down and slowly beaten to death. The more afraid they are to die, the better the taste of the meat, is the theory. This is too much even for me. And to be honest, as a dog owner or even as a casual passer-by, it's not nice to walk into a restaurant, peer into the kitchen and see a flayed dog cadaver, its face set in a terrible death grimace, lying on its back in a basin, legs stiffly pointing at the ceiling.

It's also not nice to see skinned dogs, with or without heads, hanging on hooks in markets, their blood gathered in basins underneath. Their faces, in death and without the merciful fur, look so curiously human... like stick-like corpses in the mass graves of concentration camps, heads thrown back in agony.

The first time I tasted dog meat I had no idea how the poor bugger had met its grisly death; I just did it to shock my mother. But after I found out about the killing method, it became very difficult to swallow the gristly slivers, no matter how much I wanted my host to not lose face.

And if I had any left-over affinity for dog meat lurking deep in my depraved soul, I certainly lost it forever during the Christmas of 2008 when Richard and I went on an epic journey through some of the best hovelage in China: Guangdong, Guizhou and finally Sichuan.

"Oh look! They're putting a dog in a bag into the luggage storage space!" Richard remarked, or rather shouted, just as I was settling in on the top bunk of the virtually empty sleeper bus taking us from southern Sichuan to Yunnan.

I had been looking forward to some relaxed reading and gnawing on peanut sweets when my zen-like bliss was disturbed by Richard's outburst. I could see nothing from my window, but now I could hear yelps and moans from a dog in evident distress.

Damn. I knew there had been something wrong with this bus. No means of transportation in China is 'virtually empty' and especially not in the run-up to Chinese New Year which, like Christmas in Hong Kong, comes earlier and earlier each year.

And here we had been thinking we'd hit the transport jackpot on our Christmas trip, even welcoming the fact that the journey would take five hours instead of the normal three so we could relax properly! Now we had to stare in horror as the Dog Torture Express, winding its way around the unpaved country roads of southern Sichuan at 30km an hour, stopped again and again to pick up ever more dogs trussed up like turkeys, some of them with their jaws bound with wire.

"I can't be here," I said, just as Richard was jumping off his bunk and getting his luggage.

Outside the bus was mayhem. The un-muffled dogs were yelping, howling and generally shouting for help. They seemed to understand that they were heading for restaurant tables to be gristly snacks for men who think eating dog meat makes them more virile. The yelping wasn't the worst, however, although it cut us to the marrow. It was their eyes looking at us, pleading for mercy, which really made me wish I was a huge, AK-47 brandishing bruiser, no, that I had heaps of money so I could free them and set up a doggie rescue centre and...

The driver and his gloved henchmen, wielding metal wire and shoving the dogs like so many postal packages into shallow shelves in the bus luggage hold, sniggered derisively, staring at us like we were some bleeding-heart liberal tree-huggers or something.

And really, having commented frequently during the trip on all the restaurants proudly proclaiming they served the best dog meat – where had I thought it came from? Organically reared dogs which happened to wander into the kitchen of an afternoon, accidentally impaling themselves on cleavers?

The driver's assistant, it has to be said, was kind enough to drive us to the nearest train station, where we only had to wait five hours for the next train. He also gave us 80% of our money back. He seemed almost sheepish when I commented on the fact that the upholstery in his car featured cute cartoon dogs.

So even though I still maintain that meat is meat and that the dog is not an endangered species, as opposed to many other animals which are commonly found at banquets in China, I won't be making pilgrimages to dog-meat parties before they start killing the poor dears in a so-called humane way. And not even then, probably. The dog is after all man's best friend if he doesn't have any normal ones, and chicken also tastes good. Now, if they would only stop the battery chicken treatment...

But you're in China, and sooner or later a banquet will take place. So how should you behave? Just do as the others do. *Ru Xiang Sui Su*. The etiquette is in any case not so strict, for this is the Free State of China where everything goes.

All unwanted things are thrown (or spat) straight onto the tablecloth or floor. Everything can be used as an ashtray, but the floor is recommended. To smoke and eat at the same time is okay – isn't that why chopsticks were invented? Soup should always be slurped, otherwise nobody will know that you like it, and the rice bowl should be lifted to the mouth so the rice can be shoved in with the chopsticks.

But rooting around the communal dish to find the best morsels is not good form, and neither is eating up everything; that is a sign that you are still hungry. The rice arrives last and the soup laster than last. All animals are served with heads and limbs, except those that have been chopped up and fried with other ingredients.

If, like me, you don't like your chicken staring at you or arriving at table with feet, tendons, fat or skin, you should ask for *Gai Deng* (chicken cubes). If you ask for *Deng* or *Si* (strips) you should be saved from seeing the horrible things which remind you that the food has been a living animal with personality and style.

For someone as unfussy as I am about the condition of restaurants, their toilets and of the people with whom I play cards, I'm surprisingly, irritatingly fastidious when it comes to food. I don't like soup, for example, and things with water where anything could be lurking in its murky depths, especially not soups where giant knuckles with slivers of grey meat stick out of the greasy-pearled water like the Loch Ness Monster itself.

I don't like beige, grey or brown food, no intestines for me thank you very much, and no cow's stomach (tripe) bubbling away in its cauldron all day emanating terrible fumes. I don't like boring-looking food – e.g. white fish on rice with a white sauce (popular in Hong Kong) – just looking at it makes me fall culinarily asleep.

And I can't stand hotpot.

Hotpot is gaining ground and is taking on maniacal proportions in China, especially in winter. There is Sichuan hotpot (guess what the main ingredient is) where the most tonsil-slaughteringly, throat-rippingly hot variety is Chongqing hotpot. There is Mongolian hotpot, Muslim hotpot and Hong Kong's take on all of the above. The ingredients vary but all hotpots have this in common:

A big container with one or many compartments stands boiling in the middle of the table, powered by propane gas. You put meat, fish and vegetables into the quagmire, let it churn around for a while and take it out and eat it, dipped in various sauces.

The sweat is pouring down your face both because of the chillies and because a large receptacle is steaming like a dragon five centimetres from your face, as you're forced to sit there waiting for the food to be ready. I mean – if I have to cook the food myself when I'm in a restaurant, what's the point? I think hotpot is for control freaks who don't trust the cooks to know what they're doing.

It's not necessarily that it tastes so bad; for example, lotus roots cooked in chilli sauce is something I can easily get down me. But can't the professional cooks who work in the restaurant kitchen just cook it there, in the kitchen, and let a professional waiter carry it to my table? Call me old-fashioned but I think that's what paying people to do something for you is all about.

In the same way as I don't like to cook my own food when I'm in a restaurant, I also baulk at doing my own washing-up. I know they mean well when they put bowls, cups and chopsticks on the table, and then a big glass bowl where you are supposed to wash everything with boiling tea before starting to eat. They want you to know that everything is clean (and want to avoid lawsuits?) But to me it's washing-up pure and simple, and even before the meal has started. So I'd rather risk a microbe sneaking in.

Last time I was in Sichuan visiting my friends Wang Rong, Mr. Yang and the others, they took me to a hotpot dinner to cement our everlasting friendship. Also, hotpot is their favourite, I remembered from the time before when the farewell dinner had been hotpot. I remember trying to smile through sweat and tears (and snot) while I pretended and pretended to like it.

Never tell Chinese that you like something you don't actually like. They will force it upon you again and again. This time it was the super hotpot to end all hotpots, with fresh herbs the staff had picked themselves. The herbs lay in large heaps around the hotpot cauldron which stood bubbling menacingly with something already in it. I felt myself blanch as I approached the table. In the grey and frothing water bubbled all parts of various animals. All parts, in fact, except the edible ones. There were heads with staring or half-closed eyes. There were claws and feet of various types. There were knuckles, ears and beaks. Everything was grey, brown and beige. And black.

It was without doubt the worst meal I've ever had in China, worse even than what they think is Western food, and the only time I've been hungrier getting up from a meal than sitting down to it. It was just as well that party traditions in China have changed so much and one no longer had to leave the table at the stroke of nine, for at the next table a big boozing party was underway and its inhabitants soon drifted over to our table. They had a strong and well-developed drinking constitution plus the will and strength to stay drinking until well after midnight, at which stage they ordered some food that wasn't hotpot. And so this potential culinary tragedy had a good ending.

I think that hotpot meal was my friends' little joke, that they went out of their way to pick out the most awful-looking and vile-tasting stuff in the joint just to see what I would do. I gnawed on some herbs, that's what I did.

So the etiquette, the way I see it, is this: Take what is being served with a neutral expression on your face. If you pretend to like it you'll get heaps and heaps more of the stuff, plus a big bag to take home. However, if you see something too awful to contemplate, you're allowed to say no. After all, we foreigners are strange and it can't be expected of us to understand fully the ins and outs of Chinese cuisine.

But one thing I do understand, and this is that Sichuan food is the best food not only in China, but in the universe; and that is *including* the Milky Way and Dipper (Big and Little.) It has everything you could dream of, and more.

I can never fully express my gratitude to Wang Rong, Ma and Mr. Yang for bringing me to that little rural restaurant which is still there, 'improved' by much plastic statue-ism in the garden, where I first tasted *Gan Bian Tu Dou Si*, pan-fried potato slivers with Sichuan peppercorns, chillies and a sprinkling of spring onions.

If it hadn't been for them, I would probably never have embarked upon my new career as a Sichuan chef.

And if it hadn't been for them, and for the 'Go West' campaign and everything – maybe I'd never have found out about Sichuan food at all? Because guess what had happened to Xichang the last time I was there, with Richard, at Christmas 2008 (I mean, guess what had happened *as well as* the countryside having been Shenzhen-ified.) It was just after Xichang had proudly launched one of its many Long March satellites – I forget which number.

This momentous event had attracted the usual number of foreign journalists expecting the normal five-star treatment; and indeed, a new hotel had been built and the local restaurants had been briefed accordingly.

I arrived there with Richard in sub-zero temperatures; the only thing to sustain us both during terrible bus trips for days across treacherous mountains being the thought of the Sichuan food we would soon be eating in my beloved Chuanxing.

The food arrived but... it appeared to be a light-green-to-beige boiled goo. Where were the chillies, the Sichuan peppercorn, in short, everything that made Sichuan food number one in the universe, much, much further than even China's Long March satellites can reach?

They had taken out, or rather, not added, the taste. Because we were foreigners.

With the increased exposure to foreigners over the last couple of years, and no doubt instructed by some of the same people who had harassed me over a lack of TV at the school six years before, restaurants had simply taken out everything deemed 'not suitable for *Lao Wai*.' We had to ask, no, beg staff to tell the chef to cook the food as if we were normal human beings, and even then the taste had dwindled to the proverbial mere shadow of itself.

After all these years, the Chinese still think Chinese food is only suitable for Chinese people, conveniently ignoring the one or two Chinese restaurants abroad enjoying modest success. Even in cosmopolitan Hong Kong I often get this: "So, what's best, Chinese or Western food?"

"Chinese of course! Sichuan food. In fact I cook Sichuan food for myself every day."

"... but... it's hot? Don't you know Sichuan food has a lot of chillies?"

A nadir in the food and 'only for Chinese' worlds happened only a few months ago here in Hong Kong. I was in a hurry and jumped into a taxi still clutching the bunch of fresh garlic I had just bought in the market. The driver looked back at my hand and burst into honking laughter.

"Wah, you even know how to buy garlic!"

Yes, *buying garlic* is a skill normally only associated with Chinese, that's true...

So think about that next time a Chinese asks you if you "can eat noodles." Instead of saying: "Sure, I have a mouth with teeth, right?", take the time to reflect. They honestly, *honestly* think anything Chinese is only for Chinese people. Sometimes, when in a playful mood, I've thought of going up to Chinese people in Hong Kong eating pizza with their hands (covered with handkerchiefs, hello), clapping and beaming: "Wah! You can even eat *pizza*! You're really an Old Europe Hand!"

But they would never get it. Foreign stuff is for everybody, Chinese stuff only for the Chinese.

And who would know better than the entity which knows foreign tastes and needs the very best: China Travel?

They know that Chinese food is impossible to force down for anyone who wasn't actually born in China. Most of all, they know best what foreigners eat for breakfast: Five types of dry cake. And some cheese.

I said in Chapter 1 that fighting with a hotel guard in the street was the nadir of my life, but of course it wasn't. Going on a tour organised by China Travel was.

7

Tour de Arse

Looking back, I can't in any way understand what could possibly have possessed me to go on a *tour*. A tourism *tour*. Me? Insane. I can't even stand to have a waitress ask me to wait for her to show me to a table, for God's sake. I once paid the fine for jaywalking rather than not crossing the road on a red light just because there were police around. The same way my younger brother used to jump up on my potential suitors, stabbing them with an imaginary knife and shouting in an imaginary Corsican accent: "No-one talks to my sister!" – no-one can tell me what to do, even if they're right.

So why, why God, why did I decide to go on a tourism tour with tourists?

A theory, but again in retrospect: It was something about life being a bit miserable... something about having read too many self-help magazine articles.

Yes, in 1999 I was going nowhere, it seemed. I was just drifting along, teaching Cantonese to people who didn't really want to learn it, people who, I'd come to realise, had only chosen me as a teacher because they were terrified of Chinese people.

My economy was precarious because people would call and cancel at the last moment, not paying me, and my boyfriend at the time, Ming, had just stormed out again over some perceived slight or other, the most frequent of which was that "I wanted everybody to see me naked" (by wearing skirts slightly above the knee.)

Sad and empty middle age with nothing to show for myself but a few hundred in the bank, a few sticks of furniture and a certain reputation for being the only Norwegian Cantonese teacher in my village... it wasn't much. So, as all women in that or similar situations, I naturally turned to self-help articles.

"Do something wild and unpredictable!" said the articles. "Change the colour of your toothbrush! Take a different route through the supermarket! Say hello to a beggar!"

Or! I thought. I could do something I normally *would* do, namely: Go on a train trip in China! That would take care of my existential worries, get me out of claustrophobic Hong Kong for a while and even, perhaps, give me some inspiration for what to do with my life. It would also piss Ming off no end – if he came back in time to discover I was gone, that is.

I don't know if it was that or the next day I saw the article in the *South China Morning Post* about a new railway line about to be opened, somewhere far into the inner regions of the hinterlands of northern China. A new track, as long as anything, which was to follow the old Silk Road. Was it pure serendipity? Or, because I was clearly looking for an answer; *answer*endipity?

Shivering, I picked up the map. There it was – the Silk Road. The Gobi Desert. Oh, romance! Excitement! The very name – Gobi!

The helpful newspaper said that China Travel would be organising trips on this train, complete with hotels.

The word 'organised' made me a little worried, and if I hadn't been so blinded by the word 'train' I would have thrown the paper to the floor and taken a match to it. Instead I picked up my wallet and ran to China Travel.

For Hong Kong people who want to avoid standing in unruly and quite unpredictable lines to buy train tickets at mainland stations, China Travel – the Hong Kong branch of China's official tourism authority – is the answer. China Travel has a number of outlets in Hong Kong, and has undergone quite remarkable changes over the years.

In the eighties it was manned with curmudgeonly and brusque hags whose sole vocabulary seemed to be '*mei you*' ("there isn't any, it's sold out, I can't be arsed, the man with the key is not here") and for whom every customer was a pale, disgusting insect which had crawled out from under a rock and should be shooed back again as soon as possible.

But now it's smiles all round and cries of "Can I heltchiooo?" And they now accept credit cards and debit cards, whereas the pre-modernisation China Travel only accepted used one-yuan notes, if that.

Train tickets bought in China Travel cost a little bit more than those purchased after an hour's waiting in line at some provincial station, but (so) it is worth it. As Chinese people get more money, they travel more and more, and it's no longer a case of swinging around a station of an afternoon and emerging two hours later, dishevelled and sweaty but with a ticket for the same evening's train. Now it's wise to plan your move several days in advance.

The last time I was in Lanzhou, cradle of Chinese civilisation, for example, I had to *fly* back to Guangzhou (90 kilometres northwest of Hong Kong) because the trains were packed for the next five days. Don't get me wrong, there's nothing wrong with flying. Some of my best friends are pilots. And although it takes the oil of half the North Sea and, I believe, not a few hectares of rainforest (those napkins) for each plane to reach its destination, it's not something we rich people have to worry about.

No, the reason why I don't like flying in China is this: In a country where 40 companies can get together and decide to produce a milk powder for infants without any nutrition whatsoever, knowing that the consumer will surely die after a few weeks of using their product, it's easy to imagine that guys who screw screws into the wings of aircraft may not be over-scrupulous about the amount of screws going in, and where.

Now, the train, on the other hand: Train travel in China is a perpetual party on tracks, a intoxicating joy-fest where, if a lull should ever appear, you only have to look out the window to feel you have the starring role in the world's most hilarious movie.

Because I wanted to avoid speaking English at all, I stressed to the China Travel guy that I wanted to travel in a Chinese group, *sans* Whitey. The man looked at me with surprise.

"It's more suitable for you to travel with other foreigners," he tried.

"Give me Chinese or nothing," I retorted, damned idiot as I was. He mumbled something to himself which I should have listened to, asked me to fill in some forms, and that was it.

*

Now it is August and I'm on my way. I smile, no, snigger to myself as I sit on the shaking plane to Urumqi, provincial capital of Xinjiang. I'm on my way to ten days chock-a-block full of adventure and excitement. Oh, I will hear the trumpet blows of history, with bannermen and the neighing of horses, see camels at dawn and leave my footprints on the fabled sand dunes of Dunhuang. Thinking about this is so exciting that I almost forget to worry about the wings being screwed on properly. Almost.

To fly in China is almost like being on a bus, only higher up. People wander around, sit down wherever they want, open the luggage compartments during landing and spread their belongings, notably cardboard boxes tied with blue plastic string, all over the cabin.

The in-flight meal is a lump of fried egg with half a sausage. And this is supposed to be China, food epicentre of the world! No, give me the train, I think, reminding myself that soon I'll be on a train for ten days, ten marvellous days with guys, beer and cards. And some hotel breaks. This thought is almost worth the fear every time turbulence grabs the plane in its iron fist and shakes it so passengers and cardboard boxes fly arse over tit.

For some reason I survive, and emerge in Urumqi unscathed-ish. The hotel is truly magnificent if you like that sort of thing: a grandiose monument to nouveau riche-dom totally misplaced in a warren of hovels and narrow streets, like a spray-painted, bejewelled elephant sitting down to eat with alley cats. Now I see why the ticket was so damned expensive – this is a six-star hotel owned by some Hong Kong tycoon. The place would actually, again if you like that sort of thing, have looked great among the many like-minded buildings of Hong Kong: The polished marble, the giant chandeliers, the carpets so deep you have to use a compass to find your way through them. In rough-and-ready Urumqi it just looks ridiculous.

But this kind of hotel, already spreading like wildfire through China in 1999 and the inspiration for ever more outlandishly designed shopping malls, residential complexes and not least the magnificent edifices which are headquarters for the Communist Party in each city and township, is the ideal that the nation strives for.

Oh well, the room is luxurious – and it bloody well ought to be as I've paid HK$2,000 extra to avoid sharing it with some bint, and like any woman of course I don't hate luxury. Now I'm going to go crazy in the room and use up everything in it. Write stuff on the stationery, sew on new buttons...

I check the mini bar and as I feared, a can of beer costs 40 yuan instead of the normal six.

Oh well, holiday is holiday. Cheers, you smart, independent traveller, you!

There's a knock on the door.

What the...?

"Hello'r and'r I wanna'r talk wiff yooo'r."

It's a man introducing himself as my guide. Guide? I didn't see anything about a guide. He says his name is Huang Jianguo ('Yellow Build The Country') and forces his way past me into the room. I'm not overly happy about that.

He's not so bad-looking; my age, slim, a good head of hair and white teeth. But no, not my type. And a *guide.*

I ask him to speak Chinese as the purpose of my trip is to practise Mandarin. He tells me about how terrible it is to be a tour guide and how much he hates the passengers. Not me of course, he corrects himself quickly, and starts singing my praises in various ways, all of which are fairly tedious.

"Yes, we young people must stick together," he then says.

Ha?

"We are the youngest ones in the group. Do you understand?"

No.

Then he tries the actually quite smart trick of palm reading. After studying my hand carefully for quite some time and letting his finger run up and down my life-line, he comes to the following conclusion:

"You are intelligent and have a healthy body."

Deep stuff, impressive palm reading.

"You are beautiful," he then utters, putting his hand on my thigh decidedly north of the knee.

Bloody hell!

"We Chinese men have *two* heads," he continues meaningfully when I get up and move to the chair furthest away from him. "And do you know what the other one is?"

"Oh dear, is that the time? I must sleep. Goodnight."

I push him out of the door. What a tool! The room reverberates to the sound of beer, now warm, angrily drunk and to much mumbling and shaking of head.

The next morning I'm woken by the receptionist at six and told to report to the dining room post-haste. There, the rest of the GROUP sit looking at me accusingly. Huang the guide stands there talking to them as if they were naughty children on a school trip, with much shaking of finger and many repetitions of the important words in the sentences.

He is speaking English. Or rather, that new language, Advanced American, where most of the letters are the letter 'r'.

"Nowr we're-er goirng to-er eat'r, eat'r, brearkfarst." (I don't have enough finger power to put in all the 'r's, so just do it in your head from now). "Breakfast, okay? Breakfast. And then we will going to Tian Chi, okay? Tian Chi. It's mean Heaven Lake, okay? Heaven Lake. Tian Chi."

He glances over at me, seeing nothing or possibly a cockroach where I'm standing, and goes on with his finger-wagging lecture to the GROUP, which is divided between two big round tables.

The GROUP.

Not one of them is below 65 years of age, and most are over 70.

Don't get me wrong, I have nothing against the elderly. Many of my closest relatives are old. But... when I'm on a trip in China, and other places for that matter, I'd prefer people my own age. Call me prejudiced or ageist, it's just the way I am. These people are married, into the bargain.

But they are Chinese, that can't be denied. China Travel has honoured its promise.

I've often wondered about this thing about being Chinese. Is it a race, is it a lifestyle or is it a religion? In Cantonese, to 'go to China' is called *Fan Dai Lok* ('return to the mainland') as if that was the source of all life. According to the Royal Communist Party of China, to be Chinese is something that transcends borders and generations. Overseas Chinese (*Wah Kiu*) are seen as children of the motherland living temporarily abroad, although the family might have been settled outside China since 1823.

And it is this attitude towards what constitutes Chineseness, this bond to the mythical motherland whether you like it or not, that has to be the explanation for the success of the Communist Party in recruiting Overseas Chinese to come and work for them in the early years after the revolution in 1949.

Young, idealistic and well educated they came, from all the different coloured bits of the map, to help Mao build the New China. Family and friends begged them not to go, but it was China or nothing for them; they wanted only to give their all to the motherland. The blood of China ran thicker in their veins than the water of the countries where they, their parents, grandparents or great-grandparents, had settled.

And had it not also, perhaps, something to do with the lack of enthusiasm with which the indigenous population of these countries had embraced them? Was the irresistible attraction to China based on their need to be in a place where everybody looked like them, understood and accepted them?

Whatever motives these young idealists had, they were all made to regret bitterly their decision to answer Mao's call. After the initial glorious honeymoon where they were treated as heroes and given all sorts of privileges, they started being looked at with suspicion by the very people they had come to help. Soon they were accused of being spies because of their foreign connections. Even for Chinese who had never set foot abroad, let alone established any connections with foreigners, it was enough to have glanced at the cover of an issue of *Time* Magazine while walking past a dentist's window to be accused of being a spy; this vague label which the Communist Party uses to this day when they want to chuck people in the slammer without reason.

After a while the young idealists, having aged rapidly, were then arrested, often resulting in them shooting themselves repeatedly in the back while trying to cheat justice by jumping handcuffed from a seventh-floor window.

This and many other things prove my theory: It's not always smart to be self-sacrificing.

By the way, self-inflicted death while in custody, while most popular during the Cultural Revolution, is still going on today. In July 2010, a mainland newspaper published a list of reasons the Public Security Bureau have given for young Chinese men having died while under their protection:

Death by Blind Man's Bluff
Death by Showering
Death by Nightmare
Death by Sleeping in Improper Position
Death by Drinking Water
And of course that old staple: *Death by Picking at Acne...*

Yes, it seems that 'custody' has many meanings, and that the people in my GROUP had been, if not prescient, at least very smart not to answer the call to come and be killed all those years ago. While Huang churns on and on with words filled to the brim with the letter 'r', I sit down at the breakfast table. Here I am greeted by a dismal sight: China's tourism industry's take on a Western breakfast.

Because we're a tour GROUP we have our own ready-laid table and are not allowed to take anything from the hotel buffet – table legs straining to support the weight of the most exquisite-looking Chinese food. And because our GROUP consists of Overseas Chinese and one foreigner, who "can't eat Chinese food", we get this: five kinds of cake and three kinds of biscuit, neon-orange cheddar, butter, and jam. Not to mention scrambled eggs so pale that it looks like someone has taken a nuclear-powered suction pump to the hen and sucked all the nutrition out of it. And a sixth kind of cake.

There's not even Chinese tea, only coffee. As I incredulously gnaw on a biscuit I am introduced to the others who, after the initial huffy reaction to me turning up at 6:13 instead of 6:00 on the dot, are now all smiles and affability. I can tell they're wondering what I'm doing there, but nobody asks. I also wonder what *they* are doing on *my* holiday.

Two of them, the youngest couple at only 60-something, are fortunately from Hong Kong and can speak Cantonese, although they've been living in the US for 40 years. The others are from Singapore, the US, Malaysia and Indonesia – *Wah Kiu* who have decided to take a last trip around the motherland before throwing in the towel for good.

They all have the same goal now that they have retired, their gruelling Chinese working day come to an end: To have a fantastic, relaxing and culturally stimulating holiday in the New China, on a spanking new railway line.

"Oh-er, by-er ze wei," says Huang in his 'r'-filled Advanced American. "Zose'er train'rs are full-er, unfortur'nareterly. Ye'rs, is no'rt my faulrt. Zey are overbooker'ed. We'r have'r to get zehr burs instear'ed."

The bus. Instead of the train.

In retrospect I don't understand why I didn't sue China Travel and all its descendants. When I finally came home after ten days in hell, I was so relieved to still be alive that I just sent them a long and scathing letter which they never answered, in keeping with the tried-and-tested Chinese tradition.

We gather in the reception to go on the first sight-seeing trip of the TOUR, a boat trip on the "Heavenly Lake, Heavenly Lake, Heavenly Lake... Tian Chi". I don't feel like going. No, that's a bit weak. I'd rather peel the skin off my left arm with a razor than go. So it is in the reception, in front of 14 stunned old pensioners, that Huang and I have our first quarrel. I deeply regret having asked him to speak to me in Chinese, because in an argument I'm clearly at a disadvantage in that I can't speak so fast, don't understand everything and can't speak well when I'm angry.

Is he thinking the same thing? He smiles in a sly/diabolical way and speaks extra fast.

"You can't not come. You *have to* come."

"*Have* to? It's my holiday. I paid for it." Oh, and nobody's told me what to do since I was 16?

"But it's dangerous to go about by yourself. We have responsibility for you."

"Dangerous? I have been travelling by myself in China for a long... for many..."

"It says in the contract that all the members are coming on all the sight-seeing trips."

"Yes, but I don't want to come. It's my money. The trip is expensive. I want to ride a bicycle."

"*Bicycle*?" he turns his eyes to the heavens like Francis of Assisi. "It is dangerous to ride a bicycle. It says in the contract..."

And so on and so on in a never-ending idiotic loop while the poor pensioners, who have been ready to go, are starting to sit down around the reception. They're not so sprightly any more, poor dears. I do feel sorry for them, yes even more than for myself. Almost. Huang tries to appeal to my sense of shame by pointing out how the pensioners are weakening before our eyes and that it's all my fault. I retort that if he's so worried about them he can just take them to the damned lake and leave me alone.

This is incredible. We met eight hours ago and we're already having a more or less full-blown argument like an old married couple. The old married couples, on the other hand, aren't arguing at all but are just sitting there imploring the guide silently with their eyes: Let the blighted woman have her way so we can leave!

To help them I bid a curt farewell and start walking towards the lift. Huang tries to physically hold me back. I tell him to go to hell. He grabs my arms harder. The situation is approaching, with astonishing speed, a crisis to which the only solution is murder.

Suddenly I have a flash of inspiration. "I'll sign a paper saying I take responsibility for myself," I say. Huang immediately releases me.

"Okay. You can give it to me tonight."

After this day he treats me like a disobedient and intransigent child with an uncommonly low IQ; a child who is the result of its mother having had forced intercourse with a group of one-armed sailors with dandruff. He communicates with me solely through shouting across vast swathes of reception or restaurant areas, and informs me of meeting times and places up to 20 times, because he is afraid I will "be late." Although I always turn up for departures, dinners and other group things at least 15 minutes early, he always stands outside hopping, pointing at his watch and shouting things.

Well, the group has trotted off to the Heavenly'r Lake and now I must have breakfast. Cake and cheddar – in China! Yeah right. I feel I have been temporarily removed from my dear country and thrown into some surreal, but in a bad way, parallel universe with cheddar.

I borrow a bicycle from one of the receptionists and suddenly I'm in China again. But also not China, because the place is crawling with European-looking types. They all have beards and moustaches and look like extras from the film *1900*, or they wear flowing robes and skullcaps. They stand around selling kebabs and melons.

I'm drawn to these melons as by an unseen force. Now I know why they're called honey melons. They are the kind of yellow that was ubiquitous in the 1970s on a million Smileys, and I can smell them from the other side of the street. What a difference from the anaemic, tasteless parodies of fruit we have no choice but to buy from Hong Kong supermarkets. Oh God oh God, here is one of the reasons why I was born and set down on this globe. It is the sweetest, most insanely tasty fruit into whose cathedral I have ever been privileged to enter. Has it been soaked in sugar water?

But no, the moustache guy has cut it straight from the source, a colossal, torpedo-shaped thing in a pyramid of other honey melons. I eat a half-melon on the spot and the moustache guys laugh at my groaning and rolling of eyes. The price, one yuan, I'll have to endure.

But ridiculously cheap as everything is, it's a good thing I come loaded with some extra RMB (*renminbi*, 'People's Currency'). I already have a feeling I might have to eat a lot of breakfasts and other meals away from the bosom of the GROUP.

It seems that Urumqi consists of a sharply divided upper and lower class. The Han Chinese are well dressed and have shops with walls and doors. The indigenous population is dressed in rags, seen from a Western perspective, and sit or stand around the pavements selling things. Or they are begging.

This is my first foray into a Muslim country. Yes, I have to say country, for despite the incessant churning on of the Han Chinese about Xinjiang belonging to, and always having belonged to, etc, it is very obvious that this is not China. Take the cemetery for example. The skinny gravestones leaning hither and thither are decorated with sickle moons and stars, and have Arabic writing instead of Chinese characters.

Some miserably dressed Uyghurs with scrawny beards walk furtively around the cemetery. It almost looks as if they are scavenging for food; they are that rattling.

In the middle of a barren field stand some red-brick houses which look hastily put together. Children come running out, shouting the inevitable *Lao wai!*

I duly take their photographs, cursing myself for not having bought a digital camera so I can show them their likenesses at once, and again the inevitable conversation about whether I'm an American ensues. Those damned Americans. Because they are everywhere and do everything and make everything people see on TV, all Chinese think that all Whiteys are Americans.

Now it is evening and China Travel's big dinner arrangement. I join in, in order not to be seen as a total freak. I ask the others about the trip to the Heavenly Lake. Freezing cold and with heavy drizzle in an open boat, they tell me. Many group members had asked to go back to the hotel, but the guide had refused.

I nod darkly to myself, noticing that many of the weaker members are coughing and sneezing.

Now we have to sit at long tables waiting for the evening's hilarious entertainment by ethnic minorities. The guide sits at a separate table, fortunately. We're served great hulking slabs of mutton: Bone, heads and everything. At least there is beer, and as usual in China it is excellent.

But I want to be somewhere, anywhere, else. The traditional dance routine, in which Turkish-looking people bop around in cowboy gear to the sound of *Living La Vida Loca*, can only mollify me to a moderate degree.

The next morning we have to get up at 5:30 because the guide has decided that we have to see a museum before hitting the highlight of the day: Sheep polo with ethnic Kazakhs. If I want to see the sheep, I also have to see the museum.

This turns out to be a hangar-like building with the normal shards of glass, bowls and cooking utensils typical of any museum, the viewing of which I have always found engaging to a singularly small degree. But this museum has bagged an interesting thing: A mummy. A very thin, sad and badly dressed mummy reclining in a glass cabinet, upon which a plaque proudly declares: "This is a mummified corpse from 3,000 years from now."

Can it be... yes! It's the famous red-haired European mummy which the Chinese, with that sleight of hand only they can carry off, have managed to make into a kind of ethnic Chinese, another proof that Xinjiang has always belonged to and will always... blah blah zzzzzzzzzz.

Sheep polo turns out to be young men on horses fighting to gain control over a dead goat. Fun, and also fun to see people in Xinjiang Province who are not Han Chinese but who have jobs. Of course it's a pretty meaningless job created solely for tourists and in fact the guys seem to be fed up with tourists, but it's probably better than begging on the streets of Urumqi.

We are woken up earlier and earlier every day. The third day I'm ripped out of dreamland at 4:00am, because Huang the guide has decided we have to see a fruit market before going east... by minibus. Yes.

Not train.

Not even normal bus.

Minibus.

As I stagger semi-conscious towards the reception to check out, Huang shouts, so loud the chandeliers in the reception start tinkling, that I have run away from the bill of the mini bar, trying to STEAL TWO BEERS!!!

It can't be denied – it's total war.

Now we're driving through the desert which, instead of consisting of undulating sand dunes, looks more than anything like a gigantic potato field that hasn't been tilled for years. I'm sitting in the back of the bus, which is the size of a roomy Beetle, with my knees draped around my ears because my seat is above the wheel. A staggering amount of suitcases lie stacked up behind me, and to avoid a suitcase avalanche hitting me every time the bus stops, I have to sit and hold them back with one arm.

A local guide has joined us. She sits in the front of the bus, more or less on top of the driver, talking incessantly into a microphone about how many years it took the PLA to develop Xinjiang Province and how long the river is and how many centimetres the mountain is, and how much the desert weighs...

Although the microphone possesses an awesome decibel power, it is strangely soporific, and everybody who doesn't have to hold up suitcases is soon fast asleep. Or pretending to be.

This is the first time I've ever been in a desert and, when the local guide screeches that we've arrived in an oasis and how big it is, it's my first time in an oasis. I thought an oasis was a pond with a couple of palm trees and a half-dead man dressed in rags going "water... water..." and I'm not a little disappointed to see that it is actually your common-or-garden nondescript Norwegian farmland with potato fields, a river and some not very densely foliaged trees.

We are nazi'd out of the bus to look at this. And this is the deal, and tour travel in China in a nutshell: Spending hours and hours in an extremely uncomfortable bus. Stopping at a famous place where there are 200 other buses and hundreds of other guides engaged in a fight to the death over the title 'Mr. (and Miss) Universe Loudest Megaphone Screamer.' Brisk ten-minute jog through famous place followed by two hours in souvenir shop.

The poor pensioners shop and shop, for, being old and weak, they dare not disobey the guide. Many of them have had to buy extra suitcases to fit in the hundreds of toy camels, painted mugs and colourful wall hangings the guide has more than hinted it's their moral, nay, patriotic! duty to buy.

As this is the only tour I have ever been on, I can't really compare it to any such thing as a well organised and interesting tour. People have indicated they exist. But I don't think they exist in China, at least not unless the tourism authorities have made a complete about-turn and started putting the customer first.

For foreign and domestic tourists both, China Travel's method is to herd people around at top speed, feed them sub-standard food and sell them useless crap of the kind that, when they get home, they sit shaking their heads incredulously, saying: "Norman, what in the world's bollocking bladder-burst could ever have induced me to buy an orange plastic car shaped like Mickey Mouse with 'Silk Road' written in flames on the bonnet?"

I'll tell you what: The guide, that's what. To increase his miserable income, sometimes even to have one, he will hold the tourists ransom in the souvenir shops, not letting them out before they've bought 30 plastic yaks and three mugs with pictures of Chairman Mao. Hotels, restaurants and shops are all in on the scam; you have to eat, shop and live it their way (the sub-standard way) or you will be severely punished.

For mainland tourists visiting Hong Kong, the situation is even worse because many of the trips are so cheap that only a considerable revenue from shopping can save the profit. The poor obedient mainlanders are locked into jewellers and other retail shops, not being allowed out before they have spent a certain (huge) amount of cash.

One tour guide left the entire group stranded in the middle of nowhere in the New Territories (a 'remote' area of Hong Kong) because they refused to buy more gold ornaments. When confronted, he said huffily that they should have known what the deal was; a trip that cheap was bound to have some hidden caveats.

True. But how about *my* trip, which is really, really expensive? Am I not entitled to eat some good food and to stay longer than a few minutes in some of the admittedly quite interesting places we are taken (dragged) to? Apparently not. It appears that China's tourism industry is a kind of fascist organisation attracting the bossy, solipsistic and, well, borderline psychotic, to work for them. The tourist is merely a money cow to be milked not only dry but into a kind of powder. He is more malleable thus.

The rest of the trip is a fog of minibus driving and holding up of an ever-increasing number of suitcases, pensioner chatting and guide screaming, terrible food, souvenir shops and depression, all accompanied by sarcastic comments from Huang who laughs when he sees the elderly struggling with their heavy loads.

Ah, but there is a glimmer of light. The last stretch from Xian to Beijing will be by train. First-class cabins, naturally. This also means first-class waiting rooms. Now the pensioners are made to regret being forced to buy so much crap for the grandchildren, for first-class waiting rooms in China are always on the second floor or higher, in case of floods.

A humorous (ironic?) fate has made sure the escalators of Xian Station have broken down on this day, and the elderly are made to drag their suitcases up the stairs step by step, to shouts of "hurry up" from the empty-handed guide.

Ecstasy at being just 24 hours away from freedom makes me run up and down those stairs light as a bird with load after heavy load. Being ageist I naturally don't give a toss about the old dears; no, I help them carry just to irritate the guide. What the hell? In a few minutes I'll be on a moving train.

And now I'm on it; the train, the glorious train. My journey can begin.

First-class cabins in China are made for four persons. When I get to mine, I discover I'll be sharing it with one person only.

It is the guide.

8

Upon Each Life a Little Train Must Fall

No, never again an organised tour. I would rather be dragged backwards through a toilet drain. And going through the Gobi Desert by minibus – it's like going to the toilet with skis, wearing a strait-jacket.

The only way to travel, hopefully or not, is by train. TRAIN!

When I wrote the following I was sitting in a luxury four-person train cabin I had all to myself: The two guys I shared it with – from Lanzhou, the provincial capital of Gansu (*and* cradle of Chinese civilisation) – had just left the train and I was going to have *my own room* for almost 24 hours.

> To be on a train, frequently and for long periods of time, is an inseparable part of the China Experience. If you compare, train-wise, for example Britain and China, China will emerge the undisputed winner. In Britain you get on the train (if it appears at all), sit down and have a cup of undrinkable coffee and some cardboard with ham, and then you're there. In China you can get on the train and still not have reached your destination, in extreme cases, after four days. That's the kind of train trip I like.
>
> At this particular moment I'm sitting here looking with one eye (I'm wall-eyed) at the brown and parched hills of Shaanxi Province where people live in caves dug out of the soft earth of hillsides, reinforced with splendid brick fronts. The sun is beating

down mercilessly on the brown landscape, on the meagre fields delicately bordered with stones, and on the bronzed farmers watering them with water buckets hanging from yokes. It looks like a black-and-white photograph that's been kept in a drawer for 83 years, slowly turning brown.

I'm actually a little bit three sheets to the wind, and in the middle of the morning at that, forced to drink by that relentless creator of alcoholics, Chinese hospitality. Last night, when I entered the cabin and pushed my bag under the lower bunk for which I had paid an extra 11 yuan, the two guys occupying the cabin sat looking at me a little desolately. This was after all a social situation; it was them and me in a tiny room with four bunks, so they had to say something, but knew no English.

I quickly broke the ice by asking if they fancied a game of cards, a game of *Choh Dai Di*, the famous Hong Kong staple of social intercourse.

They naturally said yes without hesitation and with some relief at the *Lao Wai* being able to do some quacking in Putonghua. After a brief introduction to the game they started thrashing me.

This seems to be the norm.

Most Chinese come equipped with a natural ability for cards that your average Johnny Foreigner can only observe wistfully and from a great depth. I think this is rooted in the innate mathematical skills of the Chinese, apparently based on the fact that they don't have 'eleven' and 'twelve,' only 'ten one, ten two.'

But the two geezers I shared the cabin with, the misters Wang and Fang, were drunk on *bai jiu*, and full of merriment as I started catching up with them again after the initial shock of being beaten senseless by amateurs. Although they were stealthy and underhand in cards, they just couldn't beat my 16 years of experience in the noble art of *Choh Dai Di*.

Still, beneath the jovial exterior they were still competitive Chinese guys, and so they decided to get me drunk too.

Beer and spirits are the order of the day on Chinese trains, and the trolleys bearing these and other necessities such as peanuts, pickled pigs' trotters and toilet paper shuttle incessantly up and down the corridors. Thus numerous bottles of beer appeared on the table, which was lovingly decorated with a plastic rose and that day's edition of *China People's Railway Daily*. It was two in the morning and I was still winning.

"Another beer, another beer," chanted Mr Wang, looking in vain for the beer trolley which, all justice be told, had stopped rolling at one o'clock. Off he dashed to the restaurant car, which was also, in a mysterious and unheard-of affront, closed.

There we sat with long faces; there was nothing else to do but roll over and lay down on the soft and comfortable bunk.

I awoke at 08:00, hangover-less, as Chinese beer is not only the best tasting in the world but also very pure and not very strong. You can quaff five or six big bottles of an evening without noticeable after-effects.

Wang and Fang probably felt it was their fault that the restaurant car had closed at such an inappropriate hour. Therefore, what I encountered when I came back to the little cabin after brushing my teeth this morning wasn't breakfast, but three big bottles of beer.

I was about to ask if they'd gone completely bonkers but remembered in the nick of time that one must never refuse Chinese hospitality, so off we went again with card playing and drinking.

That's why I'm now sitting here feeling relatively benevolent with a whole little room to myself, breathing in its soothing fumes of stale and fresh booze. I had actually bought the ticket to this first-class (soft sleeper) cabin because there are electric sockets in the corridor; I was planning to plug in my laptop there and write a word or two on the long train ride from Lanzhou to Guangzhou.

I had even bought a new 210-yuan cable for this purpose, so imagine my shock and dismay when I found that the sockets in the corridor had three legs where my plug had only two. I'm now thinking, as I have thousands of times before: Why can't plugs, sockets and, well, everything to do with electricity, be the same all over the world? Preferably the same as the three square pegs that are the norm in Hong Kong and Britain.

The staff working in the soft sleeper compartments are more service-minded than those working in hard sleepers, that is true, but even after applying my most humble train face and begging two different attendants to give me an adaptor, I was refused. Also, they insisted, the sockets in the corridor were out of power. I had paid all that extra money for first-class (soft sleeper), boring in the extreme compared to second-class (hard sleeper), in vain. I had two hours' worth of battery for a 36-hour journey (15 of which were fortunately spent playing cards.) I only had one unread book left and all was looking pretty grim.

Then the manager of the two first-class carriages appeared.

"Hello, I know you. You were on this train in April, right?"

Waaaah, what were the *chances*?

Actually quite high. The train can only ever go there and back again, due to the nature of its rails, so considering how many times I have been to Lanzhou and back, it's strange that I don't always run into train staff I know. And yes, I had been on this train in April, on an Easter holiday train trip with Richard and his brother. We'd had a very memorable trip from Lanzhou to Guangzhou, spending most of the trip in the restaurant car where we were entertained by a guy from Inner Mongolia with waist-length hair who sang and danced around, plastered.

"Well, hee hee, you remember me?"

"Yes of course I remember you. It was you and your cousin. You drank up all our beer." A strange statement considering how much the Chinese drink. But most of them get on the train laden with their own beer which costs two yuan in the shops, a third of the price on the train.

"So, where is your cousin?"

I had been forced to tell people that Richard was my cousin after the fourth person in two days had taken him for my son, an awful prospect seeing as he was only 14 years younger than me and would, if indeed he were my son, be the result of a ghastly union between me and a ginger-haired, towering whitey. But of course the Chinese can't tell how old (or disgustingly young) we beige'ies are. Also, despite reforms of this and that, they are still surprisingly strait-laced in matters of the flesh. The only relationship they can possibly imagine between a woman and a younger man, younger even by a few minutes, is therefore that of mother and son.

Another thing I've realised about the Chinese over the years is that they actually can't tell the difference between us Caucasians. So I was well pleased when the carriage master recognised me. I was even more pleased when she told me I could just put the laptop in the control room and charge away.

We had a good conversation about Chinese men. One minute I was plugging in the charger, the next I was listening to a lament about how thoughtful and affectionate Chinese guys are until they get married, but as soon as the ring is on the finger and the one child – a son, naturally – is in the bag, the scenario changes completely. Then it's whoring and drinking day and night, and, she darkly hinted, more than a little violence.

She also complained about her life as train staff, although I thought she'd done well for herself after having been 'sent down' to the countryside to dig ditches as a young and idealistic student in the 70s, managing to escape and start a train career in the dreaded *ying zuo* (hard seat compartment) with its drunken peasants sitting up three days on the trot, and working her way up to become the boss of *ruan wo,* soft sleeper.

She also got rid of her worthless and abusive husband, and now lived for her son who was studying media communication at a university in Guangzhou. If she played her cards right she could end up in an administrative position in some transport department, although these positions probably get ripped away by young whippersnappers with no train experience but with a university education, like her son.

Now it is afternoon on the train. The sun sends its orange rays slanting down on all of Henan Province and on gigantic, coal-driven power stations interspersed by fields, watered carefully with buckets hanging from yokes by the same kind of nut-brown and barefoot peasants as in Shaanxi.

Six-lane highways high in the sky on massive legs of concrete run across the fields. One should be thankful the authorities have decreed that the highways are heaven-bound and not built right on the fields themselves. As it is, the peasants can keep growing the food which will keep the train staff, the passengers, and China alive, using methods which haven't changed for millennia.

Thinking about this I become solemn, feeling strongly the echoes of generations before me, the song of the ages... or maybe I'm just sloshed. Also being on trains in China frequently makes me solemn. It is one of the greatest experiences I, and thereby the human race, can have. Sitting by the window watching China go by outside; what better cure for existentialist angst? There is not a single lull.

If a whole month goes by without any kind of train journey in the motherland, I get all paranoid and break out in a rash. I must have... give me some... please get me some *train!!!* Yes, I'm definitely three sheets, if not more, to the wind. Time to write an ode to trains:

Train addicts are the same all over the world. Show us a station and some steam coming up under a train body and we start champing at the bit. It doesn't really matter where the train goes, what's important for a trainophile is to be on the train and to stay on it. In that respect the Trans-Siberian Railway, which brought me to China 18 years ago, is the granddaddy of all train journeys.

This epic journey, immense as *War and Peace*, more romantic than *Dr. Zhivago* and *Anna Karenina* put together but without the tragedy, is one everyone should undertake at least once in their lifetime. However, be warned: The food is abysmal. As soon as the train rolls out of Moscow Station, the 10-item menu reveals its true face: it has one item and it is cabbage.

Chinese trains, on the other hand, cater to people who are particular about their food and won't be fobbed off with a few slivers of elderly cruciferous vegetable matter masquerading as Chicken Kiev. They expect the same superior standard from a six-yuan bowl of noodles cooked in the cramped and sooty kitchen of a train rattling through the great loess plains of Northern China as they do from a meal in a five-star restaurant. No matter how long the train journey, fresh produce from land and sea is therefore at hand in the dining car, more or less 24 hours a day.

While the Trans-Siberian restaurant car has strict limits for passenger use and the surly staff rips the plates away from you before you have swallowed the last miserable morsel, the dining car on a Chinese train is a veritable Free State of China. Anything goes. You can saunter in any time you like, stay as long as you like, and do what you like.

You can drink ridiculously cheap world-class beer (every little county has its own brand worth testing) and you can smoke. In fact, it might be better if you *do* smoke, as other patrons tend to indulge with abandon. Well settled over a sumptuous meal you can engage in loud banter with the grinning waiters and with the many policemen patrolling the train – telepathically from their table in the corner.

Although eating is encouraged it is not, unlike the Trans-Siberian, obligatory (not to say oligarch-ory) and you can spend all day in this pub on wheels just playing cards and drinking tea or beer – as often as not with the staff themselves.

There is another area in which Chinese trains far outshine their Russian counterparts, and that is what goes on outside the windows. Just as its train menu has one item, so Russia basically has one view: A huge and menacing sky, grey as steel, pressing down on huts huddling submissively, knee-deep in Siberian steppe. There is the occasional person to be seen, invariably a Russian peasant woman swaddled in layers of indefinable cloth, struggling grimly through mud.

This is your view for six days and it does get monotonous.

But China! If there weren't so many things to do on the train, you would be glued to the window all day marvelling at the scenery. For landscape-wise, China has everything.

There are lush and mysterious tropical rainforests and stern rocky deserts, majestic mountain ranges and mighty, raging rivers, scraggy crags shrouded in mist looking exactly like a thousand Chinese paintings, and fastidious paddy fields where peasants plod barefoot behind oxen.

China has ultra-modern cities and medieval villages, narrow, teeming alleyways and vast, empty country. You can see it all from the train.

In the northern provinces with their stark and utilitarian beauty, simplicity rules. Everything is grey. Grey-brick houses, grey earth, peasants in grey clothes shuffle down grey and dusty country roads lined with grey trees. Then, a sudden explosion of red: The Chinese flag with its five yellow stars, flapping proudly in the northern wind. It's a photographer's heaven.

And everywhere, from the wealthy east coast with its ever-increasing number of billionaires to the impoverished western provinces plagued with drought, are the people of China. Thronging the stations, waiting with their bicycles for the train to pass, squatting in silent contemplation in a field or waving enthusiastically to the train, there is no place where they are not.

The best place to meet China's teeming billions is on the train. Armed with a phrasebook and surrounded by friendly and patient people who love to talk to foreigners, you can't fail to find friends. If you're in the right kind of carriage, that is.

There are four classes of carriage: Soft and hard sleeper and soft and hard seat. Soft sleeper is the boring way to travel. You're stuck in a tiny cabin with three other people, invariably fat provincial cadres on their way home from wallowing in illicit pleasures on taxpayers' money. All they want to do is sleep and eat sunflower seeds. The cabin is freezing and you're shut off from the world.

Hard seat... is hard. It is in fact a wooden straight-backed bench which may or may not have a thin layer of upholstery, and which you share with two other people. This is the travel method of the poor, which until a few years ago meant almost everybody. Although mind-bogglingly cheap, it is not recommended for journeys of more than a few hours. But for meeting people and testing your hardiness it can't be beat.

Soft seats are just normal train seats which can recline several millimetres. Here you can't sleep *and* can't play cards, so what's the point?

No, the real China train experience where you can chat with passengers, drink beer, play cards *as well as* sleep in style, is definitely in hard sleeper. Here you share a whole carriage with the general populace, in bunks stacked three high. This is sleep made in heaven.

After a hard night of card playing and beer drinking, what could be more soporific than being carried into dreamland by the gentle rocking of the train, accompanied by the sibilant murmurs of, for example, three electricians from Shanghai…

The next morning you wake up to rousing revolutionary music and the train attendant sweeping away the debris from last night's bacchanalia. On the way to the washroom you run into two of the guys who thrashed you at Chinese poker in the restaurant car. You realise they are actually conductors, drinking and socialising on the job, not just party animals with unusual sartorial taste. None of you are looking your best, but hey, you're all on the same train. And so begins another languid, carefree day on the Free State of Chinese Train.

Forget 'hopefully'. To travel *at all* is better than to arrive when you are on a train in China.

And here I am on the train again, on the train again for God-knows-what time. Unfortunately Chinese trains are punctual to the point of fascism and the train trundles into the station at exactly 16:27 as promised. But I don't feel like getting off. I want to stay and stay on the train in China until I die.

Ode to trains: Done! If I can get that published, maybe more China-fearers will shuffle out of their little 'Home – Work – Lan Kwai Fong – Phuket' cocoon and get on the grand adventure. Probably not.

Disturbed by the bell! Or rather, a knock! It's someone in uniform wanting to see my proof of existence. A reason, or rather, another reason to avoid soft sleeper cabins is that the train staff inexplicably check the ID of those travelling in them, while hard sleeper and hard seat passengers are allowed to sleep on, unchecked. Are terrorists more likely to travel first-class? Is it because soft sleeper normally is just one or two cars, so checking people's IDs is a project that can actually be finished? Or is there another reason known only to the Chinese Interior Ministry?

That's what I had time to write that day before a blessed drunken sleep overcame me. I arrived in Guangzhou with more power on my laptop than when I got on the train. Thank you, newly divorced Mrs. Yang of soft sleeper manager fame! But I couldn't stop wondering why it is that first-class passengers come under such scrutiny by the authorities.

I noticed this puzzling phenomenon again in 2008, just before the Olympics. I was with my 'cousin' Richard on the overnight train from Urumqi to the edge of the Taklamakan Desert. For some reason – no, not for 'some' reason, it was because Richard hated the throngs in hard sleeper – we were in a soft sleeper cabin. We had just settled down with a couple of bottled beers by the corridor window, where we planned to watch yet another spectacular sunset, when a policeman turned up to check our passports. All right, but after having checked my passport, for some inexplicable reason this policeman wanted to see what was in my bag.

When he found several cans of hairspray (all almost empty; it's very windy in Xinjiang) he lit up like a Christmas tree doused in petrol and set on fire. Well not really, actually. He looked like the chief yokel at the annual yokel ball for world record holders in yokel-dom, all staring eyes and hanging mouth. He seemed to be overcome with a kind of joy and trembling with fear at the same time. Joy, because he had something to do (and perhaps that his infallible instincts for rooting out lethal weapons had served him well again.) Fear, because he didn't really know what to do when a formerly only theoretical scenario had become reality.

I, being Norwegian and not unused to dealing with police, of course started with the facts.

"Officer. It's hairspray. I use it on my hair to keep it in place." (And not clinging Scandinavianly to my head.)

"No, it's a dangerous flammable material!" he said, pointing to the skull on the canister. "You see? Skull. Poison. And explosive."

I suggested he just keep it for the duration of the journey and give it back before we got off, but that made him irate. And stern.

"This is flammable! It is illegal to carry flammable goods on a train. You have broken the law of China."

Oh dear, not again. The last time I broke the law of China was at Christmas when I took a photo of a baby *inside a train station.*

On that occasion, Richard and I were in Liupanshui ('Six Basins of Water') in the north-western part of Guizhou province, and it was here that we had felt the full, crushing weight of the Chinese legal system.

We had remarked upon the ease with which we had been able to check into hotels of late; a glance at my Hong Kong ID card with my name in Chinese seemed to be sufficient to register us both, although we stayed in separate rooms – the receptionists were only too happy not to have to bother with cumbersome passports and tricky spelling.

Wandering through a market where chillies in their myriad forms ruled the roost, we were approached by a geezer in a black leather jacket. He pulled out a police ID.

"Police. What are you doing here?"

"Walking around."

"But what are you doing here in Liupanshui?"

"Why do you ask?"

"I work at a station down the road and we've had a phone call about two foreigners walking around the market, taking photos. Where are you staying?"

Lost for words I showed him the hotel card.

Cool! 19 years of travelling in China and I was *reported on* at last! He thanked us and buggered off.

Back at the hotel, the receptionists were in a state.

"You have to fill in forms! We forgot! It's for your own safety! We need passports! Visas!... and your Hong Kong ID, how long is it valid?"

"I see. You've had a phone call from the police?"

"Er... yes. You must wait for them here. They must see your... things and er... it's for your own safety..."

Having already checked out hours before and with our luggage stored in reception, we saw no need to fill out any more forms. Ignoring the receptionists' plaintive cries about our safety we legged it down to the train station to lose ourselves in the crowds heading home for Chinese New Year. With my blonde head and Richard's six-foot-one frame, the law would never find us.

As we waited for the train in the freezing waiting hall with millions of people, I was hoping to see a police van come screeching round the corner, a SWAT team leaping out in mid-screech and swarming in, wrestling me to the ground demanding to see my ID. Richard was more apprehensive, afraid they would make us miss our train.

Unfortunately nothing happened and we just joined the crush of people trying to force their way, 60 abreast, through the narrow gate where barking ticket inspectors egged them on. On the platform we had a bit of a giggle. Safe at last!

But the rozzers got us in the end. We were just about to board the train, congratulating ourselves on our lucky escape, when a fat, rosy-cheeked uniformed policeman, a bruiser in fact, caught me by the elbow.

"Have you been taking photos in the station area?"

"Er... yes? And?" Damn! I should have said: What took you so long?

"We've been told about a foreigner taking photos in the station area. It is illegal and you have to erase them."

It was true; I had taken a photo of thousands of people fighting to get through the gates to the platform, and also a particularly incriminating one of a Yi minority woman with a baby in a sling. These I deleted amid much commenting by bystanders. Oh well, the photos were of inferior quality anyway.

Reported, no, ratted on, *twice in one day!* This was the life. I made a mental note of looking up "I am a spy working for the Norwegian government" in my dictionary.

So you see, after this unsettling experience in Six Basins of Water I was used to dealing with the police in China and secretly thought it was quite good fun; but Richard, alone with now four bottles of beer in the train corridor, didn't like it much. He just liked guys, but not guys in uniform.

No, I wasn't afraid of the police at all, and I really, really needed my hairspray. After a lot of arguing where both the policeman and I got more and more irate, he sat down in the cabin and started calling for back-up. Meanwhile, outside the train, an otherworldly beautiful dusk was slowly sinking, bathing the mountains in bright pink and blue, like the dresses of two of the fairy godmothers in the Disney version of *Sleeping Beauty*.

Richard came with more beer, but I felt the stern and irate copper in our cabin rather inhibiting for my party mood. Then I had a brilliant idea.

"How about I write a self-criticism?"

"You must be joking."

I then knew all was lost. But I could have done it – I had done it before. I was working for TV2 Norway during the Hong Kong handover in 1997, as an interpreter, translator and general fixer. We went for some reason to Shanghai, where the producer wanted to do a 'random people in the street' thing about the handover. These were the two questions he wanted to ask them:

How do you feel about the handover?

Do you like Hong Kong?

Out we went into the streets of Shanghai; the producer, the cameraman and I. I had warned the producer about cameras and microphones being like kryptonite to the mainland police – no, the opposite of kryptonite as it worked like a magnet on them – but being Norwegian he didn't believe me. "Let's go ahead and set it up! They're just some innocent questions..."

"Yeah but the police don't know that."

"Yeah, whatever. Let's go!"

We lasted about seven minutes. In the middle of the talk with the third person gushing about how ecstatic she was that Hong Kong would finally return to the motherland and how she really loved Hong Kong, the coppers descended like rain. Van, plain-clothes, uniformed, guns, everything.

After a short stand-off we were whisked to the police station where the cops watched the whole tape, including footage of the producer interviewing Governor Chris Patten on the lawn of Government House in Hong Kong. This, the policemen informed me, they would have to confiscate. We could keep the camera though. Oh, and we would have to write self-criticisms, promising never to do anything without permission ever again.

I have to say that I enjoyed it thoroughly. My first self-criticism: In 1997! About bloody time. I wrote mine in Chinese, naturally (I. Promise. Hereafter. If. Shoot Film. Definitely. Will. Ask. Police. Give. Me. Permission. If Not. Police. Can. Punish Me.) and somehow when we were finally released after about three hours, we had the tape, un-erased, and everything with us. Chinese cops are all talk, really. Unless you happen to be Chinese...

I was just telling Richard this story when, at the next station, two more policemen turned up. One of them was young and cute. Ish. He was laughing and treating the whole thing like the joke it was, and also shaking his head at the other guy's insistence on prosecuting me and possibly taking me off the train for having violated Chinese law in such an outrageous manner. He took off his hat and showed me his flat hat-hair, joking that he could do with some hairspray of his own. Ha ha.

Time went by and the sun was setting.

Now came another interrogation and the showing of my Hong Kong ID card. Because it had my name in Chinese, they concentrated on that with only a cursory glance at my passport. Yes, for them at least, I was a true Hong Kong compatriot.

"Hmm. You're still beautiful. Chinese women your age – pah!" spat the younger guy. Charmer! I liked him more and more. The beer helped too.

The flat landscape was covered in wind turbines, and with the pink and blue skies dotted with clouds and the jagged, treeless mountains on the horizon I couldn't control myself but had to take photos. This entailed going in and out of the cabin a lot, as the beautiful view was visible only from the windows in the corridor. I realised another cool thing about China: It's possible to be interrogated by the police, get drunk and do touristy things all at the same time.

An hour had already passed, amid much calling of stations, reading of the Chinese label of the hairspray canisters and sucking of teeth.

It was eventually decided that I would be free to go, or rather, stay, but that the hairspray would be confiscated and *not* returned to me. Christ on a suction pump!

But when the younger guy took my hand and lovingly put my fingerprint on the eight or so pages of the report, all of which I had signed with my Chinese name, I started feeling rather good.

Being touched by charming rozzer while drinking beer and darting in and out of cabin taking photos – I could get used to this. Two hours had now passed, it was completely dark and it was time to wrap the thing up. I was a criminal and spray-less, but had a certificate with many stamps confirming this. That was something.

The sterner cop had also begun smiling and joking after his two colleagues turned up and he was in the majority, and sat playing with my ID card round and round. Suddenly he froze.

"But… hang on. What nationality are you?"

"Ha? Didn't I just tell you, Hong Kong compatriot?"

"Yes but what minority are you?"

"Ha?"

"Yes, in China we have 54 nationalities, Han, Mongol, Hui, Yi, Yao…"

"Oh. Just 'Human'. In Hong Kong we're just Hong Kong people or non Hong Kong people." (Not entirely true, but hey.)

"Oh all right."

I saw an opening. "So I can pick up my hairspray in Korla?"

"No, we have to take it. It's for your own safety."

Oh really! Having flat, limp, village idiot hair is safer, is it? Of course, nobody was under the tiniest illusion that it was actually my safety they were worried about. For this was July 2008, three weeks before the sacred Beijing Olympics, and I could therefore only assume that their real worry had been that, after having craftily gone directly south-west from Urumqi, I would suddenly turn east, break through the heavily armed barriers protecting Beijing and then go on to spray down the entire Olympic Games.

Ha! I say. Because even if I had wanted to, I couldn't have. My three-year visa would run out just a few days before the Olympics were supposed to start, and to avoid too many troublesome foreigners at this, China's greatest moment, the authorities didn't issue any new visas between April and October that year.

Therefore, although for visa reasons I was angry with the Olympic Games and did try to sabotage them by saying things like "I think all grandiose sports arrangements like these are a waste of time and money," actual physical destruction would be out of the question.

So the magnificent Olympic Games of 2008 had to go ahead without me. And without a hell of a lot of other foreigners, as apparently even people who had bought tickets to the games were denied visas.

Beijing probably thought: "Why let a bunch of foreigners in to create trouble and maybe even support non-Chinese athletes? We have our own spectators."

The whole country thereby became more or less inaccessible to foreigners for months, and it worked: The Olympic Games went off without a hitch. The flower beds were spectacular and China won every medal.

Still – you had to wonder why the government thought there was such a threat to national security and unity (and harmony) in, say, a geezer from Belgium or Sweden trying to enter Guangzhou, 2,294 kilometres from the Games, to set up a deal involving stationery. You'd think with the security that was in force, even the most wily of foreign saboteurs would have been wrestled to the ground before they had as much as a chance to get the hairspray out of their handbag.

No! said Beijing. Stay out, you anti-harmony trouble-mongers, you.

So the result was that I couldn't even go on a day trip to Shenzhen between August and October, and believe me, it was vexing.

As well as being probably the most politicised, most fraught-with-symbolism Games since Berlin in 1936, the Beijing Olympics must have been the best-prepared and with the most far-reaching consequences. Not satisfied with making sure a lot of foreigners couldn't enter the country, leaving high-end hotels in the city deserted, Beijing shut down all factories in the area for weeks before August 2008 to ensure clean air. Private car driving was, for once, regulated to ensure smooth traffic flow and blue skies, and all the undesirable people like beggars and unskilled immigrant labourers were taken off the streets. Foreign students were 'asked' to leave the city for the duration. Journalists who had reported unfavourably or critically on the event were harassed by police long before the Games started, not to be seen in print again.

A new highway was built in Tibet – halfway up the north side of Everest, one of the most pristine areas on earth – to accommodate the bearers of the Olympic torch. Most of Beijing's *hutong* neighbourhoods were obliterated to make way for four-lane roads, shiny luxury apartment buildings and gleaming shopping malls, all in the name of "presenting a modern, international face for the Olympics."

On a more personal level, a little eight-year-old girl was forced by her father's insane ambitions to run 3,650 kilometres from Hainan to Beijing to "celebrate" the Olympics.

Oh, and the foreigners who were allowed to enter China, and actually watch the young people running round and round a track, were not allowed to wear identical T-shirts or wave banners.

I watched the opening ceremony at the Hong Kong Yacht Club. Was it impressive? Hell yes! Especially impressive was the way the authorities transplanted one girl's voice onto another girl's image, as the girl with the best singing voice was deemed too ugly to be seen on TV. "A nice little start in life for an eight-year-old" would be the normal Western reaction, but she did sacrifice herself for her country, right?

The other girl, the beautiful one, later came to Hong Kong to sing in a shopping centre. (Most acts coming to Hong Kong, the self-proclaimed "Asia's World City", perform in shopping malls. This is fitting, as most people spend their spare time in these.) The rumours about her voice being inferior, in fact not even fit for TV, had apparently been correct.

So that was 2008 out the window, along with my deeply needed hairspray (hey! *You* try having Norwegian hair, a quarter of the thickness of normal hair) but as mentioned, I managed to get a massive train trip out of it before it was too late: Hong Kong via Lanzhou to Urumqi and back. That's something like three times the distance to the moon.

Still, I wonder why, since I'm such a train lover, I don't really like boats. Well, I don't dislike boats. But once you're on one of them, crossing for example the Atlantic Ocean, that's pretty much it. You can't go anywhere and there's nothing much to look at except steely-grey water in various stages of torment.

But seeing as I'd started on this 'always try something new' rigmarole, I let myself be talked into going onto a boat deck. It was in the name of research, I hasten to add. Just like those Japanese whale catchers.

9

Three Georges: Orwell, Orwell and Orwell

The most famous victim of Modern China's destructive urges is the Three Gorges.

The Gorges is (or are) one of China's biggest tourist attractions, both for foreign and domestic tourists. It is the Yangzi River, seldom mentioned in print without being preceded by 'the mighty', that has dug out the fabled gorges, waterfalls and cliffs on its journey from the Himalayas to the Pacific Ocean. In Chinese it's called *Chang Jiang*, the Long River, and it has to be said, it's not short.

It's also not puny or a mere trickle; no, 'awesome,' 'majestic' and 'wild' are adjectives often bandied about, as well as the above-mentioned 'mighty.' Where the Yellow River is known as "China's Sorrow" because of frequent flooding and unpredictability, the Yangzi is a kind of Ganges of China; the source of most life and a mythical force towering in Chinese minds for thousands of years. So when the news came that China's government would at last fulfill its long-cherished dream of taming the mighty Yangzi by building a gigantic dam across the most spectacular part of the river, many people were left speechless. Actually, they were left speech*full;* angry protests soon flooded in from near and far.

To put the Three Gorges themselves under water – wouldn't that be like filling the Grand Canyon with cement? Turning the Niagara Falls into jelly? Redeveloping the Pyramids of Egypt into a parking lot?

And what about the 1.5 million living on the riverbanks – a mere 1.5 million people being of course a drop in the ocean China-wise, but a not insignificant amount of people – where would they go?

Ha! The authorities said, after silencing the worst protesters in the time-honoured manner of locking them up after some light beating. It was of course those very 1.5 million people they intended to save! The Yangzi has always been a temperamental gentleman who blows his top easily and frequently, causing death and devastation. By harnessing the river's awesome (and mighty) powers, they could save lives in droves. A wonderful example of 'for your own safety.'

This argument, beautiful as it sounded, was taken with a pinch of salt by many if not all. Wouldn't a more plausible explanation be that a dam on the Long River could generate 84.7 billion kilowatt hours per year?

In addition (and some suspected most importantly), wouldn't it be China's biggest showcase of engineering art ever and give the nation face in front of the whole world, not least compared to the US and her puny Hoover Dam?

Biggest! Best! Fastest!

A friend of mine in Hong Kong, a frequent China-goer who didn't speak a word of Mandarin or Cantonese, started nagging me about going on a cruise up (or down, depending) the Mighty etc, etc Yangzi to see the famous gorges, falls and cliffs. I had been on the Yangzi once, taking a local passenger boat up the flat and uninteresting-looking part just west of Shanghai and getting off at Wuhan. Although the boat had been equipped with a karaoke room, and the normal China party action (with cards) had taken place, I felt that if I had seen one Yangzi River I had probably seen them all.

I also saw that I could easily end up having adverse psychological reactions to being locked up on a boat, surrounded by tourists. Tourists from... all over the world, really, except China. I tried to avoid what I already felt could turn into a catastrophe.

"Can't we just take the train up there, buy a ticket for a normal boat and...?"

My friend, Gillian, looked at me with a hurt expression. Me and my pathological need for freedom.

"No, let's get a gang of people together and do a tour."

Tour. TOUR!!! Terrible memories from the Silk Road in 1999 came pouring into my mind like concrete at a dam-building. The guide. The pre-dawn tearings out of bed. The tourist shops. A corpse from 3,000 years from now.

But Gillian had her way as usual.

*

A few months later I'm sitting in a plane, of all things, on my way to Wuhan and the starting point of the trip up the Yangzi River – on a 'luxury cruiser' at that. Five thousand yuan I have parted with for this pleasure. So it had better *be* a pleasure.

In addition to Gillian's two friends Adam and Queenie (a name which still holds astonishing sway among Hong Kong Chinese women) I have with me the like-minded Jacq, later to be swept off her feet and out of Hong Kong by Hap Tsai the Box-boy, but for now single and interested in adventure like me. We are to share a cabin, but okay. I have to see these three wonders, I suppose, before they are buried underwater and become The Three Not Very Steep Hillocks.

As expected, the only Chinese on board the boat, sorry, luxury cruiser (whose only luxury appears to be the prices) are crew and, as I feared: Guides. Guides for two big groups of very old and noisy Americans, and a smaller group of quite elderly but very quiet Germans. They sit around the ludicrously over-priced ship bar, showing off photos of their grandchildren. They have "done" Beijing and "done" Shanghai; now they only need to do a little Yangzi River before they can bugger off home.

As I said, I have nothing against the elderly. I think they have a right to live. But when I see them in action in the bar that night, the ones not in wheelchairs swinging stiffly around to the sound of *Edelweiss* or sporting Yangzi Cruise T-shirts, baseball caps and little badges with name and number… well. I just have a feeling that this may not turn out to be the greatest China trip I've ever been on.

We are the only ones below 65, and as far as I can see, the only ones who get drunk that night.

The next day we wake to sunshine and a huge lock which the boat is supposed to go through, fifty metres straight up. A large crowd of curious onlookers is watching the spectacle, which must surely take place several times a day. But a good thing can't be seen too often I suppose. I am very relieved when I find out how we're going to go through the lock; that the water will rise and carry us through, and we won't be hauled up by chains or ropes (my experience of lock-negotiation is obviously limited.)

Breakfast is good: Noodles and fried rice, fried eggs and tomatoes. The Americans are eating cornflakes and looking suspiciously at us as we handle the chopsticks with nonchalant ease. Ha, ha, yes we're the Hongkongers, no childlike spoon-eating for us!

It is strange, travelling up the Yangzi. The riverbanks are so close to the boat that you can almost touch them; you can certainly make out the features – the handsome *male* features – of people on shore. So near and yet so far... and in such a ridiculous way, which I've *paid* for.

When the boat pulls in at the first... I suppose 'landing' is the correct word as the little wooden pontoon doesn't really qualify as a 'port', my friend Jacq and I are already standing by the gangplank with our little shore-strolling rucksacks, panting like two dogs looking at a particularly nice side of sirloin. We're off to explore!

But no, three guides and several staff members come running, asking what we think we're doing. When I tell them "going on shore to explore" they look at me as if I've just said that they are rich landowners whose entire clan must be obliterated three generations deep.

"No, you can't go ashore alone. It is dangerous."

"In what way?"

"It's dangerous. Anything can happen." Because the conversation is in Mandarin, the Americans standing nearby fortunately don't understand which face-losing situation I am exposing the guides to with my unheard-of disobedience.

"We are adults and have paid for this trip. We have the right to do what we want."

Christ, I should have known this would happen. I did know. Damn Gillian and her forceful ways! During the stand-off we are somehow manhandled into a bus and taken out to the dam. Press-ganged like two drunken sailors, and we even have to pay extra for it! I think it was 140 yuan.

If you've seen one giant dam I suppose you have seen them all, but in raw ugliness China's Great Wall of Dam must surely be unparalleled. Like the giant jaws of an enormous pike with the upper jaw missing and with scant attention to dental hygiene it lies there, gaping and waiting for prey in the polluted sunshine.

But ugly as it is, it certainly looks like the Chinese have pulled off another feat and that this is the most gigantic dam in dam-dom. In fact all those words, 'gigantic', 'huge', 'colossal' and 'enormous' seem not adequate to describe what lays before us as we stand on top of the viewing spot. Around us are hordes of domestic tourists with neon-orange baseball caps and tour guides waving flags, all participants in the Loudest Megaphone of the Year Competition.

An area the size of a small European country is about to be submerged. Houses, fields and roads as far as it's possible to see, and further, are going the way of Pompeii in just a few months. It's like standing on top of Montmartre knowing that all of Paris (a rural Paris that is) will soon be a lake.

I think of the 1.5 million people who have had to leave or will have to leave their homes. How much will they see of the money allocated to the relocation project? It doesn't take a very intimate knowledge of Chinese civil servants and other officials to figure out that most of the money will never reach those it is supposed to reach.

This is too big a chance for any self-respecting party leader, local mayor or police chief to pass up. It's a money-printing machine on overdrive.

How many millions of yuan the various uniformed and civilian-clothed kleptomaniacs will squirrel away doesn't depend on how shameless they are, but on how good they are at gathering people around them who are not likely to blow the whistle because they are too deep in the mud themselves.

But no matter how much money melts away, whether it's 20, 30 or 50 per cent, what is certain is that those kicked out of their houses and off their fields will see the least, if any, of the money.

Officials are badly paid and must make money where they can. And after all, there are not that many people being relocated; hardly the population of a small town. And they should be thankful that the authorities have taken the trouble of warning them in the first place. A less humanitarian-minded state than China would have just let them drown.

Deep in thought and very hungry we return to the boat and its dinner table. After a day of no food and no fun, I'm looking forward to a lovely healthy dinner full of garlic, ginger and chillies. But a dreadful shock awaits: The Americans have banished everything that resembles Chinese food. There's not a chilli to be seen, and the tables are buckling under hamburgers, hot dogs and what the Chinese think of as pizza: fried bits of dough with pieces of sausage and pineapple drenched in ketchup.

Gillian is allergic to chillies and starts licking her chops, but we others have long faces. Asking for normal food is impossible, we're told, because everything is pre-made for the whole tour GROUP. And that means the Americans.

Despondency descends. A relatively terrible day, where the only thing that kept us going was the thought of soon being able to eat great Sichuan food, has now turned into unfathomable tragedy-day. The death of a famous river right before our eyes, and now this.

Peanuts, beer and cards in the bar is the only way to go. This time I'm so bored that for the first time in my life I *listen actively* to the lyrics of *YMCA*, which is played at least 11 times each evening. Another favourite is the *Macarena*, and it has to be said that watching the various tour guides stomp grimly around on the dance floor to the awful tunes helps to kill several minutes waiting for bedtime in a rather agreeable way. (I wait more often and intensely for bedtime during this trip than ever before or since, with the possible exception of the days of horror on the Silk Road. I have to throw away my watch when I get home, because I've stared a big hole in it.)

Daylight is always better than the gloom of night, especially the gloom of a fluorescent-lit bar where a bottle of beer costs 12 times as much as in a restaurant on the elusive shore only a few feet away. We decide to try to get beer next time the boat pulls in and damn the consequences.

As we travel westwards, the hillsides become higher and more dramatic. The sky gets smaller as the stark hillsides plunging into the seething mass of the mighty river get higher.

The guides are in ecstasy, shrieking into their megaphones how many metres and cubic metres there are everywhere, as well as how much the various bridges have cost and how long they are. The Chinese have a curious fondness for numbers, one apparently not shared by the Americans.

They seem quite simply a little bored as they stand dutifully filming every bridge, hill and tree.

The one (apart from me) who looks the most bored is Carl, a Californian man of around 70. He is relatively youthful looking in that he has the use of all limbs as well being decked out in a Hawaiian shirt jauntily open to the waist, displaying a mat of white hairs. He wants to talk to us and I can understand that. The other people in his group sit around, virtually drooling with their walking sticks, Zimmer frames and wheelchairs. But then they have already spent two weeks under the relentless tyranny of shrieking tour guides, which can drive the sprightliest geriatric to the brink of death.

Ah! Now there is a going-ashore with prison warden guides again, this time to see a temple and a pagoda. Both Jacq and I know what temple and pagoda viewing means in terms of excruciating boredom, and we are *so* not following the groups on this outing.

It's funny – the 40-something-year-olds running China Travel, under whose leadership and planning this trip inevitably is, are the same people who not so long ago travelled the width and breadth of China, free of charge, and burnt down all the temples they could get their hands on. Now suddenly the temples, rebuilt and Disneyfied so they look like McDonald's outlets but with twice the amount of plastic, have become China's greatest gift to the tour group travelling part of mankind.

As soon as the gangplank is lowered, Jacq and I dart out from behind the lifeboats where we have been lying in wait, and sprint onto the pontoon while the staff shout after us, panic-stricken. We run as fast and far as we can, which isn't very far in this vertically built place. We are in Wu Shan, a soot-blackened town where we get to observe at close quarters what the Communists' need to create the biggest construction project in the world has led to.

After a long, long climb we're still not anywhere near the spot where the watermark will be. There's a big white sign on the hillside high above us with the number '179' burning angry red. That's the number of metres that the water will claim. 179 metres' worth of liveable, two-storey brick houses, in which soon only fish will dwell. I try to compare it with Hong Kong, and come up with the equivalent of Central to Conduit Road under water. It's too much to fathom.

Below the watermark is an orgy of destruction. There are half-houses, houses where just one wall is left, houses where only a door is still standing. Inbetween are some not-yet-demolished houses where children and the elderly still hang on, waiting for the working part of the population to come and get them.

I have never seen old Chinese so completely without zest for life. Old Chinese people have always struck me as being so much more lively than their counterparts in the West, busy as they are with their morning exercises, their board games and bird-walking. Here they just sit and stare – into the past, presumably.

I can picture the old folks of Wu Shan just one year before. They will have been sitting around in teahouses and pavement restaurants, rattling their mahjong and domino tiles, content at last in their comfortable old age after a life of toil and communism. Now they sit abandoned and alone outside the houses in which they have spent their lifetimes, waiting to be kicked out by a state that has never done anything but defecate upon them.

Far, far above the watermark lies the gleaming new town, all white tiles, blue windows and soullessness. It is a sharp contrast to the cosy chaos I can still make out the contours of, further down. I suppose the thing I love about all Chinese cities not yet succumbing to the wrecker's ball is exactly that: Cosy chaos. Hovelage. Dickensian splendour. Oh, how I wish I had visited Wu Shan earlier while it still had life.

I wonder if it was the repeated reading of *Oliver Twist* in my childhood that set me up for a life incessantly seeking out grim places full of hovels? I'm drawn to them like other tourists are drawn to beaches and dry Martinis. When I'm on holiday I want to see muddy, sooty, run-down, grey and grimy villages and city neighbourhoods with snotty children playing among stinking rubbish heaps – in other words, hovelage to rival Dickens' Isle of Dogs.

But Wu Shan isn't even grim, it's just lovely, idyllic and Chinese painting-like. Here people have lived since the dawn of time; generation after generation have climbed the steep streets carrying things to and from the river. The meandering stairs snake around the low houses, thresholds worn by grannies sitting on them for centuries, shooting the breeze.

Now the grannies are being chucked out to live in anonymity on some 27th floor or other – if they are lucky enough to be allocated a flat, that is. Most of them will have to make their own way, as usual. *Lao Bai Xing* (the common man) has never had much of a say over his life, and must follow the emperor's edict like he's always done.

I have my fortunes told by a fortune teller outside the last restaurant still standing, and it is as I suspected; I'm going to have six sons. That's a reassuring thought. China needs more boys.

When we get back to the boat, with ages to go before take-off and weighed down with normal-priced beer, we find that there has been a big to-do onboard. Our friends and the person designated as our tour leader (against our will) have been roundly criticised – yes, scolded! – because they let us go into the dangerous ghost town where *anything* could have happened to us, alone.

They were right to be concerned – we had indeed been set upon by hordes: Three five-year-olds on a tricycle who wanted to know why my hair was so yellow. There is only one thing to do, and I should have thought of it before. Fighting back smirks and with our friends circling angrily around, blaming us for ruining their day, we write and sign semi-grovelling documents proclaiming that from now on we will take full responsibility for ourselves and our insane and dangerous actions.

The next stop is Shibao, a beautiful river town untouched by the development devil that haunts every Chinese dwelling place. There are no white tiles and no blue windows. Of course, there isn't much else either after the Three Gorges Scam started, and the last inhabitants are busy taking the place apart brick by brick.

On a still-standing house with exquisite Chinese roof tiles, a large poster with a box where there's obviously been a countdown – like the one to the Beijing Olympics but manual – proclaims *Shibao Relocation Project. Number of days left: Zero.*

With our chilli-sniffing noses, sensitive as those of truffle-digging pigs, we manage to find a place where they serve food. There we play the first and only card game with Chinese guys of the entire trip. They turn out to be motorbike taxi drivers, and to further irritate the ship's staff with our recklessness, we let them drive us back to the boat, screeching to a halt right next to the gangplank.

This is fortunately the last day of the trip, and in our delirium of happiness we skip dinner, hot dogs though it is, and go straight to the bar to stuff ourselves silly with peanuts and beer (much of it craftily concealed in bags under the table).

The virile Carl comes and sits down for a chat. Out of respect for the elderly we put the cards away and sit politely/lamely nodding at his stories of how many places in China he has "done" and how stupid the Chinese are.

I might have shown him a little too much respect, I realise when we get up to go "dead tired" to bed at about ten past nine. Clutching my arm, he whispers: "You wanna come back to my cabin? My room-mate's deaf."

As a pick-up line: Unbeatable! But still it doesn't work. Am I ageist? He's only 30 years older than me. In Hong Kong, our age difference wouldn't be noticed or mentioned – if I were a Thai or Filipino woman, that is. Sometimes in Hong Kong, when I'm walking down the street or sitting in bars with friends, male or female, I can feel a frisson or titter, or perhaps just a shudder, going through our group when one of these 23-year-old, 42-kilo nymphets slinks past, all high heels and metallic micro-shorts, on the arm of an obese, sweaty 60-something 'hardship posting' geezer with hairs growing freely out of ears and nose.

But who are we to decide what constitutes true love? They must both be getting something out of it. What everyone is thinking, but is too cosmopolitan to say, is: Imagine lying in bed with that whale on top of you.

And Carl, although not overweight, belongs in that category for me. White! And old! And not my type, and not Chinese! And *white body hair!*

Now, me checking out much younger guys is of course something completely different. If they're up for it, who am I to stop them, to decide what's morally right? Youth is beautiful, there's no doubt about it. And because they are Chinese, there is no risk of people thinking they are my sons.

Unlike the damned Richard... Oh, how it irritated me to be taken for his mother. What I was hearing was of course not "That boy looks incredibly young" (which he does) but: "You're a wizened hag." Yes, yes, all women know that the day will come, just as everybody 'knows' (but doesn't really believe) that everybody must die. But does it have to come so soon? I'm just getting started in the war of the sexes!

My first younger man was Geir, whom I met when I was working in a bar in my hometown. I was 24 and fell immediately for the cocky charm of the beautiful, slightly younger than me, man. One day we were having a drink in a bar when he said: "I'm not allowed to drink here, you know." I asked if he had been banned, but no. You had to be 18 to drink in that bar, and he was... 17. It wasn't always easy to live it down. Now we're friends on Facebook and he's: Middle aged.

Anyway, the tiny seven-year age difference set me on the road to a lifetime of younger men. My only husband so far was ten years younger than me... and of course Chinese.

So yeah, I turn Carl down, running back to the cabin where Jacq is still screaming with laughter: "My room-mate's deaf! Mwahahahaha. Deaf!"

We are dizzy with joy as we gallop down the gangplank and away from the boat in Chongqing the next day. Never again tour guides. Never again American, or any, geriatrics. This awful, but at least surreal trip, has left deep scars in my soul. I still give a start when I hear *YMCA*, a song to which, against my will, I know the lyrics.

*

Oh, the Communist need for greatness and big infrastructure projects. Oh, their need to follow through with Mao's plans even 30 years after his death! It was Li Peng, that stalwart revolutionary and shadow behind the Tiananmen massacre, who was ultimately the driving force behind the Three Gorges Dam, educated in engineering and with a need to worship his ersatz ancestor Mao as he was.

Flying in the face of reason, geology and warnings from other engineers, he pushed on with the project. A few months after the dam creaked into action, we already saw the results: A build-up of silt impossible to get rid of, landslides caused by erosion, a build-up of toxic waste from the many factories lining the river (another of Mao's ideas: to relocate factories to the hinterland where the imperialists, hegemonists, spies and revisionists couldn't get to them) which before was swept away by the mighty waterway but which is now left to fester in the dam and on its wall, killing off all aquatic life.

Chongqing and the towns east of the dam soon started suffering from chronic drought, and already crowded-to-capacity Chongqing, wartime capital of China, filled up with river refugees.

In 2008 the Chinese government itself started to admit it might not have been such a good idea, and started talking about relocating (displacing) a further 4 million people from the banks of the Yangzi near Chongqing into that already overpopulated city itself, to "avoid an ecological disaster in the reservoir area which has a vulnerable environment."

Hello? Wasn't that exactly what thousands of people warned the Chinese government would happen, years before they dug the first spadeful of soil from the banks of the Yangzi?

But the reality of China today, as it has been for millennia: Whatever the leader *du jour* says, that's the law. Li Peng and Jiang Zemin, both dribbling worshippers of Mao and educated as engineers to boot, said the dam had to be built. They are mostly credited as the architects of this greatest feat in civil engineering, but the first idea of taming the Three Gorges was actually Sun Yat-sen's. He probably mentioned it at a banquet or something: "Hey, wouldn't it be totally awesome to, like, tame the Three Gorges or whatever?"

Then Mao – obsessed with the Yangzi after having swum across it (or rather having let himself be carried by its current), and because everybody said it couldn't be done – took the idea and lumbered ponderously forth with it. There was never any question of this dam not being built.

And so it was, no matter how many critical voices of those who knew better were screaming out for attention (and promptly silenced). Countless people have been beaten up and put in prison for uttering the truth that's so obvious: The Three Gorges Dam is an environmental, economical and human disaster. If it wasn't so sad, I would say this is one of the funniest things to happen in China for decades.

'The peasants are revolting' takes on a new meaning in today's China where the peasants along the Yangzi, the people bringing food to the tables of fat cadres, are seen as revolting specimens who ought to be put down or at least neither seen nor heard. What's with this strange obsession they have about staying on their farms? Don't they know that change is good? They should be thankful for being given the opportunity of a change of scenery, not only once but twice.

But the stupid peasants keep being revolting. First they complain about the new plots they've been allotted, far above the river. Apparently the soil is meagre and miserable, and doesn't yield a tenth of the fertile soil they used to till. And now when they get the opportunity to move to the big city where they won't have to do backbreaking farm work but can lie around watching TV all day, don't you think the ingrates complain again? So perhaps they'd put their life savings into buying the new farm and plot, and complain about not receiving the compensation allocated to them by the government. But have these people no compassion for a poor police chief, underpaid and overworked? They should realise that it costs money to build new three-floor houses for the whole family and keep everyone in four-wheel drives, let alone the astronomical sums you have to fork out to keep the mistresses happy nowadays.

Oh, and 'ironically' but not surprisingly: having now seen that the Three Gorges Dam is a catastrophe, the authorities pummel forth with more plans originating in Mao's 1950s. Now there will be more dam projects all along the Yangzi and its tributaries. These people won't rest until China's every waterway is ruined, a fact which proves my theory: The Chinese government can't stand to see anything whole, in its natural state – anything, in fact, unbroken by them.

*

So the earthquake arrives as warned, maybe because of the Three Gorges Scam, maybe not. In May 2008, 70,000 people in Sichuan perish, and the world's press are grovellingly thankful to the Chinese government because they are *allowed to report freely* on the tragedy.

This bizarre state of affairs doesn't last long, and soon it's back to oblique normality. Thousands of children were crushed inside the shoddily built schools which collapsed in seconds when the earthquake hit. Their grieving parents are physically kept away from the press, both domestic and foreign; some of them are beaten and locked up for talking to journalists. But who cares? Premier Wen Jiabao is on the scene, highly unusually for a Chinese leader, shedding tears and patting the few surviving children on the head. A whole nation falls in love with him because he's the first Chinese leader in history seen to be doing his job.

At the time of writing, two years after the earthquake, things are not very different from how they were two weeks after the catastrophe. People are still living in Nissen huts, most of the money flowing in from all over the world, including from my bank account, has been taken by the government to use as it sees fit; meaning that a hell of a lot of it has ended up in officials' pockets. All feeble mentioning of the shoddy workmanship of schools has been strangled. And frankly, since then there have been so many mining accidents, food scandals and people arrested for saying, sorry, *writing,* that freedom of speech is guaranteed in the Chinese constitution – but where the hell is it? – that nobody can remember the little Sichuan earthquake any more.

And nobody is asking whether the quake could have had any connection to the millions and millions of tons of water pressing down on the faultline. The Three Gorges Dam is good, has always been good and will always be good. Always. Why? Because we say so.

And more importantly: Because we have written it. For the Chinese, the written word has enormous significance and cannot be changed; except when it comes to eradicating troublesome historical figures like Lin Biao. I wonder if this adherence to the written word – in particular, the official document with big red stamps – stems from the days when all words were painstakingly hacked and chipped into stones and cliff-faces?

After a hard day of carving on a stone slab, for example, about Qin Shi Huang, China's first emperor:

Wherever the sun and moon shine
Wherever one can go by horse or carriage
Men obey the orders
And satisfy his desires

– you can imagine how you'd feel if a courtier had come running, saying: "Dude! Stop! It should say 'Wherever one can go by *boat* and carriage.' Not horse."

"What? But it says clearly here in the notes... Look, it says... Oh shit. Right. Boat."

"Throw away that stele."

"What, can't I just scratch it out? Hack it out, I mean? Or write 'boat' with ink or something?"

"Throw away that stele, get a new one, write everything again, correctly this time, and then jump from the highest tower with your hands tied behind your back while emptying a cauldron of boiling oil over yourself, you slack bastard. Scratch it out, indeed!"

"Hnnnnn. All right then. Damned waste of time."

"What was that?"

"Nothing."

How troublesome and irksome it must have been, trying to change even a single word? They were, and still are, 'set in stone' all right. I like that. None of your Western revisionism and political correctness. It is, has always been and will always be. It's stability.

I also like that everything, from tea cups to huge, 30-ton copper bells, fabric and chopsticks, shoes and city walls, is decorated with Chinese characters. Very few objects of any description have been manufactured without some kind of writing. Single words, poems or 'Made in Shenzhen' – the characters are everywhere.

Now, of course, it is English that's all the rage; no one puts Chinese characters on objects any more except some Hong Kong post-modern pre-retro manufacturers. In China, not even a notebook can be made without being decorated with some inane cartoon character saying "I happy sweet love scrotum" while the cover says things like: "This is the most comfortable notebook you've ever run into."

There are a lot of languages ending with -lish in the world. Chinglish, Singlish, Konglish and presumably Janglish, but one language clearly stands out: Manglish.

10

Tossed in Translation

When I arrived in China in 1988 as a young and adventurous woman and quickly fell in love with everything that vast entity had to offer, the Chinese language naturally played a great part. I couldn't believe I was quacking out those weird sounds, different from anything I'd ever heard, and people actually understood me. In letters and in my diary I wrote again and again: *I'm in China! Talking Chinese! With Chinese people!*

From the first character the first Chinese I met wrote down for me: *Ting* ('stop') – I was pretty much hooked. The waking hours I didn't spend cycling around Beijing, at that time the most beautiful city on earth, I sat with head buried in my dictionary, trying to make sense of the characters; sound and meaning as expressed in one drawing. It took a while of living in Hong Kong to realise that Cantonese was by far a much cooler language than the Mandarin I first learnt, and that the *real* Chinese characters used in Hong Kong were so much more beautiful and satisfying to read and write than the amputated sticks of words – simplified characters – the Communists had forced upon the already suffering mainlanders.

"When the Communists, soon after they came to power in 1949, introduced simplified Chinese characters, it was ostensibly to reduce illiteracy on the mainland. However, their real objective was to enable peasants and other illiterates to read the incessant propaganda posters the Party kept churning out.

Therefore, to this day, it is mostly words useful for propaganda such as "change," "long live" and "factory" that have been simplified. Many characters have been simplified only by removing, or even changing the position of, two or three strokes, which makes one wonder how necessary this simplification really is.

When people are learning to read and write, can't they just as easily learn 貝 ('shell' in traditional writing) as 贝? Is it really more difficult to remember 並 (combine) than the simplified 并? 參 (join) than 参? 廁所 (toilet) than 厕所?

Now mainland authorities have triumphed in their long-held campaign to make simplified Chinese the only Chinese writing allowed at the UN, to the chagrin of Taiwan, many Hong Kong people and not a few overseas Chinese, for whom even newspapers and magazines printed on the mainland are usually published in traditional script.

Many Chinese characters are put together by joining a component for meaning with the component for sound. By cutting out the meaning component from the character, you are just left with the sound component.

Thus the character for the sound *gan* – which can mean "to do" or "dry" using, in traditional writing, the two different characters 幹 and 乾 – are both simplified to 干. This has led to the ludicrous situation on the mainland where *gan* ("to do", and also in slang to "do it" which in many dictionaries is translated into English as "f***") is used in the English translation of menus as "f***" for the word "dried", as in "F*** the salt beautiful pole duck chin" (Salty dried ducks' beaks).

Instead of students of Chinese being able to roughly work out the meaning of the character by understanding the meaning component of the word, and the sound by the sound component, with simplified characters they have to know that 干 stands for both "dry" and "do" by already knowing the sound and the meaning.

Therefore, you have to already know what you're learning, which rather defeats the purpose of education.

Despite more than 50 years of simplified characters on the mainland, many restaurant and company owners prefer to use traditional characters in the name of their business, as traditional characters are considered more elegant.

A few years ago the Chinese government cracked down on the use of traditional characters on business signs, making them illegal. This has not stopped many business owners from carrying on with the practice, and especially in the southern part of China, the fronts of restaurants and other businesses are replete with beautiful traditional characters.

Indeed it seems like the mainland authorities have had as much success in banning traditional characters from signs as the French have had in banning English words from their language.

Simplified characters are at their worst downright ugly (个 instead of 個, 习 instead of 習 and 无 instead of 無) and at best incomprehensible to the casual observer.

China has come a long way since trying to educate the illiterate masses of the 1950s. Now that most Chinese children go to school, I think it's time for the mainland to bring back traditional characters to celebrate the great heritage of the Chinese language, instead of forcing the ugly and ill-thought-out simplified characters on the world. Then they can enable the masses to read the classics in their original form, as well as bringing China in line with the rest of the Chinese-writing world.

Having done this, they can leave the Chinese written language to evolve naturally, letting usage define simplification to ease understanding, like every other language on earth."

The above was one of my many missives to the opinion pages of the *South China Morning Post* that was rejected without so much as a "no". Yes, not even a single "fuck (dry) off".

Ever since the excellent male editor who published all my pieces left the *SCMP* and some woman took over, I hadn't been able to get the tiniest shadow of a piece into that newspaper.

Was I just paranoid or did she only accept the writings of men? I started to count, and out of 100 opinion pieces, only three were written by women, all of them famous Hong Kong politicians.

I comforted myself by thinking that it was probably my karma coming back to bite me in the arse, for I had said many bad things about Chinese women over the years, primarily about those who work in massage parlours.

*

When Richard and I were in China, we always headed straight for the massage parlour in whatever hotel we were staying. Richard belonged to the same category as me, namely that of preferring Chinese men over all others (it's the colouring) (no, the eyebrows) (no, the beautiful hands) (no, all of the above and more) so we always asked for *leeng tsai* (handsome boys) in Cantonese or *shuai ge* in Mandarin.

"I say, have you any *shuai ge?*" we asked, in our plummy 'Queen's Chinese'.

"Sure, just wait a minute," the ball-gowned hostesses, who always crowd the entrances to massage parlours and other entertainment venues in China, would invariably answer. After half an hour of waiting we would be taken into a darkened room with massage beds or reclining chairs… and two girls in white or pink jogging suits would appear.

"Excuse us, we asked for *shuai ge?*"

"Oh, sorry, we thought you said beautiful girls."

"No, we want *shuai ge* or nothing, thank you very much."

The hostesses would giggle in an uncertain manner. What a forward Western whore!

Another 15 minutes would pass and a scrawny-looking youth from some province would turn up, followed by a girl.

"Excuse me, we said TWO *shuai ge?*"

"Oh but you're a man! This girl is very good." Wink, wink. They couldn't fathom that Richard, a tall and handsome man, wouldn't much rather prefer a giggly pony-tailed slip of a girl to the real thing.

"We said *shuai ge*, but just forget it, we're out of here." And so it would go, from parlour to parlour. After the promise and the excruciating waiting time we would always be served up at least one girl.

Recently – perhaps since the handover, or after a terrible advert appeared on Hong Kong TV about service-mindedness: "the customer is always right" and all that – Chinese women in particular have taken it upon themselves to help Idiotic Foreigner, always, at every turn. Stop for half a second and think about, oh, I don't know, how the universe started, and one of them will come running up, twittering in that faux Minnie Mouse voice: "Can I heltchioo?"

They also show you how to walk across a floor and shout out to be careful if you for example reach up to get a magazine on a higher shelf. I'm sure many people like the lulling feeling of being taken care of at every turn, but I see it as another intrusion and extremely patronising. So I try to avoid Chinese women altogether.

That's probably what that new editor can sense. Surely my writing can't have got that much worse in only a couple of weeks?

That editor wasn't the only woman avoiding me. Two German-speaking ladies I had met while giving a talk about Cantonese at the YWCA were also leaving me, stopping the Cantonese lessons to, presumably, only speak English with Hong Kong people. Oh no! And they were in my Top 10 of The Most Fantastic Students Ever! In six months they had gone from having not a word of Cantonese to being conversational about all sorts of topics. They had good pronunciation, superb syntax, great vocabulary and could also read quite a few characters. (And: One of them was from *Liechtenstein!* Through her I met six people from Liechtenstein, half the country's population).

So what was the problem? I asked. Why stop the fun and joy when they were doing so well?

"We are sick of people screaming with laughter every time we open our mouths to speak to them in Cantonese," they explained. No matter how hard they tried, Hong Kong people would always answer them in English and even come across all sniffy because these two whiteys dared to address them in that "useless" language, Cantonese.

My students felt they were bashing their heads against a great wall of Chinese and that all their hard work had been in vain.

During my years in Hong Kong I've asked millions of locals why, when addressed in one language, they choose to answer in another. "Because it's more polite," they say. Well you know what? It's not!

I think in their eyes, Cantonese is like breast-feeding: Something their ancestors did in the rice paddies of Guangdong province, vaguely shameful, necessary at the time but too close to the earth. Also, all white people speak *English and nothing else,* ever, and if they try to stick their head out of their appointed pigeon-hole they must be stuffed back in at all cost.

For all you eager Canto-students out there, I have only one piece of advice: Stand your ground. Keep speaking Cantonese and you will eventually succeed. You're the customer and you can take your business to places where people are happy to talk to you in the local language. That should learn 'em! If Hong Kong people accepted the fact that white people can actually learn Cantonese, that it's not "too difficult for them" and that the only way to learn it is to practise, we would see a very different, less polarised society here.

And I would still have the income from Rebecca and Anna.

Apart from "It's polite to answer in a completely different language from the person addressing you" there's another answer I frequently get when I ask people why they answer me in English, seeing as I am talking to them in normal, fairly fluent Cantonese, and that is: "I was afraid you wouldn't understand."

That answer, to me, is even weirder and more insulting than "to be polite." Who can speak a language fluently but not understand it?

But this automatic answering in English – that everyone in Hong Kong is set on, like the air-con system in an intelligent building – must have a deeper meaning, I felt. And the other day it hit me like the biggest sledgehammer in town: They've been brainwashed to death since childhood. Why hadn't I put two and two together before?

I was getting on the ferry and behind me were a couple with their young child in a pram. Feeling particularly benevolent I said to the child: "細佬，你好！你去邊呀?" (Little brother, hello! Where are you off to?) whereupon the parents, like millions of parents before them, started prodding the poor tyke and pointing at me, screaming: "Say ha-lou! Say ha-lou!" in a kind of English, in that unnaturally high-pitched, over-bright way that some parents think is easier for children to understand.

The kid looked rather put out and said nothing, certainly not "ha-lou", so I walked on quickly, cursing myself for even trying.

Then: Bang! Epiphany.

Of course! This "say ha-lou" thing happens every but every bloody single time I speak to a child in Cantonese. Therefore it is to be presumed that all parents do it to all children all the time. The habits rammed down one's throat in childhood are difficult if not impossible to break, and no one knows this better than the Chinese, who start teaching children "A is for Apple, B is for Bastard" when they are still in the womb. And so it is that Hong Kong people, like linguistic Pavlov's dogs, on seeing white people invariably break into English. Or Honglish.

It's an involuntary reflex, like closing your eyes when someone approaches your face at high speed wielding a pair of scissors.

To understand everything is to forgive everything, allegedly. So after this epiphany, will I now treat people who answer me in a completely different language when I address them in their own mother tongue, Cantonese, with more compassion? Probably not. No, definitely not. But from now on I'll go straight to the root of the problem: The "say ha-lou" parents. Hoi hoi, I'm going to turn this thing around, you'll see! And in twenty years we'll have a whole generation answering people in *the same language in which they've been addressed!*

Meanwhile, every time I lose a student to local people's insensitivity, ignorance and arrogance, I become even more dead set on making Cantonese a world language. By hook or by crook. By foul means or fair. Come rain or shine.

A particularly fair means, to me, is that of the radio. I have a great radio face, if not voice, I feel. But there is one woman in Hong Kong with a great radio voice, and that is Sarah Passmore of RTHK (Radio Television Hong Kong) Radio 3.

I first met her when she interviewed me on air about my first book, *Blonde Lotus*. She had elected it to be Book of the Month, so naturally I liked her. And her voice was like honey mixed with a little bit of brandy, melting in the sun.

I thought: We should make a programme together teaching Cantonese, and amazingly she had had the same idea. Soon after, 'Naked Cantonese' was born. Every Tuesday we got together in the studio or on location (my favourite episode was recorded inside one of Hong Kong's last traditional public toilets), quacking up a storm in Cantonese.

It turned out to be quite popular, attracting listeners in places like Chile, Cuba, Madagascar and the Ukraine. And they sent us fan letters! Sometimes we got more than one fan letter a week. After they'd told us how awesome our show was, they went on to say that they had to learn Cantonese through the method of Listening to Norwegian Woman Teaching a Brit because their own Chinese spouse, from whom they should be learning, was so terribly demanding.

One listener wrote in to say that he'd been trying to learn Cantonese for 10 years as he was married to a Chinese and could "only communicate with [his] father-in law through grunts and nods" but so far had only been able to pick up a few words because of the stern treatment by his wife. If he got a single word a little bit wrong in tone or sound, she would scold him mercilessly, taunting him with unkind names. This had rather put him off wanting to learn Cantonese… from her.

If I had the proverbial one millionth of a cent for each time I've heard this story, I'd be able to travel all around China in soft sleeper for several months, staying in five-star hotels and cavorting with foot masseurs.

What is it about some Chinese, when they have given up saying "it's too difficult for you" and reluctantly accepted that the foreigner is trying to acquire their language, that they demand perfection or nothing – from day one?

It must be because they were tortured relentlessly at school by teachers for whom giving a word of encouragement was considered seriously losing face, and then harassed further by their parents when they came home. "Only an A? You call that good marks? I want to see double A double plus or you don't need to darken these doors again!" Whack.

Do they really think that belittling people, relentlessly criticising them and punishing them for not being perfect, will encourage them to do better? In the case of children, perhaps fear of being taunted and punished will make them buckle down and study every hour they don't spend at school, but they won't necessarily learn anything.

And the idiocy of criticising an adult for not having pitch-perfect pronunciation, thinking this will make him somehow put more effort into language learning; well, it doesn't need commenting on. It's a pity though. I'm sure there are more expats in Hong Kong not learning Cantonese because of spousal disapproval than for any other reason.

Forgive them though, for they know not what they do. And that's how I make a living!

I'm just thinking: What if it was the other way around? What if foreigners started laughing at and criticising Hong Kong people's English, picking on every time they said 'he' instead of 'she' (it's the same word in Chinese) and laughing when they pronounced 'doctor' as 'daughter' and 'bank' as 'behn'? There would be a merry old to-do, is what. There would be serious pissed-offness and frequent trips to the magistrate.

Guess what, Hong Kong people: Your spoken English isn't always perfect. Still, the fact that I couldn't stand listening to Hong Kong people speaking English was one of the things that spurred me on in my quest to conquer Cantonese. Many people, I'm sure, find Hong Kong-accented English charming. I don't, but then I do have many quirks.

Hong Kong and other Chinese people's written English, on the other hand, has a lot to offer. Especially after they started relying on electronic dictionaries.

The first time I saw, or at least really noticed, this language, Manglish (or sometimes Chinglish) as it's known, was on a weekend trip with Gillian – yes, the one from the Three Gorges – before our cooling-down over a river tour guide rage-debacle-incident-misunderstanding.

We were in a restaurant in Zhuhai, and because Gillian, as mentioned earlier, is 'allergic' (it's all in the mind!) to chillies, I found myself having dinner in a "Western" restaurant: All wrought-iron table legs, plastic grapes in the ceiling and voluptuous statues scattered around the room.

Gillian picked up the menu and started screaming with laughter. And believe me, that girl's laughter is screamy.

"Oh God, oh God! Look at this!"

"What?"

"Listen to this:

"The Cowboy Pics" (Beef Steak). "Siderststs" (French Toast). "Rurality Salad." "Block Pepper Sauce Retchup." "Good to Eat Mountain." "Fragrant Spring Onion Sauce Explodes Cow Son..."

And so it went on.

After dinner, which was terrible, Gillian went back to reading aloud from the menu again.

A West Bean Pays The Fish A Soup
Slippery Meat in King's Vegetable in Pillar
West the Flower Fries the Rib a Met
Domestic Life Beef Immerses Cabbage
Brazil The Carbon Burn A Meat
Carbon Burns Fresh Particularly Must

The staff started looking in our direction, concerned. We probably sounded like we were screaming in pain.

"Shall we tell them?" Gillian said, wiping away tears.

"I suppose we should, but they'll be mortified," I said. "And they will believe the dictionary more than us."

I knew this from bitter experience. Once I had pointed out to a girl whom I was teaching English that the word 'letter' as depicted in her textbook, with the drawing of a letter complete with stamp, shouldn't be spelled 'little' like the author had done. And that it should be 'fast as lightning', not 'fast and nighting.' Result, teacher told girl off, girl came home crying, I got the sack.

So we decided not to mention the slight deviation of the menu from any known food, in order to, in Gillian's words, "pass the joy on to the next Western tourist." I think she was right there. Manglish (is it 'Mandarin English' or 'Mangled English'? I googled it today and in wikipedia it said that it's actually *Malaysian* English. Well, not any more, pal) is a pure joy, which I hope can be enjoyed by generations to come. And the increase in wonderfulness the Manglish has enjoyed in recent years can be summed up in two words: Electronic Dictionary. Chinese characters go in, Manglish comes out.

Electronic dictionaries are small pocket-sized miracles. If you consider that I am still in awe of the fact that it's possible to flip a switch and the light comes on, imagine my wonderment when I first beheld an electronic English/Chinese (and vice versa) dictionary. Not only beheld but be-heard! Yes, when I prodded it with a little stick, out came a tiny little tinny voice uttering, with an Advanced American accent: "Ballarcks" (bollocks).

What a singular piece of machinery! It had many other functions such as mahjong, maps of every city in the world and some kind of valet service, but it was the dictionary that fascinated me most. How was it possible to cram that many words – with voices! – into that little space?

When I got an email from a Mr. Wong, shortly after, asking me to translate 20,000 English words into Norwegian for an electronic dictionary produced in China, I was therefore delighted. Now I would get to see the inside of an electronic dictionary and also record the words. *I* would be the little voice saying "bollocks" with a Norwegian accent! 20,000 words would be a breeze, Mr. Wong assured me. A couple of weeks of leisurely typing, plain sailing.

Or it would have been, I quickly found, if the English words had been *normal* words like 'gardening', 'slapper' or 'foreign ministry'. Those words or any like them were in fact not featured at all. No, 'ineluctable', 'impecunious', 'arthropod', 'extemporaneous', 'fimble-famble' and 'emetic' were the order of the day.

I do realise that the above words are all English words with meaning, because I looked them up. But as I worked my way down the list, I must say I was often puzzled. Nay, baffled. The words were indeed English words; the spelling was fine… so why did I find myself frequently scurrying to the dictionary to see if they existed? Why the nagging doubt?

I realised that it was all to do with the hyphens, or rather two words put together by a hyphen to create a non-word. I stood faltering before "crisis-afflicted", "heart-searching", "memory-resident" and "intellectual-historical," willing them to have meaning. When I reached "thought-free" I started wondering if there wasn't perhaps a parallel or other universe where these words existed? Yes, Mr. Wong could assure me in his soothing email voice, *this* universe. They are all common English words, widely used.

So I started doubting myself. Had I really lived this long without using the common word "memory-resident" even once?

The project went on… and on. Two weeks soon passed and became three and four. Even when I worked like a maniac without rest or food I could only put away a thousand words a day at the most. In addition I still had my day job (teaching), which was suffering because constantly having to wonder what "crisis-like" and "wine-adultering" meant was robbing me of my power of speech.

Despite the sleepless nights and my speech turning to gibberish, in many ways the translation was an edifying experience, not least because it introduced me to the world of adverbs in a big way. According to the creators of the database, not only can any two words joined with a hyphen become a new word in its own right, but any word can be made into an adverb simply by adding the letters -ly. "Town-planningly" came out as a clear favourite here, but there was also "under-challengedly", "high-prioritily", and of course the adverbial form of "intellectual-history" namely "intellectual-historically".

Perhaps anticipating puzzlement in the casual peruser of these words, the creators of the database had added explanations to facilitate a speedier translation. These came in immensely helpful. How else would I have guessed that "couldn't care less" actually meant "was unable to be careless"? Or that a "beagle" is in fact a "church officer or assistant"?

I was also relieved to find that "town-planningly" really does have a meaning, and that it is "in a way of well-planning with respect to town development." I also found that "crisis-like" means "similar to a crisis". And "tendency-wise", which at first had seemed downright daunting, at once became clear when I looked at the explanation: "Showing sound judgment and keen perception in the light of tendency".

I slogged on, word for awe-inspiring word. My social life went to the dogs as I worked every day from 5:30 in the morning to well after midnight, staggering dizzily through a world of English I had no idea existed. I only surfaced briefly on Saturdays to tell my friends about the latest new English words like "reflex-like" (that likes the reflex), "dance-like" (fond of dance), "deadliness" (no longer alive) and "deafening" (turn a deaf ear to). I found out that the real meaning of "big-boned" is actually skinny, with its inevitable adverb "big-bonedly" meaning "in skinniness". For the foreign student of English it will come as some relief to learn that both "forbidden" and "forbidding" mean "not allowed". Yes! I've always said that the English language has too many words anyway. Why not pare them down a little?

After five weeks of non-stop writing ("writing non-stoply"?) or rather, finding words I didn't know existed, I found myself in "half-relief" (semi-pain) and it sometimes felt like I'd been "mangled" (cut without permission) but I got a certain "enjoyment" (experiencing with joy) out of it as well. However, for most of the time I felt "suicide-prone" (tending to kill oneself).

Edifying and entertaining though the translation job was, I was quite relieved when I got to Z and could, with trembling hands, type in the last word. I don't know the brand of the electronic dictionary, but that it was Made in China is beyond doubt.

I still sometimes think about what "tendency-wise" could possibly mean...

In recent years and especially just before the Olympics, the Chinese government has carried out a massive campaign to eradicate Manglish, or "insane English" (their words, not mine) from – well, everywhere. Especially the big cities.

But seeing that Heaven is high and the Emperor is far away, as an old Chinese proverb says, it's going to take a while yet before all Manglish has been made to write a self criticism, then jump out from the 7th floor while shooting itself in the back. So even ultra-modern Shenzhen is still replete with good pickings.

My favourite hotel in Shenzhen is the New Times Hotel. It is beautiful. It is conveniently situated. The rooms are big. And like its service, its English is beyond reproach. Take for example the description of its rooms.

"The distinctively decorated guest rooms are all equipped with high-speed internet data hook-up, VOD system, the wide glass window that fall to the ground and individual bathroom separated by glass."

I stay in my room for most of the night hoping to see the window fall to the ground from the 21st floor, but nothing happens.

Later I swing around the "tea house" which looks like what it is: A café in a hotel. The room is dominated by a huge fake tree with branches and leaves covering the entire ceiling. What attracts me is the description of the tea house in the hotel brochure in my room:

"Decorated with modern Chinese style has several chess and card rooms and our tea ceremony professional are experts in the sealed."

The meaning of life: Chillies! I was reported to the police for walking through this market (Guizhou)

Another face of Islam: Shitfaced! (Xinjiang)

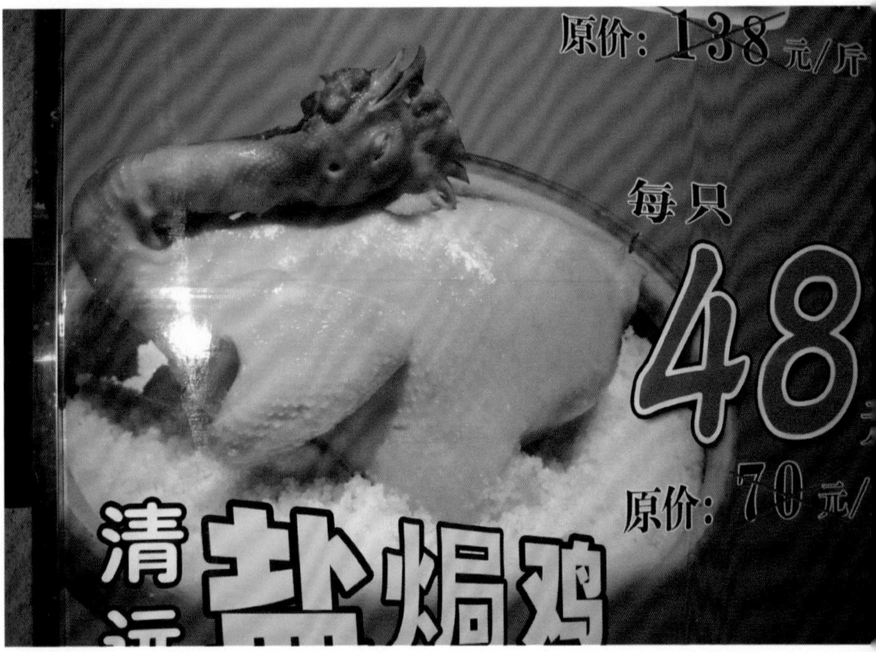

The true face of chickenhood (Ningxia)

Fish need exercise too (Guizhou)

"Hello? Yeah, it's me. Just escaped from the reform-through-labour camp." (Gansu)

Another glorious morning in train paradise (Hunan)

The Old Guard, guarding hovelage (Sichuan)

Ethnic minorities: Always colourful (Tibetan plateau)

Bride, blushing and guaranteed clean (Guangdong)

Snake wine: Drink regularly for good health (Guangdong)

iayuguan Fort: Beyond this point only barbarians (Gansu)

A smaller, untouched version of Guilin just up the road from Hong Kong (Guangdong)

Geezers of the revolution, relaxing after a hard life (Sichuan)

Hitchhiking with contraptions, a convenient and cheap way to travel (Gansu)

Poultry can be fun (Hong Kong street market)

Christmas has arrived in China with all its tinsel and enforced gift-buying, but Santa Claus will always be the father of Jesus (Guangxi)

Before, rich geezer's courtyard home; now Category 1 hovelage (Sichuan)

Cantonese people speak Cantonese! If you don't like it, off you piss! (Guangzhou)

Ah-Sin and Ah-Sa making Cantonese a world language by hook or by crook; her
broadcasting live from a public toilet (Hong Kong)

I read the copy in Chinese to find out what 'experts in the sealed' can possibly be, but am left wondering. It could be 'skilled' or 'field'.

Next to the New Times Hotel is a huge centre for relaxation (whoring) with sauna and massage (whoring), karaoke (with whores), restaurants (with happy endings) and so on. The name is Lie Fallow Agora. That took a while to work out, but I think I've got it: "Lie Fallow" – not do anything. Be at leisure. "Agora" – open space, market. Or it could just mean "Leisure City" as it's called in Chinese. It is highly recommended! Oh, and there's also a range of biscuits in the Lie Fallow brand, one of which features "forcemeat."

Oh yes, English in China has always been a great source of joy for me and other travellers. It's so charming! And the thing is: Although the spelling can sometimes be a bit wobbly (blame the printer) – the words aren't really wrong in themselves. It's just that... when they pick up the (electronic) dictionary to translate from Chinese to English, they always somehow manage to pick exactly the word a little to the left of the one they should have used. Or the word which would have been the right word – in a completely different context.

Take for example Siu Heng in Guangdong province, often called "Little Guilin" because of the scraggy crags bursting out of the ground like colossal black and gnarled upward-growing icicles.

These mountains are constantly be-swarmed by domestic tourists who climb them full of reverence and dressed in their Sunday best; skirts and high heels (with nylon socks), suits and patent leather shoes. Here the municipal authorities have put up helpful signs along the winding narrow paths. NO STRIDING! In Chinese it says: "For your own safety, please do not run."

Striding. A lovely word. A little bit further up, near a popular vantage point, a sign says NO TOSSING. In Chinese: "Please do not throw things from this point."

And when you finally make it to the top, you get a thoughtful warning about the dangers of falling off cliffs: NO PARAPETING. ("Please do not sit on the edge.")

Yes, parapet, edge – those kind of things can easily lead to verbs. Or verbing.

Of course not all English on all signs is surreal. I've never said that. On a bridge outside Siu Heng for example, 50 metres above a shallow and rocky stream, the authorities have found the right word for the timely warning without which there would be no end of trouble: NO JUMPING. This sign is also common on train windows.

For travellers in China, the menus in restaurants where the management has gone to the trouble of translating them into English are always worth a look. Reading through them adds flavour and spice to the blandest meal, and you don't even need to go into the restaurant, since many of them have photos of the food posted in the windows. One of my favourites in the outside photos department is that of an egg sandwich (whose English name is now sadly replaced with the correct term) near the Guangzhou East Station. In Cantonese, sandwich is called *saam man chee*, a transliteration of the English word using the three closest-sounding Chinese characters. But as usual they have translated the Chinese characters one by one, and "egg sandwich" becomes "Chicken Spawn Three Culture Rule." This is the kind of thing that fills the student of Chinese characters with a certain chuckling joy.

More examples from the menu:

Burn The Spring Chicken (fried chicken)
The Farmer Is Small To Fry King (fried home-style king prawn)
Benumbed hot Huang fries belly silk (tripe with Sichuan peppercorns)
Government Abuse Chicken (Gong Bao Chicken) – named after an official from the Qing Dynasty by the name of Ding Baozhen, but the name Bao is often written incorrectly in menus, with a different character for the sound *bao* – namely "explode" or "violent, abuse" – used instead.

For the reason mentioned earlier, that it uses the same character as "dry," the word "fuck" has found its way into menus all over China. It's quite... well, not shocking exactly; we urbane Hong Kong people are not easily shocked, but I have to say it's a little surprising to find this word in an innocent dish like fried vegetables with dried tofu. English translation: "Benumbed hot vegetable fries fuck silk".

Trains in all countries are full of signs, and China is no exception. The toilet doors of Chinese trains have undergone something of a facelift through the years when it comes to signs. Or signage, as it's invariably called in Hong Kong.

Many years ago, toilet door signs said 'Get Out If Not Moving', and I think that was reasonable. Seeing the toilet drains are open to the elements, or rather the train tracks, it is only natural that people don't want to see things that fall from passengers' posteriors inside the station area. Norwegian trains were the same when I was young. I'm sure I'm not the only one who discovered the entertainment value of stuffing the whole toilet roll down the hole, and then running to the last carriage to see it flapping out behind the train like Isadora Duncan's scarf.

But during recent years, 'Get Out If Not Moving' hasn't been good enough for the foreign travelling public, China Rail has decided. First the signs were exchanged for 'No Occupying While Stabling'. But not even this was quite English enough, it was evidently felt. So nowadays most toilet doors in China bear the admonition: 'No Occupation While Stabilization'. And the toilet doors are, right enough, closed before each station, to the despair of the beer-drinking travelling public. The new, airplane-like interior of the fast train from Hong Kong to Guangzhou is ultra-modern in every way, and the management keenly aware of situations which can occur when people unused to automatic sliding doors try to open them the old-fashioned way. On these doors it says: 'Beware of nipping hand'.

I have mentioned earlier the sign outside the station hotel in Chengdu: 'Welcome Bedraggled' etc. This sign was my favourite for many years.

But in 2006 in Beijing, I came across one that was, if not better, at least just as good. Okay, better.

This sign has a prologue and a rather terrible epilogue.

The Chinese, naturally, don't celebrate Easter, the most ridiculous of all the holidays. If Jesus was born on the same day each year, why did he die on a different day, eh? Eh? However, in Hong Kong, Easter is still a good excuse to take time off, and we do.

It is Easter 2006 and I am in Beijing on a book tour to promote *Blonde Lotus*. Because a considerable part of that book was about my first fantastic weeks and months in China, and Beijing with its surrounding areas in particular, and I've been doing readings from various chapters of the book, I suddenly get a nostalgic urge to visit Shanhaiguan, the place where the Great Wall of China meets the China Sea and of which I have fond memories.

I have 180 yuan and the train ticket to Shanhaiguan in my bag, and decide to get some more cash to be on the safe side. Now China is a modern country with cash points, and you can use international bank cards to withdraw money from all branches of Bank of China, so surely it will be possible in Shanhaiguan too. But my stubborn intuition still tells me to get cash, now. I manage to locate a Bank of China on the fourth floor of a business centre on Chang An Avenue. It is 8:30 and the bank doesn't open till 9:00, but there's a cash point in the corridor outside.

This stingy machine, however, refuses to cough up the cash. I see people inside the bank and knock on the glass door, which is immediately opened by a friendly and surprised clerk.

"Morning, I can't get money out of the cash point!"

"I don't know."

"Is there anyone who knows?"

"Yes but we don't open till nine."

"Oh no, I can't wait that long!"

"Well, sit down and wait a little while."

"Er... until nine?"

"Yes."

Lullophobe (afraid of a lull) as I am, I have no desire to sit and wait, and there's only the floor to sit on anyway. I take a stroll around the area instead. At the back of the building a long slope leads up to the goods delivery gates for the many restaurants and offices, and this is where I see the sign which I now understand was the real meaning of my boring bank interlude. It says:

To take notice of safe
The slippery are very crafty

I can't control myself at all and give a huge yelp of laughter alone in the spring sun. People look at me strangely but I am after all a mad *Lao Wai*. I can easily understand that 'Watch Out, Danger' in Chinese can become 'To take notice of safe.' But what dictionary can they have used to turn 'slippery ground' into 'the slippery are very crafty'?

It is in a very good, nay, exultant mood I return to Bank of China, at nine o'clock on the dot. The cash point still refuses to budge and the bank staff tells me that it is because it is empty.

"Well, then you can just fill it again, right?"

"No, sorry. The man with the key is not here."

This sentence – I think it's even the title of a book – is a typical "*mei you*" joke among *Lao Wai*. At last I have now also heard it, live.

The train leaves in 20 minutes and the station is ten minutes' walk away. I decide to put my trust in Shanhaiguan having a cash point. Even little Xichang in Sichuan has a cash point for Christ's sake, and anyway, there's always my credit card.

Shanhaiguan is like before... except that the little train station of yore has become a gargantuan Stalinesque football field of a station, an endless airport-style edifice so huge one would think it was the train hub in one of the biggest cities in the world and not a rural station with three daily departures to Beijing. The area around the station, which 17 years before was a labyrinth of narrow streets and one-floor brick houses much like the *hutong* of Beijing, looks like downtown Baghdad; several square kilometres of nothing but rubble. Here, however, the reason for the destruction is not to build a bunch of 63-floor shopping malls, but to build *new* "old" one-floor houses "more suitable for tourism." That's always something I suppose.

The hotel, which costs 100 yuan a night, doesn't accept credit cards, and neither do the other hotels in town, I discover. So it's off to withdraw money from the nearby Bank of China... which doesn't have a cash point. There are cash points but they are in the Bank of Communications and Bank of Industry, where international bank cards don't work.

Now I have 80 yuan left, 50 after purchasing the ticket back to Beijing. I'm staying a whole day and night. Only the kindness of strangers inviting me to have dinner with them saves me from death by starvation and I can't afford to go to the destination of my journey: The place where The Wall meets The Sea, as it costs 40 yuan to get in.

But never mind – there was a meaning behind this boredom and suffering, and it was to reveal to me the apparition that was the sign The Slippery Are Very Crafty. Also I got to experience how the poor live. Fun it ain't.

A couple of years ago I was in Beijing to see a Norwegian band, (incidentally called Three Little Chinese after a famous Danish children's song) and swung around the Slippery Are Very Crafty sign which I could see from a long distance, to visit it. My worst fears were confirmed: The English translation had been changed to 'Caution, Slippery Ramp'. Boring! Is there to be nothing left, I ask.

I even wrote an article and had it published in the Beijing paper *Elite Reference* where I begged the authorities not to remove all Manglish, as that would further decrease the charm of China to a not insignificant degree. Of course I can understand the Chinese wanting to get rid of screwball English, because they feel they lose face in front of foreigners when signs outside museums say "Stop Smoking" instead of "No Smoking", "Hurl Tells Box" instead of "Complaint Box" in a temple (the word "complaint" is made up of the characters for "throw" and "tell") and "Cunt Examination" instead of "Gynaecological Examination" as on a sign outside a hospital in Beijing.

Yes, I can understand it... but yet. Isn't it important to spread a little happiness and joy in people's dreary, grey lives too?

Now you may be thinking: What? Here she is, complaining about Chinese people being patronising, while she laughs at their English?

I understand that, and I agree it's patronising to laugh at people struggling with a foreign language. But really, I'm not laughing *at* Chinese people, I'm laughing *near* menus and signs. I would never dream of laughing in someone's face at the way they *speak* English. And also, the translations are made by electronic dictionaries, not caused by human stupidity. So it's not the same at all.

At the same time as Insane English is on the way out, every person in China is hard at work studying English. Apparently there are more people studying English in China today than the entire English-speaking population of the US. This bodes not well for us foreigners eager to learn and practise Putonghua. China is rapidly becoming like Hong Kong in that no matter how well you speak the local language, people will reply to you in English.

This rude and face-slapping habit has been driving me insane in Hong Kong since... well, ever since I started learning Cantonese. And now the mainlanders have started too. Like Hong Kong people, they say it is to "show respect" and because they are "afraid I won't understand." However, I and other people trying to learn Chinese don't see it in quite the same way. We rather feel they are saying: "Well, your Chinese is crap, now let me answer in my far superior English."

Also, and perhaps even worse, is a tendency among the people of Guangdong province, the very cradle and stronghold of Cantonese, to answer me in Mandarin when I speak to them in their own language. I can't count the times I've been having a long conversation with people in Cantonese, and they suddenly switch to Mandarin in mid-sentence when they realise what they're doing: Speaking lowly, gutter, uncivilised

Cantonese with an honoured Foreign Friend. When I ask them why they switch, they say: "I was afraid you wouldn't understand"...

But maybe Whitey one day will get his revenge; apparently Mandarin is now the most widely studied 'foreign' (meaning 'not English,' as in 'Academy Award for Best Foreign Film') language in the world. The day will come when the Chinese learner of English turns up at a McDonald's in London, eager to practise his English, and is snubbed by the Caucasian staff answering him in fluent Mandarin because they are afraid he "won't understand" the English he so fluently speaks.

Yeah. I would like to see that.

Meanwhile I just keep beavering away at my life's work: To make Cantonese a world language. But still, I can't completely give up the thought of teaching English to the Chinese. I must be insane. And it soon turns out: I am.

11

Done and Dusty

I often think about Xinjiang and how great my trip there could have been if it hadn't been for the miserable guide. How can they let someone like that be responsible for living creatures? Sometimes I think about articles in women's magazines. *Cosmopolitan* and *Marie Claire*, that kind of thing. Agony aunt columns.

> "Why don't I have any friends? After all, I have a car and three guns."
>
> "I am 43 years of age and have never had sexual intercourse. Should I shower more often?"
>
> "Every time I approach a woman asking for sex, she turns me down. If a woman came up to me and asked for sex, I would give it to her. What's wrong with women?"

In reply to this kind of question and others too, the agony aunt always says that the agoniser should start with her- or himself.

"Look in the mirror!" she says. "Perhaps you don't have any friends because you're actually a pile of shit? Perhaps nobody likes you because *you hate everybody?"*

I also often think about that as I struggle to draw breath in the deep gorges between the skyscrapers of Central, the business area of Hong Kong, where the sky can just be glimpsed as a tiny greyish-brown sliver far, far above. Did I hate the guide so much simply because I hate myself?

Did I in fact project my hatred of myself onto the guide because we were so similar and it's impractical to hate oneself for eternity?

Did I hell. But it doesn't really matter why. That trip was and remains my biggest mistake ever. At least in terms of travel and social interaction. However, the thought of Xinjiang province won't leave me alone. Even when I was sitting in the minibus going through the Gobi Desert with my head between my knees, using one weary arm to prevent an avalanche of suitcases, I could see that this was a fascinating, wild and untameable place with a deadly, magnetic beauty. Through the gaps between the curtains the light-sensitive geriatrics wanted drawn at all times, I could see glimpses of scenery as unlike that of Hong Kong as it is possible to get: Empty. And huge. And open. And with blue skies and, and...

I decide to go back to Xinjiang. But somehow I manage to make a huge mistake – again.

*

It was the summer of 2006, seven years after my first idiotic attempt at seeing Xinjiang province. I had contacted the same organisation that had sent me to Sichuan to teach three years earlier, and yes, they were still hard at work "developing" the western provinces. And no report about my intransigence in the face of Communist Party representatives can have reached them, for they were happy to let me be a volunteer English teacher in Xinjiang.

At this stage I had had a few excellent weekend trips in Guangdong province with Richard, who not surprisingly had turned out to be the best travel companion I had ever had, out-companioning even Jan and Ali. And that says a lot, for they were easy-going, up for anything and with a great sense of humour, eager to explore China (it was Jan who had discovered superb party town Siu Heng all by himself) and excellent at Cantonese. In fact they were just starting get a handle on the old Mandarin as well when they suddenly upped and went to Spain.

This is the scourge of Hong Kong. Every time I get a new friend, normally through teaching, he or she leaves after a couple of years or so, leaving me bereft, befuddled and bedraggled. As did the excellent Ali and Jan after only three years of fun. We had trawled Guangdong province together as well as on one memorable occasion making it all the way into Sichuan to visit Chuanxing Middle School and thence on to the north to go horseback riding (more about that later) and I had found them perfect in every way.

But at the end of the day they were a married couple, hard-drinking and adventurous though they were, and ultimately only interested in each other. Richard, on the other hand, was interested in the same thing as me, Chinese men, and I tried my best to get him to come on the greatest adventure trip in the world: Xinjiang, with free food and accommodation and heaps of male teachers who would only take a gentle nudging before storming out of the closet in which they would inevitably be hiding; thinking, as most gay men in the Chinese interior must probably think, that they were the only gay man in China and therefore the world. And stuff like that, which I kept churning out to make him change his mind.

But his father in England was not well and his brother had some grief with their father and didn't want to talk to him... Richard had to go to England and sort things out.

All right; I'd just have to go by myself. It would be fun anyway, I just knew it! Just like Sichuan or even better. Beer-filled dinners lasting long into the night, cards every day, teachers' psycho hour... I was ready to descend on Xinjiang province again.

So off I went to the same "Develop the West" bureau, and got the same spiel about how we had a responsibility to help the motherland. But this time they refused to buy a train ticket. Oh, that would have been something! A four-day train journey through the entire country, perhaps stopping here and there to look at English signs and take some photos... But this time it was fly or nothing, the stubborn devils insisted.

After a terrible turbulence-filled journey which took all day and night I finally reached Urumqi and was picked up by three guys from the school. A headmaster, another headmaster and a 'leader.'

Welcome, O Foreign Expert!

The leader, Mr. Ge, had a comb-over and a paunch, so I assumed he was a Communist Party member. Then again, they all are, otherwise they would never get the job. They would also not have been admitted to university to receive their teacher's education. To become a member of the Communist Party is no longer, if it has ever been, a matter of ideology. (Even Mao himself didn't care much for Communist thinking – he just saw the ideology as a platform from which he could control the whole of China. And it has to be said: The Communist ideology seemed particularly suited to his purpose). To join the party is now a routine matter; some papers one fills in during one's last year at middle school as a step closer to the annihilation of the self for the benefit of the family and the country.

It was late at night, almost 11, but of course we had to have dinner, which it seemed all three of them didn't want. I didn't want to eat and they didn't want to eat, but we *had* to eat. That is often the Chinese way: To do what nobody wants to do, because that's what we do.

After the world's shortest-lasting meal was arranged for me – a meal 16 people would have had problems finishing, which the men didn't eat and I had a couple of mouthfuls from – we drove off to the school just before midnight. The school was situated in Changji, an hour's drive south of Urumqi.

The guys proudly showed me the flat I was supposed to stay in. It belonged to a Filipino woman, another Foreign Expert in other words, currently on holiday. I wondered if they had bothered to tell her that her flat would be occupied by someone else while she was away. If they had, she certainly hadn't bothered to tidy up before she left.

When it comes to taste in interior decoration, few things in the universe are further apart than me and a Filipino woman. Well, from what I gather after having visited many of the Filipinas that live all around my village. But the problem with her flat wasn't that every square centimetre was covered with bric-a-brac and knick-knacks. And it was also not – not really – that there were no cabinets or chests of drawers so all her clothes were everywhere, hanging on the walls or stuffed into plastic bags.

No, the problem was that... how can I say it without sounding critical... the problem was that she, let's say, was so far behind in the line when enthusiasm for hygiene was handed out, that she was many blocks behind those who were merely far behind.

The white tiled floors were brownish-grey and covered in long black hairs. Brown water (?) had seeped out of the fridge and made a significantly sized black pond on the kitchen floor where many members of the animal and vegetable kingdom, probably never recorded, had assembled.

A sweetish, cloying smell, and, I discovered to my dismay when I licked my lips (the air is very dry in Xinjiang) *taste* of perfume permeated every room, making me gag. The rice cooker and many other kitchen receptacles still had food in them. I opened the fridge and wished I hadn't. It had several years' worth of use without cleaning, and, it seemed, with frequent power cuts.

It was difficult to sleep in the perfume-drenched bed. Couldn't they at least have changed the sheets when a new person was looming? The temperature was well above 30 degrees but there was no fan. A lesser person might have remarked: What about the lack of air-conditioning? But having lived, by that stage, 16 years in Hong Kong without this blight on the human health landscape – all that bacteria thriving in the murky pools inside the units (Hong Kong is famous for having what in Norway would be typical winter illnesses, flu and colds, in the depth of summer) – I only wanted a fan.

The next day I managed to track down Mr. Ge and asked if he could possibly send someone around to do a spot of cleaning. The unexpected result was that I was given another flat one floor up from Filipino Foreign Expert. In it, two guys from Shandong province had resided for two years, two lovely years devoid of cleaning, evidently.

But this time I didn't mind that the floors were black and the bathroom had never been in fleeting contact with soap and water. I just went out and bought stuff to nuke the place clean. For there were no personal belongings here. No cute fluffy toys, no stench of perfume and not much of the fauna which thrives in two-year-old fridge water.

I had a bed, a desk, a chair and a floor. And a lamp! It was all I wanted. But I have to say it was a surprise to see, after 17 years' travel in China, not only one but two extremely dirty homes in this country where everybody is so scrupulous about cleanliness – indoors at least. Outdoors is another matter, naturally.

Now I was about to start work. Wasn't I? I asked for a meeting with Mr. Ge, who started asking me about my achievements in life. In which famous university had I learnt everything about being a foreign expert, for example?

Er… actually I'd never been to university.

He gave a noticeable start. A veritable jump, really. Oh, me and my stupid honesty.

"OK, let's say you've studied at the University of Oslo. Understood?"

Understood! Why not? We could for example say I had majored in English literature, as I'd read several books in that language. Oh, and maybe I should also mention that I had been engaged by a bureau in Hong Kong as an expert of English? And that this bureau knew everything about my lack of formal education but didn't seem to mind? And that the school in Sichuan, whose leaders had asked me to come back the next year, hadn't minded either?... and...

What else?

I started to falter. Well, I'd taught myself two Chinese languages both oral and written, I had my own company, had just written a novel, had appeared on TV, on the radio and in the printed media several times as well as writing a regular column in a Chinese newspaper and been asked to host a radio progr...

"Yes but have you actually *achieved* anything? Have you won any famous prizes?"

Er... third prize in a writing competition in the *South China Morning Post*... Yeah, so they had called it "second runner-up" but it really was third prize.

Mr. Ge looked at me with a mixture of... could it be disbelief and scorn? Which I quite honestly felt was a bit out of order, seeing as I was going to work here free of charge. Having said that, if there is one thing I've learnt in life, it's that nobody is as demanding as those who get something for nothing.

Mr. Ge left the room, mumbling to himself.

The first teaching session took place on the stage in the big meeting hall. First I had to speak for two hours about the art of teaching, and then I would teach 60 students on the stage while the teachers looked on.

I climbed onto the stage and, using the blackboard, tried to engage the auditorium as best I could. I played the Cantonese card, the "difference between Hong Kong and the mainland where the mainland invariably comes out on top" card and every other card I had at my disposal and which had worked so well in Sichuan, trying to speak slowly and carefully to drag it out for two hours.

After this not un-harrowing experience, Mr. Ge switched to English, saying: "Well, that went very fine. The students liked you. We noticed you use a lot of body's language. Can you teach us body's language?"

Er…?

"We also noticed that you are very humour. Can you teach us humour?"

Er... sure! But I will need some time.

Clutching at a last and slippery straw he exclaimed: "We noticed you use many drawings. Can you teach us how to draw?" A low giggle emanated from the teachers in the audience who had been forced to attend the foreign expert's speech in their free time. Thank God it wasn't only me who thought the guy was a total tool.

I don't know if it was because I failed in teaching them body's language or because I didn't come bearing prizes from famous universities, but after this I got to taste the classic Chinese Ostracism. I was, not to put too fine a point on it and like Deng Xiaoping and most other leaders, ousted.

Nobody called me and nobody came to see me. Nobody invited me for dinner and nobody asked me to take them out for dinner. And, although the volunteer job was supposed to come with free food and accommodation, there was no talk of where the food would come from.

The only food I ever got out of them was the first meal which nobody wanted.

When the headmasters/leaders had picked me up at the airport they had been talking incessantly of a trip to Tian Chi, the Heavenly Lake, the fateful scene of my first non-sightseeing trip with the Group. This time I really wanted to see the lake. When the day for the planned outing arrived, I ran into Mr. Ge, who looked surprisingly surprised to see me. It was as if he'd run into a stray hippo in the middle of the school yard.

"Hello Mr. Ge, what time are we going to the Heavenly Lake?"

"Heh… we're not going. It's too cold. For you."

It was 34 degrees.

That's when I in earnest caught onto the fact that I had been well and truly ousted.

After five days in total isolation I was given a timetable and some classes to teach, two hours per day. Instead of helping them, by working for free, I got the distinct impression that they were doing me a favour by letting me teach those classes.

After a week of this and without as much as a "how is it going" from Ge or anyone else, I'd had enough. Dragging the too-huge suitcase through the school yard followed by cries of "Don't go!" I reflected that this was all my own fault. I should have known the score when nobody tried to forbid me from going outside the school gates by myself.

Now I was free and on my way to... I didn't know what, out there in the wild and unbridled Xinjiang. And there it was, just as I remembered it; mile after mile of bone-dry nothing.

I was on the train again and all was well. After so many years in Hong Kong I had almost forgotten what blue skies looked like – now I was zooming through the scenery under the biggest, clearest and most burningly blue sky I had seen since... well, since the last time I was here, probably. But this time I could actually see it.

What a province! Sun and blue skies, lovely and hot every day. The price they have to pay is of course a perpetual drought.

Xinjiang is a couple of time zones west of Beijing, but has to follow Beijing time. So if you prudently only emerge from the shade at four in the afternoon because you've heard that the UV rays are less persistent then, you have to remember that it's actually two o'clock, and bu-u-urning. Make no mistake, it is fry-egg-on-forehead hot. On the other hand it is cinder-, corpse (from 3,000 years from now)-preservingly dry, so sweat evaporates before it has time to stick its nose out of the pore. What a difference from Hong Kong where it's 34 degrees *and* 99% humidity. I wonder what 100% humidity is. A shower?

Now I'm in Korla which, apart from Siberia, is the most middle-of-nowhere I have ever been; 12 hours by train from Urumqi.

Korla looks like a festering sore on an otherwise smooth and healthy back. Amid endless sparkling-blue skies and gnarled rocks the city suddenly springs forth, a bunch of concrete and metal beneath a tight lid of grey and brown pollution. There are no suburbs, no slow build-up to the city by one house here and one there becoming more and more dense; it's just desert and desert continuing right up to the first row of ghastly high-rises.

Some Chinese friends from Urumqi have arranged for me to be picked up from the station by a Mr. Jin ('Gold'), because they think it is unsuitable for me to get around by myself. What I don't know is that they have merely told him to pick up "a friend from Hong Kong," forgetting to mention that the friend is white; the only Caucasian on the train, in the town and in most of the province.

The poor bugger must have waited and waited, looking for a Chinese woman possibly a bit better dressed than the other millions pouring out of the station in the grey dawn. Two phone calls and a lot of waiting later, he finally turns up in his four-wheel monster-drive. His face, evidently in the throes of a massive hangover and contorted with suppressed fury, says more than a thousand written Chinese characters when he realises what a hilarious practical joke our mutual friends from Urumqi have played on him.

He doesn't say a word during the long drive to the hotel.

I feel I'm intruding on his repair hangover-sleep and am ready to say goodbye after check-in, but he has been ordered by the Urumqi guys to take me to the desert, as I had mentioned to them that I'd like to ride on a camel. In China you can't refuse a friend asking for a favour. Although, as he tells me, he's only had three hours' sleep after a bout with the old *bai jiu* and appears to be unable to see straight, to the desert we're going without fail. It is to be a clenched-teeth drive.

Korla is a wild west town and Mr. Jin a wild west driver. It is obvious he wants to get this over with as soon as possible, because he thunders forth at 110 km/h and in the middle of the road, which is riddled with holes, bumps and rocks. He slides effortlessly through red lights and looks peeved when he notices me lightly gnawing on my knuckles.

"What – there are no policemen here!" he barks. "Those lights are just to show you where to speed up."

I bash my head on the ceiling every time we slam into a road crater. Will he lose face if I put on the seatbelt? I cast a discreet eye down to my right, and see to my horror, but also a kind of face-saving, fatalistic relief, that the car isn't equipped with such a thing. After that, everything gets better in a way, to the point where we're almost chatting a little.

An hour later and with my heart hanging out of my earholes, I'm proudly astride a camel in the Taklamakan Desert, of "If you go in you'll never come out" fame. (Apparently this much repeated meaning of the name is just another myth; although scholars argue about the real Uyghur meaning, they seem to settle on "Place of ruins.")

It's even more majestic than I had imagined. I feel the breath of history and can easily see the caravans trudging along the dunes bearing silk, tea, incense and all the other stuff that was fashionable in Europe at the time. Before me the immortal desert stretches endlessly; an ocean of sand beneath a neon-blue sky. This is completely different from the only other desert I've been to, namely the Gobi Desert, which doesn't look like a desert at all but like a potato field in Norway.

This is the real thing: Sand dunes and more sand dunes. There are no oases, the temperature is well below zero at night and frying in the day. If I slide off the camel and start walking, I'll be dead in a few hours.

The camel is a singular animal which only needs to eat about every third month. I've always felt attracted to men resembling camels, so I feel a great attraction to this big-nosed geezer who strides ahead with dignity with me on top. I feel I've reached the goal of the journey and many dreams: Me on a camel, howling blue skies and yellow sand, a colossal silence and, apart from that, nothing. Apart from the camel driver. And of course Mr. Jin, who somehow manages to sit on a camel, the funkiest animal in the world, *peevishly.*

I have heard that camels are supposed to be smelly and have a negative attitude to humans, but I don't notice any such thing. On the contrary, this camel, as well as those I am fortunate enough to meet later, is happy about being patted on the head as it kneels looking at me half phlegmatically, half mischievously, the way only a camel can.

"Yes, foreigners love animals," remarks Mr. Jin, an expert in foreigners and their strange ways, to the camel driver, who also shakes his head patronisingly. It is obvious that it is regarded as not quite *comme il faut* to like animals. If it's not to eat them, of course.

Mr. Jin is a man of few words. He is a tax inspector with a buzz-cut and a formidable beer gut; a man I would have guessed was 59 years old if I was in a generous mood, 65 if in a normal one. It turns out that he is 43.

This was to be a recurring theme during this journey. The Chinese, who normally look disgustingly young, age quickly in this province. If you ask a Chinese how old he is, he will always but *always* answer: "You guess!"

I quickly learnt to take 20 years off the age I thought people were when they asked me to guess, but even then I often guessed too many years, and ended up hurting them.

Off the camel and back on drier-than-dry land, it's time to eat. There's only one restaurant here on the edge of the desert and it is an outdoor

Uyghur restaurant where guys with moustaches and white skullcaps mill around. We have a choice between mutton, mutton and mutton in mutton sauce. While Mr. Jin wolfs it down and I pretend to nibble at the greasy mess, the staff come out, leading a musician with a kind of two-string banjo. He is 17 years old and blind from birth. He plays and sings hauntingly beautiful Uyghur folk songs while we eat, claiming to possess perfect tonal memory. He asks me to sing a Norwegian folk song, and suddenly I have forgotten all the songs I have ever learnt or heard.

The only thing I can think of is the jingle to a Norwegian TV advert for mountain skiing safety, which I duly sing. And shoot me if he doesn't manage to play it more or less the way I quacked it out. It is a huge moment: To sit far and beyond the middle of ultra-nowhere in Xinjiang province, where all the neighbouring countries end in –stan, listening to the melody from a thousand Norwegian TV nights strummed on a Turkish string instrument.

After this, one would think that Mr. Jin has fulfilled his duty more than satisfactorily and that we can now say goodbye. But no. With clenched teeth he takes (drags) me to meet ten of his friends for dinner. They are all middle-aged geezers (they look 65 so I assume they are around 40) who think the act of saying "hello" in English is the epitome of hilarity. Every time there's a lull in the conversation it's enough that one of them shouts "ha-lou!" for the whole table to erupt into screams of laughter.

This is the third time I've had a meal not alone during the last two weeks, and without doubt the least fun. The geezers are all braying and overbearing, and the only Chinese men I've ever felt an urge to hit and hit. Fortunately they don't pay much attention to me, and at least I can eat something that tastes good, after a long day with only greasy mutton to sustain me.

When in Rome one must of course do as the Romanians, but a lump of dead meat taken from my friend the sheep is not what I think of as a nice dinner. Vegetarians: When you are in Xinjiang, avoid Muslim restaurants like the plague; for fat mutton in fat mutton sauce is all you're likely to get. If you are lucky enough to be served vegetables, they also taste of mutton. You are hereby forewarned. But they make fantastic bread, that has to be said.

Ah yes, the food in Xinjiang province. Here on the outskirts of the empire it is as if the Chinese have forgotten all about their culinary traditions. Forget about dainty tidbits beautifully arranged – here it's big slabs of meat continually boiling on the hob. They scoff the disgusting-looking and -smelling stuff with gusto and wash it down with even more beer and *bai jiu* than is considered normal, forgetting that food should look and taste good as well as fill the stomach.

And: Where people in Changji, scene of the unhygienic school, were slim and well built, every bastard in Korla is fat. Podgy, porky or grossly obese – all variations on the theme are to be found in abundance.

Perhaps it is because they were forced to come here as teenagers to build up the western frontier and were never allowed to leave? That they simply comfort- or binge-eat because there's nothing else to do or they can't face the fact that their lives have been in vain, ruled completely by circumstance?

One of Mao's more innovative ideas was that all schooling was useless and that doctors ought to work, for example, not in boring old bourgeois hospitals or clinics but in Xinjiang province, digging latrines. By a curious irony of fate, nightsoil collectors were put to work operating on heart patients, without as much as a manual in the art of surgery. But of course they were illiterate anyway.

"Learn by doing!" was one of Mao's many slogans. That is indeed a good slogan and one by which I largely live. But still – if there was something wrong with me and I had to have an operation, I think I would prefer that it was a real doctor doing it, and not an emptier of bogs.

I'm sure Korla has its fair share of surrealism and China feeling, but I can't find it. It is probably hiding behind closed metal doors in the spanking new glass-and-tile buildings, only coming out for special occasions. I therefore leave the next day, early and with a sense of relief. Fat oil workers are not what I've come here to experience. I'm satisfied anyway, like everybody who's ridden on a camel inevitably is. And now for the train.

When you ask Chinese where is a good place to go, they will invariably tell you the name of a temple, a museum with Buddhist relics, grottoes, or of course "a mummified corpse from 3,000 years from now." These places are chock-a-block filled to the rafters with domestic tourists in their white nylon socks and plastic sandals, stripy polyester golf shirts and orange baseball caps, and incessantly screaming guides.

Those are the kind of places I try to avoid, so I search the map till I find a place which looks reassuringly small and sightseeing-less. Xinhe. ('New Peace'.) When people on the train in addition tell me that there's nothing to do there, I know I've found the right place. Emerging a day later in burning sunshine, I see nothing. No buildings and no people. Promising, but also a little worrisome. Am I to sleep under a dusty tree?

I start walking, and soon a green car the size of a matchbox draws up. The man inside, a hairy dude so large that he oozes out of all the windows, claims to be a taxi driver and that the toy car is a taxi. That'll do me, and after ten minutes' drive we arrive in a town, or rather an intersection of four wide and dead-straight highways – the staple of modern Chinese infrastructure.

When I signed up as a volunteer teacher it was as part of the Go West campaign. But if I had known that this would be the result..! The money that the central government has poured into the campaign, apart from lining fat cadres' pockets, has all gone into this: Building straighter than straight six- or eight-lane motorways which go on and on and disappear into the distance, a distance so far away that the human brain, and especially a brain living in Hong Kong, cannot fathom it.

The roads dominate the entire landscape, which takes some doing as the landscape is of the kind where you can actually see the horizon curving, like at sea. They are illuminated by concentration camp-strength lights mounted on poles, every one of which is decorated with advertising for China Mobile. The roads are wide and black. They are straight. They go on forever. And they are all empty.

The plan is probably that one day, when everybody in the western provinces is rich (except the indigenous population, but somebody has to do the dirty jobs), these roads will be filled bumper-to-bumper with lovely cars, just like in the USA. On that day we can all wave goodbye to breathing. And I'm not just talking about 'we who live in Hong Kong' but 'the whole world' we.

But don't worry. The world's oil reserves will be empty long before this happens – bled to the last drop by China.

The matchbox taxi driver takes me to the best hotel in town, and it is truly great. For 90 yuan I get 200 square metres of space, of which 60% is taken up by the bathroom, a room much bigger than my living room in Hong Kong. If I pay an additional 20 yuan, the cheerful receptionist, who is perhaps not over-used to having guests, tells me, I can get a suite with a meeting room for 16 persons. Being of a modest disposition I am happy with second best.

As soon as I've put down my suitcase I rush outside to look at the intersection – and suddenly I find myself in another country. Is it Turkey of a hundred years ago, or Romania? It's moustaches, veils, long skirts and small embroidered skullcaps as far as the eye can see, and that is, as mentioned above, far. I have never felt so totally like a foreigner. After all these years of travelling in China I'm of course used to being stared at, and normally I don't mind. Okay, normally I like it.

But here in Xinhe the feeling is different. People stare, not in a normal neutral Chinese way, but in a hostile, football hooligan "Are you looking at me? Ha? Ha?" kind of way. I can see they are talking about me, in a consonant-spitting language of which I understand not a word. Oh yes, there is one word I do understand. "Amerika."

As I walk past some intricately carved daggers displayed on a piece of red velvet, I am struck by a terrible thought. These people are Muslim separatists and they think I am an American! They are looking at me in a 'kill the American imperialist' way, that's what they are doing.

I also realise that although I'm wearing long trousers and a T-shirt, I'm more or less naked compared to the people here. They are dressed as if braced for a Norwegian winter although it's 40 degrees. The women wear jackets and long skirts, and as if that wasn't enough, longjohns. To make sure that no amount of skin will be visible, they also wear tights on top of the longjohns. Or so I think, until I see a woman pulling up her skirts well above the knee, to extract a wad of money which is secured in the elastic of the thigh-high stocking. Is it against the Koran to carry handbags? I wonder.

I'm glad I haven't followed the receptionist's advice to wear shorts. It's bad enough as it is to be blonde and showing bare arms. Now I'm going to have my throat cut in the middle of a market full of hostile strangers, just because of that nitwit George W. Bush. This is soon confirmed when a young man comes up to me and says in halting Putonghua: "USA is rubbish!"

Sometimes it's good to have Norway to fall back on.

After the Islamist attacks on the World Trade Center in New York in 2001, followed by Bush's war on terror, Beijing was given a unique opportunity to tighten the vice around every person in Xinjiang not satisfied by being led and suppressed by invaders.

With the moral support of Washington, the Chinese have classified all kinds of protest and expression of the need for cultural freedom by Uyghurs as "terrorism," and have been cracking down accordingly. According to Amnesty International, scores of Uyghurs have been executed since 2001, and Xinjiang is the only province in China where it is still customary to execute political prisoners. (Since I wrote this, scores of Tibetans have been executed after protests, but that was for 'hooliganism' so nothing political).

Historically, Xinjiang's Uyghurs have actually been the Muslims most friendly towards the USA (some say because of a misplaced hope that the Americans would somehow come and save them from the Chinese) but that benevolence ended when Beijing with gusto started its own 'war against everyone who isn't with us'. The result, as a five-year-old would have been able to tell the Chinese government, has been to radicalize traditionally more or less secular Xinjiang Muslims (they drink beer) and create many problems where before there were few.

But I can't waste the whole day worrying about American foreign policy. And when I realise that the daggers gleaming so sinisterly are for cutting melons, I relax somewhat.

"I come from Norway! Currently a Hong Kong compatriot!" I shout at regular intervals as I walk among the masses sitting around on colourful carpets looking like extras from the film *1900*.

As soon as we have established that I'm not an American, the scowling and mumbling come to an end. And when the third friendly melon-farmer has offered me some free watermelon, Hami melon and grapes, so sweet and succulent I'm moved to tears, I forget all about being murdered.

Inside a park a wrestling match, Tartar style, is in full swing. Hundreds of Turkish-looking people, yes, men and women together, which makes me feel this is a type of Islam I can live with (I've already mentioned that they love beer) sit watching and shouting enthusiastically. I ask a spectator how I can put money on the guy in the red sash because he looks marginally less scrawny and undernourished than the guy in the blue. No, they are not wrestling for money, he tells me. Have I lived too long in Hong Kong, where all forms of gambling are a national obsession?

"Not for money – then what's the point of wrestling?"

"To see who's the strongest," the patient man, who looks like Don Corleone as a young man, explains in broken Putonghua.

But of course.

I stay a few days in Xinhe because it is as far away from the modern China, with its McDonaldification, garishness and foaming traffic, as it's possible to get. Here, just a few metres away from the black and shiny intersection, it is the year 1902. Women emerge from their courtyards in the morning wearing long skirts and headscarves, sweeping the dust from the various deserts back onto the unpaved road as they've always done, while donkeys look on distractedly, waiting to be harnessed to the cart of watermelons going to market. A simple transaction like buying a pound of grapes leads to an hour's leisurely chat and an invitation to take tea. It takes half an hour to buy a stamp for the great Abroad, Norway, at the post office.

It is, in fact, just like the China I knew and loved in 1988. Funky, fun and without advertising. Further away from the hustle and bustle of the world I have never been. It is so much like a hundred years ago that telephone poles and street lamps look incongruous.

And twenty metres away from this world of yore is the dead-straight, six-lane highway on its way to eternity, empty apart from the street lights with their monotonous adverts for China Mobile, a few trucks and many carts pulled by donkeys; with Uyghurs, the real inhabitants of East Turkestan, holding the reins.

Back in Hong Kong it is August, and the rain is pounding down without stop. I miss not having mildew between my toes. But I don't miss other people's dirt.

12

Spitting Homage

Although I shower several times a year and pay a Filipina to come and clean my gaff sometimes, I don't consider myself an over-hygienic or fastidious person. Some microbes must be allowed to hang around, otherwise the immune system will get bored.

As well as not minding that I might be sharing any given toilet with pigs, I can also use toilets that aren't strictly toilets, such as a plank balanced above a cesspit. In fact I like to think I'm a bit of an old salt. After all, I once worked on a tuna boat in Australia where we had to take what we were given and be thankful into the bargain.

Now I have 21 wonderful years under my belt of toilet-going in China, a country which, okay, is not sparkling clean all the time. But how can it be, with all those people? People whose mentality sometimes is a little old-fashioned, hygienically speaking? But they are not the only ones. Don't think that Norway was always the sterile, vacuum-packed country it is today. After all, it's not that many years ago that the Norwegian idea of hygiene was to empty the commode out the window.

This 'as long as it's not in my house' attitude survives in China to this day – 'my backyard' can look any old how. People's houses and flats are shiny, dust-free, polished and rubbed down to perfection, while just outside... In mainland China the rubbish literally lies around in heaps on the streets and in Hong Kong it would do if an army of cleaners paid HK$3,000 a month and working seven days a week wasn't at it from morning till night, picking up rubbish. Also it now costs HK$1,500 to throw rubbish, to spit or crap (the latter rule chiefly aimed at dogs) in the street, so Hong Kong people have largely abandoned the rubbish-throwing habit on city streets.

In the countryside it's another matter. Every weekend Hong Kong's outlying islands are swarming with city people having barbeques – and leaving mountains of crap behind. Out of sight, out of mind.

But Hong Kong is nothing, but nothing, compared to mainland China. The train is, as always, the perfect microcosm of Chinese society, and even I, hard as nails, have been shocked at the sight of train staff walking around picking up rubbish from the aisle (the passengers' big dustbin) and putting it in big rubbish bags, only to throw them out the window. And that with the train going at full speed.

This habit has abated somewhat over the last few years, at least openly and right in front of my face. Perhaps because more and more trains have windows which can't be opened? But on the long stretches through the untouched wilderness of Xinjiang, for example, where the trains are old-fashioned, it is a national sport among the passengers to chuck everything they want to get rid of out the window.

"Oh, please don't throw rubbish out the window!" I automatically exclaim each time, shaken in my petit-bourgeois sensibilities – I just can't help it.

"That's okay, nobody lives here," they answer uncomprehendingly, and smile in *that way* in which people have smiled at me thousands of times in China: "Poor idiotic foreigner hasn't a clue, but you have to say it's quite touching."

Yes, it is true that many Chinese have a relaxed, devil-may-care relationship with rubbish. But China is not as filthy overall as many foreigners (and Hong Kong people) claim; it's mostly evil rumours put out by our enemies. People who have never been there.

But there is just one thing. One tiny little thing when it comes to hygiene and stuff, well perhaps two things but especially one thing, that I will draw attention to here. And that is the Chinese tendency of needing to remove particles – sputum, phlegm and saliva – from the larynx and nasal passages, with the help of centrifugal power.

China's spitting traditions are long, rich and all-encompassing. Yes, it seems that mainland Chinese feel duty-bound to spit as often, as hard and with as astonishingly great force and volume as possible.

And don't think you can just stand up and spit down without any more to-do. In China, spitting is an art form which takes years to perfect. Every muscle in the body is concentrated in the one purpose: To get as much slime as possible away from where it currently is, with as much power as possible, while making the process last as long as possible.

It begins by tipping one's head back a little and drawing in a great amount of air. Then follows a long hacking and roaring, like that of a helicopter approaching at great speed. The whole body is stretched to breaking point with all its energy gathered in the lip musculature, whereupon the projectile is hurled out through the mouth and away from the owner.

Perhaps this is part of the 'my house must be spotless inside but outside it doesn't matter' mentality? Some people say that the Chinese think phlegm contains devils that must be expectorated as quickly as humanly possible. But if that is the case, how do we explain why Hong Kong people, who are much more superstitious than their counterparts on the mainland, don't spit? Personally I don't think sensible adults seriously believe they have a devil-harbouring entity down their throat. I think spitting in China is merely a tradition, like smoking in the lift, walking around the streets in pyjamas and wearing one trouser leg rolled up in summer. I think it's a case of "This is the way we do it in China because it's the way we've always done it."

The spitting is everywhere, all the time and any time. It can be in a lift. It can be on the carpeted floors of a posh restaurant. It can be in the aisle on the train. But most of all, spat phlegm seems to originate from shop owners, who suddenly pop their head out the door, catapult a lump with studied precision, and pull their head back in again. And I don't know if it's my imagination or paranoia – or the truth – but I feel the catapulted globs usually land right in front of my feet. On the other hand, people spit so much and so often, and I spend so much time walking around, that statistically it is impossible for me not to have globs landing close by a few times each day. As long as they don't land *on* me I suppose I shouldn't complain.

When I first arrived in China, staying almost five months, I was so used to hearing "suuuuck, hack hack hack, roar, splat" that I seldom noticed it. But now that I only cross the border a couple of times a month, I have developed a more hyper-sensitive relationship to spitting. I notice every hacking roar, and it takes a couple of days to get into the swing of things, ignoring the threat of, or rather ceasing to be afraid of, being hit.

But, and here is the second thing I wanted to mention and which I unfortunately never get used to: The clearing of the nasal passage without using a handkerchief. Yes, I have to admit that I always turn away slightly, either in surprise or because I suddenly see something interesting on the other side of the street, when people casually place their index finger on one nostril and blow as hard as they can.

Yes, the spitting is nothing, really. The nose blowing... let's say I'm still working on it. On the other hand, the nose blowers never blow at the table or inside the lift. So I suppose it evens itself out.

During the SARS epidemic in 2003, the Chinese government – when they, after several months, admitted that yes, there was a highly contagious disease going around – tried to make people stop spitting and blowing their noses fountain-style.

Ha ha, I remember laughing then. You might as well ask them to stop smoking in the lift. At the time, there was a big to-do on the border between Hong Kong and China, with the taking of temperatures and filling-in of forms: Tick Yes or No: Do you have SARS? Yes? No? If no, please go on, or rather, to the passport control.

In front of passport control you had to stand on a pair of giant yellow feet painted on the floor, while a contraption above your head, looking like an evil glowing eye from *The Lord of the Rings*, circled around trying to work out whether you had a body temperature of more than 37 degrees. God knows what they did with those who did have a fever – many guessed they took them outside and shot them, while the health ministers who had "played down" (frantically tried to hide, lied blatantly about) the scandal for several months were let off.

But did anybody get caught at all? Many travelling flu patients claimed to have slid straight through the stringent controls, despite having temperatures of up to 39 degrees, undetected by the slovenly eye.

Behind the passport controllers people in white coats sat, writing importantly on slips of paper at desks struggling under mountains of health declarations. I wonder what they did with them, if anything. The whole health declaration thing appeared to be nothing more than a gigantic excuse to chop down millions of trees. Everybody in Hong Kong knew you mustn't dream of writing your real name, phone number or address, because the 'doctors' sold the information to crime syndicates in Hong Kong who broke into the flats of people they knew were in China.

That's one urban myth I'm inclined to believe.

After SARS was gone, for the time being at least, we still had to fill in a health declaration when we crossed the border to China. Again it was 'tick the appropriate box'. "Do you suffer from any of the following: Fever? Cough? Pulmonary Tuberculosis? Psychosis?"

Yes, I did have a touch of psychosis last week, but I'm all right now.

Then came Bird Flu, closely followed by Swine Flu, and the whole rigmarole started all over again.

It's funny really, how Hong Kong obsesses over trying to avoid SARS, bird flu, swine flu and other epidemics. Every other advert on TV is a message from the government going on about how important it is to wash your hands after you've been to the toilet, and that you must cover your mouth with a tissue when coughing or sneezing, and that it'll cost you $1,500 to gob on the street.

(These adverts, as well as those of cosmetic company *Fancl* – whose slogans are "tense up!" and "slim up!" incidentally – were what made me cut my TV cable back in 2008. I haven't thought about TV for a half a millisecond since).

Signs extolling you not to touch birds' droppings, normally an uncontrollable urge for most people, are everywhere.

Yes, we may clean and scrub, use a handkerchief and wear a surgical mask when we have a cold, buy ready-chewed chickens and pour litres of bleach over our children after they've been to the toilet, but what's the point? A few kilometres away are 1.3 billion people engaged in plucking live chickens with feathers flying while all the time spitting huge gobs and blowing their noses with their fingers, so the snot cascades around the market.

I'm not sure if there are 250,000 or 300,000 people crossing the border between Hong Kong and China every day, but let's just call it 'huge numbers of people'. So for Hong Kong people to try to protect themselves against epidemics by washing their hands, not touching poultry or wearing a mask when they have a cough (or a touch of psychosis) is like putting out a forest fire by putting up posters saying it ought to stop. It's like trying, if the Three Gorges Dam suddenly burst, to stop the water with a stern admonition.

There is simply nothing we can do, but that doesn't stop the press from screaming gleefully each time someone comes down with a nasty case of the snivels in some province. Bird flu! The fifth case in a year! It's almost as if they want bird flu, or of course SWINE FLU of which a few hundred people have died during the past five years, to turn into a lovely, roaring Black Death of the digital age.

Meanwhile China has surpassed South Korea as the country with the world's crappiest drivers, and traffic accidents claim 300 lives in China *each day*, as well as the 900 who are merely injured. But I suppose statistics and boring old traffic deaths aren't as sexy as the possibility of an epidemic.

No, I'm not afraid of a bit of dirt and grime, but I *am* afraid to die.

I'm largely afraid of dying in traffic. That's something I truly think *can* 'happen to me'. Is it my unbridled imagination or am I just being morbid when I see myself hurled across the railing from, or still sitting in, a taxi in Guangzhou thundering down one of the many narrow highways on stilts which have sprung up everywhere?

These roads shorten the travel time, to be sure, but I don't enjoy going at 120 km/h, 100 metres above the ground. No I don't. I don't even like it when I'm *on* the ground, and certainly not high up in the air.

In my younger, more gentle past, I also used to be afraid of asking drivers to slow down. Why?

1. Because the drivers are Chinese men with their masculine pride which is worse than other men's masculine pride in that it is exacerbated by a morbid fear of losing face.

2. Because they are drivers who all have the same insane illusion of sitting safely in their own little room, in their own little world so to speak, over which they have full control.

Chinese taxi drivers used to look surly when I put on the safety belt. If there was one. Or they would take the jovial tack: "No, no, you don't need a safety belt! The fine is only one yuan."

Once, in Sichuan, I walked into Chuanxing Middle School wearing a white T-shirt, ready to be taken out to dinner. "What's wrong with your clothes?" Wang Rong exclaimed, aghast. I looked down. Across my chest was a wide diagonal stripe of black grime. It took me several minutes to understand where it had come from: The safety belt in the taxi I had just been in. It had never been used before.

But over the years my fear of dying has got stronger than my fear of upsetting drivers. Now I demand that they slow down. They may have their masculine pride, but I have the money. If they refuse, I'll just jump out on one of those skyscraping highways, and then they can sit there without payment.

Actually, Chinese taxis are mostly okay as long as they stay on the ground. But buses!

Buses are even more scary than planes. In fact it's probably stupid of me to be afraid of flying in China. So what if the wings are a few screws short of a full set, or that the pilot's drunk, or, as was revealed in 2010, sometimes lack proper qualifications. (In a country where all qualifications can be bought, why go through the motions?) I've obviously never not made it through a flight in China, so why should that change in the future? I have thought and thought, and come to the conclusion that it is mostly the *thought* of falling several hundred metres that makes me go a little damp in the old palms, and then mostly during turbulence. It is a small discomfort easily remedied with white wine, as well as always avoiding setting foot on a Chinese plane.

No, it turns out not to be planes, but *buses* that I'm morbidly afraid of. Buses in general, and a bus zipping around the hairpin bends of Northern Sichuan in particular. The turbulence is constant and, unlike on a plane, you can see all too well where you are going to crash: 2,000 metres straight down to the left. Or, going back, to the right.

*

The worst thing about this trip to the innermost middle of far and beyond, in a way even further than innermost Inner Xinjiang because there is no train access, is knowing that if I survive this, I'll have to go back the same way in a few days. For you can only leave Songban, tucked away in the mountains of Inner (and Upper) Sichuan, in two ways: On the bus, or carried out in a coffin.

I'm not quite sure how I've managed to get tricked into doing this. I have said time and again that I'll never travel by bus in China; that it is, quite simply, the train or nothing for me. But here I am, hanging over a cliff and looking into a terrible abyss full of spikes and barbs.

For us Hong Kong people, not a day goes past without some story in the paper about bus crashes in China, and the words 'Sichuan Province' seem to feature more frequently than any other words.

"Sichuan Province: Driver leaves bus in mid-air to smoke – tourist bus plunges 40 metres."

"Overfilled coach slams into Sichuan mountain, driver blames 200 hours without sleep."

"Drunk bus driver kills 120 passengers in Sichuan."

We're in Chuanxing visiting the school and checking out the villages nearby, still untouched by progress. Personally I'm very happy to stroll around the softly undulating terrain of the southern part of this wondrous province, but my two friends from Hong Kong, Ali and Jan, have other ideas. They belong to the younger generation and they want high-octane action.

"Let's go up to Chengdu, get a bus into the mountains and go horse riding! It says in the *Lonely Planet* that it's really cool!"

"Yes, that will be over my dead body. I'd rather spend the rest of my life aboard a China Southern Airways jet in a typhoon," I tell the death-seeking young desperadoes.

Two days later I'm on the bus, which seems to have been manufactured in 1972 without any form of maintenance after that. It is stuffed with sunflower seed-spitting peasants and their various sacks of grain, farm animals and fruit. Their skin is so deep brown that it's impossible to see where the skin stops and the hair begins.

In the bottom of the valley I am as brave as anything, joking darkly about how everybody not on board a bus in China really is missing out. Suddenly the bus starts going up and up. And down. It's like being in a terrible nightmare at sea. My stomach plummets to unknown depths and stays there for the rest of the journey, apart from the times it flutters wildly around the ceiling. The driver is drunk, mad and blind. And insane.

This driver is without doubt the result of a daredevil coupling between a Formula 1 driver father and a mad axe murderess mother, on top of some unmanned moving truck. He seems to feel that a bus that has to resort to driving on more than two wheels doesn't have the right to call itself a bus. He also nurtures a deep scorn towards other vehicles, and doesn't just drive past but *over* every ox cart and police motorcycle brave or crazy enough to try to take up space on the road, which is *his* road. The few times he merely overtakes anyone, it is always going downhill and on a bend. Below us is the steepest drop in China, possibly the world.

Ali and I sit screaming non-stop like in 'hilarious' Hong Kong movies, with our eyes firmly closed. Every time I open them I wish I hadn't. It's like being on a roller-coaster designed by a psychopath who hates being on the ground. The difference is that roller-coasters eventually stop, while this one just goes on and on. I have only one feeble wish left: That death will come swiftly and as a surprise.

Actually, there is one little glimmer of hope: The driver is well into late middle age and must therefore have driven this route many times before. And if he has survived so far... Still, we decide to return to Hong Kong on foot if we survive. And when you think of it – although the geezer has made it until now, he is bound to snuff it sooner or later, statistically.

In Songpan, a one-yak Wild West frontier town with a large Tibetan population, I understand how difficult China can be for some tourists. Me, I'm happy wherever I am in China as long as I'm on the ground, at low speed and not too cold. But Ali! Not only is she afraid of tumbling arse-over-tit down a ravine with a sunflower seed-spitting peasant on top of her, she is also afraid of honest, innocent filth. When I awake the next morning after an ice-cold evening of yak meat and groovy Latin American rhythm in a tent disco, I can't find Ali and Jan in their hotel room. It turns out they checked out of the hotel in the middle of the night because Ali couldn't sleep due to congregations of dust balls under the bed. But who can be arsed to look under the bed when they get home from a fun party three sheets to the wind?

All right, so the linoleum floor wasn't sparkling clean, even I could see and feel that. That's the very reason most hotels in China have carpets, no? And somebody, or rather a whole lot of people, had used the floor as an ashtray. But there were no butts, no globs. What are slippers for, I ask? No, I'm more worried about what's outside the windows.

For when 1.3 or 1.4 or whatever billion people who have just discovered the fun of 'use and throw away', who feel that it's more fun to use plastic plates, glasses and utensils than washable, porcelain ones and who think biscuits, chips and grapes should be wrapped individually in plastic, have the mentality that "My home is my castle and the rest my personal rubbish tip," it can easily lead to favourable circumstances for epidemics and worse.

Sometimes one wonders what's the point in giving up smoking.

The funny thing is, though, that after this harrowing bus trip in China, my first-ever after vehemently refusing to travel long distance by bus, I kept finding myself on buses again and again.

One of those times was after I had just set foot on North Korean soil.

I chronicled that bus trip for *The Correspondent*, Hong Kong's magazine for journalists:

> So this is where I'm going to meet my maker. In balmy autumn sunshine with butterflies and other insects fluttering around, a lazy brook trickling past and a breeze teasing my hair, it seems so implausible that in a second I may be dead.
>
> Then again I am standing on North Korean soil – illegally.
>
> Who made the big hole in the not very tall or solid fence separating China and North Korea, accommodating devil-may-care tourists who want to feel the thrill of stepping onto North Korean territory, I wonder? Whoever did it has also taken the trouble of erecting a thoughtful sign in Chinese, warning people against throwing things, taking photos or using mobiles; making gestures *or laughing at* "anyone on the other side."
>
> A lone wooden board in the middle of nowhere with nobody around – and yet I, a die-hard anti-authoritarian, somehow find it best to obey it. After all, there is nothing much to photograph… and I definitely don't feel like laughing. As I stand there on North Korean soil, looking into a thorny and mysterious thicket, I can't help thinking that at this exact moment, men may be aiming at me with AK-47s.
>
> Yet the setting is so pastoral. There is birdsong, the smell of flowers and earth, and in the distance I can hear an amplified voice shouting "Shout shouty-shout shout… hamniDAAAAA!" and "Shout shout shout shout... sumniDAAAA!"
>
> Is it Radio Pyongyang's DJ saying "Goooood morning all you crazy groovers out there! Well, the traffic's heavy in the capital

this morning as usual, but before we rock up with the traffic report we're going to play Kim Jae-won's latest hit: *Sexy Comrade, I Love Your Funky Badge*"?

Maybe not.

I had been dreaming of coming here, the border town of Dandong in Liaoning province, for years, thinking it would be a remote, Dickensian, semi-Korean Wild East with Cultural Revolution characteristics. Instead I find a forest of hyper-modern high-rises with only the odd brick factory smokestack left to remind me that the town has been around for more than a couple of hours.

Here the idea of advertising has been taken to its proper conclusion. Every square millimetre of wall, floor, and ceiling space has been taken up by adverts mostly promoting, interestingly, the business of weddings; weddings up to the hilt in white satin dinner jackets and oceans of pink lace. Wedding fire crackers rat-tat-tat constantly, and there are more bridal stretch limousines than buses.

But what do I care – as soon as I get off the train from Beijing I have only one thought as I run past the gigantic Mao statue dominating the main square: To see, across the Yalu River, North Korea in all its glory.

The spanking new, pastel-coloured tower blocks on the Chinese side of the river seem to have been built specifically to taunt the drab and dreary edifices on the other side. Apparently glass-less, the windows in the grey three-floor houses on the North Korean riverbank gape darkly. There's no sign of human life and the many factory chimneys issue no smoke. It seems that nobody lives there; that it is in fact a kind of extremely unattractive Potemkin village, but what do I know – perhaps there are thousands of people milling around, hard at work trying to get something edible out of tree bark.

The Yalu River bank is the main tourist attraction of Dandong, but apart from some scattered souvenir stalls where you can pose for photos in Korean costume, there is not much to do except gaze and gaze at the other side. People use the river for clothes-washing and swimming. Many swim perilously close to the other side I feel, but then again the North Koreans and Chinese are supposed to be as close as lips and teeth.

This doesn't keep North Koreans from throwing rocks at Chinese speedboats taking tourists to get a glimpse of the tantalizing Hermit State, but trucks full of Chinese goods do keep trundling across the Friendship Bridge between Dandong and Sinuiju as proof of the brotherhood between the two countries. A few steps away there is another bridge, bombed by the Americans but left in its half-ruined state to become a great tourist attraction.

On the Broken Bridge (entry: 30 yuan) loud music thunders out of speakers posted every ten metres. The familiar tones of *Cavatina* (of *The Deer Hunter* fame) at full blast seem a bit incongruous in this setting, especially when they are followed by *Hotel California*. No less incongruous is the Ferris wheel on the North Korean side, by chance not moving that day. Nor the next.

Trying hard to find some North Korean souvenirs I trawl the riverbank, but it turns out everything for sale is manufactured in treacherous South Korea. Disappointed, I must settle for a CD with North Korean music and a packet of fags from Pyongyang Tobacco Company.

Going back to Beijing I am privileged to experience China in a microcosm: The long-distance sleeper bus. Holding a legal ticket, registered by police with my Hong Kong ID card (so reassuring in case of incineration) I am not a little vexed to see, just a few miles out of Dandong, about 50 extra mud-encrusted passengers piling onto the bus, settling on the floor and on plywood boards kindly put up by the driver between the already very close-together upper bunks. Instead of having a 20cm gap between me and the people on either side, I now have a farting bint 2mm from my face, her knee firmly planted in my stomach for the rest of the sleepless 15-hour journey.

At 1:30 in the morning, the surplus passengers are brusquely herded off the bus amid much shouting and shoving. The boards and blankets disappear and the driver and his helpers beam innocent smiles as a fat policeman sticks his head in, checking that everything is above board with only registered passengers in evidence.

A couple of phone calls and a short drive later, and back the illegal passengers flood with their farting and smoking and their softly whimpering kids. I keep reminding myself that I chose the sleeper bus over a hard seat on the train and that at least I'm able to lie down, but talking to myself now is like talking to the Great Wall.

Here is Chinese capitalism at its best – uncomfortable for everyone, with a guarantee of dying should a spark from the incessantly smoking peasants set fire to the sea of blankets – yet at the same time providing a much-needed, well-oiled service for people who are prepared to put up with discomfort and abuse.

The registered passengers look aghast as the non-registered ones pour back into the bus, but the driver scoffs at our weak protests. After all, when we bought the ticket we had only been promised a bunk bed, not that we would actually be able to sleep on it.

It's the market, innit. If you have a whole bus, largely empty by Chinese standards, only an idiot wouldn't fill it to the absolute rafters. The policemen get their cut, I get my moment of being in North Korea, and everybody gets to experience what it was really like to travel to the US on the *Mayflower*. But I have to say: Death by AK-47 suddenly doesn't seem so bad.

So here is the weirdest thing: In only a few years, I've gone from 'won't be carried dead onto a bus in China' to 'semi-actively seeking them out'.

Is it maturity, wisdom, or just a general ennui? A 'life is so dreary, one might as well get killed on a bus' kind of thing? That life had become more dreary over the years was a terrible fact.

I went to work, went home... and that was pretty much it. Although making Cantonese a world language was the best job I could think of, there were also setbacks and hindrances at every turn: Students who, after having spent six months learning Cantonese, spoke English to waiters right in front of my face. Taxi drivers who became livid with rage when I told them where I was going in Cantonese. People literally falling down laughing when I talked to them in their own language.

Well, this was my calling in life and I wouldn't budge. But surely there must be more to it than this? And how much could I, one not very tall person, really accomplish in one lifetime in terms of making Cantonese a world language?

I had to find a way to reach a greater audience. And it was a Chinese bus that made me realize how.

For years I had wanted to go to Lijiang in Yunnan province. It was supposed to be one of the last two preserved towns in China, the other being Pingyao near Beijing. I had seen a photo of Lijiang: It was a sea of traditional Chinese rooftops with a towering snowy mountain in the background. I must also shoot that photo, I decided.

By hook or by crook, I would go there and get my shot of 'China like in a painting'. And I would feel myself transported to a hundred years ago, just like I had during my first months in Beijing all those years before. Like a heroin addict I was chasing the elusive feeling of the first kick.

And I would go with Richard and it would be a huge adventure.

Richard wanted to fly from Kunming and I wanted to go by bus. What's the fun of flying, after all? It's just too fast. And it's really high up and the wings can fall off. Flying takes the joy out of travelling and it's not at all blogworthy. Yes, blogworthy: For to force myself out of my middle-aged ennui I had started a blog, just to make things happen that I could write about. The very first day of my blog-dom, my house was burgled, so that really seemed to work.

Apart from the time Richard and I had to fly out of Xian because he had to get back to work as usual – and we turned up at the airport one day early and had to stay in the airport hotel, and to comfort ourselves for having been idiots we got drunk so we almost missed the plane and were called over the loudspeakers in Mandarin using our Chinese names – we had never been on a plane together. So why start now?

And really, it wasn't hard to talk him into going on the bus, because like me he was an adventure freak, albeit a tad more fastidious. So onto the overnight sleeper bus we climbed. This was my very first sleeper bus, two years before the disastrous trip mentioned above.

Until now I had only seen these vehicles from the outside and by Jove they looked grim with their dirty windows, half-drawn curtains behind which could be glimpsed dirty-looking bed linen and even dirtier passengers... and it seemed that the top bunk was awfully close to the ceiling. Much the same as the top of three bunks in Hard Sleeper... claustrophobic sleeping!

So I was thrilled to see that inside, these barracks of the road, or this one anyway, was bright, comfortable and had been cleaned that year. Of course it was nowhere near the train (no toilets, no dining car) but definitely doable.

The driver, besides his aspirations to be a Formula 1 hero, was either a keen eater or had an inferior bladder, because we stopped at least once every hour. At one stop, where there was an outdoor waiting area, a short dark man in handcuffs and leg irons shuffled into our midst, accompanied by a couple of chain-smoking handlers.

Nobody batted an eyelid and a mother pushed her little girl down onto a chair next to the prisoner, whose face, on a scale from 1 to 10 of human expressions, registered about minus 2.5.

Was he a journalist, caught on the run from justice after having written that the party occasionally makes misguided decisions? Or was he the owner of an illegal brick kiln from Shanxi, scene of one of the bigger crime scandals that year?

A sudden, rare and unforeseen shyness overcame me and I couldn't bring myself to ask. The two guys holding him were dressed the normal way, in stripey golf shirts, dress trousers, white socks and black patent leather shoes, not uniform or anything. So instead of policemen, they could just as easily have been thugs hired by some local despot or property developer to harass a poor citizen. I hoped he was a real criminal who really needed to be kept away from society at large; by travelling on public buses.

We arrived in Lijiang in the early evening and headed straight for the Old City... and immediately came face to face with Main Street Disneyland, Graceland/Neverland Division.

Some people are never satisfied. Here I had been complaining for years about the way China's cities were going the way of the shaved head and pigtail and being razed to the ground, and how the authorities ought to preserve what few old neighbourhoods were left. I had been lamenting the disappearance of Beijing's *hutong* and the other uniquely Chinese places, asking why Chinese people think everything old is bad and why they can't understand that preserving old architecture will create much more revenue than another shiny-tiled, blue-windowed high-rise full of Starbucks and Giordano.

So what did I do when I finally found a place where there were no Shenzhen-style monsters but just one-floor, traditional roof-tiled buildings all around; a famous natural heritage Old City protected by law? I ran away screaming.

Because instead of preserved old buildings we saw nothing but New Old, built the week before to satisfy the tourist's vision of Traditional China: Beyond squeaky clean, with polished wood, faux-Chinese structures with English signs saying "West Food", "Juicy Bar" and "Whole-meal Pancake".

But: It was in Lijiang, in a crappy hotel with nothing to do, waiting for Richard to get up and shower, that I saw Da Shan for the first time. He was on the mainland's English TV channel, CCTV 9, teaching Mandarin.

Da Shan is a Canadian guy named Mark Rowswell who speaks such good Mandarin that it's better than the best Mandarin in the world as spoken by Mandarinians. He is the most famous foreigner in China and appears on every show, out-Chinese-ing the Chinese. But I didn't know that when I turned on the telly that day.

There was suddenly *Mark*, presiding over a Mando-teaching course on TV! I was really surprised to see him there in my hotel room in Lijiang, because he had been my Cantonese student in Hong Kong many years earlier, doing spectacularly well in his Canto studies but leaving after a few months to go back to the mainland.

So this was what he'd been up to in the intervening years. Wow. I sat watching and watching, drinking down cups of green tea – a wonderful feature of all Chinese hotel rooms, no matter how crappy.

Mark explained, easily and professionally, the ins and outs of various words and expressions, and then came the turn of the 'situation taken from daily life' that would illustrate how to use the words. It was two people talking about table tennis.

"Which bat do you think suits me more, pips-out rubber or reverse rubber?"

"I think reverse rubber is more suitable, because it has a more stable speed when hitting the ball, perfect for beginners."

Then back to Da Shan, sitting relaxed in his studio explaining how to use the comparative in Chinese adjectives.

A little bit envious? Oh yeah. Why couldn't I do that, I thought. I could do that. I should! Bugger me down, why couldn't I put my own course on TV, with dialogue all performed by my students... and not written by the Chinese people, apparently 200 years old, who work at CCTV 9? I would do the same, but with fun, I thought.

And so I began to write the scripts that would one day be on TV, okay, actually YouTube, watched by dozens of people. A year.

I was more determined than ever. I would make Cantonese a world language or die.

Or both.

No, hang on, I am afraid of dying, that's true, so: Not die. But after a considerable number of bus journeys in China, hanging on the edge of cliffs, tearing down one-way streets in the wrong direction and driven by drivers who stay awake for 50 or 60 hours, and on these bus journeys being exposed to millions of diseases just waiting to strike, spread generously and vigorously by millions of spitters and coughers... maybe not as afraid as before.

No, I have actually elevated the place of buses in my heart to number three after trains and motorbike taxis. And three-wheeled contraptions. And hitch-hiking... but more about that later. There is only one problem with hitch-hiking: It involves cars.

13

Car Out a Nietzsche

I have always hated cars. As a child I connected them with terrible trips to the cabin in the country during which my mother sat smoking so I always got car sick, and it was even worse to get a lift in my aunt and uncle's smelly Citroen. When I was 11 years old I was hit by a drunk driver in the middle of a pedestrian crossing on the green man. I was thrown several metres through the air, and have been like that ever since.

As a cyclist I've always experienced car drivers as being egotistical swine, and both my home town of Trondhjem and Norway's capital, Oslo, are god-awful places in winter when cars stand around with idling engines, spewing exhaust which settles at chest-height because of the cold. I didn't get a driver's licence until I was 26, and that against my will, as I was forced to drive in my official capacity as a seller of electrostatic air cleaners. These were in great demand because of pollution caused by my and other people's cars. Talk about industries propping one another up.

So, before I ended up in China, despite having no interest in the place at all, I had always been fascinated with the China of yore seen from a car-free perspective. Photos from Beijing showed six-lane avenues occupied solely by bicycles. That was clearly my kind of place.

My first memories of China are all linked to cycling. In those days, the renting out of bicycles was a big industry in Beijing, and there was a bicycle repair shop on every corner. Bicycle parking lots (called "Take Care of Station") were everywhere and for 20 fen you could leave the bike all day, safe in the knowledge that it was being looked after by bike parking guards who took their job seriously.

I wonder how, apart from for the extremely lazy or very old, driving can possibly be better than cycling. I cannot for the life of me see how it can be better to spend two hours getting somewhere, stuck in a small room that's not moving, than 45 minutes in leisurely, dignified cycling. When I first arrived in Beijing it was so easy to get around – on a bike – compared to the nightmare it is now that everyone is driving. In those days, only high-ranking party members ('leaders') had cars, which they used to maximum effect by oozing majestically down the wide, car-less avenues in huge Red Flag cars with special number plates. If there was still any doubt that a very important fat man with a comb-over was inside, the cars had black windows and curtains so the plebs couldn't see. And the plebs and most other people were all on bicycles.

Now Beijing isn't even a shadow of its former self, because a shadow indicates something that is shaped like what casts the shadow. It's just a completely different city built solely to satisfy property developers and car owners.

The Beijing I came to in 1988, despite having gone through a nasty mauling at the hands of the destruction-friendly Mao, still looked very much like it would have done after the invading Mongols who established the Yuan Dynasty had revamped it in the 13th century. At that time, it must have been the best planned and most well thought-out city in the world, with the Imperial Palace in the centre and ruler-straight avenues laid out like a chess board around it.

Eight hundred years passed and then the Communists, not satisfied with tearing down the old city walls and confiscating people's properties, had the idea that everybody must have a car each. Make that two. The car is, after all, the symbol of prosperity and progress, and that was the end of Beijing as a beautiful well-planned city. Now the car is king, and pedestrians and cyclists mere nuisances which ought to be eradicated.

All self-respecting Chinese cities are now nothing but collections of motorways where houses and shops are thrown in as afterthoughts. What used to be a leisurely ten-minute bike ride through the centre of Beijing has become a 45-minute frothing taxi ride where the driver hurls abuse out the window at anyone daring to drive alongside or, worse, past him.

Beijing's Chang An Avenue, which in 1988 was a smoothly floating river of black heads slowly but relentlessly gliding onward, weaving in and out of each other's way but forward, always forward, has become the kind of car inferno we used to see in fear-inducing photos as examples of the dehumanising effect of Los Angeles when that city's smog and traffic were at their worst.

It is no longer possible to make an appointment with Beijing people. Whereas before they used to stand waiting outside the restaurant 15 minutes before the arranged time, they now sit in taxis or in their own cars, texting apologies about not being able to make it for another hour and a half.

People give themselves two hours to get to work, and I have personally experienced people who are on their way to meet me giving up and turning back – reasoning it is better to turn around in time than to turn up three hours late.

The one thing that hasn't changed is the cadres' love of big black cars with blackened windows and curtains. No cadre is a real cadre if he ever walks as much as a step – another example of how little China has changed since imperial times.

Last time I was in Beijing, one of the above-mentioned cadre cars honked its horn at me as I was walking – on the pavement. The street was of course bumper-to-bumper and the driver, or rather passenger, probably felt driving with normal people in the street was too much of a face-losing exercise. He therefore used his 'diplomatic' status as a Communist Party member to speed things up a bit. Other pedestrians hurriedly got out of the way; I was probably the only one on that pavement who didn't know what kind of official it was who was too important to drive on the road.

Everybody in China can tell by the number plates who is a local party leader, who is a high-ranking military officer and who is just filthy stinking rich from normal corruption. What the three groups have in common is that they all have automatic right of way and God help those who don't get out of the way in time. Even inside a roundabout you have to give way if one of these bastards approaches from the outside.

I walked slowly right in front of the car for as long as I could (they never kill foreigners) and, when I finally let it pass, throwing pedestrians behind it, I was unable to avoid a little shout of "Bastard!" escaping my lips. But who was I to complain? The guy was merely exercising his right to do what he wanted on his own private driveway. For the new emperors, all of China and everything in it is their private property.

This "The Car is King and the Communist Car Kinger than Others" policy makes it difficult for me to be in mainland China and Hong Kong after I have just visited Norway. In Norway, as opposed to China, it is the pedestrian who is king, to the point where a pedestrian only has to look as if he's lazily contemplating at some point crossing the street for all vehicles to stop. So when I'm in Norway, I'm regarded as a half-wit because, used to Chinese rules as I am, I stand on the pavement waiting for cars to pass so I can cross the road.

"Drive, you bastard," I think (and sometimes say) as I stand there waiting, with the car waiting respectfully at my feet.

"Walk, you bastard," the Norwegian driver thinks, used as she is to the pedestrian having right of way. (Which is the way it jolly well should be, I think). So we both stay where we are, waiting and fuming.

Then, when after a few days in my native country I have finally got used to the thought that in pedestrian-friendly Norway I can just walk straight into the road and everybody will stop, it's time to go back to Hong Kong – where cars for one thing drive on the left-hand side and for another are the undisputed kings of the road. Now I suddenly walk straight into the road without preamble, and it's only fast-thinking fellow pedestrians with strong arms who enable me to write these lines.

*

Considering that only 5% of Hong Kong's population possesses a car, one has to say it is very nice, or kind really, of the local government to make all of society revolve around these metal boxes on wheels and their owners. In fact the whole city's infrastructure is set up to accommodate them, to the point where the last remnants of the formerly mighty harbour have now been put under concrete to enable them to quickly get to where they are going: Into another traffic jam.

In China, although cars drive on the right-hand side, the pedestrian is fair prey along with the cyclist. The only reason I am still alive is that killing foreigners is, as mentioned above, frowned upon in China. Because China's racial discrimination is normally directed against its own people for the benefit of Whitey, the punishment for knocking off a foreigner is much stricter than that for killing a Chinese, regardless of whether it is on purpose or not.

The act of crossing the street in China is nevertheless a high-adrenaline undertaking. Although I as a pedestrian have a green light, I may still be knocked down by a car coming around the corner from the right. It is only the cars going straight through the intersection across the pedestrian crossing that are temporarily hindered by the red light; all cars coming from the inside are allowed to proceed. The result is that you can never really cross the street, and are left to take your chances, running across with your eyes closed, using some local as a shield, hoping the bloodthirsty car will only kill one person at a time.

While European cities are now trying to market cycling as a healthy, convenient and not least gratis way of getting around, and places like Amsterdam use the bicycle as its main means of transportation, the Chinese government is actively engaged in removing the bicycle from city streets. The reason is that bicycles scratch up the cars and force them, on occasion, to slow down. And to please car owners, and thereby China's oil industry, many cities have banned electric bicycles whose batteries are charged with pedal power. More and more cities have more and more bicycle-free streets and roads. And today, in a time when only the most stupid illiterate can fool himself into thinking that the world's oil resources will never dry up, the Chinese have finally arrived in 1972 and they're going to make the most of it.

Of course we can't blame them for living under the illusion that The American Way is the only way – after all, most Europeans and Asians who can afford it are also going down that road. In China, a country where all religion is officially buried on the festering non-recyclable rubbish heap of history, it is no wonder that people embrace USA-style consumption as the model for society; yes, the very moral ideal everybody must strive for. One thing's for certain, when the Chinese chucked out the bicycle in favour of the Sacred Car, something terrible happened to the Chinese physique. Where everybody (except cadres) only a few years ago was slim, China is now struggling with a massive obesity problem.

In China, like many other places, being fat has long been connected with status and face. The emperors were carried around on jewel-dripping litters; the rich sported long gold nail protectors to show that they never had to lift a finger except to inscrutably scratch a hair-sprouting facial mole. The nobles never had to drag themselves all the way to the privy – they just pushed their derrières out of the bed, and there would be a person (slave) there to catch the effluent.

It is funny how in so many ways China has become a mirror image of the US, insofar as a mirror shows reality in reverse; in the US the poor people are the fattest ones whereas in China it is the rich. In the US the cheapest food is the least nutritious and highest in fat and sugar – in China, the poor have the best diet and McDonald's and KFC are the expensive and hip places to be seen in.

But no matter how much China wants to emulate the US, modern China looks, more than anything, like China 200 years ago, only with lots more rich people. And lots and lots more poor people. Now, as in imperial times, walking is seen as social death. For most people who own a car, it is unthinkable to walk even to the corner shop, and so most car owners end up obese, as car owners are often the same type of people who insist on eating fatty meat at every meal including breakfast; because they can afford it. All the lifestyle diseases of the West have therefore taken China by storm, and the problems are exacerbated by the one child policy whereby two sets of grandparents fight to stuff as much food as possible into their little grandchild, who is not allowed to lift a finger, walk anywhere or play with other kids.

Is there any hope, you ask.

No. Probably not.

But, being modern, worried Chinese parents are sending their little eight-year-old, 200-kilo monsters to fat farms, where the quivering mounds of flesh are forced to do things like tying their own shoelaces and going to the toilet by themselves. So far so good, but as soon as they get back to the grandparents' suffocating embrace, it's back to food, food, glorious food day and night while the sprog gets down to the real business of studying, forfeiting all other activities.

Meanwhile the authorities are cranking up the propaganda machinery with one giant poster every ten metres of road extolling the many virtues of the car, explaining in glowing terms how driving is somehow the key to both consumer happiness and to becoming a patriotic Chinese helping to wrest world hegemony away from the USA. (Because really – isn't that the one thing the Chinese government is geared towards? Or maybe I'm wrong. Maybe it is *Japan* they want to outmanoeuvre by any means possible).

As we all know, a family which drives together, won't pull out the... knives together? And people who are so unfit they can't walk up a single flight of stairs aren't likely to be running around throwing bricks.

But do I really care that other people get fat? Probably not. They make me look slim, which is good. Still, I really hate cars.

Probably the worst thing about cars is that they are really ugly. They clutter up streets and roads. If you want to take a photo of a beautiful building, they are always there right in front of it, messing up the picture.

Cars spew evil-smelling fumes. It's one thing when they are getting from the famous A to B and spewing their many toxins that way, but here in hot and humid Hong Kong, where the individual has a right never to get damp under the collar and indoor temperatures are always set on sub-arctic, car owners have the right to let the engine run and run while the car is parked. How else can they keep the air-conditioning on?

Cars kill more people than all the drugs in the world put together. Governments around the world are always starting the war on this and the war on that; prostitution, under-age sex, swearing. Not forgetting the war on war. Meanwhile their traffic death statistics, not sexy enough to start a war on, are left to increase every year.

Car owners, even the meekest Zen Buddhists, turn into screaming egomaniac monsters as soon as they are behind the wheel. Road rage! Wheel rage! You think you can overtake me, you fucker? Well catch a whiff of this!

Car owners think it is their holy right to use up the world's dwindling oil resources. Having paid their road taxes and other fees, they think it's only right that they should sit in a little two-square-metre room of their own, watching the pedestrian plebs choke on fumes as they try to negotiate the city's streets on foot.

Apart from golf players, no single individuals take up more civic space than car drivers.

Car drivers are ridiculous: Who else would actively choose to spend 50 minutes to get somewhere and another 20 to find a space to put their toxin-spewing beast, when they could easily have got there in 15 minutes using the underground? Or even better, in an ideal, private car-less world, the overground?

Perhaps it's because Hong Kong apartments are so incredibly cramped that such astonishing numbers of Hong Kong people insist they need their own little private room with wheels.

And not any old room, no, it has to be a tall, wide, four-wheel drive. After all, they might have to buy an elephant or a grand piano. Who wants to wait for public transport or having things delivered; it might infringe on their personal freedom and sacred rights as consumers of world resources.

But what do I know? Maybe I just hate cars because I was knocked down by a drunk driver as a child? Or maybe I connect the car with something even more traumatic: Being humiliated on TV.

*

In 2005 a publisher called me out of the blue, asking me to write a book. "Er... about what?"

"Anything!"

All right – I could do that. I went ahead and wrote a semi-biographical, fictionalised version of my early days in China, calling it *Blonde Lotus* because my Chinese name is Lotus (*Lin*), and as a play on the name Pun Gam Lin, the Golden Lotus, a famous slapper from Chinese literature.

After my book came out, or even before that, I had done a few media appearances. They were of the type: 'Foreigner can speak Chinese, we must interview her.' It has to be said: In Hong Kong it is really easy to get publicity. All you have to do is call up, for example, the *South China Morning Post*, Hong Kong's biggest English-language newspaper (of two), and say: I had a successful bowel movement today! Or: I saw a sliver of blue sky above Shamshuipo! And they will send a reporter at once.

But I didn't have to call up anybody; they came to me. All because I could speak the local language in the place where I live. This struck me as decidedly odd. Let's say you're a Bulgarian or a Kenyan living in London, and you can string a couple of sentences together in English. Imagine all the TV stations going: My God, here's a foreigner who can speak *English!* Send a team over post-haste!

Anyway, when TVB or ATV contacted me for the first time, I must admit I liked it. Have you ever had a producer call or email you saying: "We want to make a programme about you"? Well, I can tell you, for an unknown, it can be a rather heady experience. In fact, when I joined the Women In Publishing Society hoping I would learn enough about writing to get me a book deal, I had been dreaming about *being on TV.* I had pictured myself chatting away to the local version of Letterman or Oprah, having a right old giggle in Cantonese.

Still, being on TV was at this stage of my career one of my vague dreams (wanting to have my own programme about Cantonese came years later) so of course I said yes. The programmes were, as the producers had said, themed "Foreigner can speak Chinese!!!" And that was all. After a while I began to have some misgivings. For after the fourth or fifth documentary ("She can speak Chinese *and* use chopsticks! Quick, send a crew!") my euphoria about being on TV abated somewhat. I started to realise that people who work in the TV media aren't all the sharp, hard-hitting journalists I had imagined them to be.

The interviewer was always some woman who had once been Miss Hong Kong. She would sit me down in an unflattering position and ask questions like:

"You have a lot of Norwegian things in your house. Is it because you're Norwegian?"

"You have a lot of blue in your house. Is it because you like blue?"

"Why don't you teach Norwegian instead of Cantonese?"

Only one of them asked a remotely interesting question: "How do you feel about Hong Kong reverting to the Motherland?"

When I answered truthfully that I thought Hong Kong had steadily been going to the dogs since the handover and that it would be better if it was an independent country, in the same way I thought Tibet, Inner Mongolia and Xinjiang should be, as well as of course Taiwan, an uncomfortable silence descended on the living room. There was a lot of exchange of glances. "Cut, cut, yeah, this can be edited," they hastily agreed.

The last local station to interview me was TVB Jade. Armed with Richard and Alex, two of my closest and most confidently Cantonese-speaking victims, I took the TV crew to bars and showed them how I teach my students Cantonese. The producer/interviewer fell down laughing and applauded wildly every time we uttered sentences in Cantonese. "Wah! You can order beer! Wah, you can say 'Two more Tsingtao!'" she squealed, as if genuinely surprised that we actually *could* speak Cantonese and that it wasn't just something I had lied about in an email.

When I agreed to go to Shenzhen with them, it got worse. I took them to the hell-hole Lo Wu shopping centre where I let them shoot me trying on clothes at the tailor's. "Wah, you can *talk to a tailor!"* After meeting up with some mainland friends in a Sichuan restaurant with the film crew shooting our whole interaction, it was time for the deep and meaningful sit-down interview. "So, you've lived in China for almost 20 years. Have you ever had Chinese food?"

All right, I know they wanted me to say yes, and then wax lyrical about how fantastic Chinese food is. That is TV journalism. But hadn't we just had a huge Chinese meal? The next question was: "Have you ever had a Chinese meal with Chinese people?"

We got into a taxi to go somewhere so they could film me doing something as a backdrop for the documentary voice-over, like walking around in a place with Chinese people. They filmed me talking to the taxi driver while the interviewer was trying to suppress her shrieks of amazement: "You can talk to a *taxi driver!!!"*

In Shenzhen there's a huge poster of Deng Xiaoping. When we drove past it, the interviewer said with supercilious glee: "You probably don't know who that is?" And that's when I realised that no matter what I did and said, to Hong Kong film crews I would never be anything but an animal that can ride a bicycle.

So that's when I really started to combine being in cars with severe mental trauma.

A few months later I was called up by the same station. "We want to make a programme in your house with the runner-up to Miss Hong Kong 2006!"

I said no.

"But she is really beautiful!" they protested.

Yeah, right. To act as the animal that can ride a bicycle and speak Cantonese at the same time, off-setting the beauty of almost-Miss Hong Kong? No and no.

After that I must have ended up on some sort of blacklist for no local station contacted me again.

So I tried to do what Da Shan had so successfully done, and create a TV programme teaching foreigners Cantonese. I figured that with the thousands of people that had contacted me over the years, gagging to learn Cantonese without really trying, there would be a huge market. And based on all the Chinese who had written in saying they loved the radio show on RTHK, I thought this would be a show that local Chinese would watch as well.

I contacted all the stations in Hong Kong, but the few who deigned to answer me all said: There is no market. Who wants to watch boring old Cantonese which is just a gutter language and by the way not even a language but just an inferior dialect... etc.

Wah! I hadn't expected that. I decided to just keep doing what I was doing, which was slowly and steadily taking away from the local people the absurd notion that Cantonese wasn't a language, by making it a world language.

*

A few months later, a new student came into my life: The delightful Lydia.

When she came breezing into the Lok Heung Yuen ('Joyful Fragrant Garden') tea shop in Wellington Street, one of the last genuine *cha chan teng* (tea restaurants) in Hong Kong which was at that stage my office and classroom, I knew we'd be friends.

She picked up Cantonese really easily, as I had expected, and she understood where I wanted to go with the course. One day she said: "This course should be on TV!" When I explained that it wasn't for lack of trying on my part, she at once came up with a practical solution.

"Why don't you just get a film camera and make your own programmes?"

Why indeed? And more pertinently: Why hadn't I thought of that myself? But as 'they' say ('they' being of course the Chinese): When the student is ready, the teacher will appear.

Soon after I was the proud owner of a Sony Handicam, and Richard and Lydia came to my house to shoot the first episode in what was to become my show on YouTube: Cantonese – The Movie. *Episode 1: In a Bar.* Naturally.

Although I have never taken lessons in Cantonese or Mandarin, I have looked at a few textbooks over the years. The last one I looked at had as Lesson 1: "Greeting your professor at the airport." Really? Is that your most pressing concern when you want to learn a new language? Then came "Shopping for a Camera" and, in Lesson 26: "Ordering Drinks."

Maybe greeting a professor at an airport is the most important thing for people writing textbooks, but in my experience what you primarily need a new language for is to communicate with service providers. Barmen, waiters, taxi drivers; these are the vanguard in the linguistic wars.

We rigged up a bar in my living room, put on some fake stomachs and moustaches and off we went. Scene one, a man walks into a bar:

"Do you have Carlsberg?"

"No."

"Heineken?"

"No."

"San Miguel?"

"No."

See? That's what you need to learn first. In my opinion and experience. And: Film making! Filming, then editing, adding subtitles, music... I had found my calling in life. What a fantastic thing. And what a fantastic world we live in, where you can just create your own TV station and make your own films which people all over the world can watch.

But guess what? Three white people wearing fake moustaches and talking about beer in Cantonese on YouTube *didn't* attract millions of viewers! People are weird, I thought. Weird! A cat falling down the stairs attracts two million viewers overnight, while my clips, which take weeks to write, shoot, and edit, are lucky if they can get six views a year. Then again, life was never fair.

But I kept making the episodes. I have to say my students were good sports. No moustache was too '70s, no costume too ridiculous for them to go out in Central and other extremely crowded areas of Hong Kong and let themselves be filmed talking Cantonese, following a script they were only given that day. I think quite a few of them do it on an internal dare.

Check it out on *www.youtube.com/cantocourse*.

The episode that has had the most hits by far is, not surprisingly, *Episode 3: In a Whorehouse*. I should just have called all the episodes "Porn Here!" or "Whores!" "Breasts!" Then I would get the number of viewers I so clearly deserve. Yes, even when it's free, sex sells. But in China, it's normally not free.

14

A Sound of Flesh

"Sex is like drinking a glass of sewage: It tastes better the more expensive it is." – *Old Chinese proverb*

Originally, as a kind of joke, I was planning to leave this chapter empty, as in that *Intelligent Quotes from George W. Bush* book, of 100 blank pages. But on reflection I thought this would be both stupid and misleading, seeing as China is one of the countries where there clearly is the *most* sex. How else could there be so many of them?

They must have been at it something serious to go from a country of 550 million people in 1949, via 800 million in 1976 when Mao died – even after having single-handedly managed to get rid of 70 million people – to the 1.3 billion (give or take) of today. And that is after having 'saved' almost 400 million from being born by means of the one child policy.

For many years, China was a country where the state controlled and banned absolutely everything that could be vaguely connected with fun, including sex. But as soon as the Party started to loosen the reins a little in the 1980s, the Chinese wasted no time in getting rid of the 'New Victorianism with Chinese Characteristics' label they had acquired during the Cultural Revolution, and becoming a modern nation sexually.

Now, sex is everywhere. Well, not the actual act but the internationally accepted symbol of sexuality, namely the half- or completely undressed woman with moist lips, writhing in ecstasy in a room by herself. This symbol is used to sell everything from cars to washing powder, much like in other places. It is a drastic change from the China of not many years ago, when there weren't any adverts for consumer goods at all, let alone huge billboards showing women engaged in auto-eroticism.

The Chinese have, or had before the Communists came, a long and proud tradition of using sex as a method to induce health, increase physical power and enhance life. It was therefore necessary for the old emperors to keep thousands of concubines languishing in the palace, ready to be called into service at any moment, but without even workable feet to pass the time between bouts. Sometimes the emperor would have a special favourite upon whom to descend daily, but apart from that, even the lucky concubines couldn't count on being chosen more than a couple of times a year for romping with the emperor, supervised by envious eunuchs.

Many of the poor women had to go into retirement and then to their graves without having done it even once, but it was useful to keep them around just in case. And for the emperor there was of course the extra bonus of knowing that it was impossible for women living in the palace to do it with any man other than himself, the other men there being without sexual organs and all. This probably made the emperor laugh often and with much *schadenfreude* (which, unlike in English, *is* a word in Chinese).

In this as in so many other ways, Mao followed the old traditions. He preached abstinence and Puritanism to his increasingly worn-down subjects who hardly had any privacy anyway, reminding them that sex took people's thoughts away from making revolution.

To further ensure that nobody would enjoy any other pleasures than the worshipping of him and the Party, Mao suggested that married couples living in communes (slave camps) should be allowed three days together per month for (preferably joyless) couplings. Even he knew that people couldn't be completely abstemious, and besides, that this would also upset his plan of filling China with so many "stainless screws in the socialist machinery" that they could afford to lose a few hundred million in a hopeful atomic war.

At the same time, he himself out-emperored the old emperors when it came to sheer numbers of sexual partners. The man who would eradicate all religion followed to the letter the Taoist teachings of doing it as often, as long, and with as many different partners as possible. And whereas the old emperors, though omnipotent, largely had to comply with religious advisors when it came to where, when and with whom copulation would take place, Mao was supreme dictator in this area as well, refusing to take any advice from his increasingly scandalised courtiers.

This man, arguably the most autocratic and dictatorial of all China's emperors, satisfied his sexual appetite wherever and whenever he wanted, unapologetic while his advisors, local leaders and delegates from abroad waited for hours, the tea cooling in their cups. His tastes ran towards young, unsophisticated peasant girls, and almost until his dying day a steady stream of unspoilt flesh wended its way into his bedroom in Zhongnanhai, the Party's headquarters just outside the Forbidden City. His private jet and trains were also equipped with large wooden beds in case he should get the urge while travelling. His beds were all huge, to accommodate not only four or five peasant wenches at a time, but also a number of books.

Bigamy and concubinage as institutions had naturally been banned as soon as the Communists came to power, but Mao solved that problem by declaring that women should be liberated – not only to work as hard and long as men in the field and on the factory floor, but to appear in his bed in clusters. Some of them were married, but apparently the husbands didn't object to wifely infidelity as long as it was with *Mao.* At least there were no reports of any husband ever turning up at Mao's door and shoving a pitch-fork up his arse. That's superstardom for you.

*

Hong Kong has always been more tradition-minded than mainland China. Here concubinage – or bigamy, really – was part of the fabric of society until it was officially banned in 1971. Thus another tie to the old China was cut, and Hong Kong had taken a new step on the road to becoming a modern society free of barbaric customs. (Homosexuality, or rather homosexual acts, were *decriminalised*, meaning no longer punishable by life imprisonment, in *1991*. Yes, Hong Kong is truly an unstoppably progressive society). On the other hand, the concubines of rich geezers, and any children resulting from such unions, lost the rights they used to have as Wife Number Two (and Three, Four, etc.) It was now up to the guy's conscience and wallet whether he wanted to support them or not.

The rich guys, it goes without saying, carried on like they had always done – only the most naive bureaucrats would ever have thought that people would change their sexual habits just because of a new law. Then again, it is a fact that if there is something not lacking in Hong Kong, it is naive bureaucrats. Many would even say that to call them 'naive' is so mild-mannered and diplomatic that it borders on the naive.

In China, keeping as many mistresses as possible as a status symbol is now back in full force, after having suffered a slight setback in the years after 1949. In Hong Kong, of course, it was always business as usual. And in both places, keeping mistresses is completely open, carried out with panache, without shame or awkwardness. The wife is for the purpose of procreation and visiting relatives during Chinese New Year, whereas the mistress is for enjoyment.

I remember the day I married a Hong Kong guy, a handsome and kind man. His best man, Bong, brought his mistress, a simpering bint, to the wedding ceremony as well as to the party afterwards. I felt that it was perhaps peculiar manners, at least symbolically, this action of bringing the very marriage-wrecking entity itself to the ceremony marking the start of a marriage. I'm not superstitious, but that day I really felt that such behaviour could lead to nothing good. I was right – we separated two years later, purely because of Bad Luck Bong and his dubious wedding guest etiquette. Couldn't the guy have done like Norwegian Man, and kept the bint a well hidden secret?

In the China of today it is not only not a secret that all men of any standing have one or more mistresses, it is expected of them. In the same way as righteous, upright and conscientious officials get sucked into the world of graft and corruption whether they want to or not, to further their career and to avoid being ostracised by colleagues, the few faithful husbands who would actually rather go home to the family instead of boozing in a karaoke room with a couple of whores draped around them, are, if they want to succeed, obliged to play the game.

Seeing that most business deals are made during meals with lots of alcohol where part of the strategy is to get your rival shitfaced, men who want to succeed must have livers able to withstand massive and frequent onslaughts. A dinner in today's China isn't complete without a subsequent visit to a karaoke bar, and nobody would want to sing alone without two or three hostesses around to pour beer and light cigarettes for them, now would they? And seeing how these charming hostesses are underpaid like everybody else and need to make a buck where they can and therefore do anything they can to make the guy want to spend the extra yuan – well, it would be a very strong man who could resist.

In the old China, only the emperor and rich men could wallow in concubines, courtesans and 'flower girls'. Ordinary men had to make do with the one wife for whom they were able to scrape together the dowry, and perhaps the odd passer-by they could drag into the sorghum field and ravish.

The new society is far more democratic, and nowadays almost everybody can afford to buy sex.

The most expensive whores are those who live like the concubines of yore, only without bound feet. On the contrary they are very mobile, with mobile phones, cars, their own apartments and expense accounts.

Hardly a day goes by in Hong Kong without a news story about some higher official in China who, caught embezzling millions and millions of yuan, explains to the court that it was all because his "female friend" had become so demanding. It was "give me more, give me more" from morning till night until the poor bugger had no choice but to use the 50 million yuan earmarked for... compensation for the peasants kicked out of their houses to make way for the Three Gorges Dam, say, just to shut her up.

Yes, when the ladies get all unreasonable it's good to have the state coffers to turn to, and in misogynistic China it is always popular to blame men's avarice and ineptitude on the many women nagging away behind them.

Mao himself was largely excused for his insane actions including the Cultural Revolution, for which it was much easier to blame his wife, Jiang Qing, who would have had not a shred of power if Mao hadn't stood behind her. (Not in a supportive way though, just as in not lifting a finger to stop her).

Fortunately China's courts, normally not known for their impartiality or keen sense of justice, sometimes do show a bit of sense. So when somebody is to be executed or thrown in jail for corruption, it is the guy himself, or rather the man the party/courts have chosen as the fall guy, who takes the rap – not the mistress.

Having said that, and again according to the papers, it is almost always his 'secretary' the corrupt cadre takes with him when he manages to escape abroad with two billion yuan of taxpayers' money, and not the wife...

For those who haven't got the inclination, time or money to run a regular mistress, there are plenty of other possibilities to engage in extra-marital activities. Although prostitution is officially illegal in China and there aren't any red-light districts as such, you seldom have to do more than check into a hotel and everything will be sorted. As a single man in a Chinese hotel, you will find the telephone ringing off the hook with women calling day and night saying they're coming to visit you. If you don't want any visits or telephone calls, it's no good complaining to the receptionists because they're the ones handing out your number in the first place, expecting a cut of the transaction.

I also received such a call once. It was in a hotel in Shenzhen and at that time my naivety in such matters had few limits.

Ring ring.

"Wei?"

"Hi, I'm in reception. Can I come up?"

"What? Who the hell are you?"

"Ah-Keung. I'm downstairs. Maybe you can come down?"

"Who did you say?"

"Ah-Keung."

"You must have the wrong number."

"No, wait! I'm ah-Keung! I'll come up, shall I?"

"I don't know any ah-Keung."

"But I'm waiting for you."

"Oh piss off." *Click.*

It was only a long time later I twigged. He was a gigolo. Or a "duck" as they're called in Cantonese. Oh no, how could I let a chance like that go by?

So the next time someone called me in a hotel room, in Hohhot, the provincial capital of Inner Mongolia, I ran happily across the room and tore off the receiver.

"Wei. Wei?"

"Yes, this is... (unintelligible mumbling)"

"Come up at once, I've just had a shower."

"... (scratch, scratch)... wondering if... (scratch)... we... (scrape)... horse (unintelligible mumbling)"

"What? Did you say horse?"

"Yes... (mumble mumble)... horse... (scratch)... ride horse... (scratch)..."

"Come on, what do you think I am?"

The connection suddenly cleared.

"We are a company arranging horseback riding trips. Would you like to go horse riding and see a real Mongolian *ger?*"

"Piss off."

But he didn't. On the contrary, he continued calling about the damned riding trip every 15 minutes, alternating between my room and that of Richard, who would also vastly have preferred a gigolo calling. In the end we had to move to another hotel.

If nobody calls to offer their services, most hotels are equipped with a 'sauna and massage centre' whose masseurs don't mind making a bit of extra money to give the massee a 'happy ending'.

As one who thinks glancing at the cover of *Lonely Planet* is a defeat, I have of course never hired a guide, but according to reputable sources, private guides also have nothing against increasing their fluctuating and meagre incomes at the end of a hard day's strenuous wandering.

And if all this should fail, there's always the hairdressers to fall back on. Or on top of.

I always had to laugh when walking down Guangzhou's narrow and funky back street Qing Long Fang, not far from the fabled Garden Hotel, with my 'cousin' Richard, on our way to our favourite Sichuan restaurant.

He would always have an astonishing effect on the many ladies working in the hairdressing salons lining the street, interspersed only with a handful of restaurants. When I say "working" in hairdressing salons, I mean sitting around outside hairdressing salons, sparkling in their heavy jewellery, vinyl hot pants (hot pants never really became unfashionable in China) and steep cleavages of astonishingly un-Chinese dimensions.

When they discovered Richard, their faces would light up with such genuine happiness! They would smile and wave at him: Come, come! Come and have a haircut! This despite the fact that his head was virtually shaven. Whereas I, with my shoulder-length hair which was often in need of a trim, was completely ignored.

And it wasn't only women who liked (or 'liked') Richard. He was also a magnet for men. In fact, apart from the fact that he was the world's best conversationalist *and* could tell how many letters there were in a word without counting (that's right! Before you'd finished saying "surreptitiou..." he would shout "13!" Was it a form of autism? Oh how I envied that faculty), I liked travelling in China with him because he was my man-magnet. Wherever we went, heterosexual men came up to him, apparently wanting to touch him.

Oh, if Chinese men could only touch me as much, hard and often as they touch other men. Richard got men's arms around his shoulders, hands clutching his thighs, fingers holding his chin and, on one memorable occasion, was kissed on the mouth in a lift. (That guy *was* drunk, but still). I had to wait for photo ops before I could get any arms around my shoulders. But of course, when it came to the crunch they *were* heterosexual, so Richard ultimately had to sleep alone and I didn't.

In Hong Kong, it was a different story. There I had to suffer the indignity of having to live vicariously through Richard, sex-wise. Because he had Gaydar. I was truly fascinated by this excellent online gay service. The gays of Hong Kong sent each other emails saying things like: "Wanna hook up?" "Yeah, all right. Tonight."

And just like that, they were in business. I don't know how many hours I spent listening to Richard telling me about his innumerable conquests. They all seemed to want to meet up outside Marks and Spencer's in Central, often keeping poor Richard standing there for ages while they had dinner with their various family members; more often than not they would text him half an hour after the appointed time, saying they had inexplicably come down with food poisoning.

Food poisoning is a favoured staple of Hong Kong work-and-social life: Every time someone doesn't want to do something, like going to a dinner party, going to work or just meeting someone who you suspect is too far gone out of the closet for you, it's always food poisoning that's the excuse to cancel. I can't count how many dinner parties I have hosted where two or three guests, invariably three hours after the party was supposed to start, have texted me saying they couldn't turn up because they were puking their guts out in some toilet or other. Look, I'm not saying food poisoning doesn't exist. After all, I have had it too: Once in 20 years, and it was gastro-enteritis which I picked up in the five-star hotel The Excelsior.

Therefore, based on my own empirical evidence, is it statistically possible that absolutely all the people I know should have food poisoning at least twice a year? I'm not a statistician, or whatever it's called. A statistics-monger. And maybe my internal organs are superior to those of other people in Hong Kong, or just immune to the many dangers that lurk without, in that dangerous entity we call Hong Kong dining. But that *that* many people with such relentless frequency should come down with food poisoning at *exactly* the time I was giving a party or Richard was standing outside Marks and Sparks?

Hmm...

No, here is my theory. Hong Kong is a fast-food nation in every way. No one wants to commit to anything, thinking quite rationally that something better might turn up in the meantime. Therefore they say yes to everything, not wanting to seem rude. And when they invariably do find something better and want to cancel the party or whatever function they've said yes to, they come up with this brilliant idea which no one before them has ever had: Food poisoning!

Anyway, Richard managed to get a few Chinese guys to get away from their families (not out of the closet, no, that would be asking too much, but away for just one night) and that's when my vicarious living kicked in and I got to hear everything about being young and playing the field. Richard's guys, though beautiful and although homosexuality was no longer punishable by death, were bundles of neuroses. He was attracted to them physically but, I couldn't help noticing, not mentally.

They were mummys' boys. Family was everything. They cried in his lap saying they could never come out as gay because it would hurt their mothers and besides, she would disown them.

This phenomenon wasn't only going on in the gay world. One Austrian student of mine had a 45-year-old Chinese boyfriend who could never spend the night with her because he didn't want his mother to think he didn't love her enough to come home every night. "So you don't think he's actually married?" I remarked, ever the cynic. Apparently he was divorced and with two children, but, because he was back to living with his parents, he had to seem chaste.

After Richard found the love of his life and platumped (platonically dumped) me, I thought I should also give this Gaydar thing a go. Of course not the actual Gaydar, but Straight-dar, Adult Friend Finder, also known as 'the website for men who want to cheat on their wives but not with prostitutes because they're too stingy'.

I put my photo up there, lying only a little about my age, saying in no uncertain terms that I wouldn't accommodate any married men, and soon the guys started swarming in.

The first was a no-photo guy. His message to me was: "u want sex" Yeah, you had me at the "u"! I mean – not even a full stop? Come on.

Another no-photo guy had the decency to describe his status as "married," and went on to say: "I know you don't like the guy already marry but that's okay. We can meeting."

Another guy, no photo, marital status "I'd rather not say" opened with: "So, tell me all about your sexual fantasies."

"Er... perhaps you could post your photo first?"

"Come on. If you can't even share your sexual fantasies here on the web, you're not the kind of person I want to meet."

Er... all right then.

Another memorable message came from a 49-year-old man from Tuen Mun. Well to be honest, he hadn't actually contacted me, only checked out my profile. I found that a little hurtful, but eventually got over it when I saw his profile:

"Hi I am looking for a special lady who can attract me so as to give me a chance to fall in love with her. She will be the most important girl I ever met. I think my girl will be a simple one, no need to be real special, no need to be mature, the best is – she always acts like a 3 years old baby girl."

That really made me think. Is this the secret formula to winning a Chinese man's heart?

All right, on occasion I'm sure I've acted like a three-year-old. But not since I was five! Since then, 'malevolent six-year-old' is the best I've been able to come up with. And certainly not 'always'.

So I gave up on the adult 'friend' finder thing.

I still had China. And, before Richard platumped me, I used him shamelessly to get closer to heterosexual guys. They just would not stop touching him.

The most intense man-touching city in China had to be Seiwui in Guangdong province. That place is an incredible party town, where all you have to do is turn up. Walking down the pavement you will be dragged into some private room or other in one of the hundred karaoke bars, plied with beer and offered *Lao K*, just because you are beige.

Richard and I discovered this excellent town by accident one Chinese New Year. We were actually going to another good party place, Siu Heng, but realised the bus wasn't leaving for another two hours; there would in other words be a tremendous *lull*. Both of us being extreme lullophobes, we quickly decided to take the first bus available and this, the Serendipity Express, brought us straight to Seiwui. And that's where we discovered the Venus Bar, an establishment which, if it had been in any other country, would have been characterised as 'seedy', situated in 'the underbelly of' somewhere, and populated with 'sinister types'.

But of course, this being China, it was just your normal super-friendly, dunk-a-dunk-a, dice-playing, beer-soaked scream-fest with lots of male touching. At one stage Richard was dancing on the table with two guys holding onto him, all three pulling up their T-shirts to display their nipples. One of the nipple guys had been some kind of triad and chopped off half his own index finger as a young man, and as he got more and more sloshed we could see that he still had a general tendency to self-harm; doing slamming tricks with his glass he eventually broke it but carried on regardless, blood spurting from his fingers.

Then he started burning himself with a candle. We asked him why his remaining nine fingernails were so long and he grabbed Richard in what looked like a lethal head-grip, digging his talon-like nails into Richard's jugular. Everybody laughed because they had obviously seen his act many times, to the point where they were possibly a little bored.

To distract him and save the digits and limbs he had left as well as Richard's life, they encouraged the nine-fingered guy, who could be best described as a kindly thug, to get up and dance. The dance routine consisted of tearing off his shirt and soon there was a general display of male nipples which suited me fine, for there are few finer sights in this world than the male Chinese chest, and few activities more enjoyable than lightly fingering one of them.

Other people besides Richard and I had caught on to China as a paradise of nipples – female ones, that is. A few years ago, the latest trend among Hong Kong men was to make crusades to a small island just inside Chinese waters about an hour's boat trip from Central. The island was uninhabited apart from hundreds of hairdressing salons which had sprung up seemingly overnight. Illegal speedboats, whose power was just that fraction greater than that of the marine police, shuttled to and from the island all days of the week. A reporter among the hundreds writing about this phenomenon actually tried to get a haircut in each of the salons, but found that only two of them were equipped with scissors.

Since then, Chinese authorities have cracked down on this island, just like they crack down on everything that's fun. The shuttling to and from the island has ceased, to the joy of Hong Kong wives. And to the perhaps even greater joy of karaoke hostesses, masseuses and hairdressers in Shenzhen, the Wild West city across the border from Hong Kong; the only place in China where there are more women than men.

With the establishment of a whoring island right outside Hong Kong where no immigration procedures were necessary, their businesses had taken a hit, and that was hot on the heels of Hong Kong's economy going mysteriously straight down the toilet the day after the handover in 1997. Until then, they had been living the life of Riley as a direct result of the democratization and increase in overall income in Hong Kong.

When Shenzhen was declared a 'special economic zone' in 1980 and Hong Kong companies immediately started saving on wages by moving all factories across the border, thousands of men suddenly had the chance of living The Chinese Dream of being a big shot with Wife Number Two and Three. Even truck drivers could afford to set up a regular mistress in some flat somewhere. In 1997, the going rate was about HK$3,000 per month. This covered rent, clothes and make-up plus enough pocket money so the girl wouldn't have to work in a karaoke bar, or wherever she'd been plucked from, as a means of extra income.

A 'mistress village' sprang up just outside Shenzhen, and in it the lucky ladies spent their days languidly knitting, eating and sleeping while they waited for their ardent lovers to turn up with their gleaming bald pates and beer bellies.

It was inevitable that some of these alliances would result in children, but unlike during the lovely times of the old concubine system where all the wives lived under the same roof, with their myriad children and servants, the bigamist now had to scurry from one apartment to the next, back and forth across the border, trying to make everybody happy. He told the mistress(es) he wasn't married, and told the wife he didn't have a mistress.

This is where I don't understand men. Okay, so they are tired of kids screaming and wife nagging at home in Hong Kong. That's understandable. It's understandable that people want some distractions, some variation from their daily grind. What I don't understand is why they don't just have some fun with a few karaoke hostesses and hairdressers, of which there is no shortage, instead of setting up a new household with the same screaming of kids and nagging of wife?

Who can understand some people? It almost makes you suspect that men, instead of being the fickle and unreliable creatures that women complain so bitterly about, actually *want* to settle down with just one woman and some kids – simultaneously, in three different places. What is certain is that this system turned out to be not the little pastime many men wanted it to be. Mistresses found out about the wife, tracked her down and threw acid in her face. Wives found out about the mistress and threw acid in *her* face, stabbing the husband when he came home.

Mistresses killed the husband or themselves. The wives threw the children out from the 27th floor and jumped after them. Sometimes wives and mistresses became friends and left the husband together – although the latter was a rare occurrence.

Then 1997 came and, with it, Hong Kong's economic downfall from which we still haven't quite recovered. Truck drivers, businessmen, factory foremen and normal bigamists suddenly couldn't afford the upkeep of two or more families, and decided that the old wife wasn't so bad after all.

The mistress village started to empty itself of the knitting hordes, and they drifted back to the karaoke bars or villages whence they came, to live with the shame of having been spurned. Plus of course the endless fines people have to pay for having more than one child.

Now most Hong Kong men are playing it nice and safe like other men around the world, with weekend trips across the border where they sensibly take what they can get of phoning, singing or massaging women, for a fraction of the cost of a separate household.

Meanwhile China's sexual revolution goes on. Hong Kong research shows that both *university students* and *other teenagers* are at it! (Only Hong Kong seems to find this shocking, or indeed to find it necessary to ask university students if they engage in sexual intercourse). Up to 50% of girls over 15 years old would have sex with their boyfriend "if he loved her". At the same time an epidemic of syphilis, all but eradicated since 1949, is flooding the country.

There's always something.

But hello? You may ask. Whores this and prostitutes that; aren't there any normal people who want to do it, free and gratis, at the end of a fun evening?

Yes there are.

They are called men.

Women... often, even in ultra-modern China, wait a little before they go to bed with somebody. Wait for several months, actually. That's not stupid of them. How else are they supposed to get the guy to do what they want?

And what they want, more often than not, is to have the ring on their finger before venturing into the dark, messy continent of sex.

This is not very practical for the passing tourist who usually ends up having to cough up, but it has to be said: Compared to European crack whores with their indifferent hand-jobs and unfriendly attitude, the women you can get for a few coppers in China really know how to make you think they like you. And then everybody's happy, are they not?

*

Finally, I would like to share a shaggy, not to say shagg*ing*, dog story about the modern Chinese woman. This shows that what is surreal and borderline insane for me is completely normal for other people.

In my book *Blonde Lotus* there's a true story about an American man in Nanjing who'd been struggling for months to marry his Chinese girlfriend. There's a sea of documents, rubber stamps, running between the various departments, police stations and Public Security Bureaus, as well as trying to deal with various relatives.

But all that is nothing for him compared with the real problem: That he has never had sexual intercourse with the woman. That's right, eight months without even any fumbling. I remember being shocked and in disbelief. It was the year 1988! Chinese men had never acted so stubborn and difficult with me.

Oh well, each to their own, I thought. And anyway, the method worked! He *would* marry her. How many husbands did *I* have?

Then, a couple of years ago, I was shocked with a much bigger shock, so shocking that all I could do was laugh, relatively loud and barking it has to be said. I was in Shenzhen with one of my male students, a European of about 30. One beer followed another, and suddenly he started talking about the Hong Kong woman he'd been with for four years and living together for two, and whom he would soon marry.

"You must be happy now that you'll soon get married," I mumbled insincerely – goodbye to another party-partner.

"Yes, then I'll get laid at last," he sighed, taking a large swallow of beer and crushing his 50th cigarette.

"What? You mean... no!"

"Yeah, we've never done it."

"But... but you live together?"

"Yes, but she doesn't want to do it. Not before we're married."

That was when I realised how different people really are.

He would have to keep waiting away like he had been doing for four years, but fortunately the wedding was to be the week after. He still spent our whole evening in Shenzhen, ostensibly to practise Cantonese, chatting up girls. Who could blame him? But since they were Chinese girls, whose sole objective was to marry a foreigner – at least – they naturally didn't want to put out either.

The fool should have listened to me and gone straight to a massage parlour without fail, to enjoy, for a very small amount of yuan, one of the many pleasures which China has to offer.

China, whence everything originates, including sex. Still, I couldn't help wondering: Would a Norwegian guy have put up with that? Because over the years I had come to realise that China and Norway had so much in common. For example: Cantonese is more or less identical to Norwegian...

15

All the World is a Beige

"East is East. And West is also East, if you see it from the other direction."
— *Old Chinese proverb*

China and Norway: Two more or less identical countries? Superficially it can seem that way. Both countries are situated at the edge of a continent. The inhabitants of both countries are crazy about drinking and shouting out "Cheers!" And both countries have a long tradition of eating disgusting stuff. Anybody who has ever seen her own mother clutching a big, boiled cod's head and sucking out its brain will know what I'm talking about. In Norway people eat cod and sheep heads. In China: Any heads. Norway: Sheep legs. China: Anything with legs except the table.

Both peoples have an unfailing belief in their own superiority, having not long ago emerged from anonymity and poverty. And both act as if the world's resources will never be used up.

According to many Chinese, 'Norway' in this case could well mean 'the entire Western world including Australia and New Zealand.' For short, they now call these people, (as well as *lao wai* of course), 'Americans'.

When Chinese people talk to me about cultural differences or even personal things, they seldom say "you" (as in "you as an individual person"), it's always "you lot", meaning every country on the planet with a beige-coloured population. It's probably because they normally say "we

Chinese" and "our Chinese this" and "our Chinese that". They speak for the whole country and in this they can rest assured.

By the way – another thing that Norway and China have in common is that they call "abroad" the "Out-Country". (Outland). In Norway we have a saying: The Outcountry is the biggest country in the world.

I think the Chinese also, deep down or not so deep down, feel that there are two countries in the world: China and the Outcountry. And the Outcountry means the US.

But now in the techno- and fast-everything age, these two countries, China and the Outcountry, are growing closer and closer, to the point where they are almost identical. So let me explain the things, after years of studying both species, I think most separate the Chinese and *Lao Wai*.

1. Funerals. Where Beige Person sits around swathed in black, snivelling quietly into his hanky, the Chinese go full throttle with gongs and cymbals, music and noise, when somebody's kicked the bucket. There are cards and mahjong, and of course lots of good food to be scoffed, notably barbecued suckling pig. There is burning of paper houses, paper cars, people, tennis rackets, shark's fins, fine food... anything that the deceased will find useful in the afterlife. There are dentures, cigars, chocolates, swimming costumes (with goggles) for both sexes, luxury-package ginseng roots, guns, torches, video cameras, a whole McDonalds happy meal, rice cookers, bird cages… as well as stylish T-shirts for the younger generation of dead, for whom in Hong Kong suicide unfortunately is the main reason for their premature diving off this mortal coil. But what with the amount of equipment they receive for their final send-off: The dead never had it so good.

2. Hue. The Chinese are terrified of getting (or being) *brown.* You don't find Chinese people sprawled all over the beach – who's got time for that? They stay inside when the sun comes out, huddling around their air conditioners. They use umbrellas when the sun is

shining, which I thought was both strange and comical the first time I saw it, but which I now realise is not a bad idea. When the sun is broiling and it's 45 degrees, it's actually much more comfortable to carry a brolly than to wear a hat and long sleeves. The umbrella can also be used as a weapon.

The reason why the Chinese have this mortal fear of having a tan is the same as why the Norwegians are so crazy about getting one: Face and status. In China, only peasants and other outdoor workers have tans. The darker your skin, the further down the ladder of society, much like the Europe of a hundred or so years ago. And that's why the Chinese like us whites, our coming from the Outcountry notwithstanding, and why they despise Africans, Indonesians and other brown- to ebony-coloured people.

Yes, beige and fat is the best way to be; that means one works in a sedentary job, indoors.

But the sun is a capricious gentleman. He sneaks in everywhere, and umbrellas, clothes and sun creams with factors up to 44 have to give up. Therefore the Chinese cosmetics industry, to satisfy a steadily increasing middle class with *consumerism* as its main hobby, has come up in recent years with a dizzying array of products to make skin white. And not only white, but the other side of white, beyond white, minus 5 white, fish belly white. In a word: Sub-white.

There is whitening moisturiser, body lotion, face mask, eye cream and toothpaste. There is whitening foot cream, hand cream, whitening AND softening cream for elbows and knees, and whitening cream that removes hair.

For a foreigner who doesn't think God has struck if my skin takes on a light golden hue (it goes so well with blonde hair) it is difficult to understand this fascination with ultra, neon, stratospheric white. I must therefore admit I screamed discreetly with laughter the other day when I saw the following object on a shelf in Mannings, one of Hong Kong's two monopoly chains of chemists: *whitening underarm deodorant.*

But I do understand. In a society where your whole reputation hinges on whether you've swung around the outdoor world one day, with the terrible consequences that may lead to, it is obvious you can't walk around with your face and body shining like the stomach of a cod, only to lift your arm and reveal an armpit that is, watch out everybody – brown!

3. Welcoming. Chinese welcome foreigners (if they are beige) with open arms and wallets. As soon as they see a *Lao Wai* approaching on the horizon, it's pull out a chair, open the beer and, not unusually, a little handing out of presents at the end of the day.

It can get tiresome.

Foreigners visiting Norway don't have that problem. The Norwegians are discreet, non-intruding, and leave foreigners alone, always. Foreigners in Norway won't be forced by locals to eat, drink and be merry all night, no sirree. In that respect, Norway is a healthy country for foreigners to visit.

Norway is for some reason very popular in China (or actually, see point 3, being so welcoming, the Chinese probably claim to love whatever country people are from). I never cease to be amazed at how much the Chinese know about Norway. And to what degree they are prepared to tell me what they know about Norway. (I'm talking about mainlanders here. If I ask Hong Kong people to ask where I'm from and give them "whale hunting" as a tip, they guess Switzerland).

Typical conversation with new acquaintance in China:

"Where from?" (not "Hello" or anything)

"Oh, Hong Kong."

"What? You can't be from Hong Kong. You're a foreigner."

"What – I can't be born in Hong Kong?"

"No. Well yes, you can be born in Hong Kong but you can't *be from* Hong Kong. Where are you really from?"

"Hong Kong. China is my mother and the Communist Party is my father."

"... ? Oh, humour. But where are you really from?"

"For Christ's sakes... OK, Norway."

"Ah!" (triumphantly). "Norway is a rich, developed country."

"That's right."

"Norway is situated in Northern Europe. Two of its chief industries are forestry and fishing."

"Er..."

"Norway is an oil-producing country and one of the richest countries in the world. It has a small population."

"Yes, I know. I *come from* Norway."

"Norway has a population of four..."

"... yes, I know! I'm Norwegian!"

"... point three million people. Salmon is a popular export article."

"But why are you telling me this? I am a Nor..."

"Norway has a well developed social welfare system. Most people own their own house and..."

"Oh, piss off."

Of course, not everybody is like this; if they were, travelling around China would be a terrible ordeal rather than a never-ending joyous dream. But it is true that the country seems to have an above-average number of people who are above-average eager to share their knowledge about topics. Being told about topics can be very edifying, but being told about topics you already know a lot about by people who know very little, isn't quite the same.

The most common topic Chinese people want to share with me is the topic that I teach: Chinese. And I don't know about you, but if you ever met someone who said they were, oh, I don't know... an English teacher, would you then, to show that you were an interesting conversation partner, start telling them about the alphabet? Maybe you would. In which case you probably don't have a large number of friends.

But those are just my foreign, European sentiments. I'm projecting my own feelings onto others. Maybe I'm the only person in the universe who gets that restless, wanting to leave or smash somebody's face in-feeling at the following kind of conversation in Chinese (Cantonese and Putonghua both):

"Where from?"

"Hong Kong."

"Ha, ha, you can't be from..."(etc.)

"Yes I can..." (etc.)

"You speak really good Chinese, are you a teacher?"

"Yes, I'm a Chinese teacher."

"Oh really, ha, ha. Humour. You see that character?"

"Yes. It says 'One'."

"That is our Chinese character. It says 'One'. In China we don't use alphabet, but Chinese characters."

"Yes I know. I'm a Chinese teacher. I teach Chinese to foreigners."

"That character says 'One'."

"Yes, I just said that."

"And this is another Chinese character. See? Two lines. It means 'two'."

"Yes, I can read Chinese characters. I'm a Chinese teacher."

"And this means 'three', see? One, two, three strokes. Three..."

"Oh, piss off."

But, it has to be said, other times they tell me things I don't know, like the fact that China imports rocks from Norway – Norwegian Red, very popular. And bugger me if some Norwegians later don't tell me that *Norway* also imports rocks from *China*. What are these people *on?* Can't they find a better way to flush money down the toilet? Or even not, by just hanging on to their own rocks and saving on transport? For there's no shortage of rocks in China. Another way in which it resembles Norway.

Now, Norway is a fine country for those who like that kind of thing, but personally I prefer the Outcountry, and China in particular. Take for example Songpan in Inner Sichuan, where I was travelling with Ali and Jan. In retrospect it was only the altogether 20 hours on Suicide Mission Bus that wasn't a thoroughly pleasant experience on that little jaunt. Oh yeah, and the fact that I almost died of exposure... and fear.

*

According to the *Lonely Planet*, Songpan – and the mountains in which the couple have decided we are going horse riding – are *the most beautiful place in China.* That says a lot. They show me the paragraph and yes, right enough. The most beautiful. And it's not only the *Lonely Planet* bible that puts forth this claim – most beautiful this and most beautiful that; it says the same thing in hotel brochures and on every wall, sign and poster in this tourist-happy little town where every other shop is a horse rental place. So even I can't fail to believe it.

Because Songpan has a large Tibetan population there are many colourful clothes to be seen, and something I've never seen in China before: Wooden houses. I could have said they remind me of Norwegian mountain cabins, but they are too small for Norwegian weekends, and don't have as many carports.

There are also yaks, whose skins are everywhere; on people, on walls and for sale. Poor yaks! But the taste is... well, the yak is one animal that definitely doesn't taste like chicken; more like a heady blend of reindeer and dog.

Now we're on horseback and it's freezing, with a light but persistent drizzle. I have packed clothes suitable for southern Sichuan weather which is around 25 degrees; here the temperature is nudging 12. I had been counting on the horse keeping me warm, which was completely idiotic of me. I have been on horseback before, but not on a horse expedition with, bugger me senseless, tents. I hate tents.

Jan asks the horse guys how much beer we can bring.

"As much as you like!" is the encouraging reply. We therefore stack up with two days' worth of beer, and discover too late that it is the poor horses on which we will ride that are also carrying the beer. And the tents.

To ride on a horse is one thing; to sit on a horse on top of tents, food and twenty bottles of beer, something completely different. With all the luggage, we're now sitting twice as far from the ground. It is, in fact, more like perching on top of a large heap of things moving forward at a brisk trot on the edge of a 2,000-metre abyss. Oh well – back to being terrified.

Fog descends and I can barely make out the silhouette of Jan in front of me. We've all been equipped with rain ponchos (without whose protection I wouldn't be alive today) and with his hood up, and the four horse legs beneath the folds of his cape, he looks like a scene from *The Lord of the Rings*.

Sinister fog! Mordor! Orcs ahead!

Suddenly his horse buckles at the knees and sinks down in a large heap. Middle class, not to say petit bourgeois, people as we are, we take umbrage; yes, we are shaken. We declare that we want to walk the rest of the way to save the horses, while the horse guys swear and kick the poor fallen mare or gelding or whatever it is.

The oldest horse guy can smell mutiny, and explains that we have to ride because the air is so thin up here. I haven't noticed, but apparently we are 3,000 metres above sea level, 3,050 including beer and tents. So we climb back upon the swaying heights and try not to look into the gaping abyss and certain death. I'm so cold that I think it actually doesn't matter whether I live or die, but killing foreigners even through neglect is frowned upon in China, so the horse guys will probably try to keep me alive. And of course, we still haven't paid them.

Now we are on top of the mountain and rapidly approaching The Place. The most beautiful place in China (and therefore, presumably, the world). The tourist brochures go on in their normal understated way: Visitors will think they have entered a fairy tale! The sparkling lakes shine as blue as sparkling blue diamonds and make you weep with joy! This is truly a world paradise, a wonder under heaven... etc.

And yes, the mountain top is certainly majestic with its jutting crags and Tolkienesque ambience, or would be if we could have seen anything through the fog.

Descending on the other side, thankfully fog-less, we're finally allowed to get off and walk. And now I'm very excited to see all this beauty I've read so much about. It is difficult to describe my surprise when I see: A Norwegian valley. An average sad, dreary Norwegian valley with Norwegian trees, Norwegian plants and not least: Norwegian temperatures and piss-rain. Have I risked my life only to get to Inner Drizzle Valley, Southern Norway?

That means, if this dreary hole is China's (and the world's) most beautiful place, that means that Norway... er...

On the bottom of Sad Valley, next to a Norwegian-looking dirt road, we run into another horse gang. But there's nothing serendipitous about this meeting. We have actually arrived at the horse guys' meeting place, their canteen, as it were, where they can relax together after a long and horrible day with animal-protecting foreigners. Here, among sad and scrawny trees, brush and scrub and a road dragging itself forlornly forward between two high crags, we are to set up camp for the night – after an hour and a half of tottering riding.

That wasn't in the *Lonely Planet*, was it, my adventure-seeking young friends?

And in the brochures? No it wasn't. In the photos in both Lonely Pee and brochure, we saw happy, clean, dry young people in sunshine, sitting around their gleaming white tents on undulating green fields with blue mountains behind them and a kettle steaming away on the bonfire in front with rugged, healthy, clean and dry Steve from Illinois strumming a guitar. The sun shone on the shiny Arab steed, who was tapping a well-manicured hoof in time with the music.

We, on the other hand, are soaked to the skin, shivering with cold and with parodies of horses which break down at the 2,000-metre vertical drop of a hat; we are, in short, just an irritating and badly paying chore for the horse guys. Now at last they can have fun with each other and forget about troublesome us.

The other tourists are two fathers from Chongqing with a young son each, and two Korean guys who don't know English or Chinese. We think they are quite brave, but evidently the three years of compulsory military service in Korea have come in handy: Not only do they get around without any language, but they also spend the whole time in dripping wet T-shirts and jeans, stoically declining all offers from the horse guys of long yak-wool coats. We, on the other hand, welcome this offer with open arms stiff with cold, and even let the horse guys tie the sash round our waists. We are officially alive again, but can't quite bend our fingers.

So far, our big adventure has been somewhat marred by intense fear and cold, but all is forgotten as we sit crouching under a tarpaulin, wrapped in woollen coats, and see the horse guys in action. In a couple of hours they have done everything: Put up the large military-style tents, made a big fire, saved my feet from having to be amputated by giving me some military style socks, and collected enough mushrooms and herbs to cook up a huge evening meal including rice. Not a movement is wasted as these sons of the mountains go chain-smoking about their business, like experienced sailors effortlessly swinging around the masts of barques or frigates or whatever, while finding the time to laugh at us over-protected townies.

When everybody is sitting around the fire and scoffing down the best meal we've had in ages – fried mushrooms with herbs, rice, tomatoes and eggs as well as a kind of Tibetan bread they have somehow managed to bake – I feel a certain glorious satisfaction forcing itself up through the tundra that used to be my feet before the horse guys kneaded them, gave them socks and ripped them away from Death's jaws.

And when the horse guys, these rock-hard mountain men who can sleep standing on one leg in an avalanche, start to belt out hauntingly beautiful Tibetan songs, it is like we have arrived in a damp and smoke-filled paradise. I see their faces gleaming like copper in the reflection of the fire and perhaps a little from the *bai jiu* they drink as if it were water, spring water from the sparkling lakes of the most beautiful place on Earth. Suddenly I realise: It's not the place but the guys, the short and wind-dried horse guys, who are the most beautiful on earth.

Oh, and if we accidentally drank the whole trip's worth of beer that night, it was only because we felt sorry for the horses.

In the morning I stagger light-green out into another sad Norwegian day, in the same dreary Norwegian valley. Right in front of the tent of the dudes from Chongqing I see a large, fresh, newly-laid human turd.

Ah!

So yes, fortunately, although almost identical, there are some differences between China and Norway. That's why I want to live here, in the Magic Middle Kingdom, and not there, in the Land of Nog.

*

But – and not many people know this – the Cantonese language *is* identical to Norwegian. No, it's true. Word for word, they are the same; just with slightly different pronunciation.

If you compare Cantonese to English, you'll find that few if any two languages could be more different. It seems the only thing they have in common is "long time no see", which is of course Cantonese in the first place.

I think if a Martian or Jupiterian or even Pomeranian descended on Earth, trying to work with their *Earthlings' Lingo in Pictures* dictionary, sheit (she, he or it) wouldn't have much luck with English.

"Hoover?" No idea.

"Plane?" Hmm... Flat ground?

"Fridge?" Stumped!

If, on the other hand, sheit were to check the Norwegian and Cantonese dictionaries, it would at once become clear. Dust-sucker. Flying machine. Ice cupboard. ("Cooling cupboard" in Norwegian).

And why call it "liposuction" when what it really is, is "fat-sucking"? Yes, that's what we call it in Norwegian and Cantonese...

"Answer" the door? "Yeah, hello door, I'm fine thanks. See you tomorrow."

In Cantonese and Norwegian we *open* doors. See? Norwegian and Cantonese. Identical.

And this "have" everything; "have a cup of tea", "have dinner", "have some drinks" – have them where? In your pocket? On your head? In Cantonese and Norwegian we *drink* tea and *eat* food.

*Hav*ing said that; there's a delightful little book called *The Right Word in Cantonese*, written by Kwan Choi Wah but never edited by her or anyone else. This is one of the very few phrasebooks for Cantonese, seeing how most academics look down on this cool and happening language as if it were a little linguistic cockroach which has gatecrashed a 24-course Mandarin banquet.

The author has taken this 'have' thing to a new level, to the point where almost everything in the book is listed under 'have'.

Have a cold. Have a fever. Have a fire. (Meaning: A fire). Have a law suit. Have a reunion. Have a shock – mentally. Have a sad look. Have the tooth filled. And, perhaps my favourite: Have a stool. Yes, the bodily function, not as in 'owning a piece of three-legged furniture'.

Before it gets to H and the many 'haves', however, the book kicks off in style with the letter A.

A dozen. A kind of. And (but of course): A little dizzy.

Yeah, let's do it the natural way!

Want to find 'dizzy'? Look under A!

So you see, I have my work cut out. Many students have pestered me to write a Cantonese dictionary, but I don't know. Wouldn't that entail an hourly payment of about minus HK$3,000?

A few years ago I was teaching 'corporate' (yeah right) Cantonese to some Swiss people. Underwriters, as it happens.

"We want to learn Cantonese *without* having to talk to Chinese people," they complained, after I had taken them to several bars, expecting them to practise their newly acquired Cantonese on bar people and customers. After all, that was how *I* had learnt it.

"We want drills!" "We want exercises!"

All right, so I made drills and exercises. They loved them. So, after a few sessions of drills, for which they praised me for making it seem so easy, I naturally said: "Now you can go out and communicate with *Chinese people!*"

And did they? Hell, no. What they wanted was to sit in a room, a corporate meeting room in fact, 37 floors above street level, doing drills. When faced with a *real* Chinese person, they immediately slipped into much more comfortable (for them) English.

I realised that I had been too solipsistic in my dealings with students; basing my lessons on what *I* would have liked to learn if I were a victim (student) learning Cantonese… insisting, in fact, on learning by doing. Just like – good grief – Mao!

So after the Swiss brought it up, I made drill follow-ups to the 500 pages of course material I had already made about 'practical Cantonese as spoken in markets, taxis, bars and restaurants' with the same result. "We love these drills! Give us more drills!"

I did, only to see students (victims), right in front of my face, turn around to the lowliest non English-speaking waiter in the cheapest *cha chan teng*, and say (in English) "Could I possibly trouble you for a cup of milk tea, old chap?" (Okay. Not "old chap." But you get my drift).

They wanted more exercises so I gave them that, only to have many of them proudly return them, filled in to perfection by their Chinese secretaries.

"We want DVDs!" they then said. "We want computer programs!"

They were my customers so I had to do what they wanted. So many people told me that if they only had a DVD they could watch again and again, everything would be fine, that I was compelled to make the DVD they had been clamouring for: *Cantonese – The Movie.*

That took me several months of hard (but enjoyable) slog. Do you think they bought it? Some did. But do you think they watched it? No. Why not? Apparently because nobody had come into the room brandishing a large blunt household instrument, forcing them to watch it.

"We need real, live lessons to force us to learn Cantonese" was the cry after they had bought and not watched the DVD.

So I'm back at the famous 第一號方: Number One Square. My students can chat away in Cantonese with me about all sorts of topics, but when faced with even the tiniest Chinese waiter asking them what they would like to drink, it's immediately back to frozen deer in concentration camp-strength headlamp time. "Oh, it's just so much easier in English," they say. "I'm just crap at languages..."

If I had a millionth of a cent, etc. for every student who's told me she is "crap at languages," I'd be able to, etc.

Okay, people, once and for all: Nobody in the world is crap at languages. If they were, they wouldn't be able to speak their mother tongue. Of course many people are pretty inarticulate and possess a not very large vocabulary, but that's down to personal, perhaps economic and societal circumstance. Even the 300-word vocabulary Neanderthal grunters could speak those 300 words with excellent pronunciation and syntax.

"Oh, but my mother tongue – that's easy! I learnt that *as a child,*" they protest.

Exactly. When you want to learn a new language you should approach it as a child. See how the two-year-old acts: Asking the same questions again and again, driving the parents mad. They ask the question but don't listen to the increasingly impatient, short-tempered answer. What they are doing by instinct (all humans come equipped with the ability to learn language) is forging new neuron paths in the brain by constant repetition and reinforcement.

When I first arrived in China and everything was new, what I constantly and joyously returned to in my diary and letters to Norway was this: "I feel like a child again!" And learning a brand new language, so far removed from the Indo-Germanic Anglo-whatever as it was possible to get, was the main reason for this new lease on life I was suddenly given.

I went through the same stages as the slavering infant: First learning to order beer, then arguing with 'Take Care of Station' bicycle parking lot attendants ("You say I no pay but I pay!"), then learning numbers...

Then asking for directions not understanding squat of the answer but pretending to. I was linguistically one year old, then two. When I could speak like a two-year-old, I felt a great sense of achievement.

I quickly realised that *pretending* was the key... pretending to understand, just relying on people's facial expressions and body language to give me an idea of what was going on, just like the helpless child trying to work out a long and involved sentence emanating from the parents.

Because, when you talk to your toddler, saying for example: "It was really bad of you to set fire to Mommy's stack of *Cosmopolitan*, therefore you'll get no ice cream when we go to the beach on Sunday," all he can hear is: "Blah blah blah **BAD** blah blah **YOU** blah blah blah **ICE CREAM** blah blah blah, blahdi-blah."

But he can tell from your face that there's something going on, storing the words he couldn't understand away for future reference. And when you get to the beach and say "beach" again, he will understand that 'a lot of sand near water' means 'beach'.

He doesn't need a dictionary, DVD or CD-rom.

Unfortunately most of my students can't accept that they can't go from zero Cantonese to the level of a 35-year-old after one or two lessons. They are busy people who can't be bothered with going back to the toddler stage and slowly rising through the stages of linguistic proficiency. What they want is the equivalent of stomach stapling: Instant results.

It takes time to learn a language and you have to go through the stages. And the ages. You start off as a babbling infant, then graduate to toddlerhood, after which you quickly realise that every word in Cantonese you utter in the wrong tone sounds like 'penis' or variants thereof. And then you can start to have fun. Real fun, not 'idiotic Westerner quacking out "penis, penis"' fun.

After a while you can start, like me the other day, to have fun with the myriad race- and culture-based misconceptions about Westerners that Hong Kong people have.

I was just getting off the bus in my village when I overheard a bunch of young people of today talking among themselves about how they could get to Tung Chung (incidentally pronounced *Dung Jung*) and whether the bus I had just got off would get them there. I told them that it was the 3M they had to take, but that it would arrive shortly.

A lot of clapping and general merriment ensued, and they informed me that I could speak Cantonese.

"Yes, I know." (Unlike most Hong Kong people though, they told me this in Cantonese, not English).

"So, were you born in Hong Kong?"

"No, I haven't been born yet. For I am a ghost."

"Ha ha ha, great! Cool! Okay, we'll get the 3M. Cheers!" (Yes, Hong Kong Chinese still call white foreigners 'ghosts' – or 'devils', which 'gwai' also means).

*

Yeah, I have hopes for the young Hong Kong people of today. Some of them, as well as an increasing number of taxi drivers, even treat me like a normal human being, paying me the ultimate compliment of just answering me in Cantonese without any reference to the fact that I can speak the local language of Hong Kong.

My ideal taxi scenario is this:

Me (before the taxi driver has a chance to start with the painful English "you go wheeear"): "Central Plaza in Wan Chai, please."

Taxi driver: (in Cantonese) "OK."

Me: "So, that Donald Tsang, eh?"

Taxi driver: "Yeah, what a wanker I hate the Hong Kong government I wish the English would come back Hong Kong's really gone down the drain after the handover take me for example I used to only drive this taxi to make a living but now I have to work all day and night driving this taxi and working as a security guard at night but I still can't make enough money because the fucking landlord aided and abetted by the so-called government has doubled my rent and all they want to do is prop up the property developers and I have two children at university one boy one girl but they don't even know how hard I work and you live on Lantau do you or Lamma right and the last time I had a day off to go to Lantau was ten years ago and yeah we went to the beach it was beautiful but now all I do is work and that Donald Tsang yeah he claims to be a working class guy but now all he does is go to Beijing to suck up to the government there and he doesn't know that they don't like him either because he's useless and all Hong Kong people hate him and all my friends feel the same and when the English were here we could do so many things and work hard and just do whatever we wanted but now it's so different and nobody cares."

Me: "Aaaah... yes. I know. So you think the *British* should come back? Interesting."

Taxi driver: "Yeah because it was better then and I don't give a shit about politics but I tell you my life is shit now and nobody cares and I even support England in the World Cup because I tell you England has a special place in the heart of us Hong Kong people and I have police friends and they say the same bring back the English I hate those mainlanders and they come here and think they own Hong Kong."

Me: "Well, I... yeah. Well, we're here. 35 dollars, please take 40."

Taxi driver: "No way, I charge you 30, you're one of us."

That's right, people: Speaking Cantonese will make many (not all) taxi drivers tip *you!* It's happened to me so many times, it can't be a coincidence.

For no matter how many times locals answer you in English when you speak Cantonese, if you just persevere and keep up the "I can't speak English, please talk to me in Cantonese" spiel, you will succeed. Without a doubt. And, as always, taxi drivers, tea ladies and the security uncles in your building are your greatest allies.

But obviously, your best bet is to be Norwegian or at least be able to speak Norwegian. That language is so close to Cantonese, you can plonk a Wong down in Inner Trondheim armed only with a cod, and everybody will understand him. But then Norwegian does have three letters more than the English alphabet, namely æ, ø and å. Those letters really help when you want to write Cantonese phonetically.

Richard used those letters in the beginning when he was learning Cantonese, on my recommendation. It worked. After a few months he switched effortlessly to Chinese characters and then zoomed on to fluency. He was the best student I'd ever had.

He used everything I taught him, never forgetting anything, wrenching the Cantonese language away from its proprietors word by painfully extracted word. And our personal relationship continued apace as he ploughed through my course, using an hour to learn what other people needed several weeks to digest. Soon he was picking up Mandarin without really trying, and that was just as well, for our China trips started going deeper and deeper into the motherland and beyond...

16

Two Thumbs Off

"Do you realise that normal people plan for months in advance before going to Tibet?" Richard remarked as we stood up to our knees in snow on a 5,000-metre-high Tibetan mountain, trying to push a car with summer tyres out of the ditch for the sixth time in ten minutes.

They do? I hadn't known that. I thought I had prepared very well indeed and with much more care than normally by packing sunglasses, thermal underwear, scarf, gloves *and* a book with roadmaps of all the provinces in China. And a little torch! Having said that, it was probably true that if we had prepared a little better, for example by establishing that it takes five days to drive through Tibet from the capital Lhasa to the neighbouring Chinese province of Yunnan, not one-and-a-half like we had decided, the hitch-hiking trip through Tibet might not have been so frantic and nail-biting.

In fact, if we had prepared ourselves a little better, we probably wouldn't have tried to hitch-hike at all...

The hitch-hiking thing was a brilliant idea of Richard's. Actually, it all began the last time I visited Beijing, when I met an Englishman by the name of Rob Luxton. He was, in the great tradition of English adventurers, on a 25,000 km cycling trip through China. And not on any old cycle but on a recumbent tricycle.

For those who haven't seen one of these contraptions – I hadn't before I met Rob – it can be described as a veranda with wheels. You sit comfortably leaning back in a kind of deckchair, letting your legs do all the work, without the risk of a stiff neck or back pain. It is the elegant, sophisticated method of cycling.

Rob had planned to spend two years traversing all of China's provinces and 'autonomous' regions, and had so far spent six months getting from Hong Kong to Beijing.

In case anyone still doubted the genuineness of his eccentricity, he had picked up a dog on the way which now lived in a box on the back pannier. When he found it, it was a tiny puppy crying in a ditch, but it had now grown into a biggish hound by the name of Ditch, and I met him to hand over a thermal suit for dogs (unisex) he had ordered from Hong Kong. Winter was coming and that was exactly the season he had chosen to cycle through Inner Mongolia, sleeping in a tent.

He didn't do all this just for the normal reason; namely collecting money for charity. This seems to be the excuse everyone uses nowadays when they want to do something enjoyable or weird. But Rob genuinely loved China and wanted to see every inch of it from the ground. And of course, a little money for the two orphanages he supported wouldn't go amiss.

I was naturally beside myself with admiration, and not a little insanely envious. To cycle through China was a dream I myself had harboured for many years. At least around Guangdong province. Inner Mongolia in minus 20 degrees would perhaps not be quite my style... oh, but to be on wheels, to stop wherever I wanted... that would have to be even better than the train.

I started working on Richard. Chinese New Year was coming and what if? It would be fun! Us, an endless country road, lovely, sunburned peasants everywhere... the wind in our hair and a hero's welcome wherever we went. And so exciting, so free, so cheap...

If I promised not to pick up a single dog, large or small, would he go cycling around Guangdong province with me?

No, said Richard. No and no. Rain! He said. Accidents. Flat tyres. Being seen in public with sweat running down our faces. And besides: Tunnels. Long tunnels without lights, only 60-ton trucks and us.

This was a side of Richard I hadn't seen before. So far he'd been up for anything, and more. But before I had time to throw myself on the ground, screaming and kicking my feet, he came out with an utterance so brilliant it was as if it should have been wrapped in aluminium foil and sprayed with glitter.

"Of course, we could always hitch-hike."

Oh! Why couldn't that have been *my* idea? But hey – it was the best idea he'd had since I met him. And that was saying something.

We weren't completely unfamiliar with hitching rides in China; in the autumn the year before we had carried out an extremely successful hitch-hiking in Inner Mongolia. However, that hadn't been a hitch-hiking trip as such, just a last effort to save our lives on some sub-arctic grasslands where the next bus would only arrive in a couple of weeks. It was actually, more than anything, a case of a kind driver stopping on his own initiative and scraping up two frozen corpses from the side of the road. But: Seeing as his car was the only one driving on that road that day, we had to say it was a 100% successful non-hitching hitch-hiking.

Now we would hitch-hike around Guangdong province, or rather, around *in* Guangdong, which is by no means a small province, for five days.

As usual there was no shortage of warnings from well-meaning friends, who did the open-mouthed, bulgy-eyed, hair-standing-on-end thing when we mentioned "China" and "hitch-hiking" in the same sentence.

"Oh no! Mortal danger! You will get killed! Robbed!" etc, etc.

These are people who think nothing of driving a car while shitfaced or bungee jumping from Hong Kong's highest aeroplane. I tried to explain that although China is not without her share of baddies, I doubted if they would spend Chinese New Year driving around the countryside looking for rich hitch-hikers whose money and belongings they would extract in the most exquisitely painful manner.

As usual, no one would believe me.

*

Guangdong province is the richest in China. It started with Shenzhen being declared a Special Economic Zone, and since then the riches have just grown and grown; spread and spread. Just across the border from Hong Kong, what used to be fields is now mile after mile of factories and residential areas, many of which are never occupied. The train trip from Hong Kong, formerly more than three hours through charming farmland, is now just over an hour's zooming through a giant industrial suburb, and a not very attractive one.

In China, the acquisition of wealth always means an immediate breakdown in aesthetics.

However, as soon as you get beyond the capital Guangzhou, you find a different world from the extended factory-cum-dumping ground that is southern Guangdong.

In the undeveloped hinterland of Guangdong is a Beatrix Potter kind of world with sparkling lakes, ducks, geese, small woodlands and rolling hills, red-brick houses surrounded by bamboo and free-range chickens.

This area we swept through in the first car that picked us up, a car so large and beige (even the steering wheel was beige) and with so many gadgets – video screen, digital direction finder and ice cream maker – that the driver just had to be a high-ranking official. Only people with direct and unlimited access to public coffers can afford such a car.

I asked him what he did, but he was so busy plotting in the direction on the computer that he didn't hear me. There was only one road in this particular countryside, so I couldn't really see why he couldn't navigate the old-fashioned way: By looking at the road in front of him. Men, eh?

Yes, progress has arrived with blasting horns and crashing cymbals. Where before only long-distance buses had video screens, showing old Hong Kong films dubbed into high-octane Mandarin, every self-respecting taxi and private car nowadays has a TV screen embedded on the back of the driver's seat, so that the person in the back can follow the latest stock market information or watch adverts about how one can become 10 cm taller. Or lose 20 kilos. (Both of which, interestingly, can be achieved by wearing a special kind of trainer. And although it is surely possible to lose 20 kilos by running, these ads show people whose surplus kilos just melt away by wearing the shoes while sitting in front of their computers, occasionally ambling aimlessly around on the floor. The advert also doesn't mention that the increase in height, 10 cm or more, is really achieved by sawing off the legs and putting them together again with extensions, an operation to which many people desperately subject themselves to get out of the dreaded 'below 160 cm tall' category. Yes! This operation does exist and was developed in Russia. Thousands of Chinese have undergone the operation; however it is not clear how many have been permanently handicapped by going under the saw.)

And now more and more bigger and stronger jeep-like cars sport a video screen on the inside of the windshield. Is that to enable the driver to relax with a good movie while negotiating the hairpin bends of northern Sichuan province, perhaps?

The video screen in this particular car was turned off, and that was probably just as well. I felt marginally safer with the driver merely punching in information with one hand, while occasionally glancing at the road in front of him, than I would have if he should also have been watching movies.

When we got off with profuse thanks a few kilometres further on, the driver turned around and went back. He had only driven us here because we had said we were going here.

Hitch-hiking is not unknown in China among the poor, who are often seen on the side of roads hoping to be picked up. And they are: By bus staff whose relentless search for money makes them actively chase down passengers, picking up people who aren't really going anywhere but are too polite to say it. But to give people lifts, gratis, in private cars, seems not so prevalent. Was that why people were so quick to stop for us even though they didn't have enough space? Was that why they drove us to places they weren't really going? Or was it just that we were foreigners and therefore to be pitied? Were Richard and I, in fact, the equivalent of the first black people to turn up in Norway in the '50s? These, I've been told, weren't allowed to pay for anything because people felt so sorry for them for being black.

Now it was Chinese New Year's Eve and all nice and decent people were ensconced in the bosom of their families eating luck-generating food: Long noodles for a long life, fish (*yu*) because it sounds like plentiful, *gam-gat* (kumquat, a kind of orange) because it sounds like Golden Auspicious, etc. Or, they would be, if this hadn't been the New China.

Only a few years ago, China during Chinese New Year was a wasteland where everything was closed and even the trains rattled emptily along. If you wanted to be in China without the throngs, hordes and staring squads, you couldn't find a better time than Chinese New Year.

Each city would have only one open restaurant where you would be the only customer, grey and silent in a sea of empty tables and staff dying to go home. The train stations, normally the most packed places in packed-to-the-ceilings China, lay vastly gaping and sinister with empty benches and empty floors, lonely beneath the fluorescent lights.

But after money came to town, combined with some of society's many rigid rules being loosened a little, Chinese New Year has become a time for shopping, a time to mill around the streets and go to restaurants with one's family and, increasingly, friends. A quick duty meal with the family, and then – party.

That was just fine with Richard and me, because we didn't like to feel we were the only two people alive in the entire country. No lull! Must party!

Now we are in a bar and although it isn't packed, it is like a normal week night, a Wednesday for example. But since it is Chinese New Year's Eve, the biggest night in the Chinese calendar, the bar owner has rigged up a gigantic video screen so people won't have to miss any New Year TV just because they happen to be in a bar. And it's certainly quite an extravaganza CCTV is serving up. As usual it is the USA (Las Vegas) that is the role model, with hundreds of frantic dancers bustling around on a stage decked out like a giant rhinestone-studded, plastic toy-strewn wedding cake while a stern-eyebrowed opera diva dressed in the gala uniform of the People's Liberation Army piercingly screeches out a patriotic song.

The male presenter is also in full uniform minus hat, while the female one – 20 years younger than him, naturally – has wiggled into a glittering blue body condom with peacock feathers. Together they sing the praises of... could it be... Yes! The eternal friendship between China and Tibet, a friendship the Chinese have cultivated hard, always. And bugger me if a picture of the Potala Palace isn't now projected on the stage backdrop, while another singer dressed in uniform, stuffed like a sausage, jogs lumbering up to the microphone followed by 30-40 dancers in Tibetan garb.

And my, how happy they are! They smile and smile while spinning around with long billowing sleeves and fur-trimmed hats. And it soon becomes apparent why the Tibetans are so happy; it is of course because the Chinese have been kind enough to build a railway line to the Tibetan capital Lhasa. An image of the train is imposed on the backdrop screen and the Tibetans smile and smile as broadly as only an ethnic minority can, until the whole thing explodes in a shattering crescendo of music, happiness and eternal gratitude.

And here I had been thinking that the Tibetans wanted to *get rid of* the Chinese! How wrong one can be. The simple, backward but sensitive Tibetans, unable to verbally express their deepest feelings, *dance* the railway line and the People's Liberation Army welcome.

Yes, Chinese New Year is in every way a big day for the People's Liberation Army. The next item is a 100-strong choir from same army. Standing on a model of the Great Wall they sing it out for the motherland in young, baleful voices: "When the enemy comes, what will be your true face? In the heat of battle, will you fight for your loved one and your race?" (It was actually "your country and your loved ones" but I wanted it to rhyme).

That is surely a question many ask themselves on a New Year's Eve. Another one is: Which enemy? Definitely not the Tibetans, that's for sure.

The next day our adventure continues in a light drizzle. We set up for our hitch-hiking expedition beneath a giant poster declaring in writing and in charming symbolic painting of a soldier hugging children in front of the Forbidden City, the vast concrete expanse in front of which has been miraculously transformed into a lush meadow, that the PLA and the People are one. That the People are, in fact, the very water in which the fish, the PLA, swim.

We extend all we have of thumbs and chests, and after a couple of cars whose drivers also grin broadly, raising their thumbs – they seem to think we're signalling "nice car" – three young guys stop. They wonder what we're doing in the light drizzle, and don't we know that the central bus station is on the other side of town? We explain that we're trying to get free rides, and after a discussion among themselves they drive off. But they did stop first, and that counts!

And when they come back five minutes later and stuff us and our luggage into the tiny car, it most certainly counts. They take us far into the middle of the proverbial nowhere, which is their ancestral village, and here we are introduced to the driver's father and given breakfast.

The father seems to be someone important in the Party, for he insists on getting in the car again and driving past the huge and imposing, even ostentatious, shiny-tiled and green-windowed gigantomaniac building where he works. It looks wonderfully out of place among the scruffy village houses; like an overly made-up supermodel surrounded by coal miners. The business cards he presses into our hands bear the proud symbol of the Chinese state: Tiananmen Gate with five stars above it, embossed in red and gold. With many exhortations to call him at any whiff of trouble he waves us off and we hitch-hike on to great merriment among the children of the village. And the adults.

The further we get from civilization, the more quickly we are picked up each time. We hardly have time to get out of one car, let alone stick out any fingers or organs, before another one, sometimes two, stops.

Meanwhile the road has given up all pretensions of ever having had tarmac. Only my underwired bra saves me from serious injury as I'm thrown about in the steering compartments of trucks. On the map in *Car Book For Self-Driving Motorists* (28 yuan in the Xinhua Bookstore in Guangzhou), the road is marked in green: 'National Highway', the second best road after 'Expressway'. But the road reminds me more than anything of The Grapes of Wrath. And Cannery Road.

And that makes us enjoy our trip even more. It is in every way the journey we had envisaged – a voyage along the neverending country road of yesteryear with pointing children, quacking geese, the odd gawping donkey, and sleepy lakes blinking among the bamboo thickets.

By this time, so many drivers have taken us to where we've said we're going, only to turn back once they've dropped us off, that we've started saying we're going to the next village so the poor buggers won't have to waste a whole day driving to where they're not going.

So when two guys in the smallest car in southern China pick us up just as we're leaving the car of a kind family of three who have spent New Year motoring around the sights of Guangdong, I tell them wisely that we're going to Mocun, 20 km down the road. The truth is we're going to Siu Heng, party town extraordinaire but 150 km away.

Neither Richard nor I are particularly small people and with his giant rucksack and my wheelie bag we have to fold ourselves into the car, sitting with our knees wrapped around our ears. The back of the car sags noticeably under our weight. The driver takes it in his stride, but with gritted teeth, I can't help noticing.

Listening in on the guys' conversation I hear that they are actually going to Siu Heng. Really? That's where we're going too! I beam. A decidedly morbid atmosphere descends upon the car. After much prodding I get it out of the driver: Yes, they are indeed going to Siu Heng, but with the additional weight of us on board they won't be able to drive fast enough to get there in time for work.

Oh, the Chinese penchant for hospitality! We have to beg them to let us off in Mocun so they can get to their destination on time. They drive off, hesitantly at first and then at increasing speed, flying over the many bumps and holes in the road now that 200 kilos of foreigner is gone.

*

Living in Hong Kong you are overwhelmed by holidays. As soon as Christmas and New Year are out of the way, along comes Chinese New Year with its extended festivities, and almost immediately after that, depending on which day Jesus died that year, Easter. Richard, being a teacher, got two weeks off for all of these holidays, and now here he was again, raring to go on a trip. "Why not North Korea?" we shouted in unison.

I had been wanting to go there for ages due to the extreme surrealism factor, as well as there being no cars. But as the emails flew back and forth between me and the travel agent and it appeared that not only would we be followed by two guides wherever we went, but also would have to ask for permission if we wanted as much as to stick our heads out of the hotel window, I started having second thoughts. Bringing a laptop would be out of the question, as would taking photos of "non-authorised things" and writing a word about the trip; if we did, the guides would be executed or worse.

"Richard," I said. "We don't even like being told where to sit in a restaurant – how are we going to stand having to pay $20,000 for a holiday where we won't be able to go to the toilet without permission?"

And so it was that we decided to take the train to Tibet and hitch-hike from Lhasa back to Guangzhou. In the self-driving car map book we saw a green road, a national highway, leading out of Lhasa, so it couldn't take long. Only 1200 km from Lhasa to Kunming in Yunnan province, the last 100 or so kilometres on an expressway! If even the sophisticated and jaded people of Guangdong province were so thrilled to pick up hitch-hikers, what rousing welcome would we receive from the simple and trusting Tibetans?

In the map book I found good advice about travel in Tibet. Sunglasses, tick, suncream, tick, altitude sickness, okay, warm clothes... and avoid by all means discussing religion or "sensitive issues". Don't try to sneak in on sky burials and don't take photos of people without permission. Done!

*

Armed with such good advice we feel well prepared when we get off the train in Lhasa, marvelling at the, naturally, colossal, ostentatious and spanking-new train station built in 'Tibetan' style – sombrely brown-tiled on the outside and with brown glass windows.

On the way to Lhasa, crossing the endless grasslands of northern Tibet, we had noticed the national highway from Qinghai province; a not wide but covered road where the odd four-wheeled monster jeep zipped briskly along. A road perfect for hitch-hiking. The future had arrived in Tibet, and on this kind of road it would take one day, tops, to hitch-hike from Lhasa to the border of Yunnan. That meant we would have time to swing around one of China's only two cities preserved in the old style, Lijiang (our aforementioned trip to that monument to new-old and subsequent deep disappointment was undertaken the next year) and relax there with long rambling walks before going home.

In our modern life it is common to have seen most famous places in pictures or documentaries before we get to see them with our own eyes, and it's not unusual to feel disappointment at finding the reality not as airbrushed as the images imprinted on our brains. I've heard people express disappointment on seeing the Pyramids of Egypt (the pictures don't show screaming tourist hell and buses) and the Taj Mahal is apparently also much smaller than we have been led to believe. I therefore wasn't surprised to see that the famous Potala Palace was much smaller than in the Michael Palin documentary. But I could never have imagined that it wouldn't be the main attraction of Lhasa.

Yes, the palace is imposing enough, beautiful to be sure and without doubt lovely to live in for the Dalai Lama before he was forced to run away to India in 1959. But to my astonishment it turned out that the real tourist attraction for *real* tourists – Han Chinese sporting red baseball caps and herded by screaming guides – is the enormous concrete expanse in front of the palace; Potala Square, a marginally smaller version of Tiananmen Square.

Along one side of the square, right up to the very picket fence of the palace grounds, a four-lane motorway decorated with China Mobile-festooned streetlights runs proudly and ruler-straight through the city. At the other end of the square a colossal monument reaches for the cobalt blue Tibetan sky; a phallus-like granite symbol of the Chinese people's solicitude in taking the trouble of liberating Tibet from her backward and barbarian ways. Around the foot of the monument stand statues of rifle-thrusting Chinese workers and peasants – and one Tibetan herder – all staring grimly and with much clenching of eyebrows at the Chinese flag in the middle of the square.

While browsing through the goods in the tourist shop of a new hotel built in the style of an old Tibetan palace, we find some old postcards showing that where the square and the four-lane boulevard are today, there used to be a beautiful lake fringed with weeping willows. As if this wasn't reactionary enough, there was also a cluster of old Tibetan houses on the banks of the lake. Is it any wonder that the Tibetans dance around with wafting sleeves, welcoming progress and the future, Chinese style? On the train we had also been informed by a bookish cook that Lhasa had been nothing but a swamp before the Chinese arrived and that the Potala Palace had been built by a Chinese emperor "in 1463."

Verily, does this not prove more than anything that Tibet has always, and will always be, an indisputable part of China?

Yes, the Chinese have truly invented everything and discovered everything and -where. Gunpowder, America, golf and football... and I'll be damned if it doesn't also turn out that the fearsome Genghis Khan, terror of the world and formerly assumed to be a Mongol, was Chinese as well! Yes indeed, recent Chinese research has showed that he was actually born in Inner Mongolia, a place which, as every child knows, has always been a part of China. Ipso facto: he was Chinese!

If it hadn't been for all the Tibetans who stubbornly cling to their traditional garb and bizarre Buddhist customs, Lhasa would have looked like a typical Chinese town with awful shiny-tiled shopping centres and over-wide roads, flashing neon lights and fashion shops with insane English names. But the natives keep walking around like they've always done with their prayer wheels, bronzed weather-beaten faces and braided hair fastened with red ribbons, looking like an issue of *National Geographic*. They make the silly buildings and streets look like it is the Chinese who don't fit into the Tibetan world instead of the other way round, contrary to the Chinese world view. After all, progress with Chinese tasteless characteristics has worked so well elsewhere.

Now more than 50 years have passed since the Liberation of the mountainous country in the West, but not one of the ten or twelve Han Chinese we ask knows how to say "hello" in Tibetan. We think that is quite an achievement, but when all is said and done, not so different from the imperialist role model of the Chinese, the British, with their supercilious disdain for all the countries they conquered.

Mandarin is the new English and everybody who wants to make something of themselves, whether it be in Tibet, Xinjiang or other areas the Chinese have embraced under the big China umbrella, must speak the language of the master race. I read somewhere that if you write an address in Tibetan on a letter you want to send to somewhere inside Tibet, it will never get there. There is no education in Tibetan, and gifted Tibetan children are sent to study elsewhere in China to ensure they forget their own language and culture. Did I say that? I meant: "For greater success and national harmony."

After the new railroad from Qinghai to Lhasa opened, a wave of Tibetan culture-worship swept over China. Funny dances and costumes in hastily assembled "Tibetan" bars became all the rage, and shops played

Tibetan music; a welcome relief from the dunk-a-dunk disco music to be sure, but all the lyrics were in Mandarin.

In Lhasa, only a few streets have been allowed to keep their original architecture, namely those around the Jokhang Temple, crawling with tourists and a larger than usual contingent of fat policemen. Here the Tibetans prostrate themselves in front of the holy temple, wearing aprons made to withstand hundreds or thousands of kneelings and prostrations each day.

Lhasa is the only 'Chinese' city I have been to which stinks of piss everywhere. But then again Lhasa is in Tibet, which is not, I repeat *not*, a city in China, so it is as it should be. When one considers that there is a massive problem of alcoholism, unheard of before the Chinese came, as well as a dearth of public toilets, the unbearable stench becomes only more poignant. Perhaps the Tibetans piss everywhere in quiet protest against their Chinese overlords? Or perhaps it is the Chinese themselves who feel free to let it rip because they aren't at home?

Outside the Jokhang Temple a young German ambles up to us, dying to speak English it seems. This is unusual, because so far all the foreigners we have seen have studiously avoided our eyes, as we have done with them. What we're all thinking is: Foreigners, here? How rude! Only we are allowed to be foreigners here. At least we won't acknowledge them; it's not as if we must greet and talk to each other by hook or by crook. Are we Livingstone and Stanley or something? Go away.

But we can't avoid this guy. He says he's driven here on a motorbike from Shanghai and that the green national highway, along which we have planned to hitch-hike, is a sub-human dirt track almost un-negotiable by wheeled transport, and that anyway nobody will pick us up because it is illegal to have foreigners in the vehicle. He goes on to say that the road frequently climbs across 5,000-metre-high mountains and that it is a wonder he is still alive.

He is travelling with his Chinese girlfriend who, he says, is the only reason he was able to get into Tibet at all. Every time they came to a police checkpoint, of which there were many, she had taken off her helmet and talked to the police, while he kept his full head helmet on.

Hmm...

Richard and I listen incredulously to him as he forges ahead in his peculiar English which he obviously hasn't been able to unleash for weeks, while we glance at each other with much discreet eyebrow action.

Afterwards we agree that he must have been exaggerating to make himself interesting. Terrible roads – nothing! Haven't we just observed the most beautiful green national highway? These Germans. We are going to follow our plan and hitch-hike out of Tibet, no matter what.

In a Sichuan restaurant the same evening I happen to look out the window to see a small example of how the liberation of backward areas, Chinese style, really works. I see an old Tibetan monk in maroon robes, holding a walking stick, arguing with the same Chinese waitress who has just happily served us our meal amid much banter and many laughs.

Clearly not happy with the monk's attitude, she starts pulling at his walking stick, tearing it away from him and proceeding to whack the old boy with it so his hat flies off, rolling down the pavement. When he starts trotting away, looking nervously for his hat, she follows, bashing away with the walking stick.

Richard sits with his back to the window and doesn't see a thing, and looks very surprised when I suddenly get up and run outside.

"What the hell are you doing, stop hitting him!" I shout at the wench, only to get the sulking response: "He hit me first."

All right, so I hadn't seen the prelude to this drama, but: A 70-something-year-old Tibetan monk suddenly starts hitting a Chinese waitress? I would wager that the real explanation was that he had tried to get into the restaurant to beg, an irritation to be sure, but perhaps not irritating enough to set in motion a spectacle which, with my middle-class Western prejudices, I would call somewhat excessive violence. I can't help thinking that the Chinese have succeeded in the purpose of their invasion: To dehumanise the enemy to the degree that he becomes a thing, thereby making it easier to justify the atrocities. For if the Tibetans,

Uyghurs, Tartars, Mongols and all the other minorities were real people like the Chinese, wouldn't it be that much more difficult for the thinking, feeling human being to invade and conquer them?

Probably not, actually.

The next day we are still feeling a little wistful and disappointed that the liberation of Tibet should have taken such a shape. And when on top of it all it starts snowing bucketfuls, and the Potala Palace, up to whose summit we had got up at six to reach, turns out not to open before nine (Lhasa is different from other Chinese cities in that everything opens late – but then again it's not a city in China) we decide to leave.

That was a wise decision, because it turns out we need every second left of our holiday if we're going to have a hope in hell of getting home.

The night before, after the walking stick incident, we met a geezer who had a car, and who invited us to drive with him to the next town, Linzhi. In retrospect I have laughed many times at how scared I was when he thundered forth at 140 km an hour, wearing sunglasses despite the low-hanging clouds and intermittent rain, while watching a movie on the video screen on the inside of the windshield, all the while talking on his mobile and rooting around in his collection of DVDs in the glove compartment.

As if that was anything to be afraid of – the road was after all tarmacked and more or less straight. The guy had driven the same route hundreds of times. It was his job. If I had known what lay before us, I wouldn't have glanced nervously at the speedometer, the road, sunglasses and all the other things. I would quite simply have sat back and enjoyed the idiotic movie about a guy who wanted to get a divorce because he was bored in his marriage, and who, helped by an angel with a mobile phone, suddenly could get all the women he wanted, with the inevitable result that after much trying and hilarious, hysterical failing, he saw the light and 'accidentally' ended up with his ex-wife. Moral rectitude restored. (All films in China must be morally correct. In 2008 a communiqué was actually issued by Beijing saying films must be straightened out; from now on only morally correct endings will be tolerated. There will be no more depictions of murder, incest or adultery).

Linzhi is a weird place. In the middle of nowhere, surrounded by 5,000- (or maybe 6,000? Who goes around with a tape to measure the height of these giants?) metre mountains, the city lays there as a monument to all modern Chinese architectural beauty: Green-tiled, whole-block-covering buildings surrounded by empty six-lane highways.

Apparently Linzhi is supposed to be a kind of Silicon Valley with Chinese characteristics, a totally artificial town built last week with money from Guangdong and Fujian (a rich province on the east coast). Every building bears the legend *Guangdong Develop And Teach*. We see no Tibetans here, but they would have fitted poorly into all the modernity, looking as if it was created for a future hopeful invasion of thousands of cars and robots. The three hapless taxis driving round and round looking for passengers were bound to be frustrated; it takes about ten minutes to cross the entire town on foot. But modern it certainly is.

The next day we catch a lift with the first car we see; a representative of the Guangdong Develop And Teach Bureau. He drives us for miles before hastily turning around and going back the way we have come, after having done his bit for the motherland. The foreigners must be accommodated no matter what. The next car that comes rolling also picks us up. The driver and passengers are Tibetans, and have a picture of Mao done up like a Buddhist symbol dangling from the mirror. As soon as we get out of the car, it does a perfect three-point turn, screeching back in the direction whence we have come.

And that is the end of private car ownership in Tibet. Richard and I drag ourselves, followed by a number of children, down the road for mile after mile, waiting for the next lift. But there are no more cars. Not one. Not even half a car. After a couple of hours in the rain (at this stage I have wisely acquired an umbrella – so much for Tibet being dry!) we start thinking that the national highway of Tibet might not be as easy to negotiate as we had thought. Richard starts muttering about not being able to get back to work in time, a muttering that is to increase in intensity over the next few days.

We are now standing at the foot of a not inconsiderable mountain, having just gnawed down the last of the peanuts we bought in Linzhi and drunk the last drop of water, when a pickup truck appears. A Tibetan. Cross the mountain? No problem. Only 100 yuan per person.

And so it is that we spend the next four days hitch-hiking through Tibet... by hugely overpriced taxi. And we are cringingly, grovellingly happy to pay any price they ask. The few not very tall snow-clad mountains we passed in the first taxi turn out to be a doddle compared to what lies before us. Yes, it soon becomes apparent that the national highway going eastwards out of Tibet, the 1200 km we had laughingly thought we'd pack away in a day, yes the very same kilometres which we, in our extreme and pathological optimism, had thought the German motorbike rider had lied about, quite rightly turns out to be a hastily hacked-out dirt road of the kind only seen in mining period dramas from Yorkshire anno 1893.

Except that this one has several-hundred-metre vertical drops on one side and thousands of metres of overhang on the other. The road, if one wants to call it that, is just wide enough for an optimistic car, and any meeting with a vehicle travelling in the opposite direction results in hundreds of metres of reversing. Now we realise why the road isn't covered: Any attempt at laying asphalt would lead to the road having to be closed down with no possibility of detour or passing. Here is the road: 50 cm wide, dug out of the mountainside by the People's Liberation Army to facilitate its entrance into and eventual control of Tibet, riddled with stone avalanches and treacherous holes and with a two-kilometre sheer drop to the right. Take it or leave it.

Yes. Instead of a leisurely jaunt with time out for strolling around, taking photos and having light discussions about the meaning of life, we have to drive hell-for-leather for four days straight, without as much as a second's stop to go to the toilet or eat as much as a tiny little thing. We have (or rather, Richard has) to be at work on Monday! The longest stretch takes 17 hours. That particular driver had just nipped out to get some fags of a morning when we accosted him; he was wearing slippers and had probably thought that when he got up in the morning it was only to return to bed a few minutes later. That was the seriously under-equipped car we found ourselves pushing and pushing incessantly out of snowdrifts.

Why does this driver, wearing slippers and sporting smooth tyres for light city driving, have to be the one meekly giving way to every bloody vehicle on the road?

"Push!" the slipper-wearing geezer screams. That is easy for him to say from where he sits comfortably inside the car. We are outside, now up to our waists in snow, while four-wheel drives slide past and a 120-piece colonnade of People's Liberation Army trucks – on their way into Tibet to deal with the uprising that is to take place the year after – takes their good time passing us, while not one of Lei Feng's selfless soldier colleagues gets out to give us a push.

It is beginning to get dark and we are still stuck in the snow-covered wilderness. That's when I realise how stupid I had been in being scared of a driver occasionally glancing at a measly morally correct video, and that on a covered road.

Here we are knee-deep in freezing snow and nobody knows where we are or where the next town is – certainly not the driver.

But nobody can beat a Norwegian when it comes to pushing-cars-out-of-snowdrifts techniques. Only five hours later we roll proudly into the next collection of houses, Mangkang, a town everybody we have talked to has assured us has a cash point. People aim to please, that's true. There's not even a bank, let alone a cash point.

After paying the driver we suddenly have only 200 yuan between us, 100 after having paid for a terrible room where we undignified-ly have to share the bed.

We learned a lot that day about always carrying stacks and stacks of money while travelling in Tibet. People: When travelling in Tibet, always carry stacks and stacks of money!

Richard has to go with the 'hotel' owner to the police station to register us mad aliens, only to be told that we can't stay in Mangkang overnight unless we pay 200 yuan "for our own safety". But as it's almost midnight and we have no money, the police moderate their demands to asking for zero yuan in return for us leaving the next day. Yes, I have no truck with mainland police. Square to the death, they are.

The poor slipper-wearing driver (who, if there had indeed been a cash point in Mangkang, all justice be told, would have received a 200-yuan tip, sorry mate) had been mumbling about having been forced to pay 300 yuan at one particular police checkpoint to somehow increase the foreigners' safety. However, as he was unable to present a receipt we just started talking about something else, and no more mention of this bribe is made.

Two days later we can at last get off the bus after a ten-hour drive from Shangri-La (formerly a figment of an author's imagination but now a town in Yunnan) – a bus trip which gave us the pleasure of watching *Pirates of the Caribbean* dubbed into Mandarin – and suddenly the air was normal again. Chewable. It covered my contact lenses like a thick film. Funnily enough I hadn't noticed how fresh the Tibetan air was before I was back in normal Chinese brownish-grey soup.

Hitch-hiking in China is easy; all you have to do is make sure you're hitch-hiking in a province where there are private cars. That province is not Tibet. But I'll say it again: Tibet is *not* China! Call me old-fashioned, but I'm for Free Tibet. And also I'm for Free Inner Mongolia and Free Xinjiang, and Free Everywhere where the indigenous population is not Han Chinese.

Free, free, and get rid of the invading Chinese with their dubious taste in buildings and monuments, and their queer compulsion to build wide roads where there are no cars. Surely all those roads can't be only for the purpose of carrying Chinese soldiers into areas which they feel need to be controlled? But as it stands, at the moment of writing this chronicle of surreal China, insanely wide roads are criss-crossing the entire Chinese landmass except for the place where a road, one single-lane road, is really needed: On the green national highway number 380, from Lhasa to Kunming.

*

There's another national highway in another 'China which isn't China', namely G315 in Xinjiang, and don't you think I've hitch-hiked along that one too? Richard and I had one goal on this two-week epic journey from Guangzhou to Xinjiang and back, namely to travel through an infamous stretch of sand the size of France. As mentioned before, the name of the desert, 'Taklamakan', was formerly taken to mean 'If you go in you can never come out', but now that's been debunked along with the idea that the Great Wall is the only man-made structure visible from the moon. We went in and, after some very hot boredom, certainly came out, dusty and with sand between our teeth.

No, it should be: 'When you go in and come out, you can't go any further'. For there really is no transport south of the desert, like the locals have been telling us with escalating urgency.

Right, we have no choice but to hitch-hike, another goal of ours. Like a mad dog and her Englishman we rock up at the highway at the height of the midday sun, waiting for the locals to start fighting for the privilege of picking us up. But there isn't a single car. Are they having lunch? After 25 minutes we are starting to hallucinate when two Uyghurs in a beat-up pickup truck take pity on us. Their Mandarin is so guttural and drowning in moustache that I can hardly make out a word they're saying. Oh yes: *Pi jiu*. Beer.

We're whisked away to a kind of brand-new hovel put together with skirting boards and plywood, where a beer-drinking party is in full swing. Yes, make no mistake; Uyghurs are Muslim but they drink like the parched desert itself. They also dance with *members of the opposite sex* and generally behave like they can well afford to wait for the heavenly pleasures promised their more jihad-oriented brethren, preferring to take them here on Earth instead.

But when we see the way Muslims drink, we realise they might as well be Koran-thumping fundamentalists. We are 11 people with at least 20 bottles of beer, but only two glasses between us. And this is the drinking etiquette of the indigenous people of Xinjiang, which would have been East Turkestan if the Chinese hadn't suddenly remembered that the place is, has always been and will always... (etc): The leader pours the two glasses full of beer, points out which two lucky bastards get to drink, and they then sluice it all down amid much shouting of *"Kosheh!"* (Drink!)

Among these flat-capped, facial-haired locals is a Chinese, Li Zhiwen. He is in his late thirties, with military-style hair and eyes the colour of his skin; deep salmon. They must have been at it for hours. He tells me that he only hangs out with Uyghurs and doesn't like Chinese at all. Hmm! This is my third trip to Xinjiang and the first time I've seen friendship between locals and Han Chinese.

"Kosheh! Kosheh!" Oh dear, is it our turn again? Richard, I and of course our driver seem to get the lion's share of the warm liquid, and it's maybe just as well, because one of our hosts falls asleep at once and the others sit there with heads lolling. With several litres of beer sloshing inside us we set off down the ruler-straight road at 120 km/h, screaming through the desert in a car held together with string and sticky tape and with a windshield which hasn't been cleaned since they bought the car around 1992.

But hey, we don't really need to see anything – the only vehicle on that road is the one we're in. We cover almost 400 km that day in eight hours including a long beer break, which is good going, seeing as the next lift we get is on a hay truck going at exactly 50 km/h. Even here, three days' drive from Beijing, the blasted Olympics holds sway. At a police roadblock we are flagged down and with many polite explanations, searched. That is to say, the smiling policeman runs his hand through the pocket on the inside of the driver's door – there is no searching of the several tons of hay which could have held all sorts of explosives, nor our bags. Perhaps the cops who confiscated my hairspray five days before have sent out a communiqué saying we are now clean.

Then again, if that hay truck had indeed been full of contraband going to sabotage the Sacred Olympics, moving at maximum speed (that of a souped-up donkey cart), it would have reached Beijing exactly two years after the closing ceremony.

In the next town there is actually a bus, and we get tickets to Delinghe in Qinghai province, a mere 14 hours' haul away. But as we board the bus, the driver shouts that Delinghe is off-limits to foreigners. Dumbfounded, I forget to point out that I'm a Hong Kong compatriot, and we docilely exchange our ticket for Xining, making the bus trip 21 hours long instead of 14. There are times when plane travel doesn't seem so unattractive.

At Delinghe there's a one-hour break and I flag down a police van asking how it could possibly be that we can't be here, as we actually *are* here. The cops have never heard of this edict and neither has anyone else. Could it be because of the Olympics?

Back in Lanzhou I google Delinghe and it turns out the place is allegedly a nuclear missile site. At last something is really done for us to "protect our own safety."

Even I know this nuclear stuff is bad for you; yes, possibly worse than the Sacred Olympics.

But there's one thing that's even worse than that, and that's being platumped.

17

Better to have lost in war than never to have lost at all

Richard was a man with a Protestant work ethic, and proud of it. Although he was popular at work, I got the impression that his colleagues were a bit afraid of his relentless labour routine; marking and marking through the lunch breaks, at night and during holidays. They also didn't like that he wanted to have meetings finished within half an hour so everyone, instead of endlessly circling around the same topics without making a decision, could go back to work which was basically marking.

(When I saw how much of a teacher's work was marking, I was glad I hadn't chosen that profession, having briefly considered it in high school, but instead drifted aimlessly through life until I acquired so much Cantonese vocabulary that I could make a living from that. Marking seemed to me about as life-giving as doing the dishes; as soon as you had finished a huge batch, another one, equally disgusting, came along).

It turned out that Richard used the same work ethic in every aspect of his life. He was, for example, committed to the task of finding a real boyfriend, and to achieve this he decided to go out with every guy in the Gaydar pantheon until he found the right one. And he did. Week after week he met up with four or five of them, weighing and finding too light or heavy one "mincing poof" (as he called them) after another.

It was fun to hear him talk so scathingly about all these people, whose number one sin always seemed to be that they fell in love with him, but also a bit worrisome. What was he saying about me to other people?

I was never to find out. After about 25 Gaydar misses, he made a big hit: Harry. Harry wasn't Chinese at all but English, and after three weeks of this relationship Richard announced that this was it: He had found the love of his life.

I knew of course what it was to be in love, and made sure I only texted him about once a week instead of several times a day as had been our habit before, and then only in a breezy manner. I knew China was now out, but I was glad Richard had found someone and with Harry on board I was hoping for more card playing. Richard, Harry, me and Lydia, two fags and two fag hags. What could be better? But every time we arranged a party or card meeting, one or both of them always came down with a mysterious illness, food poisoning usually, just when the party was about to start.

After a while, Richard just said that they were busy, and so I stopped inviting them.

One Monday I texted Richard saying I really needed to talk to him because my mother had just died, and he answered: "Maybe on Saturday." Then I knew I'd been platumped. He didn't need me any more.

I missed Richard terribly but didn't forget one of the business rules I'd learnt from my business guru Robert Ringer: "Don't deal with people who don't want to deal with you." It was true in real life as well as in matters of commerce. If a student stopped coming to lessons without notifying me, for example, I only ever sent her one email; if she didn't answer that, it meant she didn't want to deal with me.

So I was glad to get more and more students; students who were interested in exploring China and who didn't mind dealing with me although they already had husbands, partners or even children. And I was double glad when George arrived on the scene: Gay, funny, understanding my humour, picking up Cantonese as easily as my dog Piles picked up ticks, and immediately starting a vigorous campaign to teach himself the written language.

Great! Would George perhaps be my new travel companion? I didn't dare to ask. Also he was living with a guy and they frequently jetted around the world.

So imagine my joy when George suggested we go to Xinjiang together. We would both be on a mission, I to film and take photos, and he to scour the area for carpets, perhaps even with a swing around Yunnan on the way back to look for tea, in which he also took great interest. Oh, how he would love the four-day train trip. I just knew he would! Richard had tended to get testy after a second night on the train.

It would take my mind off all the sad stuff that had happened that year, and we would eat melon and at night sit and drink beer and talk to guys, play some cards... Oh! My lovely China awaited another pair of eager worshippers from Hong Kong. And the air would be dry.

All I had to do was finish my DVD, have the launch and we were off.

Yes, *that* DVD. I had finally caved in to my students' demands and made a DVD: "Learn Cantonese the Natural Way – From a Norwegian! All you ever need to learn about Cantonese, including how to look up characters in the dictionary and how to write them, in just 90 minutes" or as the slightly shorter title went: *Cantonese – The Movie*. Now they would stop nagging me, now they would have no excuse but to learn Cantonese in what they thought was the *natural* natural way: Shuttered up in a room by yourself.

I invited everyone I knew to the outdoor launch, regretting not having staged it in an office or shopping centre or something, because it was the hottest, most humid and windless night of the year. So ultra-dry Xinjiang with George a mere five days later would suit me just fine! It was that day, the day of the launch, that I received the email from George about him being unable to make it because his boyfriend was "taking him on a weekend trip to Tokyo."

So that turned out to be a very different trip indeed. On it I learnt that I don't enjoy travelling for weeks at a time by myself any more. It was fine in 1988, but not now. Something about "a young girl travelling by herself" looks different to people from "a middle-aged woman who's travelling by herself because she has been dropped at the last minute and is quite vexed and has something to prove."

*

At least here I was in Kashgar and had reached my goal. With all communication cut off so I couldn't email, blog or text, it was perhaps even a tad worse than it ought to have been, but I got on with Kashgar, or what was left of it. For there would be no "seeing the old city of Kashgar before it's razed to the ground." It had already happened.

Kashgar was the furthest west in China I had ever been and of course this wasn't even China but so obviously still East Turkestan.

It was Central Asia and make no mistake. On my earlier trips to this vast and mysterious 'province' I had met many Uyghurs, and they had, as mentioned, mostly looked like East Europeans of many, many years ago. Old-fashioned in dress, but ostensibly more or less like the Chinese in behaviour. Here, where Uyghurs were still in the majority, it was a different matter. Here it was full veil, women walking a little behind the men, and no music, no wine. Of course it was only a few weeks after a rather serious incident of riots and there were Chinese soldiers everywhere, so they must have thought I was an American spy or something come to... spy on them. No other tourist was in sight – in one of China's biggest tourist attractions.

Before I went on this trip, I had read in the *South China Morning Post* that the tourist industry and people of Xinjiang were gagging for us big spender "Americans" to come back, but I could see little evidence of this. On the contrary, most of the locals looked at me as if I were a big and nasty cockroach or roasted pig, glaring at me with murder in their eyes. I asked a butcher to pose for a photo, and he did, but looked as if he wanted to butcher *me*. However that could have had something to do with the moustache and mono-brow action. With those, even the friendliest geezer can easily look like a murderer.

Talking of moustaches, have you noticed how men in places where the moustache is a predominant feature always need to check/look for/rearrange or just feel their testicles? Without stop? The Uyghurs of Xinjiang, and especially Kashgar, are no exception. It's check, check, feel, feel, every few seconds. I have a theory: Guys with moustaches need them as a kind of bulwark against the world because they are deeply unsure of their masculinity, hence the constant need for reassurance that nether regions are still in place. Do Chinese guys ever check their tackle in public? No need! They know it's there.

Kashgar seemed to be much more overtly Muslim than the other towns on the Silk Road, close to every place ending in -stan though they are. I have to say I got a bit tired of seeing all those women wrapped up like Christmas presents with only their eyes peeking out – eyes hidden behind sunglasses mostly. Some just had a brown table cloth covering their whole head. How they got around was a wonder. Many of them sat around begging, and I felt like saying: Yeah, I'll give you ten yuan, just take off your towel, you burq!

But I'll give them this: The guys also walked around dressed in traditional gear from head to toe; not like in Hong Kong and Europe where they sashay around in T-shirts and shorts, with the wife lumbering behind in a black tent with an eye-slit like some throwback from 1209.

Still, after the 300th person had glared at my T-shirted arms as if they were pork, I couldn't help thinking: You know what? This is China. Women can wear anything we like here. It's 2009. Deal with it! Yes, that's how inconsistent I was in my loyalties. I wanted to be on the side of the underdog but not if it was going to look at me like that.

*

I have to hand it to the Chinese government; when they say they're going to do something, for example making the backward and medieval Kashgar more suitable for tourists, they do it. It was only a few months before that the newspapers had written that the government was *planning* to raze old Kashgar, of "one of China's main tourist attractions" fame, to the ground.

When I arrived, the warrens and bazaars and markets and Central Asian glory had already been Shenzhen-ified with brand new enormous buildings covered in tiles in what the Chinese felt was... Arabic? style, and green windows with aluminium frames. The markets had given way to supermarkets selling fun, ethnic trinkets, and the chaotic alleys and back streets had been made nice and wide to accommodate… armoured vehicles?

There were certainly enough of these around town, with lots of army posts everywhere complete with sandbags and soldiers armed with machine guns, sub-machine guns and shields. Outside the Tai Kai something Dance Hall seemed to be a particularly hot hotspot – here the army had really bunkered down with dozens of soldiers behind sandbags and metal fences. That must have been where those pesky Uyghurs threw rocks or something at the Chinese, who had come out in force to avenge the honour of the two Chinese women who hadn't been raped by gangs of crazed, hairy Uyghurs in Guangdong province the month before.

So what if that particular rumour turned out to be untrue? Fighting is fun and the Uyghurs must be taught who runs the place. I stopped outside the Tai Kai something Dance Hall to gaze at the beautiful soldiers (after all I am partial to a good man in uniform), only to be told by an admittedly widely grinning soldier: No standing!

What – outside the fence? On a public pavement?

The main mosque in town, now overlooking a "panoramic view tourist something or other" was another place where the soldiers had congregated. I helped an old geezer in a skullcap feed a flock of doves on the steps of the mosque, and I don't think the irony was lost on him as the white doves crowded around us while 60 or so soldiers, none of them a day over 20 except the surly commander, looked on, guns at the ready.

The geezer and I lifted our collective eyebrows and shook our heads in weary resignation as the soldiers nervously stared at my camera. Would the foreigner take photos? Yes, she would, actually. Of the doves. The expected frantic arm-wave and angry eyebrow action duly occurred, and the commander came running up, ready to defend his post to the death. Fortunately, when it became clear that he was a Cantonese speaker as was I, everything was all right again.

We agreed that dry heat was better than the humid heat of our respective hometowns and that *Choh Dai Di* was the best card game in the world. We bemoaned the lack of Pearl River Beer in Xinjiang and agreed that it was a damned shame that we wouldn't be able to get online until the end of October, and parted on excellent terms.

Of course, the "Improvement" of Kashgar wasn't all done and dusted yet. Walking around where the aforementioned warrens, bazaars and markets used to be certainly satisfied all my curiosity about what it's really like to live in a war zone – without the risk of being bombed. Here was everything I had seen in documentaries about the second world war. Half-demolished houses stood naked and roofless with a doorframe or other as sole witness to an earlier life; here and there a wall gaping empty with its carefully arranged mosaic tiles – an aesthetic "up yours" to the 80-floor shiny new building mastodons towering up behind them.

And just like in the grainy black-and-white footage from the bombings of a thousand European towns, I could see people picking their way carefully across the debris, perhaps on their way to work, maybe 'happy, colourful Uyghur dancing and singing for Chinese tourists'.

The little shops stood abandoned with metal grilles pulled down, and the few meat, vegetable and artisan shops still open had been equipped with glaring signs in typical Chinese tour group lingo: "A Traditional Knifeancarpet (sic) Shop For Tourists." "Street display for sale to tourists." "Original art for tourists." But no tourists were forthcoming. At least not while I was there.

Was I paranoid, or had everybody been warned against talking to strangers? In front of each heap of building debris, each gigantic crater where not long ago had been homes inhabited by people whose lifestyle hadn't changed much since Mohammed wore short trousers, stood local Uyghurs looking expressionlessly at the destruction. When I asked them if this used to be their home or how they felt about being thrown out of their houses, they suddenly couldn't understand Mandarin. The brave ones mumbled something about this being too sensitive to talk about, before hurrying away.

Only a Chinese worker on his way into a crater chatted openly.

"Yes, we had to tear down these awful old things to build new things!" He pointed proudly to a monster tower block in the background: "Look at that! We did that. We are going to help the Hui (Uyghurs) to get somewhere to live!"

I asked him if they had asked the Hui if that's what they wanted.

"Asked them? Hee hee. Everybody wants to live in a new house, right?"

That wasn't what I had heard. Then again, with no Uyghur willing to talk to me, I only had the article that George had sent me to back up my claim.

"We have never been asked if we want to live in a high-rise. We Uyghur Muslims want to live with only the earth below us and only heaven above," one of the few citizens of Kashgar willing to be interviewed for that particular article had said. Allegedly.

Also: When I looked at the pink- and beige-tiled high-rises lording it over what was left of the old city of Kashgar, I thought: The Uyghurs will never be able to afford to live there. If the train, the microcosm of China, was anything to go by, I had seen this during my four trips to Xinjiang: The Uyghurs never travelled soft sleeper, extremely rarely in hard sleeper, and, if they travelled by train at all, only on hard seat.

What they did travel on, though, was the bus.

And so did I. Having already conquered my youthful fear of travelling by bus in China, I would take the day bus to Kuche, stay one night and then onto the overnight bus to Urumqi. There I would meet the only person I knew in Xinjiang: Ah Mak from not only Hong Kong but from my own village, Pui O. A Hong Kong guy as fond as I was of Xinjiang and a friend of the people who had, two years earlier, set me up with hung-over Mr. Jin, he was the only person I had been able to communicate with by mobile phone during my lonely and ultimately rather fruitless trip to this province, so cut off from civilization it might as well be Mars. Or Jupiter. Whichever is furthest away.

Because we couldn't text inside Xinjiang, I had stayed in contact with ah-Mak by actual telephone calls, him warning me at every turn against going to Kashgar, Kuche, Korla and all the other places I had gone to. "Dangerous! So many soldiers! You'll get killed! And the toilets...!"

The last time I had heard from him was two days before; he was in Yili, supposedly the most beautiful place in Xinjiang and fond topic of many a song by my favourite singer Dao Lang, a Sichuan guy who had become a megastar in China by pretending to be from Xinjiang, and also by having a marvellous voice.

Now ah-Mak was making his way down to civilization, Urumqi, and we would meet there in two days' time.

Oh glory, oh friendship! All I had talked about with anyone for the last week was the old:

"Where from."

"Hong Kong."

"No."... etc.

Now I would party with Hong Kong guys, speak Cantonese and generally have a fantastic time.

After having fought with a hotel reception guard and been forced to pay 900 yuan for a three-hour sleep at the Lido, I got on the overnight bus and settled into the lower middle bunk (when I bought the ticket I had asked for an upper window bunk), right behind the driver. This bunk was the one where the television set was. They turned it on at about 11:30pm. The TV was right above my knees and my face is – oh, I don't know – 50 cm from my knees, at least in the semi-upright position that these bunks, 40 cm wide, force you to adopt. The show was a screechy cartoon and, I'm embarrassed to say, I couldn't stand it. After only a few minutes of screaming rabbits or mice or whatever, I said to the driver: Please turn it off.

"What, you don't want to watch *TV???*" (You insane foreign woman, you?)

No, I do not.

"But how about the other people?"

If they want to watch it, you can move me to another bunk. Do you want to move me to another bunk?

Head-shakingly, they turned it off, and I drifted into blissful sleep.

To deal with the once-every-five-minute roadblocks, the driver and his assistant had sensibly just collected and kept our ID cards, not collected and given them back again each time like on the other buses I had been on. Which, at this stage, were incredibly many.

At about 3:00am I was woken up by the bus shaking and veering all over the road. The driver seemed to be behaving erratically. He was shaking his arm violently backwards and forwards, swinging his body from side to side as well as slapping himself in the face, hard. But still he kept nodding off, bringing the bus back from the edge of the road each time. Oh dear.

I sat down next to him to try to keep him awake by talking, but it was no good. His male ego couldn't stand such an affront. On we went with nodding off, almost going off the road into the desert, bringing the bus back to the road with a jerk, nodding off again. The highways of Xinjiang are just too good and smooth – not like in Tibet, for example, where they can only accommodate the width of half a car and where there's inevitably a 2,000-metre drop to the right. Or the left, depending on which direction you're going.

In the end I thought: Well, I've had a reasonable life. Why not end it here? I got up and on my way back to my bunk sort of pointed with my chin to the sign above the door where the bus policy, starting with "Your safety is our sacred duty!" was displayed, remarking: "Well, safety *is* of course number one." I felt quite pleased with myself for ending my life on a sarcastic note.

That made him finally wake his fellow driver who had been snoring away in the bunk next to mine. Another male Chinese ego shattered but

I didn't care. The freshly woken driver drove smoothly without incident all night until we reached Urumqi and I could check into the excellent Royal International Hotel, 60% cheaper because of the lack of tourists. That's right; discounts. That's how you attract tourists to a province, *not* by kicking them out of hotels in the middle of the night! I had to snigger as I checked in; last time I had been at this same hotel with Richard, it had also been 60% cheaper because the air conditioning system had broken down. Was there no end to my luck with this town and this hotel?

When I got to the room I thought I should immediately call ah-Mak, to arrange for that evening's Cantonese-speaking, *Choh Dai Di*-playing extravaganza.

That was when I realised I had lost my mobile phone on the trip between Kuche and Urumqi.

Had it slipped out of my pocket as I crouched down in one of the squatting toilets on the many stopovers? Or had it fallen from my waist-bag as I lay on the bus bunk, willing the driver to stay awake? The phone was gone, and I had no way of contacting ah-Mak, as I couldn't get online and couldn't call out of the province to perhaps find someone in my village who could get ah-Mak's mainland phone number.

I sprinted back to the bus station where the customer service person, a Uyghur woman, immediately set a huge thing in motion, ending with her personally taking me to the bus from Kuche which, amazingly, was still there. But my phone wasn't.

Back in Hong Kong I could sense that ah-Mak didn't believe me when I told him I had lost my mobile. He had called me hundreds of times and been extremely worried when all he got was: "This number has been disconnected." If I were him, I wouldn't have believed me either. Lost my phone on the bus? It was the equivalent of "I can't come to your dinner party because of food poisoning." I'm still trying to live it down.

But I'm happy to say that I eventually forgave George and went on to enjoy a superb trip to Guangdong province with him. As I had suspected, he turned out to be an excellent travel companion all round, and it was only awful fate and the nature of Hong Kong companies that made his boyfriend's firm suddenly relocate to London this year, thus depriving me once again of a good friend. That's the nature of Hong Kong. You meet people, get to like or even love them; then they leave.

However, I carried on regardless with the people I did have, i.e. my students (victims), but bugger me if the Chinese Communist Party didn't come to my aid again.

To accommodate the Asian Games in Guangzhou late in 2010 the Party not only started to raze to the ground all that was good and great about Guangzhou, namely the old, untouched by 'progress' neighbourhoods just north of the Pearl River, no, in the name of 'national harmony' they also decided to get rid of the Cantonese-language TV and radio stations, making all media in Guangzhou Mandarin. Just to help outsiders, you understand, as the mainland government has always been keen on a high level of communication.

They have frequently showed this willingness to share information, for example each time a highly contagious disease has broken out in the country.

Anyway, this time it was our sacred Cantonese language at stake, and as soon as the news broke, the local media started calling me, wanting to interview me as an 'expert on Cantonese'. You see? This is how lowly Cantonese ranks in the minds of Hong Kong people.

After the first newspaper article, my latest film on YouTube got 10,000 hits in 40 hours (outnumbering the most viewed film which had been up for two years) with young Hong Kong people of today swamping me with messages saying things like "Thank you for saving our language", "You are a foreigner but cares more about Cantonese than we do, I'm embarrassed" and "Thank you, Norway friend." In English, of course.

Next week there will be a demonstration in Guangzhou fighting for the Cantonese language. Of course I'm going! I must fight and fight for the coolest language on Earth. The next day I'll be getting on a train with my new travel companion, Peter. Although he's heterosexual and not likely to be willing to sit and gaze and gaze at beautiful Chinese guys like George (and Richard, whom I will always love no matter what)

– what the hell. We're still going to Lanzhou with its Yellow River, the cradle of civilization, and after that, into the wilderness of the Tibetan areas beyond.

Of course we will have to communicate by Mando, but we'll deal with it. When we get back to Hong Kong, I expect the Cantonese language debate will have taken off in earnest.

Make no mistake, I'll be there to fight the good fight. And I'll keep wandering along the wild and wacky roads.

But I expect the fight to be long and hard, for making Cantonese a world language is not exactly a downhill battle. But who wants to fight downhill? It's too easy – as when you joke on the stairs – to "slip and fall".

Epilogue

One of the great regrets of my life is that I wasn't in Hong Kong during the Tiananmen massacre in June 1989. Yes, I know, it's been officially downgraded to an "incident", but you know what, I think it's right to call soldiers killing thousands of their own people a massacre.

I don't regret not being in Beijing at the time – that would have been asking too much – but why oh why did I have to go and live in South Korea just that year?

As I watched the drama unfold on the TV screens in the schools I was teaching at, and in bars and restaurants in the evenings, I experienced the greatest pain and sorrow of my life so far. As I cried and bemoaned the fate of the people and city I had come to love so much, the Koreans just shrugged. "That's nothing," they said. "We've had much worse, in Kwangju in 1980." It was true that the South Korean government hadn't been slouches when it came to mowing down students in that city's uprising, but during the six months I lived in South Korea, for various reasons I never warmed to the Koreans the way I had to the Chinese. Quite frankly I felt the food was the best thing about Korea, and left as soon as I could, going back to Hong Kong to settle for good.

Thus I missed possibly the biggest demonstration in Hong Kong's history, when more than one-and-a-half million people turned out to swamp the streets, marching in anger, grief and disbelief for the fate of their countrymen up north.

So when I receive an email from an unknown source in Guangzhou saying a demonstration, a real demonstration, will take place there in two weeks to support no less than the Cantonese language, there is no way I am going to miss it.

For years the Communist government has been working to undermine the regional languages and dialects of China, promoting Mandarin as the "civilized language" and making sure that the only way to get ahead for people all over the country, from Tibet to Xinjiang, from Shanghai to Sichuan to Guangdong and even Hong Kong, is to speak that imperialist language consisting mostly of "sh" sounds. As well as, of course, "r".

And after 1997, although more subtly than the 'speak Mandarin or die' approach they have been using in occupied territories of China, Beijing has been pushing for Hong Kong too to convert to the civilized language. I can't tell you how surprised I was, stepping into my local branch of HSBC (formerly known as Hongkong Bank) with its 20-square-metre premises and three teller windows, to be greeted at the door by a staff member wearing a big badge saying "Promote Putonghua Campaign Month" and chirping *"Ni Hao!"* in terrible Mandarin.

What – a Cantonese-speaking Hong Kong person talking Mandarin to a Cantonese-speaking foreigner, in Hong Kong? In little sleepy backwater Mui Wo? I looked at her aghast, and she had the decency to look a bit embarrassed. That campaign died a quiet death, as even the docile Hong Kong people just ignored this effort by a privately owned company to be the errand-boy of Beijing in seeking to obliterate their mother tongue.

That was years ago, and since then the 'everybody must learn Mandarin or they will never get a job and will die a horrible death of starvation' campaigns, not only in Hong Kong but all over the world, have been escalating, reaching something of a crescendo this year.

So now I'm on my way to Guangzhou to stand up and be counted for Cantonese. Only yesterday I have received an email saying the demonstration has been cancelled because the organisers have been, surprise, arrested. Therefore I assume that it will go ahead anyway – this is too big to be stopped by some puny arrests. In the days leading up to the demonstration I have been deluged with calls from various Hong Kong media wanting to interview me about this momentous event, as a

'Cantonese expert'. I think this is a little sad – don't they have their own people?

Even TVB asks me to make a video which I am to hand over to them free of charge, presumably because they are too pusillanimous to go up there and film the demonstration themselves.

Plaintive cries are heard all over Facebook: Be careful! Don't go! You'll be arrested! Killed! Or worse!

But as we all know, they never kill foreigners, and this is too huge to be missed.

I go with my good friend Ellen, my publisher Pete and two Hong Kong journalists who interview me in the train restaurant car. "How do you feel about Cantonese, how come you like Cantonese, isn't Mandarin much more useful and have you ever used chopsticks?"

Installed in the hotel, we take a taxi to the demonstration venue.

The tension is great.

Is it because we're afraid there won't be anybody there, seeing the thing has officially been cancelled? No.

Is it because we're afraid to be arrested? Is it hell!

It is because, to accommodate the upcoming Asian Games, the local government has been busy (not as busy as Beijing before the 2008 Olympics but very busy) razing large swathes of Guangzhou to the ground, and we are therefore stuck in the worst traffic jam ever. It would have taken less time leisurely walking from Hong Kong to Guangzhou than this, the last leg of our journey from the Venice Hotel to Gong Lam Sai metro station, the scene of the demonstration, normally a five-minute drive.

When we finally get there one hour late, we hear the sound of thousands of people shouting long before we see them. And then we're engulfed in a seething sea of humanity; a quagmire of joyous, raucous youth bellowing out their salute to Cantonese language and culture, thousands and thousands of young people, iPhone-waving 20-somethings, sick and tired of being dictated to by Beijing.

If I'd been two or three metres tall, I would have been able to capture this scene, unheard of since June 4th, 1989, of young people in peaceful protest against, or rather a peaceful fight for, that wondrous entity that is Cantonese. As it is, and despite standing on tiptoe and holding the camera high over my head, I only get shots of other people filming and taking photos; as well as more and more people pouring into the street every minute.

Naturally there is a large presence of police, but they seem not to know exactly what to do, in the end resorting to saying "This way, please" and stuff like that. Most of them are smiling and laughing. Is this the beginning of something new? But, as I said to the journalist on the train: Cantonese makes people more lively. It is its nature.

Being all Canto speakers, we three foreigners quickly join in the chorus of "Support Cantonese!" and "Cantonese people should speak the Cantonese language!"

Being the only foreigners there, we are immediately mobbed, swamped, photographed and filmed. And interviewed.

Oh, it is beautiful. A completely peaceful, joyous and fun demonstration in China, whereas if you're in the Tiananmen Square of today reaching into your pocket to take out as much as a handkerchief, you will be immediately wrestled to the ground by three guys in fake leather jackets and whisked away to face hours of interrogation. Here we are among thousands of like-minded people and the police can't do a thing. And they don't seem to want to do a thing.

After about an hour of shouting, filming and modern technology-ing (*everyone* has an iPhone) it seems the police have received some kind of orders, because they start to gently and politely nudge people away from the demonstration grounds. And as it is a road, a major thoroughfare, they can't really be blamed.

What a fantastic victory. What a delirious moment. I feel so good about my life's purpose, to make Cantonese a world language, now that I know I can hand the baton, as it were, over to the young people of today.

The next day I meet up with Peter and we set off on our epic journey to the north, with the Hong Kong media calling me for comments every day. I do comment, but only on my blog: "A historic moment and a triumph. I'm telling you now: You haven't heard the last from the youthful Cantonese movement! It will spread to Hong Kong. Fast."

And yes! The week after I get back, there is indeed a demonstration in Hong Kong in support of the Cantonese language. I get four of my students to come with me although it's a Sunday – truth be told, I'd rather be at home as well, but I cannot miss this momentous occasion.

We arrive at Wan Chai sports ground, probably big enough to accommodate the thousands of Hong Kong people coming out in force to fight for their language. We are four foreigners, all dressed in white as requested.

The number of Hong Kong people who have come out in force to take a stand for their mother language:

Three.

Language Notes

(p) = Putonghua, (c) = Cantonese

Chapter 1

喀什 (p) Ka Shi, (c) Haak Sap: Kashgar. People say the name means "variegated houses." My question then is, naturally: Who are these people? And what does "variegated" mean? "With many gates"? (One google later: Bugger me, it is a word meaning "of various colours".) The Chinese name is just a transliteration.

新彊 (p) Xin Jiang (c) San Geung: New Frontier.

北京 (p) Bei Jing (c) Bak Geng: Northern Capital. There's a 南京 (p) Nan Jing (c) Lam Geng, Southern Capital in China, and a 東京 (p) Dong Jing (c) Dong Geng, Eastern Capital, namely Tokyo, in Japan. But there's no 西京 (p) Xi Jing (c) Sai Geng, Western Capital, anywhere in Asia. There is one in Europe though: Oslo.

庫車 (p) Ku Che (c) Fu Cheh: Warehouse Vehicle. Kuche, famous Silk Road oasis town.

阿克蘇 (p) A Ke Su (c) Ah Hak Sou: A Gram Become Conscious Again (transliteration, hallo!) Real meaning: White Water. Akesu. Another trading place on the Silk Road – now a tiled and blue-windowed monster.

香港同胞 (p) Xiang Gang Tong Bao (c) Heung Gong Tong Bao: Hong Kong compatriot. Tong Bao means also someone who's born of the same parents.

烏魯木齊 (p) Wu Lu Mu Qi (c) Wo Lo Muk Tsai: Urumqi. Means "Beautiful Meadow" in Turkic. Urumqi is the capital of Xinjiang province.

漢 (p) Han (c) Hon: Han Chinese. The Han Dynasty (206 BC to 220 AD) was huge – most things happened then with some great wars, great wall-building and a lot of one country, one system, and the Chinese really established themselves. The ethnic majority in China calls itself Han, and the character also means "real man" or "hero."

Chapter 2

中國 (p) Zhong Guo (c) Jong Gok: China, the Middle Kingdom. I don't know why I didn't put that word first in the notes for Chapter 1, as it is the most important country in the world and becoming more important every day. Why else would it be called the Country in the Middle, eh? But there it is: Jong: Middle, Gok: country. Some other countries have been honoured with the term Gok, notably 英國, Ying Gok, Hero Country (Britain); 法國, Fat Gok, Law Country (France); and 德國 Dak Gok, Virtuous Country (Germany). But most countries are just good old transliterations, like Norway: 挪威, Lo Wai (Shift Strength). All the countries' names mean something good though. The only exception I can find is 非洲, Fei Jau, Evildoing Continent (Africa). But then again it isn't a country.

老百姓 (p) Lao Bai Xing (c) Lou Bak Seng: The Old One Hundred Surnames, the common man. There are about 700 surnames in China, of which only about 20 are widely used. The surname comes first, then the generation name, and the personal name last. Take for example Mao Zedong. Mao (hairs) is the family name, Ze (brilliant) is the generation name which is given to all the sons in the family, and Dong (East) is the guy's personal name. By friends he may be known as Ah Dong, which in English would be something like "Our East" or "The Eastster."

Now Chinese names have been in circulation for quite some time, and Mao Zedong, Deng Xiaoping, Zhou Enlai and the others are household names. So I was a bit surprised the other day when I saw, in an English-language magazine, Jiang Zemin referred to as Mr. Zemin.

Another somewhat peculiar thing about China today is that during the last 15 or 20 years it has become very popular to have just one name. Perhaps this is connected to people not having any sisters or brothers, but it must create a total headache for the authorities. Even after decades of the one child policy, it can't be denied that the Chinese population is growing steadily. These people bear, in 90% of cases, one of 20 surnames. One would think it would be advantageous if they had two given names, so that four different men would be called for example Mao Zedong, Mao Zhidong, Mao Judong and Mao Jiandong. But no, to show that they are modern and hip (and perhaps to get the taxman off their backs), all are called just Mao Dong. And there will be about three million other guys in the country also called Mao Dong.

蘭州 (p) Lan Zhou (c) Laan Jau: Orchid Land. Northern China's transport hub number one. If you ever go there and want to leave by train: Go to the station first thing. Before you check into the hotel, even. They're selling the tickets up to two weeks in advance now, so get your ticket as soon as. Everyone in China who is anything in the travelling world will want to be on YOUR train.

內蒙古 (p) Nei Meng Gu (c) Loy Mong Gu: Inner Mongolia, which the Mongolians call South Mongolia. Now some politically correct people want it to be that Mongolia, an independent country over which not even the Russians have any influence any more, is somehow called "Outer Mongolia". Give me a break! 蒙, by the way, means "ignorance" according to the dictionary, and 古 "ancient". Hmm... Mongolians have been ignorant for a long time? No, it must be a coincidence. And a transliteration of the Mongolian word Mongol.

黃河 (p) Huang He (c) Wong Ho: Yellow River. 黃 is one of the most common surnames in Hong Kong, 香港 (p) Xiang Gang (c) Heung Gong. It's the accepted fact among foreigners, and perhaps the Chinese who keep feeding them wrong information, that Heung Gong means "Fragrant Harbour". But that doesn't make sense. Although the harbour in those days was probably less foul-smelling than now, the origin of Heung Gong isn't the whole city/special autistic zone (what does SAR stand for again?) but a small bay on the south side of what is today Hong Kong Island. In those days most geographical spots were named after the trade that went on in them, and as 香 (Heung) – good smell, fragrant, good taste – also means "incense" (joss stick), I think it's much more plausible that the city is named after a bay where incense-making went on. "Incense Harbour" in other words.

廣州 (p) Guang Zhou (c) Gong Jau: Wide Open Land, Guangzhou, capital of Guangdong province. When I say "land" (as you read through these notes or look at a map of China, you'll see that untold place names end with 州, Jau, land) I don't mean as in "country" but "geographical feature". The character is put together by river and earth, and Jau actually means "administrative district in ancient China". But I can't write that every time, therefore "land".

深圳 (p) Shen Zhen (c) Sam Jan: Shenzhen, shopping paradise right across the border from Heung Gong. Talking about geographical features – it means "Deep Drain"!

老外 (only p) Lao Wai: "Old Outside", white foreigner. And when I say white, the Chinese think "British/American". I used to think "old outside" was a kind of term of endearment, as the Chinese call each other "Old Wang" and "Old Li" as a term of address. And "old" doesn't always mean "advanced in years", by the way, but more like "venerable". But then I was told off by some 17-year-olds, not only for having a fuddy-duddy, "village" name (Lotus) but also for "allowing" people to call me Lao Wai. It seems it's a racial slur after all. Oh well. At least it beats the shit out of 鬼婆 (c) Gwai Po: Devil Hag, which Hong Kong people call me.

中國文明的搖籃 (p) Zhong Guo Wen Ming De Yao Lan (c) Jong Gok Man Meng Dek Yiu Laam: Chinese Civilisation's Cradle. I've stood on it! And: It rocks.

兵馬俑 (p) Bing Ma Yong (c) Beng Ma Yong: Soldier Horse Funereal Statues, the Terracotta Army. Since I started writing this book, I've actually caved in and gone to see them. I don't want to tell people what to do but: Unless you're fond of throwing money out the window, look at photos of them instead. But if you love and adore tackiness, screaming crowds and shrieking guides, plus you absolutely worship knick-knacks and would love nothing more than wading through tourist crap for three kilometres before you even get to the hangar where the figures are stored – by all means go now!

普通話 (p) Pu Tong Hua (c) Pou Tong Wah: common or ordinary language – Mandarin. In Cantonese normally known as 國語, Gok Yu, National Language. When people ask me why I don't like Putonghua, I of course never say "because it sounds like two cockroaches fighting in an arse" – no, I just say "太普通, tai pou tong" – too ordinary. And anyway, I don't *not* like it – it's just that I vastly, by a million times and to the death prefer...

廣東話 (p) Guang Dong Hua, (c) Gong Dong Wa: Cantonese. Also known as 廣州話, Gong Jau Wah (Language of Guangzhou); 白話, Bak Wah, White Language; 粵語, Yuet Yu (Yuet is the old name for Guangdong province); 廣府話，Gong Fu Wah (Canton-official Language), and of course just 中文，Jung Man, Middle Language.

Chinese. For it's Cantonese that's really Chinese, and not Mando! Get it?

川菜 (p) Chuan Cai (c) Chuen Choy: Sichuan food. Chuan means river and Si Chuan four rivers. Cai or Choy actually means vegetable but together with the name of a province or area, it becomes "cuisine".

共產黨 (p) Gong Chan Dang (c) Gong Chan Dong: Common Produce Party, the Communist Party. As a Norwegian, I have to say I'm not a fan of capital letters for so many things. In fact people seem to be using them more and more, as in "I read many Book's (sic)." It seems that people want to return to a time when common nouns had capital letters, and liberally sprinkling adjectives and adverbs with them as well. Me, I think few nouns should have capital letters, and certainly not the Communist Party – the dullest, most destructive party ever. It doesn't deserve them.

Chapter 3

蘭桂坊 (p) Lan Gui Fang (c) Laan Gwai Fong: Orchid Cassiabark Tree Neighbourhood, Lan Kwai Fong – a steep (and steeply priced) watering hell-hole in Hong Kong, inexplicably in vogue for the whole time I've been here. When will it end? And why does the fact that a pint of beer costs three times as much there as almost anywhere else make it so much more attractive? It's just a glorified ski jump without the snow.

羅湖商場 (p) Luo Hu Shang Zhang (c) Lo Wu Seung Cheung: Net Lake Commerce Park. That Hades on Earth and therefore so alluring – Lo Wu Shopping Centre. Not many people (that I know, naturally) know that Lo Wu means Net Lake – reflecting the status of Shenzhen just a few years ago, a sleepy backwater to out-sleep the sleepiest backwater anywhere. I don't know, given that I hate that shopping centre so much, why I go there so frequently. I hate being harassed by touts and above all, having little binty fingers plucking at my sleeves, or worse, at my arms. I think I just go there to keep the repulsion alive. Anyway, the fact that Lo Wu means Net Lake and Shenzhen means Deep Drain – that's the kind of stuff I find fascinating. I think it's weird and quite incomprehensible that people can live in a place maybe their whole lives and not bother finding out what the name of it means. Hence these notes. That's right: You're going to find out what stuff means whether you like it or not.

建設路 (p) Jian She Lu (C) Gin Jit Lou: Construction Road. The main drag from the Lo Wu station to... I'm not sure where it ends really. I think it just changes names further north and probably becomes something inventive like Liberation Road (every single town in China has one) or One Child Policy Road. A(nother) terrible result of the Communist takeover in 1949 was that China's formerly charming and colourfully named streets and roads all became depressingly the same. Beijing Road. Nanjing Road. Liberation Road. Workers' Road. Not like Bubbling Well Road, Whispering Bamboo Street and Whoremonger Alley, is it?

青島 (p) Qing Dao (c) Cheng Dou: Green Island, Qingdao, or more commonly known (beer-wise) as Tsingtao. "Tsingtao" is neither Cantonese nor Mandarin. So why call it that? One has to wonder.

元 (p) Yuan (c) Yuen: the currency of China. 1 yuan is about US$0.75. However, the Chinese seldom say "yuan", preferring to name prices in 塊 (p) kuai, which means "rectangular flat piece", an abbreviation of 塊錢, kuai qian, meaning "piece of money" (notes). In the China of 1988, all money came in notes, down to US$0.07. It was easy to feel rich then. Cantonese doesn't use "yuan" at all except in writing. In Hong Kong the currency, which in English is called dollar, is called 蚊 (c) Man, which actually means mosquito.

火車站 (p) Huo Che Zhan (c) Fo Cheh Jaan: Train station. 火車 literally means Fire Car.

Chapter 4

燒餅 (p) Shao Bing (c) Siu Behng: a kind of flat, deep- or pan-fried cake with various stuffing, with or without sesame seeds.

廣州東站 (p) Guang Zhou Dong Zhan (c) Gong Jau Dong Jaam: Guangzhou East Railway Station. A lovely station with some good restaurants and great hotel service. Right near the exit you can have hotel rooms organised for you, not only for up to 30% less than if you should have found the hotel by yourself, but you will also be driven there, free! This took me about eight years to discover, because of my pathological independence and aversion to people helping me. No "service" for me, thanks, I'd rather stay out in the rain. What a tool!

天河 (p) Tian He (c) Tinn Ho: Heavenly River, the Milky Way. I think "Heavenly River Station" is a somewhat more romantic name for a train station than "Guangzhou East".

好，好，好好 (p) Hao, hao, hao hao (c) Hou, hou, hou hou: Good, good, very good. Yes, Chinese is a practical language. One word means practically everything. "Hao" means good, well, fine, OK, as well as "very". And many other things.

紫禁城 (p) Zi Jin Cheng (c) Ji Gam Seng: Purple Forbidden City, the Forbidden City. This is the original name in use from about the 1420s. Purple was the colour of military bravery. Nowadays though, if you want to ask for directions to the Forbidden City you should say...

故宫 (p) Gu Gong (c) Goo Gong: the Former Palace. Also known as the Forbidden City or the Palace Museum.

天安門 (p) Tian An Men (c) Tin On Mun: the Heavenly Peace Gate (or door).

明朝 (p) Ming Zhao (c) Meng Chiu: Bright Morning, Ming Dynasty. There is that 朝 word again. It means "morning" but *also* Imperial Court *and* Dynasty! And when you see how the character is put together by "ten, sun, ten and moon" – well, you get an idea of how the Chinese looked at their dynasties. They loved them! At least in writing.

沙偭島 (p) Sha Mian Dao (c) Saa Min Dou: Shamian Island, a small spit of land in the Pearl River running through Guangzhou. Here the British, Germans and other foreigners had a sanctuary while they were engaged in swapping opium for silk, tea and other stuff they were so crazy about in those days. Well, not really a sanctuary – it was in fact the only place in China in which they were allowed to stay. Many of the stately colonial-style buildings are still left, and the island is also home to a bunch of giant banyan and other trees up to 200 years old. Shamian is also the last stop on the journey of mostly American couples who have bought, I mean adopted, Chinese children, mainly girls."Tobacco, beer, film, adoption" it says on the wall of one of the many souvenir shops which have spurted forth in the last seven or eight years, ruining the neighbourhood for me.

I myself have always tried to avoid having children, feeling that there are enough of the blighters, so I don't know how it feels to be childless but wanting a child intensely. These newly-minted adoptive parents who, seen by the casual observer, seem to consist of an overwhelming percentage of grotesquely obese people, probably feel they're doing China a great favour by taking these girl children, whom nobody wants, out of the country. But I don't know. If there's something lacking in China today, it is girls. Some places I read that China has 70 million more men than women, other places a more modest 40 million. But even if only 40 million, it is still a significant number. 40 million men; that is ten times the population of Norway, to use a global yardstick. 40 (or 50, 60 or 70) million sexually frustrated men who will never get married or have a family – that kind of thing can easily cause violent scenes. Wouldn't it be better to build good orphanages for girls and keep them in China until they are ready to get married in their own country? Perhaps even convince Chinese couples to become adoptive parents? Now we have the ridiculous situation that girls are sent out of the country as adoptees, while young girls are kidnapped and sold into sexual slavery, exported around the world, "forcing" Chinese men, especially farmers, to buy women from poor countries like Laos, Cambodia and Vietnam to carry on the family name. It goes against all logic and reason. It is almost... dare I say... surreal?

毛澤東 (p) Mao Ze Dong (c) Mou Jak Dong: Hairs Brilliant East. That's right! His surname means "hairs", as in "body hairs". Also "fur", "feathers", "down", "gross, untouched, unpolished" and, interestingly, "panic-stricken"! Panic-stricken Brilliant East – I wonder if any of the Mao worshippers think of him in those terms. Probably not.

鄧小平 (p) Deng Xiao Ping (c) Dang Siu Peng: Deng (I can only get "family name" out of this one although I know more meaning lurks behind this character – part of it is a geographical feature meaning city) Little Peace. "Little Peace" also sounds like "Little Bottle" in Chinese, and apparently during one of Xiaoping's many periods of being ousted, people used to put small bottles here and there to show their support. However, after the Tiananmen massacre, people started putting small *smashed* bottles everywhere. And too bloody right! I love the subtlety – still, wouldn't it be better if they could just come out and for example write a letter to the editor: "Yeah, that Xiaoping? I think he's not a perfect leader." That would save a lot of people from stepping on broken glass, among other things.

Chapter 5

成都 (p) Cheng Du (c) Seng Dou: Becoming the Capital, capital of Sichuan province. Chengdu is an excessively over-trafficked, pancake-flat city in the north of the province with 11 million people as I write this sentence, a number which will probably have increased to 12 million by the time I get to the end of it. It's difficult to breathe in Chengdu because of all the cars and an almost insanely vigorous construction programme. The city used to be famous for its plethora of street snack stalls but has now been sterilized and scrubbed clinically dead, and looks like all other big cities in China, without any funky neighbourhoods but with marginally higher car-to-human ratio. Still, there are some beautiful bamboo parks where the old teahouse tradition still holds forth. Knowing Chinese city "planners", these tea gardens will soon be put inside air-conditioned glass and concrete boxes with plastic bamboo.

西昌 (p) Xi Chang (c) Sai Cheung: Western Brilliance. You thought only "ze" as in "Mao Zedong" meant "brilliance"? Oh no. In the Chinese language there are more words meaning "brilliance" than you can swing a dead kangaroo at. And that's interesting, because "kangaroo" in Chinese is the same word as "mouse". Well, "bag mouse" really.

白酒 (p) Bai Jiu (c) Baak Jau: White Alcohol/Wine – bai jiu. In Hong Kong, if you ask for white wine you actually get white wine, whereas in China you'll be served the vilest brew that ever tore asunder a billion brain cells. Beware, I say. Beware.

王榮 (p) Wang Rong (c) Wong Weng: Wang means King and is one of the most common surnames among the Old Hundred Surnames. Rong means Honour. A relatively unusual name for a girl as they are normally named after a flower or some word for grace, beauty or to sit in the corner and shut up.

馬富漒 (p) Ma Fu Qiang (c) Ma Fu Keung: Horse Rich and Strong. Ma (Horse) is my favourite surname. I don't know why. And give me a geezer whose name is Ah Keung! But it has to be in Cantonese, obviously. Qiang just doesn't have the same ring to it.

鋤大D (p) Chu Da Di (c) Choh Dai Di: Play Big Two, "Chinese Poker". An exciting, challenging and adrenaline-boosting card game for four players where the two is the highest card. There are many underground Choh Dai Di cells around the world and in northern China, all initiated and trained by me.

天壇 (p) Tian Tan (c) Tin Taan: the Temple of Heaven in Beijing.

川興 (p) Chuan Xing (c) Chuen Heng: River Joy. Small village in southern Sichuan.

喝 (only p) He (pronounced like "murder"): Drink. In Cantonese, "drink" is 飲, yam.

雷鋒 (p) Lei Feng (c) Loy Fong: Thunder Knife's Edge. Wah, imagine being called Thunder! A surname almost as good as Horse.

大地塘 (p) Da Di Tang (c) Dai Dei Tong: Big Ground Reservoir, Tai Tei Tong village on Lantau Island, Hong Kong, one of my former homes. And a good example among hundreds, if not thousands, of how place names in Hong Kong – "Hong" (Heung) "Kong" (Gong) being another one – are spelled in a ridiculous fashion. 大, daai, "big" and 太, tai, "too" or "supreme" are both spelled "tai" in the ludicrous Romanisation of Hong Kong place names. How can "tai" mean both "daai" and "tai"? There is no "tei" in the Cantonese language, so how can "Daai Dei Tong" become "Tai Tei Tong"? Small wonder Hong Kong taxi drivers can't find the addresses foreigners direct them to, when the real sound is so far removed from the spelling.

魚香茄子 (p) Yu Xiang Qie Zi (c) Yu Heung Keh Tsi: Fish-fragrance aubergines. Please come to my personal restaurant to savour them.

士多 (only c) Si Doh: store. A store where you can also drink beer and eat noodles. Almost like a "Bia Hoy" in Vietnam.

Chapter 6

啤酒 (p) Pi Jiu (c) Beh Jau: Beer.

不吃肉 (only p) Bu Chi Rou: I don't eat meat. In Cantonese: 唔食肉, M Sek Yokk.

素食 (p) Su Shi (c) Sou Sekk: Vegetarian. Literally, Pure Eat. This is totally different from "I don't eat meat" which is almost a guarantee that you will be served beef, chicken and ducks' heads. Because in China only pork is "meat". I can't stress this vigorously enough.

肇慶 (p) Zhao Qing (c) Siu Heng: aptly named Begin Celebrations. "Small" town in west Guangdong province and China's best party town; before they tore down all the bars to make way for luxury flats. Damn money grubbers.

入鄉隨俗 (p) Ru Xiang Sui Su (c) Yapp Heung Seui Sok: Into the village, follow customs. When in Rome do as the Romans. Yeah, but if the custom is to drink the bile of bears which have been kept in tiny cages all their lives with tubes permanently lodged inside their gall bladders and their whole lives are unstoppable torture, should one then follow it? Personally I don't think so. I'm against cruelty to animals actually. So I take that proverb with a pinch of MSG.

卡拉O.K. (p & c) Ka La O.K.: Karaoke. Still very popular after 20 years. Well, well, well.

吃飯了沒有 (only p) Chi Fan Le Mei You: Eaten yet? Cantonese: 食咗飯未, Sekk Jou Faan Mei.

桂林 (p) Gui Lin (c) Gwai Lam: Cassiabark Tree Forest. Guilin, city in Guangxi province famous for its weird mountain formations, or scraggy crags as I call them. They really are weird, and if I knew anything about geology I would have held forth at length. But if you've ever seen a typical Chinese classical painting with some crags and bamboo and drifting mist or fog, you'll know what I mean. These are mountains to my taste – half an hour to get up and ten minutes down.

狗肉 (p) Gou Rou (c) Gao Yokk: Dog meat. Take it easy – you'll be told what it is if it's being served. And yes, if it's the cook's wife too.

雞丁 (p) Ji Ding (c) Gai Deng: Chicken cubes. Not a trace of bone! No skin! And above all: No eyes. Ah, that's the way chicken should be served, I think, if at all. I feel sorry for those little bastards too sometimes.

絲 (p) Si (c) See: Silk. Slivers. Another safe, eye-less method of preparing meat. Yes, yes, I'm so fussy. But when I go into the village I want to go out of the village with a smile on my face. Know what I mean?

老K (p) Lao Keh (c) Lou Kei: Old K, Ketamine. A horse tranquillizer. Another example of how "old" is used affectionately in Chinese, just like in English, really. As in "You're a funny old 21-year-old drug addict, aren't you?"

强 (c) Keung: means Strong. One of my three favourite Canto-names. My other two are 龍, Long (Dragon) and 海, Hoy (Sea).

Chapter 7

中旅社 (p) Zhong Lü Se (c) Jung Loy Seh: China Travel Society, China Travel. You are hereby forewarned.

沒有 (p) Mei You: Don't have, it doesn't exist, it's sold out, I can't be arsed to walk the few steps to get it, I don't have time now and also not tomorrow... etc. Apart from Pi Jiu (beer), Mei You was the one Chinese expression guaranteed to stick in rabidly anti-linguist foreigners' brains during the 1980s. This was a time when China really cared about the working human being, in that everyone who had a counter to stand behind, a waiter's uniform to wear, an armband which said Neighbourhood Rottweiler, or a broom, spade or mop, had power over other people. Nowadays the customer is at the centre of everything even in China (except in tour groups) and people in the service industries have sunk back into their former powerlessness. But the 80s were their glory days, and they wasted few opportunities to bark out a shrill "Mei You!"

People said that this was due to communism and the Iron Rice Bowl allowing people not to work or provide any kind of service as they couldn't be fired and made the same money whether they worked or not. But I think the Mei You mentality is inbuilt in all of us and that we'd all treat irritating customers ("irritating" meaning "wanting something from you" such as a ticket) like that if we weren't afraid of them complaining to our superiors.

天山 (p) Tian Shan (c) Tin Sahn: the Heavenly Mountain. Very high mountain range in Xinjiang, from which most water for irrigation comes. The water is used to grow grapes and melons, and I tell you, I could spend the rest of my life eating those grapes and melons. "Sweet" doesn't begin to describe them. The wine, on the other hand, is mouth-tearingly sour. One of the mysteries of nature, I suppose.

山東 (p) Shan Dong (c) Saan Dong: East of the Mountains. An Eastern province famous for its tall and strongly built men.

黃建國 (p) Huang Jian Guo (c) Wong Ghin Gokk: Yellow Build The Country. In China, like in many other countries, it's relatively easy to judge people's ages when you hear their names. Build the Country, Strong Country, Bright Country and Glorious Country are typical names of people (men) born in the 1960s.

天湖 (p) Tian Chi (c) Tinn Ji: Heavenly Pond, i.e. Lake, 110 km north of Urumqi. The lake reminds one of a Norwegian fjord in that it is framed by high mountains and the weather is unpredictable – you don't know if it's going to be rainy, windy, snowing or hailing. Just one thing is for sure: It won't be sunny. But it looks great in photos not taken by me.

華僑 (p) Hua Qiao (c) Wah Kiu: Overseas Chinese. Hua is one of the many names for China, which in addition to the country's name means Brilliant, Magnificent, Splendid, Prosperous, Flourishing, Thriving, Flashing, Extravagant, Best Part, Cream, the Essence.

漢人 (p) Han Ren (c) Hohn Yan: members of the Han people, the ethnic majority in China. And therefore, the world. "Han" also means man and hero, as in Nan Zi Han, a real man.

Chapter 8

陝西 (p) Shaan Xi (it should be Shanxi but there's another Shanxi province next door so the problem is solved by sticking in an extra "a". Looking in the dictionary I can't find a meaning for Shan. It must have a meaning! All Chinese characters have meaning. Time to consult the ultimate in dictionaries, "10,000 Characters". No, it just says "province"). (c) Sim Sai: Northern province, dry, rocky and poor. And like all the northern provinces, victim of increasing water shortages.

硬坐 (p) Ying Zuo (c) An Choh: Hard Seat.

軟臥 (p) Ruan Wo (c) Yuyn Oh: Soft Lying Down. Soft sleeper. If you like to have very few people around you when you sleep, Soft Sleeper costs about 30% more than Hard. You'll be close to the dining car and there are fewer people using the washroom and the toilet, but apart from that it's pretty much the same as Hard Sleeper (see below).

硬臥 (p) Ying Wo (c) Yeng Woh: Hard sleeper. Not so very hard, in fact exactly the same level of hardness as Soft Sleeper.

河南 (p) He Nan (c) Ho Lam: South of the River, Henan province.

黃土 (p) Huang Tu (c) Wong Tou: Yellow Earth or loess. Reddish, meagre earth more like dust, covering more and more of northern China due to desertification.

軟坐 (p) Ruan Zuo (c) Yuyn Choh: Soft seat. Zuo means both sit and seat. English, eh! So many words for the same thing!

上海 (p) Shang Hai (c) Seung Hoy: Above (or on) the Sea, Shanghai.

Chapter 9

三峽 (p) San Xia (c) Saam Happ: Three Gorges. No longer existing.

麵條 (p) Mian Tiao (c) Min: Noodles. Direct translation: Wheat noodle strips. Why does "mian tiao" taste better than "spaghetti"? Because it does!

巫山 (p) Wu Shan (c) Mou Saan: Witch Mountain.

秦始皇 (p) Qin Shi Huang (c) Cheun Chi Wong: China's first emperor. An old favourite of Mao's for his ruthlessness and hatred of intellectuals.

茄汁 (p) Qie Shi (c) Keh Jap: Tomato Juice, Ketchup. Yes, it comes from Cantonese!

石寶 (p) Shi Bao (c) Sek Bou: Stone Treasure, now under water.

Chapter 10

停 (p) Ting (c) Teng: Stop. The first character I learnt. It's a genius character in that it reflects the meaning and sound and what it is, in one. If you take away the left-hand component (that looks like the number 1 but actually means 人, yan, person), you get 亭, teng, which means pavilion. So it's something that *sounds* like teng but *means* something else, something to do with people. On the other hand, what did the person do when sheit reached the pavilion? Stopped, innit!

復活節 (p) Fu Huo Jie (c) Fuk Wot Jit: Back to Life Festival, Easter. The most important of the Easter days is, naturally, 耶穌受難節 (p) Ye Su Shou Nan Jie (c) Ye Sou Sau Laan Jit: Jesus Experiences Difficulties Festival, Good Friday. Yes, I can see Jesus on Easter Morning, coming out of the grave and flicking dust off his tunic sleeves: "Yeah, I suffered a few difficulties on Friday, but I'm all right now!"

山海關 (p) Shan Hai Guan (c) San Hoy Gwan: Mountain Sea Pass, Shanhaiguan.

Chapter 11

中環 (p) Zhong Huan (c) Jung Waan: Middle Circle, Central, one of the ugliest and most people-hostile areas of Hong Kong. Canyons of ridiculously tall buildings, the bottoms of which are bathed in perpetual half-light. There are no trees, and no building is lower than 40 floors. The authorities want all pedestrian traffic to take place on flyovers high above street level so cars won't get scratched when they mow people down, but there are still some stubborn individuals to be seen, defying the toxic gases as they insist on getting around on the ground.

格 (p) Ge (c) Gakk: Mr. Ge's surname, meaning to correct, reach, influence, resist... and many other things.

昌吉 (p) Chang Ji (c) Cheung Gat: Prosperous and Lucky. City in Xinjiang not far from the capital Urumqi. An hour-long bus trip between the two cities means almost an hour's opportunity to admire the magnificent Tianshan ranges. That little bus trip is worth the whole journey to Xinjiang – as if the whole place isn't a constant source of wonder. I'm so going back.

庫爾勒 (p) Ku Er Le (c) Fu Yi Lok: Korla, former hub of trade on the Silk Road, now a polluted dump.

金 (p) Jin (c) Gam: Gold. A surname. And a first name. My ex-husband, for example, is called "Easy to Find Gold".

新和 (p) Xin He (c) Sann Ho: New Peace. Yes, peace always occurs where the Chinese go forth – the kind of peace that is the result of all opposition having been crushed.

Chapter 12

丹東 (p & c) Dan Dong: Red East. Dandong, industrial town on the border of...

朝鮮 (p) Zhao Xian (c) Chiu Sin: Morning Brightness, North Korea. Interestingly (for me) the Chinese call South Korea 南朝鮮 – "South North Korea". It's to the North their loyalties still lie, I suppose. Weird.

吐 (p) Tu (c) To: Spit, cough up.

鼻屎 (p) Bi Shi (c) Bei Sii: Nose Shit. Snot.

非典型肺炎 (p) Fei Dian Xing Fei Yan (c) Fei Dinn Yeng Fei Yimm: Atypical Style Lung Infection, SARS. Not the Hong Kong Special Administrative Region of the People's Republic of China (ah, how our bureaucrats adore catchy names) but the horror disease to end them all.

松潘 (p) Song Pan (c) Chung Ponn: Conifer Water-that-rice-has-been-washed-in. Most suitable for people unafraid of death.

Chapter 13

自行車 (p) Zi Xing Che: Self-going vehicle. In Cantonese, 單車 (c) Dan Cheh: Single vehicle. Bicycle.

美國 (p) Mei Guo (c) Mei Gok: The USA. Means "beautiful country" and the first character is composed of "sheep" and "big". Well, what could be more beautiful than a big sheep?

樂香園 (p) Le Xiang Yuan (c) Lok Heung Yuen: Formerly Hong Kong's coolest cha chan teng – tea restaurant – now an idiotic... something-shop. Selling bags, maybe. They all look the same to me.

Chapter 14

青龍坊 (p) Qing Long Fang (c) Cheng Long Fong: Green Dragon Neighbourhood. The best street in Guangzhou, if it's still around. Probably not. *2011 update:* No, it's not. My favourite restaurant is closed and the others have become indoor restaurants. Sigh.

四會 (p) Si Hui (c) Sei Wui: Small town in Guangdong province which has long since taken over from Siu Heng as the best party town in China. It's screaming even at Chinese New Year.

Chapter 15

一 (p) Yi (c) Yat: The number 1.

二 (p) Er (c) Yi: The number 2. The fact that "1" in Putonghua sounds more or less the same as "2" in Cantonese has led to untold grief when I venture into Mando territory. "What? TWO HUNDRED per night? Outrageous!" "That's right. One hundred." "Oh yeah, excellent! Very reasonable."

韓國 (p) Han Guo (c) Hon Gok: (South) Korea.

Chapter 16

西藏 (p) Xi Zang (c) Sai Jong: Tibet. Western Storage. Or "Hidden in the West." It's not a joke that China is the Kingdom in the Middle, you know. Look at the countries around it: Vietnam – "Beyond the South". Mongolia – "Ignorant from Old" and now Tibet – "Hidden in the West." They certainly knew their place!

魚 (p) Yu (c) Yu: Fish, sounds like 餘, excess, plentiful.

金橘 (p) Jin Ju (c) Gam Gat: an orange-looking fruit which in Cantonese sounds like 金吉, gold and happiness.

青海 (p) Qing Hai (c) Cheng Hoy: Green (or blue) Sea. Qinghai province. It certainly lives up to its name as it's more or less empty apart from rolling green hills or, in spring, rolling yellow hills haunted by blizzards. But it's named after China's biggest salt-water lake: Green Sea.

林芝 (p) Lin Zhi (c) Lam Tsji: Forest of Sesame. Nothing could be further from the truth.

雲南 (p) Yun Nan (c) Wann Lam: South of the Clouds. Yunnan province.

昆明 (p) Kun Ming (c) Kwan Meng: Manifold Brightness. Kunming, capital of Yunnan.

Chapter 17

珠江啤酒 (p) Zhu Jiang Pi Jiu (c) Jyu Gong Beh Jau: Pearl River Beer, the best in China. And that says a lot! But make sure you get the traditional kind with the green and gold label – they do a lot of fancy-schmancy stuff with "Ice" and "Light" now. Not good. I'm a beer Luddite.

麥 (p) Mai (c) Mak: Wheat. A surname.

ABOUT THE AUTHOR

Cecilie Gamst Berg was born in Norway but soon escaped its icy grip, arriving in China in 1988. A long-time Hong Kong resident, she has spent most of her adult life trying to go everywhere in China and meet everybody.

When at home in Hong Kong she works hard to make Cantonese a world language – through direct teaching, making films on YouTube and hosting radio programmes on RTHK. Visit her website at *www.happyjellyfish.com.*